Landmark
Essays

Landmark Essays

on
Classical Greek Rhetoric

Edited by Edward Schiappa

Hermagoras Press
1994

Landmark Essays Volume Three

Published 1994 by Hermagoras Press,
P.O. Box 1555, Davis, CA 95617

Cover design by Kathi Zamminer

Typesetting and Camera-ready Production
by Graphic Gold, Davis, California
Manufactured in the United States of America
by KNI Inc., Anaheim, California

ISBN 1-880393-06-9

2 3 4 5 6 7 8 9 0

For George A. Kennedy

About the Editor

Edward Schiappa is Associate Professor and Director of Graduate Studies in Communication at Purdue University. His work on classical and contemporary rhetorical theory has appeared in such journals as *American Journal of Philology, Rhetoric Review, Quarterly Journal of Speech, Philosophy and Rhetoric, Rhetoric Society Quarterly*, and *Communication Monographs*. He is author of *Protagoras and Logos: A Study in Greek Philosophy and Rhetoric* and editor of *Warranting Assent: Case Studies in Argument Evaluation.*

Rhetoric and knowledge
truth
philosophy
dialectic
sophism
oratory

Acknowledgements

I wish to thank John T. Kirby and James J. Murphy for helpful suggestions for articles to include in this collection. I am especially grateful to Omar Swartz for his research and editorial assistance and his help in preparing the index.

Table of Contents

Introduction

Essays

Section 1: Earliest Greek Rhetoric

Section 2: Sophistic Rhetorical Theory

Section 3: Platonic Rhetorical Theory

Section 4: Isocratean Rhetoric

Section 5: Aristotelian Rhetorical Theory

Introduction

by Edward Schiappa and Omar Swartz

The purpose of this collection is to provide students and scholars of classical rhetoric with a set of exemplary works in the area of Greek rhetorical theory. Many of the articles included here are not easily accessible and have been selected with the intent of providing graduate and undergraduate students with a useful collection of secondary source materials. This book is also envisioned as a useful volume for scholars who will benefit from having these sources more readily available.

Scholarship in classical Greek rhetorical theory typically is aimed at one of two goals: *Historical reconstruction* is work that attempts to understand the contributions of past theorists or practitioners. Scholars involved in the historical reconstruction of Greek rhetorical theories attempt to understand the cultural context in which these theories originally appear. A scholar involved in historical reconstruction may try to answer questions such as: What did Homer think about language and persuasion? How did Isocrates describe the purpose of education? What did Aristotle mean by "enthymeme"? What theory of style did Theophrastus articulate?

Contemporary appropriation is work that attempts to utilize the insights of past theorists or practitioners in order to inform current theory or criticism. Rather than describe rhetorical theory as it evolved through the contingencies of the past, scholars who attempt the contemporary appropriation of classical texts do so in order to shed insight on rhetorical concerns as they are manifested in today's environment. A scholar involved in contemporary appropriation tries to answer questions such as: In relationship to modern-day compositional and literary practices, what can be learned from the efforts of persuasion found in Homer? Can Isocrates' vision of higher education serve as a useful model today? How might we use the notion of "enthymeme" in contemporary public speaking classes? Is stasis theory an adequate inventional device for nonjudicial discourse, such as composition and presentational speeches? Are the categories of style that Theophrastus identified still useful today? Such questions function to direct and develop the concerns of classical authors in a way perhaps never anticipated by those theorists. Rather than being a response to the conditions of ancient Greece, these theorists' ideas are appropriated as a way of addressing and edifying contemporary concerns.

As can be seen in the following articles, historical reconstruction and contemporary appropriation differ in terms of *goals* and *methods*. Since the goal of historical reconstruction is to capture the past, insofar as possible, on its own terms, the methods of the historian and, in classical work, the philologist, are appropriate. As a result, many of the essays in this collection draw heavily on the original Greek terminology to describe a given theorist's contributions. All Greek words have been transliterated in this edition in order to improve readability. In addition, where the meanings of the Greek words are not explicitly discussed, a bracketed translation has been added to make the text more accessible for non-Greek reading audiences.

The careful reader will notice that, in the articles that attempt a contemporary appropriation of classical Greek theory, philological precision and fidelity to the original Greek text is a less central concern. Since the goal of contemporary appropriation is to provide critical insight to contemporary theorists and teachers, the needs and values of current audiences justify less rigidity and more creativity in the process of interpreting how long-dead authors through their texts "speak" to the needs and interests of contemporary audiences. *Both* sorts of scholarship—historical reconstruction and contemporary appropriation—are useful and important. Both sorts of scholarship are found in this collection, sometimes even within the same essay.

The essays that follow have been arranged into six sections that focus on some of the major trends in the theorizing of Greek rhetoric. The three essays included in the first section, *Earliest Greek Rhetoric*, discuss some of the earliest notions of rhetorical practice and persuasion in Western history. John T. Kirby identifies the earliest concepts we would now call "rhetorical" in the constellation of three key ideas that permeate early Greek literature: persuasion, force, and love. His study suggests that a thorough account of early Greek rhetoric requires a historical understanding of the relationships among these three terms. The earliest Greek texts that survive today are the poems by Homer that were originally composed and performed orally. Homer created his epics in a mostly nonliterate society and, as K. E. Wilkerson and Andrew J. Karp note, an incipient rhetorical theory can be seen in the social tensions found within the mythic, oral tradition. While both Wilkerson and Karp explore the notion of Homeric rhetoric, they come to very different conclusions. In the process of exploring the points of agreement and disagreement between these two essays, readers may want to explore such questions as: What is meant by the word "rhetoric"? Is there a necessary connection between rhetorical *practice* and rhetorical *theory*? Is it useful to distinguish between *explicit* and *implicit* rhetorical theories?

In the second section the reader is provided with two award-winning articles that construct a dialogue about the notion of a discrete *Sophistic Rhetorical Theory*. John Poulakos provides what he believes to be a distinct and useful "sophistic definition of rhetoric" while Edward Schiappa questions the historical basis of any notion of a distinct "sophistic rhetoric." One possible way to resolve the differences between these two essays is to see each as answering different questions that reflect the differences between historical reconstruction and contemporary appropriation. The articles represent key positions in the recent renaissance in scholarship about the Sophists that has taken place in the disciplines of Speech Communication and English. Questions raised by this material include: To what extent might we view the Sophists' theorizing about *logos* as constituting an incipient rhetorical theory? To what degree is "sophistic rhetoric" a historically valid concept? What notions of "sophistic rhetoric" might be usefully appropriated for contemporary theories of rhetoric?

The third section of this volume, *Platonic Rhetorical Theory*, introduces the reader to conflicts over Plato's treatment of rhetoric that have spurred debate for over two thousand years. The two essays included in this collection review the dominant themes within contemporary interpretations of Plato in an effort to further delineate his position on rhetoric. Edwin Black argues that Plato presents a consistent and coherent view of rhetoric in the *Gorgias* and the *Phaedrus*. Black's interpretation of Plato presents a view that appropriates Plato as a critical ally of rhetoric. Black's view is contrasted with Charles Kauffman's cautionary note that such enthusiastic receptions of Plato's "philosophical rhetoric" may be unwarranted and undesirable. Though both Black and Kauffman are interested in understanding Plato's texts historically, they also want to inform contemporary theorizing about rhetoric. Readers may want to consider such questions as: What counts as *evidence* for a particular reading of an ancient theorist's texts? How does Plato's ideological doctrines become emphasized and deemphasized in both Black's and Kauffman's interpretations? To what extent do all rhetorical theories contain an implicit or explicit theory of politics?

In the fourth section of this text, *Isocratean Rhetoric*, the reader is presented with two historical reconstructions of Isocrates' texts. Classicists Werner Jaeger and Erika Rummel explore Isocrates' cultural theory of rhetoric and philosophy in relationship to the intellectual milieu of his time. Ironically, Isocrates' texts never use the Greek word for rhetoric (*rhêtorikê*). Nonetheless, both Jaeger and Rummel demonstrate the usefulness of analyzing Isocrates' texts as contributions to ancient Greek rhetorical theory. Questions readers may want to consider while reading these essays include: To what extent can a theory of rhetoric inform a complete theory of pedagogy? Can Isocrates' vision of higher education serve as a useful model today? Can past theorists' ideals of rhetoric provide criteria for evaluating contemporary discourse?

It is arguably the case that Aristotle's writings about rhetoric have influenced twentieth-century rhetorical theory more than any other Greek author. The fifth section of this collection, *Aristotelian Rhetorical Theory*, provides three of many possible important and influential examples of modern scholarship about Aristotle's *Rhetoric*. The essay by Carnes Lord provides a historically-grounded argument about a point typically assumed rather than proven: Why did Aristotle write the *Rhetoric*? James H. McBurney and Richard C. Huseman offer historical reconstructions of Aristotelian contributions to rhetorical theory, the enthymeme and Aristotle's topics, that also aim to inform contemporary theory and criticism. The most fruitful area of discussion students may want to consider while reading these essays is how Aristotle's ideas might be most profitably used in the contemporary teaching of writing and speaking.

In the sixth and final section of this collection, *Post-Aristotelian Rhetorical Theory*, the pair of articles included attempt to reflect two of the

dominant approaches to rhetoric presented by the Hellenistic world. Following the time of Aristotle, the Greek rhetorical theory of the Hellenistic period
often focused on invention and style (both of which became emphasized in
Roman rhetorical theory). Both articles reflect these emphases and serve as
bridges from Greek to Roman theory. George A. Kennedy's discussion of
Theophrastus provides readers with a sense of how Greek rhetorical theory
became transformed through an emphasis on style and delivery. Theophrastus' writings on style are an excellent example of how one hallmark of
increasing specialization or the "disciplinizing" of rhetoric is a proliferation
of concepts and terminology. In addition, Kennedy's article serves the
purpose of tracing clearly the diffusion of Aristotelian perspectives on style
into the Latin arena. Otto Dieter's discussion of stasis takes as its starting
point Hermagoras' heuristic system of inventing arguments and explicitly
develops the theory of stasis in light of prior Greek and later Roman theore-
ticians. Readers may want to consider such questions as: Was the development of stasis theory and theories of style the inevitable evolution of previous
theories? What needs and interests did such theories serve for the teachers of
rhetoric of the time? What aspects of stasis theory are useful today? Are the
categories of style that Theophrastus identified still useful today?

As a last note, this collection was not designed to provide a compre-
hensive overview of the development of Greek rhetorical theory and practice.
Readers interested in such an overview should consult one or more of the
following sources: James J. Murphy, *A Synoptic History of Classical Rhetoric*
(New York: Random House, 1972; Davis: Hermagoras, 1983); Thomas Cole,
The Origins of Rhetoric in Ancient Greece (Baltimore: The Johns Hopkins
University Press, 1991); Thomas Conley, *Rhetoric in the European Tradition*
(New York: Longman, 1990); George A. Kennedy *Art of Persuasion in
Greece* (Princeton: Princeton UP, 1963); and Kennedy *Classical Rhetoric and
Its Secular Tradition from Ancient to Modern Times* (Chapel Hill: University
of North Carolina Press, 1980).

Section 1:
Earliest Greek Rhetoric

The "Great Triangle" in Early Greek Rhetoric and Poetics

for CDS

by John T. Kirby

In speaking of a "Triangle," I have in mind a particular constellation of three concepts—one might call them psychosocial phenomena—that recur in Greek literature from its very earliest stages on: namely, peitho, bia, and eros.[1] "Peitho," which originally drew me to this study, is the word for persuasive communication, both as a process and as the state resulting from that process; it was early hypostatized as the goddess Peitho, persuasion personified.[2] "Bia" means force, physical strength, and (most especially) violence; the goddess Bia is mentioned in tandem with a kindred deity, Kratos ("Strength" or "Power").[3] "Eros" refers to any strong desire, but particularly sexual passion, and is itself hypostatized as the god of Love. In the Hesiodic canon he is a mighty and fearsome power, at once beautiful and terrible; a god who can create, a source of life and growth, but also a source of potential devastation.[4]

If the treatment of peitho in ancient Greek literature is taken as a whole, certain patterns of thought emerge. It is not simply that Greek writers persist in addressing the topic of peitho (which they do): what we find is that peitho

---

Reprinted from *Rhetorica,* volume VIII, number 3 (Summer 1990). Used with permission.

[1] *Peithô, bia,* and *erôs* are—like all significant words—polysemous; and they will occur frequently in my discussion. Because of their polysemy, I have decided not to entrammel any of them in a single translation, but instead to transliterate them (and to elaborate their variable meanings as appropriate). Because of their frequency, I print them in roman type, without marking long vowels: peitho, bia, eros.

[2] See, e.g., Hesiod *Theogony* 349, *Works and Days* 73; the scholiast on this latter passage of Hesiod reports that Sappho called Peitho the daughter of Aphrodite (Sappho fr. 200 [Lobel-Page]). See too Sappho frr. 1.18, 90.8, and 96.26-29 (L-P); Ibycus 288 (Page); Pindar *Pythian* 4.219 and 9.39; Aeschylus *Suppliant Women* 1040; Herodotus 8.111.

[3] *Theogony* 385; [Aeschylus?] *Prometheus Bound* 12. Homer uses "bia" + genitive as a periphrasis for a strong man *(Iliad* 2.658, 4.386, *et passim).*

There is a tremendous amount to be learned about certain aspects of bia from René Girard's *La Violence et le sacré* (Paris 1972), translated as *Violence and the Sacred* (Baltimore: Johns Hopkins Univ. Press, 1977).

[4] *Theogony* 120–22. M. L. West, *Hesiod: Theogony* (Oxford 1966), 195, writes: "The position of Eros here in the very first generation of created powers strongly suggests a quasi-demiurgic function."

A profound book on the topic of eros is Anne Carson's *Eros the Bittersweet: An Essay* (Princeton: Princeton Univ. Press, 1986).

is diagnosed, again and again, in parallel with eros or with bia.[5] Given such striking juxtapositions, it is only a small step to the realization that eros and bia are themselves strongly associated as well. So the three concepts enter into a relationship that we may usefully consider as triangular. I will not say that the Triangle as a whole is consciously recognized in all periods, or by all writers, but there seems to be an evolution toward the formulation of this triad as such.

And we will find repeatedly that a story focuses on not just one or another of these three concepts—peitho itself, bia itself, eros itself—but on the *dyads* constituted by virtue of their juxtaposition: peitho/bia, peitho/eros, eros/bia. That is, it is the sides of this Triangle, as much as the vertices themselves, that become the matter, the issues, treated in the great works of classical Greek literature. One might think of the Greek mind as running along recognized axes of thought. I like the image of an *axis* because, on any given line, there is an infinite number of points: so too the juxtaposition of A and B is not merely a (single) new fixed *topos*; rather it allows for infinite considerations of the relationship between A and B.

When peitho, bia, eros, and their various combinations are traced through the Greek corpus, it becomes clear that they function as governing principles of both rhetoric and poetics, from Homer to Plato. In this respect they conspire, in fact, to unite rhetoric and poetics as disciplines. While Plato shows signs of dissatisfaction with the poetic/rhetorical tradition he receives, and makes an attempt to transcend it, he finds himself at a philosophical impasse; it is Aristotle who first succeeds in making a major break with this virtually pervasive ideology.

Peitho/Bia

The first axis to be considered is that connecting peitho and bia.[6]

---

[5] The love for parallel structure manifests itself quickly in Greek culture, in the plastic arts and in architecture as well as in literature. The designs on vases of the Geometric period, the rows of columns on a temple, evince a desire for order *(kosmos)* and arrangement *(taxis)* that proves one of the most characteristic traits of Greek classicism. So it comes as no surprise that such a principle should also be manifested in the Greek language. Binary parallelism is by no means an exclusively Greek phenomenon; but in its conjunctive form *(both A and B)* as well as its disjunctive *(not A but B)*, it lies very close to the heart of Greek syntax. Nor is it sheerly a matter of structure. Concepts themselves may be juxtaposed in an associative or dissociative way, even when there is no parallelism at the syntactic level. Such juxtaposition is useful because it clarifies thought: if we want to know more about A, it may help us to know that A is like B, or that there are bonds of association between A and B. Or, if we are told that A is *not* like B, that A is implacably opposed to B, or that A and B are mutually exclusive, then B serves as a foil, a ground against which A can be figured more clearly.

  The best-known study of this as a phenomenon of language is G. E. R. Lloyd's *Polarity and Analogy:Two Types of Argumentation in Early Greek Thought* (Cambridge, Cambridge Univ. Press, 1966).

[6] For explicit use of the antithesis see, e.g., Isocrates *Plataicus* 8, *Nicocles* 22, *Philippus* 15–16; Lysias 1.32–33, 2.19; Plato *Laws* 722b; and (much later) Plutarch *Themistocles* 21. The dyad may be implicit in Nestor's words to Achilles and Agamemnon at *Iliad* 1.274: *peithesthai* is preferable *(ameinon)* to coercion. In this context it is worth noting that the threat of physical force may be used as peitho.

  Sometimes the word used to designate the bia-element in this dyad is *anagkê* (or *anagkaiê),* "force," "constraint," or (most familiarly) "necessity." For early examples of this concept personified,

Typically this collocation of ideas is antithetical: I will try to persuade you, but, failing that, I will force you. Such a disjunction is rooted in our most fundamental concepts of civilization. The wild beasts settle their disputes by bia; it is a mark of our humanity, we feel, that we can use persuasion to effect change, that we are not limited to the use of coercion. The writer of the *Rhetoric to Alexander* observes, "All other living creatures have passion and anger and such urges, but only humans have *logos*."[7]

The peitho/bia axis is at the base of some of our most ancient literary and rhetorical formulations. It determines Homer's overall structural poetics in the *Iliad*; the trajectory of the story-line as a whole is a kind of arc from bia to peitho, and books 1 and 24 represent the opposite extremities of this arc. In a fundamental sense the whole poem is *about* the peitho/bia antithesis. Book 1 begins with the wrath *(mênis)* of Achilles, who is face-to-face in conflict with another mighty lord, or *anax*:[8] Achilles and Agamemnon are quarreling over who is going to take the girl as his war-booty. Peitho having failed, or not even having been attempted, Achilles is on the verge of committing an act of violence (bia) against Agamemnon, and must be restrained by force (bia)— Athene pulls him back by the hair. In book 24, by contrast, Achilles is confronted by yet another *anax* who wants something (someone) Achilles has: Priam wants the body of his son Hector, which Achilles has attached to his chariot so that he can drag it around and around the walls of Troy. Here the peitho of Priam prevails, and Achilles puts aside his bia. He could have killed Priam on the spot, as he came alone and defenseless to Achilles' camp, but he looked so much like Achilles' own aged father that this aroused compassion in Achilles, who next does the one thing we should never have expected him to do: he relinquishes the body of the man who had killed his soulmate Patroclus. Against all odds, the unquenchable *mênis* of Achilles is assuaged. Overall, then, we find a movement from bia to peitho. Indeed Priam's visit represents *the triumph of peitho over bia*: Achilles is induced to abandon the frenzy of his revenge and violence, and to reach a new level of human understanding.

Within this arc there are other recognizable points, in somewhat symmetrical arrangement.[9] Book 9 represents an attempt at the use of peitho on Achilles, which fails; all the rhetorical stratagems of the Greek generals

---

see *Iliad* 6.458, Herodotus 8.111. It is perhaps significant, in this light, that for Aristotle the crucial element in the deployment of peitho will turn out to be the enthymeme or rhetorical syllogism (*Rhetoric* 1354a, 14–15); and, of course, the operative force in syllogistic is none other than *anagkê* (*Prior Analytics* 24b, 18–20; cf. *Topics* 100a, 25–27). The taming of bia?

[7] *Rhetorica ad Alexandrum* 1421a. The converse idea is a familiar *topos* of invective: the heaviest aspersions may be cast upon another person's humanity by denigrating his or her very humanity, by calling such a person a "beast" or the equivalent. For examples of this in Roman drama and oratory, see John T. Kirby, *The Rhetoric of Cicero's* Pro Cluentio (Amsterdam: J. C. Gieben, 1990), 144 and nn.

[8] The use of this word, which was already archaic in Homer's day, itself draws attention to the fact that Achilles, Agamemnon, and Priam are comparable in poetic as well as in social and military status.

[9] This observation is consonant with, but does not depend upon, Cedric Whitman's analysis of the structure of the *Iliad* in his *Homer and the Heroic Tradition* (Cambridge, Mass.: Harvard Univ. Press, 1958), chap. 11.

fail to persuade Achilles to come back with them. This is balanced further by its mirror-book, 16, where Patroclus puts on the armor of Achilles in order to masquerade as that great hero:[10]

> Give me your armour to wear on my shoulders into the fighting;
> so perhaps the Trojans might think I am you, and give way
> from their attack, and the fighting sons of the Achaeans get wind
> again after hard work. There is little breathing space in the fighting.
>
> [40-43]

This is bia used as a kind of peitho: by the threat of what would appear to be the return of Achilles to battle, Patroclus hopes to turn aside the Trojan onslaught.

Interestingly, the *Odyssey* seems to yield an exactly opposite trajectory. It begins with peitho and moves toward bia. At the beginning the suitors are dealt with civilly—pleaded with to be reasonable, but meanwhile fed and entertained. By the end their presence has become intolerable and indeed dangerous, and Odysseus and Telemachus have no alternative but to resort to force (bia) in order to remove them.[11]

Much of Greek tragedy runs along the peitho/bia axis. Often the critical turns in the plot arise from a failure of peitho that issues in an act (or acts) of bia. In Sophocles' *Oedipus the King,* Jocasta pleads in vain with Oedipus to desist from his persistent inquiry into the secrets of his parentage:

> Why ask of whom he spoke? Don't give it heed;
> nor try to keep in mind what has been said.
> It will be wasted labour.
>
> . . .
>
> I beg you—do not hunt this out—I beg you,
> if you have any care for your own life.
> What I am suffering is enough.
>
> . . .
>
> O be persuaded by me, I entreat you;
> do not do this.
>
> [1056-64]

---

[10]Quotations from the *Iliad* are taken, or adapted, from the translation of Richmond Lattimore (Chicago: Univ. of Chicago Press, 1951); quotations from tragedies are taken, or adapted, from the edition of Grene and Lattimore, *The Complete Greek Tragedies* (Chicago: Univ. of Chicago Press, 1959). But my line-references, in all cases, correspond to the original Greek texts in their Oxford (OCT) editions.

[11]This brings to mind, but does not of course answer, the question of whether the same person could have composed both the *Iliad* and the *Odyssey*. Gregory Nagy, in *The Best of the Achaeans* (Baltimore: Johns Hopkins Univ. Press, 1979), discusses the remarkable mutual exclusivity of the two epic narratives: ". . . their sheer size would make it seem inevitable for them to overlap in their treatment of at least some events related to Troy—unless there was a deliberate avoidance of such overlapping. If the avoidance was indeed deliberate, it would mean that the *Odyssey* displays an awareness of the *Iliad* by steering clear of it. Or rather, it may be a matter of evolution. Perhaps it was part of the Odyssean tradition to veer away from the Iliadic. Be that as it may, the traditions of the *Iliad* and the *Odyssey* constitute a totality with the complementary distribution of their narratives and, to me, there seems to be something traditionally self-conscious about all this. It is as if there were a traditional suppression of anything overtly Iliadic in the *Odyssey*" (20–21). This may be related to the fact that rhetorically, their plot-trajectories are mirror-images of one another.

He will not be dissuaded; he persists until he comes to that dreadful revelation which induces him to commit an act of violence more terrible, more punitive, than suicide itself, and even to call for further bia against his person:

> What I have done here was best done—don't tell me
> otherwise, do not give me further counsel.
> I do not know with what eyes I could look
> upon my father when I die and go
> under the earth, nor yet my wretched mother—
> those two to whom I have done things deserving
> worse punishment than hanging. . . .
>
> . . .
> . . . I beg of you in God's name hide me
> somewhere outside your country, yes, or kill me,
> or throw me into the sea. . . .
>
> [1370-1412]

The *Hecuba* of Euripides illustrates powerfully the effects of the breakdown of peitho. Hecuba, the august queen of Troy, is trapped, like a wild animal. In her attack on Polymestor and his children, she resorts to bia, not to solve her problem—for the tragedy of her situation is that there *is* no solution, either in peitho or in bia—but out of rage and vengeance:

> . . . See the bodies of his sons,
> killed by my women and me. His debt is paid
> and I have my revenge.
>
> . . .
> Why shouldn't I rejoice in my revenge over you?
>
> [1051-53, 1258]

She rejects *logos* for *ergon*, word for deed, and in so doing rejects the possibility of peitho for an ineluctable program of bia:

> . . . The clear actions of a person,
> Agamemnon, should speak louder than any words.
> Good words should get their goodness from our lives
> and nowhere else; the evil we do should show,
> a rottenness that festers in our speech
> and what we say, incapable of being glozed
> with a film of pretty words. There are men, I know,
> sophists who make a science of persuasion,
> glozing evil with the slick of loveliness;
> but in the end a speciousness will show.
> The imposters are punished; not one escapes
> his death.
>
> [1187-94]

At the end of the tale, in a remarkably tense passage of stichomythia, Polymestor answers *ergon* with *logos*. Instead of reciprocating her act of

violence directly, he makes a prophecy of violence to come, in the deaths of
Hecuba, of her own child Cassandra, and of Agamemnon:

POLYMESTOR. Hear my prediction.
                                                  I foretell that you—
HECUBA. Shall be carried on ship across the sea to Hellas?
P.—*shall drown at sea. You shall climb to the mast head
and fall—*
H.   Pushed by force?
P.   *You shall climb the mast
of your own free will—*
H.   Climb the mast? With wings?
P. —*changed to a dog, a bitch with blazing eyes.*
. . .
H. Shall I live or die?
P.   *Die. And when you die
your tomb shall be called—*
H.   In memory of my change?
P. *Cynossema, the bitch's grave, a landmark
to sailors.*
H.   What do I care how I die?
I have my revenge.
P.   *And your daughter Cassandra
must also die—*
H.   I spit your prophecies back.
Use them on yourself.
P.   *—killed by this man's wife
cut down by the bitter keeper of his house.*
H. Clytemnestra? She would never do it.
P. *Then she shall lift the dripping axe once more
and kill her husband too.*

                                                        [1259-79]

Once again, in this bizarre prophecy we see the association of bia— Hecuba's
violent suicide—with the loss of humanity, by means of her mythical
transformation.

Sometimes peitho and bia are gruesomely related. In the *Agamemnon* of
Aeschylus, the chorus makes the jarring statement "*biatai d'ha talaina
Peithô*"—"Persuasion the persistent overwhelms him" (1n. 385).[12] Later in the
same play, Clytemnestra must use all her powers of peitho to induce

---

[12]This is Lattimore's translation. A more literal one would be "Peitho, the bringer of wretchedness,
overpowers [the one who resists justice]." Here, as elsewhere, peitho is Peitho, the divine
personification of the power of persuasion. She is described in the next line as "*proboulou pais
haphertos Atas*," "child of scheming *Atê*, unable to be resisted."

Agamemnon to step on the purple tapestries, as an Eastern potentate would. He himself is reluctant to do so because of the intimations of *hubris*:[13]

> And all this—do not try in woman's ways to make
> me delicate, nor, as if I were some Asiatic
> bow down to earth and with wide mouth cry out to me,
> nor cross my path with jealousy by strewing the ground
> with robes. Such state becomes the gods, and none beside.
> I am a mortal, a man; I cannot trample upon
> these tinted splendors without fear thrown in my path.
>
> [918-24]

But eventually he does, and the outrage of his act brings down gory death upon his head, even as Polymestor had prophesied And this interchange between Clytemnestra and Agamemnon is not the beginning of the process: throughout the story of the house of Atreus a nauseous pendulum swings between peitho and bia. At the start of the Trojan War, Agamemnon had sacrificed his own daughter Iphigenia to appease Artemis—an act of bia as an act of peitho. Nor is Agamemnon's death the end. As a result of it Orestes is motivated to kill his mother Clytemnestra, an act which (in turn) generates the plot of the *Eumenides*. And it is not until the *Eumenides* that the conflict is resolved: the bia of the avenging Furies is assuaged in a triumph of peitho, when Athena persuades them to relent:

> It is my glory to hear how these generosities
> are given my land. I admire the eyes
> of Peitho, who guided the speech of my mouth
> toward these, when they were reluctant and wild.
>
> [968-72]

Peitho/Eros

Another axis of thought runs from peitho to eros. Whereas the peitho/bia axis is typically antithetical or disjunctive, the peitho/eros axis is quintessentially conjunctive. This must be so, it seems, because of the nature of eros: it is at base a desire, and for that which is not—or not yet. The moods of the Greek verb well illustrate for us the dynamics of eros: the indicative speaks of the realm of *fact*; the subjunctive treats of the realm of *non-fact*; and the imperative is the mode by which non-fact is made factual. Eros—desire—exerts an imperative upon that which is not, to transmute it into fact according to the dictates of desire. For such a task eros will turn to peitho, and for the accomplishment of such a design peitho works hand-in-

---

[13]Students of Aeschylus will know that Agamemnon's exact reasons for not stepping on the tapestries are a notorious chestnut for critics. For a useful summary of the various positions see Haruo Konishi, "Agamemnon's Reasons for Yielding," *American Journal of Philology* 110 (1989): 210–22.

glove with eros.[14]

The peitho/eros axis is so extensive (and intensive) as to defy comprehension. First and foremost is the use of peitho to fulfill eros: Come live with me, and be my love. Penelope's suitors, in the *Odyssey*, engage—not very successfully—in the use of peitho toward this end. Calypso is somewhat more successful, if only temporarily, with Odysseus. Phaedra's nurse, in the *Hippolytus* of Euripides, is miserably (I should say tragically) unsuccessful in procuring the favors of Hippolytus for her mistress. But over and over the theme is propounded, for eros wells up like an unquenchable spring, and demands fulfillment again and again.

Eros may itself sometimes be used as a sort of peitho, as in *Iliad* 14, where Hera wants to distract Zeus from the goings-on of the war, so that Poseidon can help the Achaeans without Zeus' preventing it. In a famous scene, she manipulates Zeus into making love on the slopes of Mount Ida, where he then falls asleep:

> Then in turn Zeus who gathers the clouds answered her:
> "Hera, there will be a time afterwards when you can go there[15]
> as well. But now let us go to bed and turn to love-making.
> For never before has love for any goddess or woman
> so melted about the heart inside me, broken it into submission,
> as now. . . ."

[312-16]

For Plato, if I may jump forward several centuries, eros is an informant of peitho. The whole complex concept of Platonic love, as exemplified in the *Symposium* and *Phaedrus*, is closely related to the dialogue between the teacher of philosophy and his or her student(s). That is, the practice of Platonic dialectic is not unlike a kind of lovemaking. For Plato's Socrates, philosophy is to be embodied in, and driven by, a hankering—an eros—for the Form of the Good. He would doubtless admonish us that what we perversely see as a series of sensory stimuli and endocrine responses is really (if we only knew) the powerful call of our eros for what is fine and honorable and eternal and divine and perfect.

A thorough reading of Plato's *Phaedrus* must include an assessment of its relationship to the earlier dialogue *Gorgias*, for as a pair they examine a

---

[14]On the meaning of eros, particularly for Plato, see David M. Halperin, "Platonic *Erôs* and What Men Call Love," *Ancient Philosophy* 5 (1985): 161–204, and "Plato and Erotic Reciprocity," *Classical Antiquity* 5 (1986): 60–80. Broader treatments are to be found in David M. Halperin, *One Hundred Years of Homosexuality and Other Essays on Greek Love* (New York: Routledge, 1989); David M. Halperin, John J. Winkler, and Froma I. Zeitlin eds., *Before Sexuality: The Construction of Erotic Experience in the Ancient Greek World* (Princeton: Princeton Univ. Press, 1990); and John J. Winkler, *The Constraints of Desire: The Anthropology of Sex and Gender in Ancient Greece* (New York: Routledge, 1990).

[15]*Scil.* to the house of Tethys and Okeanos; "I shall go to visit these, and resolve their division of discord, / since now for a long time they have stayed apart from each other / and from the bed of love, since rancour has entered their feelings" [304–306].

problem and offer a tentative solution to it. The *Gorgias* is a statement of
Plato's dilemma over a particular potential misuse of rhetoric: here we find
ourselves faced with a peculiar manifestation of the peitho/bia controversy.
The Sophists, we are given to understand, are propounding a false use of
rhetoric—*eristic*—which is, as it were, a verbal bia. Socrates is determined to
shun this at all costs. In the hyperbolic manner characteristic of his
philosophical method, the Socrates of the *Gorgias* at first condemns
"rhetoric" wholesale and then proceeds to a careful analysis and definition of
what rhetoric actually is; then, aligning it unconditionally with Goodness, he
stipulates that rhetoric must be understood right down to its roots: the
philosopher must discover and examine its first principles. This is his way of
saying that he wants rhetoric to be closely associated with dialectic—which
is, as I have said, far more erotic to Plato than mere genital contact. How
such a project is to be undertaken is not specified in the *Gorgias,* because the
method of dialectic is not spelled out there; it may not even have been fully
crystallized in Plato's own mind at that time. It is a project to which he
returns in the *Phaedrus*, where we learn much about the nature both of eros
and of dialectic, and of course, a good deal about peitho itself. But he does
not complete the project: he does not establish a truly dialectical approach to
rhetoric. And this is a point to which I myself shall shortly return.

Eros/Bia

Once all three terms have been introduced, a third axis may be drawn,
between eros and bia. (As it is somewhat less central to our realm of inquiry,
I shall comment only briefly on it here.) The ramifications of movement
along this axis are unsettling and sometimes macabre, but the mechanism is
clear: eros sometimes motivates to bia, particularly when peitho is useless. It
was the abduction of Helen by Paris that put into motion all the engines of
war, issuing in the Trojan conflict.[16] There is something of a family pattern
here, since Zeus had found it necessary to resort to bia in ravishing Leda,
who thus became Helen's mother.[17]

Occasionally it is eros thwarted that results in bia. This is the case with
Phaedra in Euripides' *Hippolytus*: driven simultaneously by self-loathing and
by eros for Hippolytus, she hangs herself and leaves behind a written
indictment which, she hopes, will destroy him. The entire play is prefaced by
the remarks of a savage and implacable Aphrodite:

> Such as worship my power in all humility,
> I exalt in honor.

---

[16]We mentioned Aeschylus' *Agamemnon* as an illustration of the peitho/bia axis. It might well be
considered along the eros/bia axis too, since Clytemnestra's eros for Aegisthus (and, one might say,
for her lost daughter Iphigenia) motivates her to act in bia against Agamemnon.

[17]Cf. too his abductions of Europa and Ganymede—archetypal moments in eros/bia.

But those whose pride is stiff-necked against me
I lay by the heels.

[5-6]

And the choral odes are much occupied with the potentially violent power of eros:[18]

Eros distills desire upon the eyes,
Eros brings bewitching grace into the heart
of those he would destroy.
I pray that Eros may never come to me
with murderous intent,
in rhythms measureless and wild.
Not fire nor stars have stronger bolts
than those of Aphrodite sent
by the hand of Eros, Zeus's child.
. . .
. . . he keeps the keys
of the temple of desire,
. . . he goes destroying through the world,
author of dread calamities
and ruin when he enters human hearts.
. . .
Kupris is like a flitting bee in the world's garden
and for its flowers, destruction is in her breath.

[525-64]

Even Hippolytus himself, who purports to have renounced eros, speaks constantly of Artemis in terms that can have sexual overtones: and his renunciation of eros brings him death with terrific violence.[19]

---

[18]Or Eros, the divine personification of passionate love. The description of him in the first stasimon, cited here, syncretizes him rather smoothly with Aphrodite (Kupris) herself.

There is a psychoanalytic theory asserting, essentially, that eros *is* bia: "In the absence of special physiological factors (e.g., a sudden increase in androgens in either sex) and putting aside the obvious effects that result from direct stimulation of erotic parts, hostility, overt or hidden, is what generates and enhances sexual excitement and its absence leads to sexual indifference and boredom. . . . The same sorts of dynamics, though in different mixes and degrees, are found in almost everyone. . . ." (Robert J. Stoller, "Sexual Excitement," *Archives of General Psychiatry* 33 [1976]: 899–909; my citation is from 903). This seems to be a hypertrophy of Freudian theory, as propounded in *Drei Abhandlungen zur Sexualtheorie* (Leipzip 1905). The social psychologist is liable rather to see sex and aggression as related but distinct behavior systems, whose relationship is susceptible to the influence of learning variables (Neil M. Malamuth et al., "Sexual Arousal and Aggression: Recent Experiments and Theoretical Issues," *Journal of Social Issues* 33 [1977]: 110–33); cf. the excitation transfer theory of Dolf Zillman, as set forth in (e.g.) *Hostility and Aggression* (Hillsdale, New Jersey: Erlbaum Associates, 1979) 335ff. The eros/bia axis, as we have delineated it, is expansive and complex enough to accommodate all these perspectives.

[19]Charles Segal, in "The Tragedy of the *Hippolytus*: The Waters of Ocean and the Untouched Meadow," *Harvard Studies in Classical Philology* 70 (1965): 117–69, demonstrates how the vocabulary of the *Hippolytus* is used to make this point; see especially 151–52.

The Triangle

These concepts—peitho, eros, bia—recombine in endless ways throughout Greek literature. (All three are to be found in Gorgias' *Encomium of Helen*, under the umbrella of Divine Will.) Particularly along the peitho/bia and peitho/eros axes, they persist in shaping the conceptualization of rhetoric from the earliest period on. The Triangle is not, however, a closed system. Each pair may be triangulated with yet another concept; bia/eros, for example, with *death*, as in the *Hippolytus*.[20] Peitho/bia may be triangulated with *dikê* (justice), as in the *Eumenides* (or in *Agamemnon* 385).[21] Such a strategy emerges as early as Hesiod, and continues down to Plato. And peitho/eros, curiously, are sometimes triangulated with *writing*.[22]

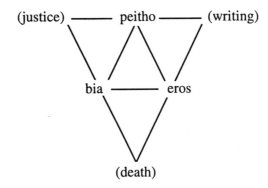

So the Great Triangle continues to grow. At its center, peitho, eros, bia, these three, abide; but from such a beginning, myriad new directions suggest themselves. One might supply secondary triangulations different from those I have suggested above. Doubtless the whole structure could be expanded indefinitely, even into three dimensions. In fact, it is at this level—when the geometry of our conceptual framework passes from plane to solid, and the Triangle becomes a Tetrahedron—that we begin to perceive the issues that are most critically at stake: what shall we put at the fourth point, at the top of the pyramid? Under what encompassing rubric shall we lodge our whole contemplation of the Great Triangle?

For Plato, the problem of peitho is a thorny and painful one. He makes

---

[20] A similar situation obtains in Euripides' *Medea*. It is out of the dynamics of her eros for Jason that Medea turns bia upon their own children, resulting in their death. And we must not forget Freud's famous eros/thanatos dyad.

  The reader may find it intriguing to peruse Georges Bataille's *L'Erotisme* (Paris: Editions Minuit, 1957), translated as *Erotism: Death and Sensuality* (San Francisco: City Lights Books, 1986).

[21] On *dikê* see Eric Havelock, *The Greek Concept of Justice* (Cambridge, Mass.: Harvard Univ. Press, 1978); also Michael Gagarin, *Early Greek Law* (Berkeley: Univ. of California Press, 1986), particularly chap. 5. Nagy, in chap. 20 of *The Best of the Achaeans*, discusses the antithesis of bia to *dikê*.

[22] A line of thought pursued in the later work of Roland Barthes, and, more recently, in Carson, *Eros the Bittersweet*.

great strides in the *Phaedrus*—the understanding of the *psukhê* as fueled by eros, the method of definition and division that provides a format for dialectical analysis—but he is tortured by humanity's proclivity to evil.[23] As far as Plato is concerned, this is the Serpent in the Garden of peitho, and eros is a shiny apple waiting to be eaten. How then to ensure a true and philosophic rhetoric, one noble and unsullied by the urges of the dark horse? These questions are not answered by Plato, and indeed he cannot answer them, for, despite his yearning for absolute Knowledge, he (like all his predecessors) has placed Power at the top of his Tetrahedron. As long as the Great Triangle is treated under the discourse of power, Plato can find no exit from the ethical problems that beset his understanding of rhetoric. Peitho is bound in the shackles of eros and bia. Had he only realized, he held a solution all along. But it was not for him, but for his greatest and most recalcitrant student, to see it.

That solution lies in providing the Tetrahedron with a different vertex: not Power, but Knowledge. Plato's Socrates defines rhetoric as a *"psukhagôgia dia logôn"*[24]—"leading-the-*psukhê* by means of words"—which is tantamount to saying, the use of peitho. Such a skill is obviously fraught with danger for one's audience, both the individual *psukhê* and the *polis* as a whole; hence the need for it to be used aright. This entails, most particularly, knowledge of the truth and commitment to goodness.[25] Even the latter is reducible, in the Platonic system, to knowledge, since knowledge of the good is held to produce virtuous behavior.[26]

Thus in his programmatic insistence on knowledge (as opposed to, say, right opinion) Plato sets the stage for Aristotle to make one of the boldest moves in the history of the philosophy of language: to redefine rhetoric, not as the *use of peitho* but as the *study of peitho*, the *dunamis peri hekaston tou theôrêsai to endekhomenon pithanon.*[27] Aristotle's "rhetoric" is in effect a metarhetoric. In this fashion, safely ensconced in the purview of dialectic,[28] rhetoric is disentangled from its immemorial encumbrances and associated with *theôria*, which for Aristotle is the supreme pursuit of the philosophic life, the principal parameter of happiness, and in fact the sweetest and best thing of all.[29]

The issues now couched in the discourse of knowledge, the axes of the Great Triangle are at last broken asunder. Free from the vagaries of eros and bia, Aristotle is able to examine the phenomenon of persuasive

---

[23] See *Phaedrus* 246ff. for Plato's famous comparison of the *psukhê* to a charioteer with a team of two horses.

[24] *Phaedrus* 261a. Cf. also *Gorgias* 453a, where rhetoric is defined as the *peithous dêmiourgos*. I take this genitive to be objective, and peitho here to mean persuasion as result.

[25] *Phaedrus* 262c, 273d-e.

[26] *Philebus* 20d; cf. also *Laws* 731c, 860d, and of course the *Protagoras*.

[27] *Rhetoric* 1355b, 26-27.

[28] *Rhetoric* 1356a, 30-31: *esti gar* [scil. *rhêtorikê*] *morion ti tês dialektikês kai homoia*. Here I prefer Kassel's reading to that of Ross (*homoiôma*).

[29] *Metaphysics* Λ.7.1072b, 24: *kai hê theôria to hêdiston kai ariston*. Cf. *Nicomachean Ethics* 1.5.1095b, 10.4.1174b, 10.7.1177a.

communication in serene perspective with all other human activities, and indeed with all other aspects of the phenomenal universe. A similar goal is accomplished, by similar means, in that curious little treatise, the *Poetics*. Just as, in Plato's *Gorgias*, rhetoric was accused of being not a *tekhnê* but a mere knack, so mimesis was excoriated in the *Republic* on the grounds that the mimetic artist can have no real philosophical understanding of imitation.[30] By providing a metapoetics within the discourse of knowledge, Aristotle can assert that poetics, no less than rhetoric, is indeed a *tekhnê* with demonstrable principles. He thereby achieves, to his own satisfaction, the liberation of poetics from the suspicion and shame heaped upon it by Plato. In addition, it is established (for the first time ever) as a discipline discrete and independent of rhetoric.[31]

Aristotle's solution is not, to be sure, one calculated to please everyone. I surmise that Plato would find in Aristotle's *Rhetoric* both more and less than he had bargained for. But it cuts the ethical Gordian knot in such a way that Aristotle finds himself free to pursue other issues. What a splendid irony. No sooner does he obtain his freedom than he presents us with another triad of his own devising: ethos, pathos, logos.[32]

---

[30]*Gorgias* 500e–501a, *Republic* 601c–602b.
[31]Though still intimately related to it: see John T. Kirby, "Aristotle's *Poetics*: The Rhetorical Principle," forthcoming in *Arethusa*.
[32]*Rhetoric* 1356a, 1-25.

From Hero to Citizen: Persuasion in Early Greece

by K. E. Wilkerson

Now do you know how we may best please God, in practice and in theory, in this matter or words? —Plato

Cultural concepts, especially those that are value-laden and that run deep in the currents of civilization, do not appear suddenly and fully developed. It is sometimes convenient and perhaps reassuring to account for their origins as if they did, but such explanations belong to the world of mythology and not to the methodology of history.[1] Traditional accounts of the origin of rhetoric declare that it made a precipitate appearance on the Greek scene about the middle of the fifth century B.C. Prior to that time there was no art *(techne)* of persuasive discourse but merely persuasion; or as H. D. F. Kitto puts it, before the Sophists, persuasion "had been a matter of native wit and practice."[2]

But scholars who have written about the unprecedented appearance of rhetoric in the fifth century are aware that skilled public speaking was to be found in Greek society at a considerably earlier time. Although preliterate speaking, they say, was uninformed by theory, it did not differ very much from the speaking that was so informed in the fifth century. Thus Walter Ong can say: "Once writing made feasible the codification of knowledge and of skills, oral performance, enjoying the high prestige that it did, was one of the first things scientifically codified."[3] George Kennedy, the reigning authority on Greek oratory, finds that "techniques of rhetorical theory are already evident in the speeches of the Homeric poems," but these precepts were

---

Reprinted from *Philosophy and Rhetoric*, 15. (1982): 104-125. Copyright 1982 by The Pennsylvania State University. Reproduced by permission of The Pennsylvania State University Press.

[1] Myths may sometimes illumine a shadowy cultural landscape. Ancient Israel, we must assume, was not one day lawless and the next governed by a moral code spoken by God to His prophet atop a stormy mountain. But the myth that relates these "events" dramatizes the special significance a set of practical laws had for a loose-knit group of Semitic tribes struggling to become a united people. Law for the ancient Hebrew was transcendent and suffused with spirit; thus it was regarded quite differently than was the code rather arbitrarily imposed upon the Athenians by Solon at a not much later time.

[2] *The Greeks* (Baltimore: Penguin Books, 1951), p. 168.

[3] That is, its rules were written down, not invented or changed. *Rhetoric, Romance, and Technology* (Ithaca: Cornell University Press), p. 4. See also Eric Havelock, *Preface to Plato* (New York: Grosset and Dunlap, 1967), pp. 304-5.

known, he thinks, only tacitly.[4]

These accounts tell us little about the development or even the condition of persuasion in Greece prior to the critical time when rhetoric itself could emerge in the forms of manuals for speakers and of speeches artfully designed for their audiences; they suggest instead that no significant development took place, or if it did, it is lost to our view in the dark age that preceded Homer.

Surely this complacent view of persuasion in archaic Greece overlooks more than it clearly sees. A close similarity between forms of discourse found in the eighth century and those found in the fifth is contrary to our expectations: poetry in the same interval had undergone radical change from epic to tragedy; the Greek intellect had experienced what Peter Green describes as a "rapid, tension-ridden, and spiritually fraught evolution";[5] revolutionary social and political changes had occurred. We can only marvel that persuasion could have enjoyed special immunity from the forces of change.

Apart from such general considerations, there are indications in the extant literature that persuasion in Homer's time was differently conceived and practiced than in the time of Socrates. There is, for example, the extraordinary interest expressed by Athenians of the fifth century in the Sophists and particularly in the art of speaking they practiced and taught. If their speaking and its precepts contained nothing strikingly new, how can one account for the excitement they generated? Another indication is that although the beginning of rhetoric can be located historically, the beginning of persuasion cannot; the Greeks accounted for its origins mythically in relation to their gods. *Peitho,* the Greek word for persuasion, can also mean temptation. Each meaning appears to have its own ancestry, for *Peitho* (persuasion) is the name of a Greek goddess, the daughter of Ocean and Tethys, according to Hesiod;[6] but *Peitho* (temptation) is the name of a demon, the offspring of Ruin, according to Aeschylus.[7] Whether goddess or demon, these identifications indicate that persuasion was linked with religion for the early Greeks. Homeric man believed the gods were instrumental in the conduct of his daily life; and although Athenians in the fifth century may have believed in the gods, most, if not all, of the Sophists were agnostics who believed human decisions are free of divine intervention and can be guided by reflection on rational criteria.[8] Since decision is a central concept of

---

[4] *The Art of Persuasion in Greece* (Princeton: Princeton University Press, 1963), pp. 35-40. This influential work was reprinted for the fifth time in 1974.

[5] "Answering Service," *The New York Review of Books,* 26 (April 5, 1979), p. 12.

[6] *Theogony,* 345.

[7] *Agamemnon,* 385. See Kitto's discussion of this distinction. *Poiesis: Structure and Thought* (Berkeley: University of California Press, 1966), pp. 47-49.

[8] Fifth-century enlightenment has been praised far in excess of what historical data will support, yet it is clearly evident from many sources, including the speeches of the early Attic orators, that added scope had been gained for the role of reason in the conduct of human affairs.

classical rhetoric, this belief of the Sophists must have influenced their concept of persuasion just as Homeric man's polytheistic belief must have influenced his. To paraphrase Peter Green, the world of human discourse bears one aspect in the *Works and Days* and quite another in the *Peloponnesian War.* It is a duty of the student of rhetoric to chart such distinctions.[9]

I

The animated portrait of Sophists found in Plato's *Dialogues* shows them to be characteristically hubristic and opportunistic. Protagoras, Prodicus, Gorgias, Thrasymachus, and Hippias—there were others not mentioned by Plato—were all alien teachers of rhetoric in Athens during the latter half of the fifth century B.C., and all seem to have prospered there. Plato was interested in their educational system,[10] which he attacked through the dramatic agency of Socrates, arguing that it was irrational and immoral. But despite his hostility toward them, Plato never fails to present the Sophists as being popular and admired for what their devotees perceived as wisdom and cleverness in speaking. In the *Gorgias* and the *Protagoras* these eponymous characters are surrounded by admirers who evince, as Jacquelin de Romilly has described, "how deeply these Greeks of the fifth century were, at all levels, enthralled by the power of speech."[11]

Given Plato's bias against the Sophists, we can assume that his portrait was not a perfect likeness. Its general accuracy, however, is supported by older contemporaries, notably Xenophon and Aristophanes, and by later writers in antiquity, including Aristotle;[12] there is also first-hand evidence regarding Gorgias to indicate that Plato accurately described his teachings.[13] Of all the Sophists Gorgias was the best known and most influential.[14] The heterodoxy of their ideas and their blatant appeal to self-interest seem not to

---

[9] "Answering," p. 12.

[10] Eric Havelock argues convincingly that the Sophists collectively created a system of education. *The Liberal Temper in Greek Politics* (New Haven: Yale University Press, 1957), p. 165.

[11] *Magic and Rhetoric in Ancient Greece* (Cambridge, MA: Harvard University Press, 1975). p. 37.

[12] According to Xenophon *(Anabasis,* II, vi, 17), one Proxenus paid Gorgias to teach him to be a man capable of dealing with great affairs. He appears to have become confident if not competent. The Sophists drew their most scorching fire from Aristophanes who, in *Birds* (1695), envisions a city completely overtaken by them: "In the fields of Litigation,/ Near the Water-clock, a nation/ With its tongue its belly fills;/ With its tongue it sows and reaps,/ Gathers grapes and figs in heaps,/ With its tongue the soil it tills./ For a barbarous tribe it passes,/ Philips all and Gorgiases./ And from this tongue-bellying band/ Everywhere on Attic land,/ People who a victim slay/ Always cut the tongue away." Philip was likely the son or a disciple of Gorgias. Trans. Benjamin B. Rogers. The Loeb Classical Library Edition (Cambridge, MA: Harvard University Press, 1924).

[13] See his "Encomium to Helen," trans. George Kennedy in *The Older Sophists,* ed. Rosamond Kent Sprague (Columbia: University of South Carolina Press, 1972), p. 52.

[14] Isocrates, who founded a successful school of rhetoric in Athens, had been his pupil. Philostratus says in *Lives of the Sophists*: "Gorgias [was] a man to whom as to a father we think it right to refer the art of the sophists." *The Older Sophists,* p. 30.

have lessened the demand for their teaching and performances.[15]

Athenian interest in the Sophists clearly ties in with other late fifth-century developments of moment for the study of rhetoric. Before about 460 B.C. there was no publication of speeches in Greece. Antiphon, another Sophist, was apparently the first to submit one of his speeches to the public in written form.[16] Among the first Greek works published in prose are the histories, the earliest of which we know from a few scattered fragments which tell us little or nothing about speaking; but Herodotus, in about 450 B.C., included reports of speeches which he considered to be efficacious in the historical events he recorded. He mentioned only what is necessary for his reader to be able to follow the development of events, unless the wording or the argument is unusually clever or otherwise interesting.[17] A generation later Thucydides evinced a quite different attitude toward speeches and their historic significance. He attempted to include in his history complete and, where possible, verbatim reports of public orations which he judged to be significant in the preparation for and conduct of the Peloponnesian War.[18] His painstaking care to preserve not just the most pertinent content of speeches but also the styles of their speakers suggests the attitude that deliberative speeches are in themselves significant cultural achievements. By the end of the fifth century, manuals on the art of rhetoric were readily available in Athens, and in the most significant development, rhetoric was well on its way to replacing poetry as the mainstay of educational discipline.[19]

I do not mean to suggest that public speaking was insignificant or of little interest to the Greeks prior to the fifth century. On the contrary, political and judicial arrangements described in Homer and Hesiod three centuries earlier indicate that speaking was already an often exercised and necessary feature of these institutions. Both an assembly of tribes and a council of elders are present in the *Iliad,* and both observe the institution of the sceptre: he who holds it is the speaker of the moment. In *Works and Days* Hesiod appears

---

[15]However exaggerated, Aristophanes' *Clouds* suggests that the Sophists' mercenary bent was a commonplace subject in the Athens of his day.

[16]The practice may have started when, as in the case of Antiphon, professional rhetoricians wrote forensic speeches for clients: since he had troubled himself to write the speech, he would have had copies made for public distribution. These would at least serve to advertize his persuasive skills. The oldest of Antiphon's extant speeches is assigned to the middle years of the fifth century (he was born about 479 B. C.), on stylistic grounds.

[17]Communication of a particularly graphic sort appealed to him. For example, his account of messages exchanged by Apries, an Egyptian king, and a faction of rebellious soldiers is richly detailed: the king "sent Amasis to the rebels, to appease the tumult by persuasion." But a rebel "put a helmet on his head, saying . . . that he thereby crowned him king." Amasis liked the idea and prepared to march with them against Apries. The king in turn sent Partarbemis, a courtier of high rank, to bring Amasis to him alive. When Partarbemis had delivered his message to Amasis, the latter "farted and said, 'Take that back to your master.'" *The Persian Wars,* II, 162, trans. George Rawlinson in *The Greek Historians,* vol. I (New York: Random House, 1942). Later references to this edition are parenthetical in the text.

[18]*The Peloponnesian War,* I, 22. Trans. Benjamin Jowett in *The Greek Historians,* vol. 1. That speeches were sometimes memorized is apparent from Plato's *Phaedrus,* 228b.

[19]Eric Havelock, *Preface to Plato,* pp. 47-49, 303-5.

troubled by the wrangles in court, which are noisy features of the social drama he describes. To be well-spoken was an evident virtue in the eighth century, and although a particularly pleasing voice might have been thought to be a gift of the gods and speakers from time to time were thought to have been inspired like the poets, speech training was not unknown.[20] The archaic Greek seems to have regarded public address as important, as something established and a stable feature of his society; but he took it for granted unless something momentous called for its exercise, as frequently happens in Homer, or it was abused.

In what ways, then, had public speaking changed that could account for the excited, positive interest Athenians expressed toward it early in the classical period? It is almost certain that the major changes occurred during the turbulent century which began with Solon's liberal reforms (circa 575 B.C.) and ended with the creation of the Delian League (477 B.C.). As Athens moved from the strictures of Draconian law toward her vivid, if brief, experiment in democracy, conditions were created that greatly favored sophistic rhetoric. Primary social and political realignments were necessitated, which must have altered the attitudes with which citizens of the polis regarded each other; as the polis became a more discrete political entity, mutual dependence was increased and class distinctions became of less consequence, but there was no significant lessening of mutual distrust.

Rhetoric, as the art of persuasion and compromise, was tailored to fit this new social milieu, and it was soon observed to be an effective social instrument for maintaining status and, frequently, for obtaining it. This tailoring had involved especially an alteration in the relation between speaker and audience, so much so that it bore slight resemblance to that which characterized earlier public address. Plato saw, perhaps more clearly than anyone else, that the essence of the art of persuasion developed by the Sophists resided in its psychology. In the dialogue that bears his name, *Phaedrus*, one of the excited admirers of the orator Lysias, says to Socrates: "I have heard that one who is to be an orator does not need to know what is really just, but what would seem just to the multitude who are to pass judgment."[21] That such was the cast of early classical rhetoric is attested to by Aristotle in his review of works on rhetoric: "The only thing to which their attention is devoted is how to put the judge into a certain frame of mind."[22]

---

[20]Phoenix claims *(Iliad,* IX, 443) to have been assigned by Achilles' father to teach the boy "to be . . . a speaker of words [*rhetor*]." All quotations from the *Iliad* are translated by A. T. Murray, in the Loeb Classical Library Edition, 2 vols. (Cambridge, MA: Harvard University Press, 1924). Later references are parenthetical in the text.

[21]*Phaedrus,* 260a. Trans. Harold N. Fowler, in the Loeb Classical Library Edition (Cambridge, MA: Harvard University Press, 1914).

[22]*Rhetoric,* 1354b. Trans. John H. Freese, in the Loeb Classical Library Edition (Cambridge, MA: Harvard University Press, 1926). All quotations from the *Rhetoric* are from this edition. Later references are parenthetical in the text.

To be persuasive the speaker is governed by the values, expectations, and feelings of his audience; he tells them, insofar as he can consistent with his goals, what they wish to hear.[23] But if these descriptions of sophistic rhetoric stress its shallowness and self-interest, it must not be overlooked that such discourse contemplates a decision based upon what is said, upon factors inherent in the speaking itself.

A conception of persuasion such as that described by Plato and Aristotle would have been anathema to Homer and Hesiod and to most of the lyric poets of the archaic period. Speakers in Homer are manifestly ingenuous: they speak from the *thymós,* the center of their feelings.[24] This same transparency of self is evident in Hesiod and the archaic lyric poets and appears to have been an almost universal desideratum of discourse within Greek culture until the appearance of sophisticated rhetoric in the fifth century.

Before examining the Homeric speeches, I wish to stress the peculiarly moral cast of the heroic attitude toward speaking. Eric Havelock's notable examination of the transition from an oral to a written mode of cultural devolution may suggest that changes in the attitudes of speakers toward themselves and their audiences are to be accounted for by changes in the technology of communication.[25] But it is abundantly clear that all the means necessary to develop an art of rhetoric are to be found in the Homeric poems; what was missing was the determination to use them in ways comparable to their uses by sophisticated speakers three centuries later. The heroic *areté* could not be compromised except by divine intervention in the practice of the two activities of highest repute in Homeric culture, fighting in battle and speaking. It can be argued that speakers in Homer, having only tacit knowledge of rhetorical principles, could not consciously employ them as did fifth-century orators whose literacy had made it possible for them to conceptualize those principles. I find no convincing reason to think such was the case. In a work of rare insight into the development of Greek thought Marcel Detienne and Jean-Pierre Vernant have shown that Homeric man was fully capable of the sort of thinking which the Sophists exploited in their speaking.[26] In Book XXIII of the *Iliad,* Nestor instructs the inexperienced

---

[23]Evidently rhetoricians in the fifth century were already image-makers and manipulators of appearances.
[24]"*Thymós:* the spirited, aggressive and impassioned aspect of the soul." H. D. Rankin, trans. *Archilochus of Paros* (Park Ridge, NJ: Noyes Press, 1977), p. 6.
[25]*Preface to Plato.* See esp. "The Homeric State of Mind," pp. 134-44.
[26]*Cunning Intelligence in Greek Culture and Society,* trans. Janet Lloyd (Atlantic Highlands, NJ: Humanities Press, 1978). "*Mêtis* is a type of intelligence and of thought, a way of knowing: it implies a complex but very coherent body of mental attitudes and intellectual behaviour which combine flair, wisdom, forethought, subtlety of mind, deception, resourcefulness, vigilance, opportunism, various skills, and experience. It is applied to situations which are transient, shifting, disconcerting and ambiguous . . . which do not lend themselves to precise measurement, exact calculation or rigorous logic." Pp. 3-4.

Antilochus in the tricks of chariot racing so that he can win though his horses are mediocre. Nestor sings the praises of *mêtis* (cunning), but not with regard to speaking. The authors are convinced that cunning intelligence was well developed before Homer's time and that it remained relatively unchanged through the whole of classical antiquity, although the Sophists "occupy a crucial position in the area where traditional *mêtis* and the new intelligence of the philosophers meet."[27] Perhaps the Platonic forms had to await the conceptual development which widespread literacy made possible before they could be articulated, but the stratagems which characterized the Sophists' manuals on rhetoric surely did not. The heroes' *areté* had been replaced by the Sophists' audacity.

II

A critical analysis of the Homeric speeches must consider that they are quasi-fictive creations of a poet (or poets), a folk genius who sang of "a god-like race of men," as Hesiod described them, and not of the "iron race" who labor and are full of sorrow, among whom Hesiod included himself.[28] Thus it is not likely that merely human speakers in the eighth century were "master[s] of refined forms of social intercourse [who spoke] with astonishing skill," as Hermann Fränkel describes Homeric man.[29] With Homer epic poetry had reached its fullest and most satisfactory expression; but its formulaic phrases, deliberate archaisms, elaborate similes, and complex, artificial hexameters are hardly suitable for the practical business of speaking in court[30] or before a deliberative assembly. Homeric speeches do not develop as speeches according to consistent principles of arrangement; that is not to say they are formless or hard to follow, but merely that if a would-be speaker studied them hoping to learn how to organize a persuasive speech, he would find little that is instructive. Kennedy says of Odysseus' speech to Achilles in *Iliad* IX that it is well arranged rhetorically,[31] but he does not say why he thinks so. I take him to mean that its structure is suited to its purpose—which it probably is—rather than that it corresponds to later rhetorical principles of

---

[27]Ibid., pp. 4, 12.

[28]*Works and Days,* 159, 176. Trans. Hugh G. Evelyn-White in the Loeb Classical Library Edition (Cambridge, MA: Harvard University Press, 1914). All quotations from Hesiod are from this edition. Later references are parenthetical in the text.

[29]*Early Greek Poetry and Philosophy,* trans. Moses Hadas and J. Willis (New York: Harcourt, Brace, Jovanovich, 1975), p. 76.

[30]There was forensic speaking of some sort in Homer's time. The famous description of Achilles' shield includes this scene: "The folk were gathered in the place of assembly: for there a strife had arisen, and two men were striving about the blood-price of a man slain: the one avowed that he had paid all, declaring his cause to the people, but the other refused to accept aught; and each was fain to win the issue on the word of a daysman" (*Iliad*, XVIII, 497-501).

[31]Kennedy, p. 37.

disposition. There are arguments in the speeches which are suggestive of what judicial argument may have been like in the eighth century, but these defy analysis in standard rhetorical terms: they do not appear to have the purpose of proving anything, which is not to say they are illogical. It happens that there is little to be proven by means of argument in Homer. The characteristic argument is one in which the speaker attempts to clarify and perhaps justify why he did something or why he persists in a particular mode of conduct, usually the latter. There are some interesting exceptions, however, which I will mention below.[32]

A marked consistency of Homeric speakers is their outspokenness, their propensity for unabashed emotional expression and lack of secretiveness. Since this quality is discernible in Hesiod and the earliest lyric poets,[33] it is safe to assume that it reflected both an ideal of discourse and, to some extent, speech performance in the eighth century. The attitude a speaker assumes before his audience is critical to all that follows in his performance and their responses; thus I am surprised that this salient feature of the epics has not received more attention. It has been discussed, of course, particularly by scholars whose subject is Homeric psychology, but little has been said of it with reference to speech situations as such. Kennedy, for example, does not mention it directly. Fränkel, one of the foremost authorities on Greek poetry, is interested in the attitudes of speakers but discusses them mainly in connection with a shift he finds from ingenuousness in the *Iliad* to worldly sophistication in the *Odyssey*. Given certain extremes in Odysseus' behavior in the younger epic—his lies and disguises—Fränkel's opinion is plausible and deserves consideration.

According to Fränkel, Achilles is the representative hero of the *Iliad* as Odysseus is of the *Odyssey*: Achilles is great because he is "wrathful and stubborn," Odysseus because he is "'versatile.'"[34] "Even deception and falsehood are now [in the *Odyssey*] legitimate weapons in the struggle for existence,"[35] Fränkel says, and directly to the point states that "the epic personnages . . . are far from expressing themselves frankly."[36] For him Odysseus is not only the model of "Ionian cunning and boldness"; he also represents "the modern ideal of the clever and experienced man who makes his way by all means, straight or crooked."[37] But if the hero uses crooked means, it is surely incumbent on the reader to notice the contexts in which he does, and if he is dishonest, to ask to whom. That the *Odyssey is* a travel

---

[32]See n. 49 and 52, below.

[33]See, e.g., Hesiod's remarks on judges, *Works and Days.* 37-40, 248-51, and 263-64. Archilochus is said to have been so potent a writer of vituperative verse that he caused a family to commit suicide. Rankin discusses the probable truth of the legend. (*Archilochus,* pp. 47-56.)

[34]Fränkel, p. 85.

[35]Ibid., p. 86.

[36]Ibid., p. 91.

[37]Ibid., p. 86. This modern ideal was clearly the ideal of the Sophists.

adventure filled with the fancies of a seafaring people Fränkel notices early in his critique.[38] He describes it as romantic and mythical in contrast with the historical and political cast of the *Iliad,* yet his judgments of their heroic ideals rests upon an unwarranted assumption that Odysseus behaves differently in the later epic in situations that are comparable to those in which he appears in the *Iliad.* But he is also of "many wiles" in the earlier epic, where he does not appear as the central character and where he is depicted in few situations which call for the exercise of his craftiness. Even in the *Odyssey* his wiles are evident only in the most extreme situations, in which extraordinary measures must be taken, usually for the sake of survival.[39] But when I compare the speeches he makes to friendly peers in both epics, I find an even consistency in his words and actions. Odysseus is presented as a gifted speaker in both, he speaks copiously and well in both, and his skills do not make him disingenuous; he tries but is unable to hide his tears from the assembled Phaecians.[40] Nor is Odysseus wanting in outspokenness. When Euryalus mocks him before the assembly saying, "'Thou dost not look like an athlete,'" Odysseus, although a stranger dependent upon the hospitality of the Phaecians, replies "with an angry glance . . . 'Thou hast not spoken well; thou art as one blind with folly'" *(Odyssey,* VIII, 164).[41]

The fullest examples of debate before an assembly of peers in the *Odyssey* do not feature the man of many wiles but his son, Telemachus, who lacks neither wrathfulness nor stubbornness, the special characteristics of Achilles. After the youth has spoken for the first time before the Achaean assembly, the poet comments: "Thus he spoke in wrath, and dashed the staff down upon the ground, bursting into tears" *(Odyssey,* II, 80). He is answered by Antinous, a wooer of his mother: "'Telemachus, thou braggart, unrestrained in daring, what a thing hast thou said, putting us to shame, and wouldest fain fasten reproach upon us!'" *(Odyssey,* II, 85). He hides neither his feelings nor his intentions even though they are directed against the audience of suitors: "'Now that I am grown, and gain knowledge by hearing the words of others, yea and my spirit waxes within me, I will try how I may hurl forth upon you evil fates, either going to Pylos or here in this land'" *(Odyssey,* II, 315). Thus even if the later epic better represents attitudes found

---

[38]Ibid., p. 49.

[39]For example, in his encounters with the Cyclops and the suitors, but he is also wily when Nausicaa finds him naked on the beach.

[40]*Odyssey,* VIII, 85. Trans. A. T. Murray in the Loeb Classical Library Edition (Cambridge, MA: Harvard University Press, 1919). All quotations from the *Odyssey* are from this edition. Later references are parenthetical in the text.

[41]Consistency of characterization is pointed to by Sir Maurice Bowra as a primary reason for seeing "a close connection" between the epics. He says of Odysseus: "In the *Odyssey* [he] is ten years older than in the *Iliad,* but he is unchanged in his courage, resourcefulness, courtesy, vigorous appetites, and capacity to deal with other men." "Composition," in A *Companion to Homer,* ed. Alan J. B. Wace and F. H. Stubbings (London: MacMillan, 1962), pp. 66-67.

in the poet's own time, it is not established that cleverness was then replacing frankness as a desideratum of human discourse.

I do not mean to suggest that archaic speakers were never strategic or deceitful, but only that if they were known to be so as a rule, they were not therefore admired, as Fränkel appears to suggest. The heroes themselves are aware of these possibilities in others. Achilles says in reply to Odysseus' appeal to him to be reconciled with Agamemnon: "Needs must I verily speak my word outright . . . for hateful in my eyes, even as the gates of Hades, is that man that hideth one thing in his mind and sayeth another" *(Iliad,* IX, 310-13).[42] Oaths are frequently required of those who promise aid. Odysseus, with good reason, makes Calypso and Circe swear they will not harm him *(Odyssey,* V, 178; X, 343). Although wary that someone may lie, the heroes show no awareness that they might be misled by means of psychological stratagems of the sort recommended by the Sophists. Odysseus may disguise his appearance, but he speaks from the same heroic stance, his mettle undiminished; his lies are blatant misstatements of fact. Neither he nor any other speaker in Homer concedes anything to any audience beyond their acknowledged worthiness. Proteus could change his shape but not his character.

As Kennedy points out, "later antiquity found formal rhetoric everywhere in Homer."[43] "Menelaus [was regarded] as an example of the plain style, Odysseus of the grand style, and the honey-sweet speech of Nestor as the model of the middle style."[44] The broadest generalization in this regard that Kennedy's own analysis yields is equally rewarding: "Oratory in the Homeric poems is always represented as extemporaneous and as fitted together out of words or groups of words known to the speaker."[45] Such attempts at rhetorical analysis illustrate a cautionary remark made by Fränkel that an examination of the speeches in Homer could "produce rich and surprising conclusions [but they] must not be approached with the narrow and superficial categories of formal rhetoric, as has often been attempted with no substantial gain."[46]

It should surprise no one to find in Homer what were later thought of as rhetorical elements, because the early rhetoricians, Gorgias in particular, turned to the Greek poets for techniques adaptable to speechmaking.[47]

---

[42]Hesiod echoes Achilles' thought in an epigram: "Do not let your face put your heart to shame" *(Works and Days,* 713).

[43]Kennedy, p. 35.

[44]Ibid., p. 36.

[45]Ibid. To his credit Kennedy recognizes that the speeches should be viewed at least partly in other than rhetorical terms. He notes that Homer treats speech as an "irrational power," the product of "inspiration, a gift of the gods." But he does not pursue this point.

[46]Fränkel, pp. 83-84, *n.*

[47]"It was a poetical style that first came into being, as that of Gorgias" (Aristotle, *Rhetoric,* 1404a). "Gorgias transferred poetic expression to civic discourse because he did not think it right for the orator to be like a private citizen" (Dionysius of Halicarnassus, *On Imitation,* trans. George Kennedy, in *The Older Sophists,* p. 40).

Argument, which Aristotle considered to be the basis of rhetoric, is not wanting in the epics, although he makes no reference to them in this regard. On the contrary, verbal contention between peers is at the center of development in both poems, whether on Olympus or the plains of Ilium. Achilles, whose valor at arms may have overshadowed his prowess as a speaker, is capable of sustaining a complex and consistent argument. His speech in *Iliad* IX in reply to Agamemnon's offer of gifts through an emissary, contains a line of argument with no fewer than ten steps and a quite varied set of appeals, including this touching simile: "Even as a bird bringeth in her bill to her unfledged chicks whatever she may find, but with her own self it goeth ill, even so was I wont to watch through many a sleepless night" (323-27). He concludes his argument with an overstatement that the translator describes as "splendid rhetoric":[48] "Some [spoil] he gave as prizes to chieftains and kings, and for them they abide untouched; but from me alone of the Achaeans hath he taken and keepeth my wife, the darling of my heart" (333-36). But the burden of this is simply to state his vehement opposition to any offer from the humbled king; an Aristotelian analysis of it in terms of logical proof would not further our understanding of its peculiar features but rather obscure them. No question of fact, value, or policy is at issue: there is nothing for his hearers to decide.

More typically a Homeric argument lacks complex development—is the barest of enthymemes—even if it concerns a substantial and momentous issue. The opening quarrel between Agamemnon and Achilles illustrates this. The king demands recompense for the maiden he has surrendered to appease the wrath of Apollo, resting his case on a single appeal: it would not be "seemly" for him, the king, to do without (*Iliad*, I, 119). Achilles' rejoinder is equally singular: it would not be right to take from someone booty that has been properly apportioned to him (125). In retaliation Agamemnon says he will have Briseis, a maiden allotted to Achilles. The speakers mainly denounce and threaten each other with violence before the assembly until Nestor, "the clear-voiced orator of the men of Pylos," joins the fracas. Agamemnon, he advises, should not seek to take the girl from Achilles for she was properly given to him by the Achaeans; Achilles should not strive against the king for "he is the mightier, seeing he is king over more" (275-82). These are arguments only in the most rudimentary sense, consisting of simple appeals to well-established rules of conduct or to facts apparent to all. They do not represent the highest level of Homeric reasoning as the exceptional arguments prove,[49] but they do suggest that Homeric society did

---

[48]*Iliad*, vol. 1, p. 406, *n.*

[49]Nestor comes at least close to developing an argument based on probability. He advises the king to separate his men by clans so that clan allegiance will be an incentive for each man to fight at his best (*Iliad*, vol. 2, 360-66). Had he been speaking before Athenians three centuries later, he might have added: "for it is evident that a man will usually fight harder if he has the honor of his clan to uphold." See n. 52, below.

not view argumentation as an effective means for settling disputes. The real policy decision was made before the quarrel began when Agamemnon agreed to return the priest's daughter,[50] a decision based on a seer's determination of Apollo's will.

The disputes in the *Iliad* are mostly like quarrels between young boys: the speakers are controlled by their emotions; they do not check them nor do they manipulate them to impress their hearers; they are in no sense given to using what Aristotle describes as emotional proof. Most often the speaker directs his anger against the audience or some part of it. If an emotion is eloquently expressed, it is so in poetic terms and not because of the practical requirements of rhetoric. The speaker is not artfully displaying emotion as the Sophists later advise; i.e., its expression is not under the control of the audience.[51] When Agamemnon replies to Nestor in *Iliad* I, he acknowledges that the old warrior has spoken "according to right," but it makes no difference that he has because Achilles wants to give the orders, and that is sufficient affront for him to continue to be outraged.

A commonplace type of statement in the speeches that may be viewed as evidence of speaker strategy is the statement in which the speaker attempts to shame his audience or some part of it. References to shame occur so often in Homer that the subject requires careful attention. Since the act of shaming may imply to us an attitude of moral superiority in the person who undertakes it, we might think shaming is a persuasive strategy related to ethos or character, one of the types of proof discussed by Aristotle. But the concept of ethos would not help us understand this feature of Homeric discourse since shaming is attempted before assemblies by an untried youth (Telemachus), by a warrior universally despised as a speaker (Thersites), by a maiden in the house of Odysseus (Melantho), as well as by those who are much respected as speakers and as men of wisdom.[52] Nestor is quite given to the practice but never evinces specifically moral superiority, and he is no more successful in making his listeners ashamed than is any other speaker. Odysseus causes Thersites to shed "a big tear" but appears to do so with the blows he lands on the rowdy's back rather than by his speech. When Agamemnon at last relents in *Iliad* IX and acknowledges to Nestor that he had been "blind," it is long after Nestor's attempt to shame him, and after many defeats at the hands

---

[50]I will look at the suasiveness of oracles, auguries, etc., in Homer below.

[51]Thrasymachus wrote a treatise on pathos of which Aristotle seems to have approved in principle (*Rhetoric*, 1404a). Aristotle's own discussion of style contains advice on using the language of the emotion appropriate to a particular subject *(Rhetoric*, 1408a).

[52]In *Odyssey* II Telemachus, still unfledged, tries to shame the suitors into leaving with a rather subtle argument: he suggests that if they are truly angry with him they will not wish to stay, then adds, "if this seems in your eyes to be a better and more profitable thing, that one man's livelihood should be ruined without atonement, waste ye it" (138-43). Thersites calls the assembled Achaeans, "Soft fools! base things of shame, ye women of Achaea, men no more" (*Iliad*, vol. 2. 235-36). Melantho, in front of the suitors, says to Odysseus, who is disguised as a beggar: "Surely wine has mastered thy wits, or else thy mind is ever thus, that thou does babble idly" (*Odyssey*, XVIII, 329-30). He calls her "a shameless thing" in response (333-34).

of the Trojans (114-16).

There is an anomaly here: attempts to control conduct by means of shaming pervade the epics, but they are shown to be largely ineffective if not disruptive. E. R. Dodds and A. W. H. Adkins in separate works maintain that the society described by Homer is a "shame-culture." For Dodds this means in particular that individuals project onto others (the gods included) attitudes, impulses, and conduct they consider improper; thus much of the shaming undertaken in the epics, in this view, is a sort of scapegoating.[53] This interpretation suggests that shaming is more a matter of habit than of persuasive strategy, so that when Nestor tells the unruly Achaeans they are holding assembly like silly boys, such words would have been expected by them and are thus commonplace and impotent. According to Adkins a shame culture is one in which the sanction "is overtly 'what people will say.' "[54] What should be stressed in Adkins's definition is the requirement of overtness. Athenian society in the fifth century recognized the sanction, but it was covert; Athenians, as Pericles boasted, had come under the rule of a more or less coherent legal system that was splendidly overt. Lacking such, Homeric man, in his ready tendency to shame others, was encouraged to do so by his society. I think the general ineffectiveness of shaming to control behavior that Homer reveals was related to the prevailing conditions of disorder and confusion that characterized his own time, conditions which marked the end of a cultural age. At such a time one would expect to find forms of behavior that were still followed although their utility had long since been dissipated.

Aristotle discusses shame as an emotion relevant to the epideictic speaker who seeks to censure or demean someone or something. In his dry and unremitting prose he tells us who can inspire it, under what conditions, about what matters, etc. (*Rhetoric*, 1383b-1385a). But the speaker's attempt is seen to direct the emotions of the audience toward someone or something and not to shame the audience. There is much to suggest that the sanction of "what people will say" was a far more effective means of social control, although covert, in classical Athens than it had been overtly in Homeric Greece. Creon, for example, in Sophocles' *Oedipus Tyrannus,* is a revealing character with regard to this notion; in his demonstration of civic virtue and his concern to keep unpleasant things hidden, he might be viewed as a model Athenian

---

[53]*The Greeks and the Irrational* (Berkeley: University of California Press, 1951), p. 17.

[54]*Moral Values and Political Behaviour in Ancient Greece* (New York: Norton, 1972), p. 12, *n.*

[55]Kitto comes close to this view aligning Sophocles with Pericles and, after noticing Creon's concern with ordered civic life, ending his discussion of the tragedy by remarking: "The modesty of Creon is a better example [of conduct] than the towering self-confidence of Oedipus" (*Poiesis*, pp. 233, 242). Rankin makes a pointed observation with regard to the same tragedy. "The suicide of a person irredeemably shamed may be observed in the case of Iokasta (Epikaste in Homer). Homer's version simply relates that she kills herself for shame, as a result of finding out the nature of her relationship to Oedipus; Sophocles' Iokasta only decides to kill herself when it becomes apparent to her that the incestuous relationship is inevitably going to be published at large" (*Archilochus,* p. 55).

citizen of the fifth century.[55]

As Aristotle observes, there were important exceptions to the rule of covertness in classical Athens, namely, satire and the old comedy *(Rhetoric.* 1384b). Writers of these genres, he says, are chiefly occupied with the failings of their fellow men. They did not always escape censure for their efforts: Cleon unsuccessfully prosecuted Aristophanes for high treason, according to Sir Paul Harvey;[56] for libel, according to Peter Green.[57] Socrates, too earnest for satire, was yet one who concerned himself with the failings of men. He was not convicted for atheism, but as he says in his defense, because he had made certain of his fellow citizens feel bitter hostility toward him as he searched for a wiser man than himself *(Apology,* 38c-39d). His defense is an exceptional instance of an extant public speech delivered in classical Athens in which the speaker deliberately and directly shames the audience whose decision is critical to his own welfare—with what result all the world knows.[58]

It is instructive to compare Pericles' rhetorical defense of his conduct of the war with Socrates' unaccommodating stand. Pericles acknowledges to the assembly he has hastily called that they are angry with him; he goes so far as to say they have accused him of following the wrong policy because their own characters are weak. But he immediately rationalizes their behavior for them, saying in effect, "I understand why you have weakened." In Thucydides' rendition he says, "Your minds have not the strength to persevere in your resolution, now that a great reverse has overtaken you unawares. Anything which is sudden and unexpected and utterly beyond calculation . . . cows the spirit of a man" *(Peloponnesian War,* II, 61). Pericles was the definitive orator, a man steeped in rhetoric who could face an angry audience, blame them, praise them, and appease them to the point that they would again do his bidding.[59] Socrates, who referred to the necessity he was under to speak the truth, shunned rhetoric and did not let his audience off the hook. Homeric man would have found both Athenians strange; he would have

---

[56]*The Oxford Companion to Classical Literature* (London: Oxford University Press, 1962), p. 43. Sir Paul is the compiler and editor.

[57]*The Shadow of the Parthenon* (Berkeley: University of California Press, 1972), p. 30.

[58]Fifth-century Athenian concern to maintain a favorable public image is vividly illustrated by Critias, one of the Thirty Tyrants, who was hardly above reproach. He wrote of Archilochus: "If he had not published such a reputation of himself amongst the Greeks, we would not have learned that he was a son of Enipo who was a slave-woman; or that he left Paros through poverty and lack of means and went to Thasos; or that when he arrived he was hostile to the people who were there, speaking ill impartially of both friends and enemies. Nor would we have known, in addition to these facts, that he was an adulterer, had we not learned it from himself; nor that he was a sex maniac and a rapist; nor (what is even more disgraceful than this), that he threw away his shield. So Archilochus did not prove to be a good witness in his own cause, leaving such a fame and repute behind him." Critias did not see fit to credit him with having been a frank and honest witness *(Archilochus,* p. 11).

[59]Thucydides comments that following the speech the Athenians "took his advice, and sent no more embassies to Sparta; they were again eager to prosecute the war. . . . The popular indignation was not pacified until they had fined Pericles; but, soon afterwards, with the usual fickleness of the multitude, they elected him general and committed all their affairs to his charge" *(Peloponnesian War,* II, 65).

applauded Socrates' courage and bluntness but not fully understood his moral position; that Pericles excused his audience would have surprised him, but he would have admired the orator's results.[60]

Kennedy, following Maurice Croiset, finds that the "artistic proof [of] ethos ... is often illustrated in Homer." I suppose there is some sense in which one can say that the most highly regarded of the Homeric speakers rely upon character and status to be convincing, but these are very nearly the same in Homer. It would be more precise to say they have won the right to speak as they do having demonstrated their worth through success in the grand and grave trials set for them by their culture. There is no artistry in their "displays" of *areté*. Aristotle says that "the orator persuades by moral character when his speech is delivered in such a manner as to render him worthy of confidence. ... But this confidence must be due to the speech itself, not to any preconceived idea of the speaker's character" *(Rhetoric, 1356a)*. In Homer the relative worth (worthiness) of everyone is already determined and is taken into account by speakers and listeners alike; the self is established and transparent. Thus nothing could be said to make its qualities more apparent. But we should be wary of applying even the nonartistic sense of character to the Homeric heroes since it is tied into our notions of moral goodness which are quite foreign to those found in the epics. Above all, the heroes are men of violence whose highest virtues are attainable only in victory over the enemy. There are moral notions in Homer, of course, but they have a mien far different from the middle-class virtues we approvingly find in the *Nichomachean Ethics*. Thus when Nestor acclaims himself before the assembly, he boasts of having fought with the Lapiths, not of being a law-abiding citizen.

III

If to persuade becomes necessary in the epics, the means employed tend to be extraordinary from a classical point of view.[61] When in *Iliad* IX Agamemnon acknowledges the worth of Achilles and his own folly, he moves to make amends by sending sumptuous gifts to the young warrior. Since that is the form prescribed by his culture for the purpose, he expects it to be effective. Nestor agrees that the gifts are sufficient recompense (he obviously has considered Achilles' measure of worth, his *areté*). That the gifts are not persuasive attests to the magnitude of Achilles' anger and, I should think in the poet's eyes, to the sublimity of his personal worth. Kennedy comments

---

[60]As Adkins stresses, "Homeric man lives in ... a 'results-culture'" *(Values, p. 12, n.)*.
[61]When, according to Hesiod, the gods created Pandora, Persuasion *(Peitho)* gave her gold necklaces. Hermes gave her speech *(phonen)* together with crafty words and a deceitful nature *(pseudea th aimylious te logous kai epiklopon ethos)*. This passage from *Works and Days* suggests that persuasion was not primarily thought of as an end of speaking (73-79).

that the prizes and not the speech of Odysseus who describes them "are the considerations principally intended to persuade Achilles." No one would deny it; but he adds that they "take the place of arguments,"[62] a statement I find misleading. No argument is called for since the king has confessed his error and resorted to the means dictated by the situation; arguments would have been equally futile and, given the circumstances, fatuous.

The most extraordinary and successful instance of persuasion occurs near the end of the *Iliad* (XXIV, 432-692). Aided by Hermes, Priam comes as a suppliant to Achilles, who is "seized with wonder" at the sight of the old king. He "clasped in his hands [Achilles'] knees, and kissed his hands, the terrible, man-slaying hands that had slain his many sons" (477-79). He entreats Achilles to return Hector's body by asking him to recall his own aging father. They sit awhile crying together. Achilles returns the body with apologies to the ghost of Patroclus and grants the Trojans an appropriate time free of hostilities in which to bury it. But it must be stressed that Priam has paid "a countless ransom for Hector's head" (578-79) and Achilles has concluded that the mission itself is under the protection of a god. Kennedy thinks Priam's appeal succeeds because it is pathetic in the Aristotelian sense.[63] The scene is pathetic but that should not blind us to other motives prompting Achilles' behavior. Humility and earnest pleading, if done according to custom, could be persuasive where clever argument or mere emotional appeal would certainly fail, and the suppliant is protected by Zeus himself. Achilles warns Priam: "Stir my heart no more amid my sorrows, lest, old sire, I spare not even thee within the huts, my suppliant though thou art, and so sin against the behest of Zeus" (567-70). The custom appears to have endured into the fifth century, but it does not seem to have greatly influenced the discussion of rhetoric.

When Achilles is restrained from harming Priam in part at least because he senses that the suppliant is being helped directly by a god and because he acknowledges the will of Zeus, his conduct indicates how potent is the causal agency of the Olympians, an agency at work throughout the epics. It takes many forms: dreams, oracles, omens, and especially, the direct appearance of a god or goddess, frequently disguised, who persuades a mortal to do or not to do something of consequence. The significant decisions, those that affect the conduct of the war or Odysseus' return to Ithaca, are all influenced by divine agency.[64]

---

[62] Kennedy, p. 37.

[63] Ibid.

[64] For a thorough archaeological account of the Homeric gods see Part 2 of Martin P. Nilsson's *The Minoan-Mycenaean Religion and its Survival in Greek Religion,* 2nd rev. ed. (New York: Biblo and Tannen, 1972). For interesting interpretations of the roles of the gods in Homer see Dodds, *Irrational,* pp. 1-63; Bruno Snell, *The Discovery of the Mind,* trans. T. G. Rosenmeyer (New York: Harper Torchbooks. 1960), pp. 23-42; Joseph Russo and Bennett Simon, "Homeric Psychology and Oral Epic Tradition," pp. 41-57, and M. M. Willcock, "Some Aspects of the Gods in the *Iliad,*" pp. 58-69, in *Essays on the Iliad,* ed. John Wright (Bloomington: Indiana University Press, 1978).

The significance of the gods for Homer is as great as it appears to be in the poems. That may seem a trivial statement, but there are interpretations which would reduce their functions to merely mechanical ones, either to move the plot along or to vivify the presentation of thoughts. In a recent paper on Homer's psychology, the authors state: "It is our opinion that the demands of the poetic performance, with its special rapport between audience and poet, encourage a psychological world-view which finds it most natural to portray private mental activity as a process of continuous interchange between persons."[65] ("Persons" for them refers also to gods.) They claim support for their view from Dodds, who opines: "How much more vivid than a mere inward monition is the famous scene in *Iliad* I where Athena plucks Achilles by the hair and warns him not to strike Agamemnon!"[66] It is, indeed. But Dodds's support for their general view is surely doubtful since the burden of his great work is to prove that myth, religion, magic, etc., were of major cultural significance in Greece even at the height of classical enlightenment. Bruno Snell, whose study of Greek psychology is highly regarded by the same authors,[67] thinks the gods are more important in Homer than they allow for. Snell refers to the above scene in which Athena stays Achilles and generalizes: "Homer's man does not . . . regard himself as the source of his own decisions; that development is reserved for tragedy. When the . . . hero, after duly weighing his alternatives, comes to a final conclusion, he feels that his course is shaped by the gods."[68]

The poems reveal the saliency of divinity throughout. Consider the dramatic development of *Iliad* II. The book begins with Zeus sending Agamemnon a dream that bids him arm his men and attack the Trojans, who, the dream says, have fallen from favor with Zeus. The king hastily summons the Achaeans to gather. He describes the dream to his council of elders, who agree that its command should be followed. Before rallying his army to fight, however, Agamemnon makes "trial of them in speech" (73-74). He faces an unruly audience: "The place of gathering was in a turmoil, and the earth groaned beneath them . . . and a din arose" (95-97). As the king stands before them, the poet digresses on the sceptre, the symbol of authority to speak, held by Agamemnon, and details its descent from Zeus (100-9). Agamemnon tells the warriors that Zeus now bids him "return inglorious to Argos" (114-15). Their response is immediate and direct: "Their shouting went up to heaven, so fain were they of their return home; and they began to take the props from beneath their ships" (151-54). Athena prompts Odysseus to rally the homesick host, but when reassembled they are even more unruly. Thersites, an unfavored man of the people, with a mind "full of great store of disorderly

---

[65] Russo and Simon, p. 56.
[66] Dodds, p. 14.
[67] Russo and Simon. p. 41.
[68] Snell, p. 31.

words," reviles Agamemnon with "shrill cries" (215-41). Odysseus scolds, then whips the malapert, to the delight of the crowd. In this chaos Odysseus speaks. His first effort, not surprisingly, is to shame them: "Like little children or widow women do they wail" (289-90). But he nourishes their weakened resolve by recalling to them the prophecies of Calchis. He recounts how Zeus had sent "a great portent: a serpent, blood-red on the back, terrible," and carefully details the events of that fateful day, ending by quoting the prophet who had foretold that Zeus would grant them victory in the tenth year of the war (300-30). It is enough. The Achaeans shout praises of Odysseus' words until "the ships echoed wondrously" (333-35). Nestor then also recalls to them the signs of eventual victory sent by Zeus (352-56). The assembly ends with sacrifices and prayers to the gods.

Clearly Homeric man believed his course was shaped by the gods. If persuasion, in particular the artistic persuasion governed by rhetoric, contemplates decision, we should not be surprised to find that in Homer either it is ineffective or, if effective, it is directly related to divine sanction or activity. The suppliant succeeds because Zeus commands his host to grant hospitality; the gods are persuasive because they possess extraordinary powers to influence human behavior. Telemachus, however, fails to persuade the suitors to leave his house, not for want of good reasons or skilled presentation but rather because they would persist in their pleasure until there was some sign to indicate divine displeasure. As one of them says to Telemachus, the matter "lies on the knees of the gods" *(Odyssey,* I, 400-2). This primary condition for the development of the art of rhetoric—belief in the efficacy of human decision—missing in Homer was not fully present in ancient Greece until the fifth century. I cannot agree with Snell that it remained for the tragic poets to develop it, although they clearly dramatized its development. I think that it evolved through the attitudes of the lyric poets and the unprecedented adventures in thought of the pre-Socratics, and under the influence of political changes which saw the rule of law well established in the polis of Athens.

Homeric Origins of Ancient Rhetoric

by Andrew J. Karp

It will be the argument of this paper that the elements of an implicit if sketchy theory of persuasion can be drawn from the Homeric poems. The interest of such an investigation into Homeric rhetoric is threefold:

1) The investigation will proffer a new reading of Homer.
2) It will provide evidence that Homer was a forerunner of, if not an influence on, later explicitly philosophic formulations of theories of persuasion (in particular, those of Plato and Aristotle).
3) It will offer some insight into the Greek conception of justice, by considering what Homer understands the relation of rhetoric and justice, and rhetoric and truth, to be.

To alleviate the confusion which surrounds the concepts of persuasion and rhetoric, and to delimit the sphere of this study, I will outline at the outset the five theses which are assumed and argued in this paper. The following two (I-II) theses are assumed:

I) The uncontroversial thesis that the poet Homer both employed rhetorical figures and was understood in antiquity to have been a master of rhetorical figures.
II) The uncontroversial thesis that Homer's characters, when speaking, frequently employ rhetorical figures and techniques for the purpose of persuading one another, and that they often explicitly talk of persuading one another.

Arguments are presented to prove the following three (III-V) theses:

III) The thesis that persuasion is an important, if not central, theme in both the *Iliad* and the *Odyssey*.
IV) The central thesis that the different instances of persuasion in the Homeric poems constitute an implicit theory, or at least a set of consistent claims, about how effective persuasion functions, and on whom it functions.

Reprinted from *Arethusa* 10 (1977): 237-258. Reprinted by permission of The John Hopkins University Press.

The necessary element for such a skeletal theory of persuasion (following Aristotle, *Rh.* 1356a ff. and 1358a36-1358b1) is a recognition of the tri-partite character of persuasion; viz., a recognition that persuasion, to be effective, must take into consideration the relation of speaker—speech—audience and, more broadly, that effective persuasion must take the relation of agent of persuasion—means of persuasion—object of persuasion[1] into consideration. If Homer can be shown to allow that effective persuasion depends upon the manipulation of these three factors, then, I submit, we will have shown that the Homeric poems implicitly contain the skeleton of a theory of persuasion.

V) The thesis that Homer was at least sometimes read in antiquity as a rhetorical theorist.

Part A of this paper will discuss persuasion as a theme in the Homeric poems (III above, with passing reference to I). Part B will analyze elements of a theory of persuasion in the Homeric poems (IV above) and will form the bulk of the paper. Part C will conclude the paper with a brief mention of a Socratic interpretation of Homer (V above). The following five insights of Homer into the nature of rhetoric[2] will be discussed in sections 1-5 of Part B:

B.1. The "language" of rhetoric—
> Concerning the means and the agent of rhetoric, Homer recognized that rhetoric is not limited to verbal persuasion but may be non-verbal as well.

B.2. The psychology of rhetoric—
> Concerning the object and the agent of rhetoric, Homer believed that rhetorical methods must conform to the character of the audience in order to persuade effectively. He also held that:
> a) Effectiveness of persuasion is dependent upon the character of the speaker.
> b) Under certain circumstances rhetoric must give way to force as the most efficient way of effecting action.

---

[1] The phrase "object of persuasion" is of course ambiguous. I intend it to denote the person to whom persuasion is directed, not the goal or aim of the persuader.

[2] As will be evident below, I am using "rhetoric" in its very broadest sense, as "discourse or actions directed primarily toward influencing the beliefs or actions of an audience," viz., as persuasive "language" (where "language" may indicate any consistent method of communication). Such a definition of "rhetoric" avoids imposing upon Homer distinctions about "rhetoric" that are drawn later in antiquity.

B.3. Rhetoric and truth—

Concerning the means of rhetoric, Homer held that:

a) Truth is often unpersuasive.

b) In order to persuade effectively, one must often suppress or distort the truth; thus falsehoods or deceptive semblances of truth must often be employed in order to effect persuasion.

c) The ability to fool men into trusting false appearance is attributable to an ability to create likenesses of things in words and deeds (e.g., lies and disguises).

B.4. Rhetoric and theology—

Homer believed that persuasion is the gods' primary tool of contact with men and involvement in human affairs. Through persuasion, gods can reveal their will to men and manipulate them, without jeopardizing human free will. Men, in turn, must make attempts at persuasion through propitiation in order to affect the will of the gods.

B.5. Philosophic implications of rhetoric—

Homer subscribed to the views that:

a) Rhetoric is often just and beneficial to those on whom it is practiced. Since most men do not know what is in their own best interest, they will neither understand nor act upon what is good for themselves. In order to motivate acts beneficial to men themselves and to the community, those who know what is good (wise men and gods) must employ persuasion. Homer, consequently, subscribed to paternalism, for the practice of which rhetoric is a primary instrument.

b) Truth and rights of individuals can and should (under certain circumstances) be suppressed in the interests of social justice.

A. Persuasion as a Theme in the Homeric Poems

Homer was recognized in antiquity as a master manipulator of language and his poems were frequently used to exemplify the variety of rhetorical elements. Quintilian considered Homer the source and foundation of ancient formal rhetoric. (*Inst.* 10.1.46)[3]

---

[3] Cf. *Inst.* 2.17.8; Cic. *Brut.* 40, 50; Ps.-Plu. *Vit. Hom.* On Homeric rhetoric, see G. Kennedy, "The Ancient Dispute over Rhetoric in Homer," *AJP* 78 (1957), 23-35; *The Art of Persuasion in Greece* (Princeton 1963) 35-39, particularly notes 21-23.

Igitur, ut Aratus ab Iove incipiendum putat, ita nos rite coepturi ab Homero videmus. Hic enim, quem ad modum ex Oceano dicit ipse amnium fontiumque cursus initium capere, omnibus eloquentiae partibus exemplum et ortum dedit.*

Moreover, Aristotle reports that Homer first employed lies and faulty inference as effective persuasive techniques and, "above all taught the others [the other poets] how they should lie," (*Po.* 1460a18-19).[4] Homer's concern with persuasion, however, goes beyond his use of language. The verb *peithô* (I persuade) and its passive counterpart *peithomai* (I am being persuaded, I am obeying) occur countless times in both the *Iliad* and the *Odyssey*. The passive is frequently used to indicate an audience's response to a speech, e.g., "He spoke and they were persuaded/they obeyed," or "He spoke and they were not persuaded/did not obey." The preeminent man, as Phoenix suggests (*Il.* 9.443), must be a speaker of words as well as a doer of deeds, and a speaker's success is measured by the degree of persuasion/compliance he elicits in his audience. A speaker persuades his audience by using the right tactic to win them over to his particular opinion or plan. To persuade is to succeed in persuading; in Classical Greek, as in English, 'persuade' is an achievement verb (see Ryle's well-known distinction between task and achievement verbs).[5]

In the Homeric poems verbal persuasion is central to any decision procedure. Thus attempts at persuasion highlight the attempts to resolve the famous conflicts surrounding Agamemnon and Achilles in the *Iliad* and Odysseus in the *Odyssey*. Homer's concern with persuasion, however, goes beyond a concern with mere speeches. The question by whom and by what one should be persuaded, and to whom one owes obedience, are central to the struggle between Achilles and Agamemnon, to Odysseus' struggle to return home and to the very relationship between men and gods. The plot of the *Iliad* revolves around three attempts at persuasion:

1) The attempt to persuade Agamemnon to give up Chryseis and to then give up Briseis.

2) The attempt to persuade Achilles to return to battle.

3) The attempt to persuade Achilles to return Hector's body.

---

*I shall, I think, be right in following the principle laid down by Aratus in the line "With Jove let us begin," and in beginning with Homer. He is like his own conception of Ocean, which he describes as the source of every stream and river; for he has given us a model and an inspiration for every department of eloquence. (trans. H. E. Butler)

[4] On Homer's skill at mixing lies with truths, cf. Str. 1.2.9. and Hor. *AP* 151.

[5] See G. Ryle, *Concept of Mind* (England 1949). Also J. N. Garver, "On the Rationality of Persuading," *Mind* 69 (1960). For a discussion of the semantics of *peithô* in Homer and a brief discussion of the theme of persuasion in Homer, see G. M. Pepe, "Studies in Peitho" (Ph.D. Dissertation, Princeton University, 1966). Also A. P. D. Mourelatos, *The Route of Parmenides* (New Haven 1970), Ch. 6, "Persuasion and Fidelity."

The distinction between the ways Agamemnon is persuaded and the ways by which Achilles is finally persuaded outlines a fundamental difference between Agamemnon and Achilles. Whereas Agamemnon can be persuaded to return Chryseis only on the condition that he receive another prize, and can be persuaded to return Briseis only as a result of his fear of defeat, neither goods nor fear can change Achilles' mind. He refuses to be persuaded by (obey) Agamemnon. Since Achilles denies that words or gifts (in his own case) are the necessary or sufficient conditions for persuasion, he will accede neither to Agamemnon's persuasive words nor to his persuasive gifts. Achilles says that he will not be persuaded to return to battle until Agamemnon pays for all his heartrending outrage against him (*Il.* 9.386-387). But what can make up for past human suffering or convince Achilles of Agamemnon's remorsefulness? Unlike Agamemnon, Achilles cannot be persuaded by the gambits of compensation, threat or public interest. Achilles will accede to persuasion only out of piety toward the gods, or out of love for his friends (e.g., Patroclus) or relatives. Love for his own father along with the will of the gods persuades him to take pity upon Priam and return Hector's body (see *Il.* 24.507-508 and 371). An analysis of the justifications for, and the causes of, Achilles' resistance to persuasion is central to an understanding of the *Iliad*.

Similarly, the *Odyssey* records Odysseus' resistance to countless attempts to persuade him to relinquish his homecoming. He must mentally steel himself against Circe's erotic charms and Calypso's temptation to immortality, and literally bind himself against the enchanting speech of the Sirens that "takes away men's homecomings" (for Circe see *Od.* 9.33, for Calypso 7.258, for the Sirens 12.39-40). The mind of Odysseus, however, is *akêlêtos*; it cannot be charmed or persuaded (10.329, if this line is authentic); he must resist persuasion in order to return home and reassert his role as ruler, husband and father.

Resistance to persuasion is only one side of the persuasion theme in the wanderings of Odysseus. Unlike Achilles, who insists upon speaking frankly and refrains from fooling others, Odysseus is a master of persuasion and deception. All lying is as hateful to Achilles "as the gates of Hades" (*Il.* 9.312-313); only lying compelled by poverty is equally hateful to Odysseus (*Od.* 14.156-157). Odysseus does not consider lying in itself reprehensible. The *Odyssey* is filled with elaborate examples of Odysseus persuading others to believe lies about his identity and his adventures. It is, moreover, a testimonial to Odysseus' mastery of rhetoric: he not only knows how and when to lie, but he knows when the truth must be suppressed (see *Od.* 12.222-225 and below) and when it must be revealed (e.g., to the Phaeacians, *Od.* 9-12, and see particularly 11.363ff. and below).[6] The issues of persuasion

---

[6] It might be argued that the use of such terms as "lie" and "deceit" in describing the actions of Homeric characters (particularly Odysseus, see sections B.3. as well as B.4. below) imbues those actions with a moral baseness foreign to Homer and to the Greek terms for intentional falsehoods. Such a criticism

which center about Odysseus will be discussed in part B.

In *Iliad* 2.1-210 occurs a scene of paramount importance for illustrating the theme of persuasion in the Homeric poems—a scene to which we will return in our discussion of persuasive theory as well. It depicts, in quick succession, no fewer than five separate attempts at persuasion. This sequence of successful and unsuccessful attempts at persuasion is as follows:

1) Zeus persuades Agamemnon to attack the Trojans by convincing him (in a deceitful dream) that the gods have abandoned the Trojans and that his attack will therefore be successful (1-72). Knowing Agamemnon, Zeus knows that just such a dream of divinely sanctioned conquest will persuade him to act. Nestor and the other kings are persuaded that Agamemnon is telling the truth about his dream because they also believe that they know Agamemnon's character (79-83).

2) Agamemnon attempts to persuade his troops (with words) to fight by pretending to give up the battle. His attempt at persuasion fails, however, since his troops take him literally and flee to the ships (73-74, 110-141). Agamemnon, persuaded by the deceit of Zeus, tries to persuade his troops to arm for battle by a deceitful show of cowardice (139). But Agamemnon's ploy is unsuccessful for, unlike Zeus, Agamemnon misunderstands the character of those he is addressing and unlike Odysseus (see below), Agamemnon believes that words are sufficient for persuading the many (75). Instead of shouting down Agamemnon's cowardly excuses, the crowd shouts out with joy and heads for its ships. The effect of Agamemnon's speech is just the opposite of the effect he intended; in this case, deception is totally unpersuasive.

3) Athena persuades Odysseus (with divine "words") to stay the flight of the men caused by Agamemnon's speech (155-181). Agamemnon must be bailed out by the gods and Odysseus. Hera advises Athena to try to persuade Odysseus to stop the panic flight of the troops.

4) Odysseus persuades the kings (with gentle words) to stay their flight (188-197).

5) Odysseus persuades the people/demos (with harsh words and a blow) to stay their flight (198-210).

The issues which this scene raise about the nature of rhetoric will be

---

would suggest that these terms impose a modern moral standard upon ancient morally neutral concepts and would replace "lie" and "deceit" with terms such as "fabrication," "fictionalization," or even "falsehood," (I owe this point to an anonymous reader and Professor John Peradotto). The difficulty with such terms, however, is that they fail to convey the sense, indispensible to my analysis, of actions or speeches performed with the explicit *intention of distorting or withholding the truth* from some particular group. While "lie" and "deceit" may contain connotations alien to Greek culture, I find the denotation of these terms still closest to the meaning and spirit of the Greek. Because of the differing evaluation of terms between different cultures (which is my point), we must be satisfied with imperfect translation. (For a discussion of the problems surrounding the translation of value-terms from Greek, see A. W. H. Adkins, *Moral Values and Political Behaviour in Ancient Greece,* [New York 1972] Ch. 1). By using these terms, therefore, I do not mean to settle beforehand the case of the moral status of lying in Homer; this subject and the concomitant one of the moral status of lying and deception in modern society are highly controversial and outside the scope of this paper.

discussed in part B of this paper. At this point we need only conclude from this scene that persuasion is a prominent means of interaction between men and gods here as elsewhere in the Homeric poems.

The theme of divine persuasion (i.e., persuasion of men by gods) will be considered in section 4 of part B. Nonetheless, it is worth noting here that whereas the gods rarely intervene physically in human action, they frequently employ verbal or non-verbal methods of persuasion in order to affect human actions. The most famous incident in the *Iliad* of divine "intervention" in the world is the staying of Achilles' hand by Athena. Intervention here only appears to be physical. In fact, Athena stops Achilles' hand just to persuade him to pursue a more reasoned course of action; "I have come down from the sky in order to stay your anger, if [in the hope that] you will obey [be persuaded]," (*ai ke pithênai, Il.* 1.207-208). The goddess' qualification of her action cannot be explained away by the formulaic character of Homeric verse. It is Achilles' piety and not Athena's physical force that finally prevents Achilles from killing Agamemnon. Were Achilles' character other than it is (for example, had he the character of Thersites), Athena's attempt at persuasion would have fallen upon deaf ears. Thus, even in this most famous incident can be seen recurring themes of persuasion and persuasion's motivation in the Homeric poems.

B. The Theory of Persuasion in the Homeric Poems

B.1. The "Language" of Rhetoric

There are two points to be made here: the first concerns the agent of persuasion. It is a linguistic fact that Homer does not restrict the agent of persuasion to persons.[7] Just as in English one can speak of being persuaded by reifications of words, facts or circumstances, so too in Homeric Greek can one be persuaded by similar reifications. One can, for example, be persuaded by night (*Il.* 7.282 = 7.293; 8.502 = 9.65 = *Od.* 12.291) or by old age (*Il.* 23.644-645); similarly Phoenix wishes Achilles to be persuaded by the gifts of Agamemnon (*Il.* 9.111-113). Homer recognizes that those things which appeal to self-interest can be said to be persuasive (e.g., money). Moreover, if "persuasion" be taken in the broad sense of "(the act of effecting) a change in or shaping the set of beliefs or dispositions to action of the audience by neither purely rational (*viz.*, instruction) nor purely physical (*viz.*, coercion) means," then Homer can be said to admit the properties of objects and persons, as well as objects and persons themselves, to persuasive agency. Thus it is Helen's beauty and not Helen herself that nearly persuades the elders that the Trojan War is worthwhile (*Il.* 3.156-158). Her beauty arouses

---

[7] The middle or passive *peithomai* can take a dative agent that is either a person or an inanimate object. As far as I know, however, there are no occurrences in Homer of inanimate objects as subjects of the active form of the verb *peithô*.

an erotic feeling in men which affects their souls; they become charmed and lose control of themselves. Similarly it is Achilles' anger at Hector or his love for Patroclus that persuades him to return to battle—no words could have persuaded him.

The more important point about the "language" of rhetoric concerns the means by which living agents (men or gods) persuade. Although there is slight linguistic evidence for this claim, there is ample textual evidence that Homer allows agents to use other than verbal means to effect persuasion (taking "persuasion" in its broad sense). Just as it seems possible for sign-language to effect persuasion, so Homer thinks it possible that the gods (in particular) can and actually do employ signs as rhetorical "language." A number of suggestive examples are available from the text. The "words" by which the gods communicate with men (for the purpose of persuading them) apparently border upon non-verbal communication since they are heard only by the person to whom they are directed. Moreover the signs and omens sent from the gods, such as the dream that Zeus sent down to Agamemnon or the position of birds in the sky, are non-verbal attempts to affect the actions of men. Plainly then at least this modest conclusion is admissible: Homer does not preclude non-verbalizing agents, nor non-verbal means, from effectiveness in persuasion. Thus Homer can be said to have delimited the initial elements in a skeletal theory of persuasion: he has identified the proper agents and means of persuasion.

B.2. *The Psychology of Rhetoric*

The most important illustration of Homer's understanding that persuasion, to be effective, must conform to the character of the audience addressed,[8] occurs in the scene in Book 2 of the *Iliad* cited above (page 40). Agamemnon, you will recall, had failed utterly in his attempt to persuade the troops to arm for battle. He had wanted merely to test and stir their mettle; he had instead roused their cowardice and their desire to return home. Agamemnon had seriously misread the character of his audience by making an appeal to shameless men on the grounds of shame.[9] He was unjustified in

---

[8] For a discussion of the role of the character of the audience in persuasion, see Arist. *Rh.* 1377b24-1378a5 and the details which follow, 1378a19ff.

[9] Cf. *Rh.* 1383b11-1385a13 on the conditions for and causes of shame. The opening section of Book 2 of the *Iliad* has occasioned much controversy. Agamemnon's seemingly gratuitous test of the army has led many scholars to treat that incident as a separate level of the *Iliad* (independent of Agamemnon's dream of victory) and as a serious suggestion to flight. Such a view is espoused, for example, by W. Leaf, *A Companion to the Iliad* (New York 1892) 66-69. Wilamowitz and Reinhardt, however, argue convincingly for the internal consistency of the opening of Book 2. Wilamowitz argues that Agamemnon's speech contains veiled suggestions of hope and endurance rather than flight and is "wirklich eine Versuchung," *Die Ilias und Homer* (Berlin 1920) 269. Reinhardt points out that Agamemnon directed a speech to the people that was suitable only for the leaders (*Die Ilias und ihr Dichter* [Göttingen 1961] 113). Thus Agamemnon's test of the people develops an important point about the inability of *all* the Achaeans to be persuaded by an appeal to shame.

believing his troops would be ashamed to flee. Because Agamemnon was ignorant of the souls of his men, he was not able to persuade them to act as he wished.[10] Agamemnon reveals himself as a man who can be persuaded but cannot persuade. Just so does he distinguish himself from Achilles and Odysseus, both of whom can persuade[11] but cannot themselves be persuaded.

Upon Odysseus falls the task of counteracting Agamemnon's folly. Athena tells Odysseus to draw *each man* back to the ship with gentle words (*Il.* 2.164 = 2.180, *sois aganois epeessen erêtue phôita hekaston*). Athena tells Odysseus both what must be done (check the flight) and how to do it (persuade each man with gentle words). Odysseus, however, while accepting the end that must be accomplished, alters the means. The kings and the preeminent men he persuades with gentle words (*Il.* 2.188-197); the common man (*anêr dêmou*, the demos, *Il.* 2.198) he persuades with harsh words and the thrust of a blow (*Il.* 2.198-206). Odysseus disobeys the particulars of Athena's instructions precisely to avoid a second fiasco. He recognizes that gentle words will not persuade everyone to turn back but only those who can feel shame and who loathe the label "coward." Odysseus, in knowing the souls of those he must address, knows that he cannot employ the same means to persuade the demos as to persuade the kings.[11a] All men's characters are not the same and, therefore, different means are necessary to effect the same end (e.g., to instill the same belief or arouse the same action) in different men. Odysseus chooses to persuade the noble men by telling them the plain truth (that Agamemnon was testing them) and by threatening them with the wrath of a Zeus-nurtured king. The demos he forces and rebukes.

Unlike Agamemnon,[12] Odysseus recognizes that force (or, more accurately, the show of force) must accompany persuasion in certain circumstances if one wishes to effect the desired end in the souls of certain men. He brandishes his sceptre, a symbol of sovereign right and power, to persuade

---

[10]Agamemnon may also be guilty of an inability to inspire belief in his own character, either through a lack of good judgment (*phronêsis*) or a lack of goodwill towards his audience (*eunoia*). See *Rh.* 1378a6-13 and section B.3. below.

[11]Odysseus, of course, is the master of persuasion. Although Achilles hates lies and deception, he is skilled in words and capable of persuading when he so chooses. He knows how to stir his troops with words (*Il.* 16.200-209) and occasionally tells different stories to different men. For example, he gives Odysseus and Ajax different accounts of when he will leave Troy (cf. Pl. *Hp.Mi.* 371bff.). Similarly he gives different accounts of his instructions to Patroclus when speaking to Patroclus himself (*Il.* 16.80-96), when praying to Zeus (16.233-248) and when talking to himself (18.13-14). I owe this point to Seth Benardete. For a brief discussion of the rhetoric of Achilles and Odysseus, see O. C. Cramer, "Speech and Silence in the *Iliad*," *CJ* 71 (1976) 300-304.

[11a]Cf. K. Reinhardt (above, note 9) 113: "[Odysseus] weiss, wie anders man zu Fürsten als zu Gemeinen redet." Xenophon makes a similar point explicitly in *Anabasis.* 2.6. Proxenus was capable of commanding the noble men in his company but found that many of his soldiers plotted against him. He believed that to be a good general it was sufficient to praise those who act nobly and to withhold praise from those who act unjustly. He failed to control the majority of his soldiers, however, since he mistakenly imagined that the same speech could have the same effect upon the noble and the base. Hence he was incapable of impressing all his soldiers with feelings of respect and fear for their leader.

[12]Agamemnon makes the mistake of using words with the common man and force with the kings (e.g., he takes Briseis from Achilles by force, *Il.* 1.430). instead of vice-versa.

Agamemnon's men to obedience. Thus Odysseus' form of persuasion, in this instance, is both non-verbal and forceful.[13] Homer, through Odysseus, shows that he recognizes that effective persuasion depends on the speaker's (the agent of persuasion's) adaptation of his rhetorical methods to the character of his audience (the object of persuasion).

A correlative point is also illustrated in the *Odyssey* by the different stories that Odysseus tells to different men,[14] and in particular by his recognition that only certain men will be disposed, by faith in the speaker or by native discernment, to believe the truth. Thus it is only to the god-like Phaeacians (9-11) and to his wife Penelope (23.310ff.) that Odysseus dares tell the true stories of his adventures. He knows that Penelope will believe him because he knows that she trusts his character. He knows that the Phaeacians will believe him because they are god-like and sharp of understanding. Alcinous, the king of the Phaeacians, shows that Odysseus' belief was justified when he declares, after hearing Odysseus' tales, that Odysseus is a man beyond lying and deceit (11.363ff.)! These incidents will be discussed again in section B.3 below.

Homer recognizes that the character of the speaker (persuader), and thus the attitude of the audience (objects of persuasion) to the speaker, play an important part in persuasion. The incident mentioned above concerning Penelope is illustrative. Whereas Odysseus in disguise tells Penelope truths (e.g., *Od.* 19.273-282) mixed with lies, he tells her only the truth after he has revealed himself (23.310ff.). Odysseus knows that Penelope will be persuaded that his stories are true because he knows that she trusts him as her husband and is familiar with his character. Similarly Nestor tells Agamemnon (*Il.* 2.79-82) that the Argive leaders believe that Agamemnon is telling the truth (when he tells them about his dream from Zeus) only because he who is recounting the dream is Agamemnon, best of the Achaeans. Had he been any other man, the Argive leaders would have called him a liar and not been persuaded that he had dreamt such a dream. Therefore, a persuader's ability to secure the compliance of his audience depends not only on his ability to gauge the character of his audience, but also on his ability to gauge his audience's opinion of his own character (cf. Arist. *Rh.* 1377b22-1378a19). He must suit his means of persuasion to both measures.

Thersites is an example of a man who cannot persuade anyone as a result of the disrespect in which he is held by those he is addressing. Regardless of

---

[13] A show of force (threat) is by this account a legitimate form of persuasion in contradistinction to physical force itself. Aristotle hints at the effectiveness of combining verbal persuasion and force (particularly as a means of calming men who have acted rashly) when he suggests that a verbal attack should precede a physical attack when trying to calm a slave who recognizes that he is being punished justly (*Rh.* 1380b18-20).

[14] A feeble attempt to explain how the differences in Odysseus' lies depend upon Odysseus' intentions and the character of the person addressed is given by R. B. Woolsey, "Repeated Narratives in the Odyssey," *CP* 36 (1941). A somewhat more convincing attempt is made by C. R. Trahman, "Odysseus' Lies," *Phoenix* 6 (1952).

the truth of what Thersites says, the kings will not be persuaded by Thersites' words. Thus he charges Agamemnon (*Il.* 2.212-242) with those very crimes for which he (Agamemnon) could be held accountable: selfish abuse of power and use of force for his own ends rather than for the good of his people (e.g., stealing Briseis). Moreover Thersites' charges against Agamemnon are very similar to Achilles' charges; they both see through Agamemnon's hybris. Thersites' observations, however, are met with harsh words (2.245) and the sceptre (2.265), rather than with gentle words. The truth spoken by the common man Thersites is met with derision and punishment; the same truth spoken by Achilles seemed both just and acceptable.

Thersites' ill luck raises some specific questions about the relation of truth and rhetoric (which will be addressed in section B.3. below). We can conclude from Thersites' case that the truth is not simply persuasive regardless of who is telling it. Thersites, but not Odysseus, would have persuaded kings more effectively had he spurned the truth. The analysis in this section leads to the conclusion that Homer recognizes that effective persuasion must take both the character of the speaker and the character of the audience into consideration. Thus the Homeric poems contain another element essential to a skeletal theory of persuasion: a recognition that effective persuasion depends upon the relation of the agent of persuasion to the object of persuasion, and a recognition that the means of persuasion must be accommodated in this relation.

B.3. *Rhetoric and Truth*

The case of Thersites illustrates one way in which Homer recognizes that truth is not always (or even often) persuasive. A man's character and relation to his audience can reflect upon what he says and consequently overshadow the truth of his statements. One is reluctant, for example, to be persuaded by a man one hates, even if that man is telling the truth. Homer also recognizes, however, that truth is itself often unbelievable and unpersuasive, regardless of who tells it. Odysseus expunges the fantastic from his lies in order to make them more believable than the fantastic truth. His elaborate lies about his identity and adventures (e.g., *Od.* 13.154-286, 14.199-359, 19.172-202, 24.304-314) are more convincing accounts of what might have happened than would be the accounts of Odysseus' true adventures with gods and monsters. Odysseus understands that truth is often more unbelievable than well composed lies.[15] Homer realizes that the probable and the truthful are not one and the same, and that persuasion is often more effective when based upon the probable. In the Homeric poems, only the gods and the god-like can hear

---

[15]Cf. Arist. *Po.* 1460a26-27, *proaireisthai te dei adunata eikota mallon ê dunata apithana*: "[In writing stories] one should choose incidents that are likely but impossible over those that are unlikely but possible."

and believe the truth, for only they have enough understanding to realize the gap between the probable and the truthful. Thus, as, mentioned above, only the god-like Phaeacians and the faithful Penelope are able to be persuaded by the truth when they hear it. Effective persuasion directed to most men must be based upon lies and deceit.

Homer's claim is made through Odysseus, who also expresses his understanding that the truth must sometimes be suppressed if persuasion is to succeed.[16] We have seen how Odysseus recognized that truth would have no persuasive effect upon the demos. In order to persuade his crew to act in their own best interest, Odysseus refrains from telling them about the unavoidable danger of Scylla (*Od.* 12.222-225). The truth would have merely roused their fear, slowed their rowing and resulted in a greater loss of life. By suppressing the truth, Odysseus persuades his crew to continue rowing and consequently acts for their own good.

There are frequent examples in the Homeric poems of persuasion accomplished through lying and deception. Many of these examples are instances of the gods lying or deceiving men in order to persuade them to act in accordance with divine will.[17] Zeus' deceptive dream to Agamemnon cited above is such an example. Zeus persuades Agamemnon by telling him just the opposite of the truth: he tells Agamemnon that the Achaeans will conquer the Trojans when, in fact, evils are planned by Zeus for the Achaeans and not for the Trojans.

Athena is said to have persuaded the mind of Pandarus in its folly (*Il.* 4.104: *tôi de phrenas aphroni peithen*) when she brings Pandarus to shoot the treacherous arrow at Menelaus. Her method of persuasion is to make Pandarus believe that he will win great glory by killing Menelaus. Yet Athena knew all along that Pandarus would not kill Menelaus. She plays upon the Trojan's desire for glory by persuading him with a deceitful promise. Similarly Agamemnon says that he was mad and persuaded in his wretched mind (*Il.* 9.119: *all' epei aasamên phresi leugaleêisi pithêsas*) when he admits the folly of his theft of Briseis. In the case of both Pandarus and Agamemnon, persuasion (by a god or god-sent *Atê*) leads man to act against his own apparent best interest by convincing him that some act *is* in his own best interest (e.g., shooting at Menelaus, stealing Briseis).[18] The gods, like men, apparently employ persuasive images and words which are enmeshed with lies and deceit. The question of whether these divine methods are intended ultimately to serve man's own best interest will be taken up in the next section of this paper.

Odysseus in the *Odyssey* gives us a somewhat deeper analysis of how one persuades (i.e., the means of persuasion) than has been offered so far.

---

[16]Cf. Aristotle's lament that the deficiencies of audiences compel the orator to appeal to non-apodictic elements in his speech, *Rh.* 1404a5-8.
[17]See section B.4. for further discussion of this point.
[18]See also Agamemnon's association of deception and persuasion, *Il.* 1.132.

Odysseus persuades by imitating what is true. That is, Odysseus' persuasive expertise consists in his ability to make convincing likenesses of himself in deed (e.g., through disguises) and in speech (e.g., through lying). He is able to fool all but one of the Trojans by likening himself to a beggar (4.247-248: *allôi d' auton phôti katakruptôn êiske/dektêi*). Most importantly, Homer describes Odysseus' ability to persuade in speech as an ability to make likenesses by making false things look like they are true (19.203: *Iske pseudea polla legôn etumoisin homoia*).[19] Even the physical likenesses that Odysseus carries about seem real. As he tells Penelope, the dog and the fawn pictured on his golden clasp moved and struggled like real animals (19.228-231; note how soon after the previously cited passage this occurs and cf. the activity on Achilles' shield, *Il.* 18.490ff.). Both in word and in deed, Odysseus' likenesses are indistinguishable from that of which they are likenesses; his pictures of animals are like real animals, his lies are like truths. The persuasive ability of Odysseus is ascribed to his skill at making likenesses, at making what is false look like it is true. It is but a small step from this skill to the rhetorician's skill of making what is a weaker argument look like a stronger argument. Homer has isolated likening (or imitation) as central to the method of persuasion.

Odysseus' ability to liken one thing to another lies at the heart of his resourcefulness and persuasive talent, and is a key to his characterization as *polutropos*. In order to be able to create likenesses, one must be able to recognize resemblances and comparisons between things (*viz.*, one must have the ability to compare, cf. *Od.* 6.151-152). Hence the expert in making likenesses should also be an expert at recognizing likenesses (i.e., at recognizing likenesses as likenesses). He should not be able to be fooled into thinking that something which is a likeness is actually not a likeness. Thus the expert liar should never himself be taken in by a lie, nor the expert camouflager fooled by a disguise.

In order to avoid further confusion, let me restate my argument. If, (1) the ability to recognize likenesses is a necessary condition for the ability to create likenesses, and if (2) the ability to create likenesses is a necessary condition for the ability to persuade, then (3) the ability to recognize likenesses is a necessary condition for the ability to persuade. Thus, (4) the master of persuasion should also be a master of recognizing likenesses and (as stated above) will consequently not be taken in or fooled by likenesses.

Furthermore, if to liken is to persuade, then to be taken in by likenesses

---

[19]Cf. Hes. *Th.* 27 where the Muses rather than man have this ability. Wilamowitz takes this as evidence that Hesiod preceded and is being recalled by Homer; Odysseus can thus create likenesses as well as can the Muses (*Die Heimkehr der Odysseus* [Berlin 1927] 49). There is some dispute over the meaning and necessity of *iske*, but it has little or no effect on the meaning of the sentence as a whole. Almost all editors accept the line as genuine. On the knowledge of truth required for Odysseus' ability to lie, cf. Pl. *Hp.Mi.* 365ff. On the art of rhetoric as an art of likening, cf. Pl. *Phdr.* 261d ff. and *Rep.* 382.

is equivalent to being persuaded. Hence the master of persuasion will himself be most resistant to persuasion. Our earlier examples of Odysseus and Agamemnon uphold this conclusion. Odysseus, who is persuasive, is immune from mortal persuasion or persuasion against his will;[20] Agamemnon, who cannot persuade, is persuadable. Homer seems to believe that there is some common factor that connects the ability to persuade and the ability to resist persuasion.

The relation of likening to persuasion is not unproblematic. The ability to liken is clearly only a part of the ability one needs in order to persuade effectively. Not all cases of likening are cases of persuasion, and our analysis has not identified the especially persuasive character of those which are. Moreover even a master of persuasion is not immune to the persuasion of the gods. As the next section will demonstrate, the gods themselves are masters of likeness and persuasion as well as being adept at resisting persuasion. Despite the qualms, however, it still seems fair to add likening to Homer's roster of the proper means of persuasion. Thus Homer has identified another indispensible feature of a skeletal theory of persuasion by recording the elements and tools necessary for making something persuasive.

With this admission we can now say that Homer has at least sketched in the outline of a fledgling theory of persuasion. He has considered the three elements necessary to such a theory: (1) the character of the agent of persuasion, (2) the character of the means of persuasion and (3) the character of the object of persuasion. He has, moreover, considered how these three elements must interact in order to effect persuasion.

B.4. Rhetoric and Theology

The ability of god-like Odysseus to create persuasive images is preeminently an art of the gods. Athena is expert in making images (*Od.* 4.796) and in making herself appear in different likenesses that delude men (*Od.* 13.313, *se gar autên panti eiskeis* and *Od.* 17.485-486: cf. the power of Proteus, *Od.* 4.417-419). It is this power of making images, likenesses (e.g., Apollo, *Il.* 5.449-450), dreams and signs that characterizes the power of the gods, for it is not directly or forcefully or entirely that the gods reveal themselves (and their will) to men but only darkly and obliquely through persuasion. Persuasion is the gods' primary tool of contact with men.[21] Only to the

---

[20]"Against his will" is a serious qualification here. "Persuasion" in Homer can be used merely to indicate assent or consent. For a discussion of the role of consent and assent in the Homeric usage of *peithein*, see A. P. D. Mourelatoes (above note 5). Odysseus is, of course, at times persuaded by other men in the sense that he agrees with their reasoning and will act upon their advice. Even in this sense, however, it is only infrequently that Odysseus is persuaded. Although persuasion may entail assent, this does not eliminate the role of deception in persuasion. I may willingly be persuaded (i.e., agree) that the beggar is a Cretan when in fact he is Odysseus. Compare, for example, *Il.* 4.104: Athena persuades Pandarus to shoot at Menelaus by making him think, erroneously, that he will kill Menelaus. His consent, if there is any, is based upon a misconception. If consent is a necessary part of persuasion, then only subconscious persuasion is eliminated.

privileged few and only to them rarely do the gods appear visibly (*enargês*),[22] and the visible appearance of the gods is still only a likeness which they have assumed. Athena appears *enargês* to Odysseus (*Od.* 16.161-162) yet still in the likeness of a woman (16.157; cf. 13.288 and 20.31). Only from a human viewpoint are the Homeric gods truly anthropomorphic. The gods appear in so many different forms that even Odysseus finds it difficult to recognize all the images of the gods (*Od.* 13.312-313).[23]

We have already cited a number of examples of persuasion employed by the gods and take it as established that the gods are frequent and expert users of persuasion. It is also evident, since men have neither the strength nor means to compel or instruct the gods, that they must try to persuade the gods to favor human ends. This is accomplished through propitiatory sacrifices and prayers. The gods, however, cannot be deceived by man and therefore cannot be persuaded against their will. Thus persuasion was, for Homer, a religious as well as a political concept.

Many of the instances of divine persuasion are directed to the overall benefit of some individual man or some community, even if those men do not themselves realize that benefit. It is as a result of the persuasion of the gods that Achilles does not trample completely on justice and human custom. Athena stays the hand of Achilles when he is about to slay Agamemnon and persuades him to restrain his anger. Similarly Thetis brings a message from Zeus (*Il.* 24.133-137) that persuades Achilles to return Hector's body and give over his furious revenge. Were it not for the persuasion of the gods, Agamemnon would have been killed and the Greek host thrown into chaos; were it not for the gods, Hector's body would not have been returned to Priam and burnt on the pyre. The persuasive dream which Zeus sends to Agamemnon is also ultimately intended to right the wrong done to Achilles. Through persuasion, the gods appear to protect men from anarchy and to help to uphold the claims of justice and human law. They appear to be necessary to maintain man in his humanity.

Athena also frequently withholds the truth from men, and cites this same benign purpose to justify her deceit. She refuses to allow the dream image of Penelope's sister to enlighten Penelope about Odysseus (*Od.* 4.836-837) in order that Penelope might be given the opportunity to reveal her true courage and fidelity in the face of utter uncertainty. To Odysseus' amazement, Athena refused to tell Telemachus about Odysseus' whereabouts but preferred that he go and find out for himself (13.417). As Athena tells Odysseus (respecting Telemachus, 13.416-424), it is often for man's own good that the gods conceal the truth; had Telemachus known about the fate of his father he

---

[21]The gods do, of course, snatch up heroes from out of battles every now and then.

[22]*Il.* 20.131: *chalepoi de theoi phainesthai enargeis* and *Od.* 16.161: *ou gar pôs pantessi theoi phainontai enargeis.* They do appear thus to the Phaeacians: *Od.* 7.201-2. Cf. *h.Cer.* 111, *chalepoi de theoi thnêtoisin horasthai.*

[23]*argaleon se, thea, gnônai brotôi antiasanti, /kai mal' epistamennôi. se gar autên panti eiskeis.*

would not have travelled and, by learning, grown to manhood.

By this statement Athena implies that Odysseus' wanderings too were meant for his own benefit. Odysseus fears that the travels of both himself and Telemachus (note the *kai* in 13.418) bring only suffering. Athena, however, says that Telemachus' travels were for his own benefit and thereby implies that the same may be true of Odysseus' travels. The gods often afflict men in order to arouse and edify their natures (cf. 22.236-238, Athena delays the victory of Odysseus and Telemachus in order to test, i.e., develop, their strength). By concealing the truth and by employing persuasion instead of force or instruction, the gods can help to direct men's lives without impinging upon human independence and free will. The end of divine persuasion is apparently to help men to help themselves and to keep them on the path toward moral and intellectual development.

A passage previously cited may throw some further light on the method of divine persuasion. Athena was said to have persuaded the mind of Pandarus in its folly (*Il.* 4.104, *tôi de phrenas aphroni peithen*). It is by the oxymoron *phrên aphrôn* (mindless mind) that Homer perfectly characterizes persuasion. Persuasion affects the mind by making one mindless; it makes one act willingly in one sense and unwillingly in another. This, though, is just the way one can characterize human freedom and the undeniable interaction of men and gods. Just as men and gods are said to be jointly responsible for actions instigated by gods and carried out by men (e.g., Athena staying Achilles' hand), so too one can say that any persuader and persuaded are jointly responsible for the action of the persuaded. In both cases, the man who acts both is and is not a willing actor. Persuasion is not only employed by the gods but may be the very model for the effect of gods upon men. Just as man's mind is affected by the powers of persuasion, so may his mind be affected by the powers of the gods.

We have argued that (a) persuasion is the most prevalent method of contact between gods and men and (b) persuasion is often employed by the gods for man's own benefit. Consequently it is true, for Homer, that the gods frequently appear to act "unethically" (they lie and deceive) in order to accomplish "ethical" ends (acting for man's own benefit). The following section will suggest some of the provocative philosophical questions raised by Homer's theory of persuasion. The past section has been intended not as a further contribution to an enumeration of elements crucial for theories of persuasion, but as argument for the centrality of the notion of persuasion in the Homeric poems. Homer reveals the (to us) unlikely association of a mundane concept of persuasion with the enlightened activity of the gods in the determined course of human affairs.

B.5. *Philosophic Implications of Rhetoric*

From our investigation into Homer's theory of persuasion, it is fair to surmise that Homer rejects egalitarianism. All men are not capable of ruling others, says Odysseus (*Il.* 2.203), and by this implies that all men are not capable of ruling themselves. Some men must be led, some dragged, along the path of righteousness and justice. The rule of many is not a "good" thing (2.204: *ouk agathon polukoiraniê*). It is the right or duty of the best men to rule and the duty of the lesser men to follow. Odysseus turns the people aside from their self-willed flight for their own good. Athena stayed the hand of Achilles for his own good. Wise men and gods alike, knowing better than all other men what is in man's own interest, have the right to suspend all individual rights on behalf of social justice. Homer thus subscribes to paternalism on both the human and the divine spheres. Persuasion is that just means by which the best men and the gods motivate men to act in ways beneficial to themselves. Persuasion is just in that, unlike force, it allows some measure of independence to the men on whom it is practiced and encourages assent rather than dissent among men.

Persuasion is thus a kind of benign coercion which masks its anticipation of benefit and its forcefulness behind the consent which it elicits from its audience; it is a safe and efficient method of effecting action. As Socrates says (Xen. *Mem.* IV. 6.15), Odysseus is a safe speaker (*to asphalê rhêtora* from *Od.* 8.171, *ho d' asphaleôs agoreuei*),[24] because he knows how to base his speech upon the opinions of those he is addressing. Thus, in Homer, persuasion can actually be pursued for the sake of social justice although it appears to be a kind of injustice (because a kind of deception). This idea reappears with striking frequency in Greek literature ranging from Aeschylus to Plato to Xenophon.

C. Conclusion

Let me conclude with a story from Xenophon which stands as evidence that at least Socrates understood Homer as a master of persuasive theory. In the *Memorabilia* (I.2.58-59), Socrates' accusers hold it against him that he was wont to cite the passage of Homer in which Odysseus addresses kings with "gentle words" and common men "harshly" and with an added blow of the sceptre. Xenophon explains that Socrates quoted this passage as an example of how certain men functioned as mere liabilities to the welfare of others and had to be restrained and compelled to obedience. Socrates, moreover, quoted Homer's heroes as models for the effective use of different persuasive methods upon different men; he attributed to Homer the judgment that one speech would neither be understood nor believed by all types of men.

---

[24]Although in Homer this is said not about Odysseus but by Odysseus about some man in general, it is brought up by Odysseus in order to distinguish one man (beautiful in speech) from another (beautiful in appearance) and to illustrate that the gods do not bestow the same graces on all men (*Od.* 8.167-168). For this phrase, cf. Hes. *Th.* 86, where it is said of the king who has been given the power of persuasive speech by the Muses that *ho d' asphaleôs agoreuôn*. Cf. F. Solmsen, "The 'Gift' of Speech in Homer and Hesiod," *TAPA* 85 (1954) 8-15.

This very insight of Socrates is illustrated by the way in which Socrates' accusers misinterpreted his quotation of Homer. They believed that Socrates was using Homer to teach his followers to be evil-doers and tyrants (*Mem.* I.2.56); they believed he was quoting the speeches of Odysseus as praiseworthy examples of how violence must be used against the commoners and the poor. Whereas Socrates understood that Odysseus' harshness was beneficial to the souls of the commoners themselves, Socrates' accusers believed that such harshness was intended to benefit Odysseus himself and, by analogy, Socrates. Thus the same speech of Socrates (and of Homer) is interpreted in two drastically different ways by the accusers and by the followers of Socrates; a difference in the character of the audience accounts for a total divergence in the interpretation of Socrates' single example. In order to have avoided such misunderstanding, Socrates would have had to tell a different story to his accusers than the one which he told to his followers. Only then could he have been confident of persuading both groups. Socrates interprets Homer as the source for the distinguishing techniques necessary for effective persuasion.[25]

---

[25]I would like to thank M. E. Karp and S. G. Benardete for comments on an earlier draft of this paper.

Section 2:
Sophistic Rhetorical Theory

Toward a Sophistic Definition of Rhetoric

by John Poulakos

When Hegel undertook to reanimate the Sophists,[1] he established with poignant observations that the message of those itinerant teachers of culture was a natural as well as a necessary link between Pre-Socratic (especially Anaxagoran) and Platonic thought.[2] Thus, he endowed their views with intellectual integrity on the one hand, and gave them a place in the history of philosophy on the other. The recent plenitude of sophistic studies shows that Hegel's work was not an instance of philosophical lightning but an origin of things to come. But whereas he and others[3] after him have placed the Sophists' views historically or topically, the meaning of their rhetorical perspective has not received adequate attention.

This essay presumes that without the Sophists our picture of the rhetoric that came out of the Greek experience is incomplete. For over two millennia we have relied almost exclusively on the Platonic and Aristotelian notions of discourse while we have treated the sophistic position as an obscure but interesting historical footnote. And despite Hegel's and others' efforts to rehabilitate the Sophists, we are still bound to the directives of Plato's system of Idealism and Aristotle's system of Development. But because rhetoric came about as an activity grounded in human experience, not in philosophical reflection, we must approach it by looking at those who practiced it before turning to those who reflected about it.

In recent years the above position has been espoused by many students and teachers of rhetoric. Thus far, however, it has led mainly to studies enabling us to better understand individual Sophists. But if Greek rhetoric is indeed a trilogy, we need to concern ourselves with its first part, which to this day remains fragmentary. To do so, we must reexamine the surviving

---

Reprinted from *Philosophy and Rhetoric,* 16 (1983): 35-48. Copyright 1983 by the Pennsylvania State University. Reproduced by permission of The Pennsylvania State University Press.

[1] By "Sophists" I refer to those commonly recognized as the major figures of this group of teachers of rhetoric i.e., Protagoras, Gorgias, Prodicus, Antiphon, Hippias, Critias, and Thrasymachus.

[2] G. F. Hegel, *Lectures in the History of Philosophy,* trans. E. S. Haldane (New York: Humanities Press, 1963), pp. 352-54.

[3] See Mario Untersteiner, *The Sophists,* trans. Kathleen Freeman (New York: Philosophical Library, 1954); Laszlo Versényi, *Socratic Humanism,* (New Haven, Conn.: Yale Univ. Press, 1963); E. M. Cope, "On the Sophistical Rhetoric," *Journal of Classical and Sacred Philology,* 2 (1855), 126-69, 3 (1856), 34-80, 253-88. For a more detailed list, see W. K. C. Guthrie, *The Sophists,* (London: Cambridge Univ. Press, 1971), pp. 9-13.

fragments of and about the Sophists and seek to articulate on probable grounds their view of rhetoric. This essay purports to do just that. More specifically, it purports to derive a "sophistic" definition of rhetoric and to discuss some of its more important implications.[4]

Although not as rigorous systematizers of thought as Plato or Aristotle, the Sophists were the first to infuse rhetoric with life. Indebted only to the poetry of their past, not to any formal rhetorical theory, they found themselves free to experiment playfully with form and style and to fashion their words in the Greek spirit of excellence. Aware of the human limitations in the acquisition of knowledge, they sought to ground the abstract notions of their predecessors[5] in the actuality of everydayness. Conscious of people's susceptibility to each others' language, they taught eloquence whose peculiar characteristic is "to show the manifold points of view existing in a thing, and to give force to those which harmonize with what appears to me to be more useful."[6] As practitioners and teachers of rhetoric, the Sophists made Greece aware of her culture and demonstrated to the rest of the world that rhetoric is an integral part of the social life of all civilized people.[7]

The definition I wish to advance is: *Rhetoric is the art which seeks to capture in opportune moments that which is appropriate and attempts to suggest that which is possible.* Very briefly, this definition intimates that rhetoric is an artistic undertaking which concerns itself with the how, the when, and the what of expression and understands the why of purpose. Further, this definition links rhetoric to a movement originating in the sphere of actuality and striving to attain a place in that of potentiality. The following discussion focuses on key notions and terms which, if seen together, constitute a coherent and defensible position on rhetoric. The example of the Sophists suggests that the notions and terms to be investigated are rhetoric as art, style as personal expression, *kairos* (the opportune moment), *to prepon* (the appropriate), and *to dynaton* (the possible).

The Sophists conceived of rhetoric primarily as a *techné*[7] (art) whose medium is *logos* and whose double aim is *terpsis* (aesthetic pleasure) and *pistis* (belief).[8] The evidence supporting their artistic view comes from several sources. According to Philodemus, Metrodorus seems to make it clear enough

---

[4] When I say "sophistic" rhetoric, I do not mean to disregard the fact that in many cases the Sophists differed in their views on rhetoric. Rather, I mean to emphasize those common elements among them which permit us to regard them as a group.

[5] Hegel, p. 355.

[6] Ibid., p. 358.

[7] Regarding the meaning of the term *techné*, Guthrie remarks: "No English word produces exactly the same effect as the Greek *techné*. 'Art' suffers from its aesthetic associations, and also from the opposition between 'the arts' and the natural sciences. Those who know no Greek may be helped by the term itself: its incorporation in our 'technical' and 'technology' is not fortuitous. It includes every branch of human or divine (cf. Plato, *Soph.* 265e) skill, or applied intelligence, as opposed to the unaided work of nature." *The Sophists*, p. 115, n. 3.

[8] For an insightful discussion on the relationship between *pistis* and *terpsis* see Charles P. Segal, "Gorgias and the Psychology of the Logos," *Harvard Studies in Classical Philology*, 66 (1962), 119ff.

that "the rhetoric of the Sophists has the status of an Art."[9] On a more specific comment, Philostratus claims that within Antiphon's forensic speeches "lies all that is derived from the art [of rhetoric]" (87 B44a). Similarly, Suidas informs us that Thrasymachus wrote, among other things, "a rhetorical art" (85 A1). In Plato's *Protagoras* (317b), Protagoras discloses that he has been many years "in the art" while Gorgias asserts in the *Gorgias* (450b) that "the rhetorical art is about words" and boasts in the same dialogue, (456b), that he often persuaded reluctant patients to submit to medical treatment "through no other art than the rhetorical." In his *Encomium to Helen* (13), Gorgias extends his conception of rhetoric by implying that if a speech is to be persuasive it must be "written with art."

Conceiving of rhetoric as art is important because on the one hand it designates the sophistic view proper[10] and on the other it helps place the controversy between Plato and the Sophists in the right light. In particular, one may argue, rhetoric as art does not admit criteria appropriate to strictly epistemological or axiological matters; nor does it call for the same considerations which rhetoric as argument does. Thus, some of the well-known Platonic charges against rhetoric become inapplicable.[11] In distinction to *episteme*, rhetoric does not strive for cognitive certitude, the affirmation of logic, or the articulation of universals. Conditioned by the people who create it, rhetoric moves beyond the domain of logic and, satisfied with probability, lends itself to the flexibility of the contingent.[12] Because the sophistic notion of rhetoric as art is a topic too large for the purposes of this essay, the following comments will be limited to the sophistic concern for the artistic aspect of discourse, or style.

The story of the Sophists' preoccupation with style is too well-known to be recounted here. Collectively, they were held in contempt for dealing with "the non-essentials" of rhetoric.[13] However, this preoccupation seems to have arisen from the realization, expressed later by Aristotle, that "the way a thing is said does affect its intelligibility."[14] Antiphon is quite explicit about the

---

[9] Philodemus, *Rhetoric* II, 49. Cited in Hermann Diels and Walther Kranz, *Die Fragmente der Vorsokratiker*, (Berlin: Weidmannsche Verlagsbuchhandlung, 1952), 85 B7a. All subsequent fragments are from this source. The translation of this fragment is by Francis E. Sparshott in Rosamond K. Sprague, ed., *The Older Sophists*, (Columbia: Univ. of South Carolina Press, 1972). Unless otherwise specified, the translations which follow are mine. I have taken fewer liberties with the texts than have other translators and have tried to remain as faithful as possible to the Greek. As a result, the reader will note, the English in several cases is awkward.

[10] In the *Gorgias* 463b, Socrates refers to rhetoric as *kolakeia* (flattery) and refutes Gorgias by saying that rhetoric is not art but *empeiria* and *tribé* (habitude and knack). On the other hand, Aristotle, although he does refer to rhetoric as art (*Rhetoric* 1402a), conceives of it primarily as a faculty (*dynamis*) (*Rhetoric* 1355b and 1359b).

[11] For Plato's criticism of rhetoric see the *Gorgias* and the *Phaedrus*.

[12] A useful discussion of the notion of contingency is provided by Robert L. Scott, "On Viewing Rhetoric as Epistemic," *Central States Speech Journal*, 15 (November 1967), pp. 9-17.

[13] Aristotle, *Rhetoric* 1354a.

[14] Ibid., 1404a. This is Rhys Roberts' translation and I have included it for syntactical purposes. A more literal translation is given by E. M. Cope: "for it makes *some* difference in the clearness of an explanation whether we speak in one way or another" in John E. Sandys, ed., *The Rhetoric of Aristotle*, (London: Cambridge Univ. Press, 1877).

grave consequences of effective or ineffective style when he says: "it is as unfair that a bad choice of words should cause a man of good behavior to be put to death as it is that a good choice of words should lead to the acquittal of a criminal."[15] Of course, there is room to argue that stylistic emphasis in discourse, that is, emphasis of the how over the what, displays a preference indicative of misplaced values. But however small its value, style is an inescapable reality of speech, one which must be attended to necessarily. Aristotle himself, who insists on the primacy of facts and their proof,[16] acknowledges the reality and necessity of style when he writes: "it is not sufficient to know *what* one ought to say, but it is necessary also to know *how* one ought to say it."[17] So, to the extent that style is allowed to be seen primarily as an aesthetical issue, the question of its superiority or inferiority to content, essentially an axiological question, becomes secondary.

The evidence of the Sophists' excellence in style is plentiful. Protagoras, who on some matters held the same opinion with Diagoras, is said to have "used different words in order to avoid its extreme forcefulness" (80 A23). Philostratus reports in the *Lives of the Sophists* that Gorgias, who did for rhetoric as much as Aeschylus did for tragedy, "was an example of forcefulness to the Sophists and of marvels and inspiration and of giving utterance to great subjects in the grand style, and of detached phrases and transitions, through which speech becomes sweeter than itself and more pompous, and he also introduced poetical words for ornament and dignity" (82 A1 [2]).[18] Xenophon, after recreating the tale of Hercules' dilemma between Virtue and Vice, tells us that Prodicus, its original author, "embellished the [above] thoughts with still more magnificent words than I [have done] just now" (84 B2 [34]). Dionysius of Halicarnassus writes that Thrasymachus was "clean-cut and subtle and formidable in inventing and expressing tersely and extraordinarily that which he wants" (85 A13). According to Philostratus, Hippias "used to enchant Greece at Olympia with varied and well-heeded speeches" (86 A2 [7]). Philostratus praises Antiphon's *On Concord* by saying that it contains "brilliant and wise maxims and narrative elevated and flowered with poetical names and diffuse exposition like the smoothness of the plain" (87 B44a). Philostratus also praises the speech of Kritias for being "sweet . . . and smooth like the west breeze" (88 A1).

As the historical record indicates, the Sophists were master rhetoricians. That their excellence in the area of style has often been construed as a liability is due partly to Plato's influence on posterity and partly to the

---

[15]J. S. Morrison's translation in *The Older Sophists.*
[16]Aristotle, *Rhetoric*, 1404a.
[17]Ibid., 1403b. Emphasis added.
[18]With the exception of minor changes, this is George Kennedy's translation in *The Older Sophists.* On a more focused comment, Suidas writes that Gorgias "was the first to give to the rhetorical genre the verbal power and art of deliberate culture and employed tropes and metaphors and allegories and hypallage and catachreses and hyperbata and doublings of words and repetitions and apostrophes and isokola" (82 A2) (Kennedy's translation with minor changes).

excesses of some of their successors. But if it is agreed that what is said must be said somehow, and that the how is a matter of the speaker's choice, then style betrays the speaker's unique grasp of language and becomes the peculiar expression of his personality.[19] If this is so, the Sophists need no longer be misunderstood. As some of their artifacts reveal, they were highly accomplished linguistic craftsmen with a heightened sense of the nature of *logos*, their medium.[20]

As the suggested definition of rhetoric implies, the Sophists were interested in the problem of time in relation to speaking. At least one of them, Gorgias, asserted that situations have a way of revealing themselves to man and of eliciting responses from him. As he states in his treatise *On Non-being or On Nature*, "the external becomes the revealer of *logos*" (82 B3 [85]). But Gorgias was not alone in asserting that situations exist in time and that speech as a situational response does also. The Sophists stressed that speech must show respect to the temporal dimension of the situation it addresses, that is, it must be timely. In other words, speech must take into account and be guided by the temporality of the situation in which it occurs.

For the most part, what compels a rhetor to speak is a sense of urgency. Under normal circumstances, that is, under circumstances in which we are composed and things are "under control," there is no pressing need to speak. But during times of stress, we feel compelled to intervene and, with the power of the word, to attempt to end a crisis, redistribute justice, or restore order. In his *Defense of Palamedes* (32), Gorgias has the speaker say, following a lengthy statement of self-praise: "But [ordinarily] it is not for me to praise myself; but the present moment necessitated . . . that I defend myself in every way possible." Illustrating the same point, Thrasymachus, we are told, once addressed the Athenians by saying: "I wish, Athenians, that I had belonged to that time when silence sufficed for young people, since the state of affairs did not force them to make speeches and the older men were managing the city properly. But since our fortune has reserved us . . . misfortunes . . . one really has to speak"[21] (85 B1). In the former example it is urgent that the defendant reinstate his threatened reputation while in the latter it is crucial that the citizens protest against the injurious practices of their civic leaders.

Both of the above examples imply that ideas have their place in time and unless they are given existence, unless they are voiced at the precise moment

---

[19]Georges Gusdorf, the phenomenologist, says that "style signifies the task given to man of becoming aware of perspective. Each of us, even the most simple of mortals, is charged with finding the expression to fit his situation. Each of us is charged with realizing himself in a language, a personal echo of the language of all which represents his contribution to the human world. The struggle for style is the struggle for consciousness (la vie spirituelle)" in *Speaking (La Parole)*, trans. Paul Brockelman (Evanston: Northwestern Univ. Press, 1965), p. 76.

[20]Bromley Smith demonstrates how this is so in his article "Gorgias: A Study of Oratorical Style," *Quarterly Journal of Speech Education*, 7 (1921), 335-59.

[21]Sparshott's translation in *The Older Sophists*.

they are called upon, they miss their chance to satisfy situationally shared
voids within a particular audience. Moreover, the two examples seem to
restrict speaking to only those times calling for it, and to suggest that silence
be the alternative at all other times. In fact, Gorgias praises the dead in his
Epitaphios for having known when to speak (*legein*) and when to be silent
(*sigan*) (B6).

Clearly, speaking involves a temporal choice. The choice is not whether
to speak but whether to speak now; more precisely, it is whether now is the
time to speak. When a rhetor speaks, he responds to a situation. But the fact
that he speaks now, the fact that he has chosen this moment over another
reminds the listener that the situation is ephemeral, urgent, and, by
implication, significant. But if the rhetor chooses to address the present, he
also agrees to confront the contingent elements of the situation as they
unfold. As such, he is taking on a risk, the risk that his timing might not
coincide with the temporal needs of the situation. According to Philostratus,
Gorgias, who held in contempt those who spoke about "things that had been
said many times," devoted himself to what was timely (82 A24). Further,
Gorgias "was the first to proclaim himself willing to take this risk . . . that he
would trust to the opportune moment to speak on any subject" (82 A1a). That
addressing the present requires courage and involves the taking of a risk is
apparent in the compromise of extemporaneous speaking, the kind which
literally occurs out of time. Prepared speech texts betray our insensitivity to
and insecurity about all that is contingent in the act of speaking. Prepared
texts have a designated time in the future and a prefabricated content. But by
designating the time and by prefabricating the content of a speech, we are
essentially setting the parameters of a situation to come and prepare ourselves
in advance to treat it in its fixity. This compromise we make out of our
apprehension regarding the indeterminate aspects of a situation to which we
have no immediate access.[22] The example of several Sophists, most notably
that of Gorgias and Hippias, suggests that an accomplished speaker has no
need for notes or a text, rehearsal, or presitutional practice.

The sophistic insistence that speaking be done with respect to time does
not stem from a philosophical position regarding the nature of *logos* but from
the observation that if what is said is timely, its timeliness renders it more
sensible, more rightful, and ultimately more persuasive. Reportedly, Protagoras was the first to expound on "the power of the opportune moment" to give
speech advantages it otherwise would not have (80 A1). In the anonymous
sophistic treatise *Dissoi Logoi* 2(19), the author is quite explicit about this
point. Specifically, he states that "nothing is always virtuous, nor [always]
disgraceful, but taking the same things the opportune moment made disgraceful and after changing [them made them] virtuous." Clearly, the notion of

---

[22]For a discussion of the merits of impromptu speaking, see Alcidamas' *On Those Who Write Written
Speeches or On the Sophists*. Since Alcidamas was Gorgias' student, it is not unreasonable to suppose
that some of his views coincide with those of other Sophists.

kairos points out that speech exists in time; but more important, it constitutes a prompting toward speaking and a criterion of the value of speech.[23] In short, *kairos* dictates that what is said must be said at the right time.

In conjunction with the notion of *kairos*, the Sophists gave impetus to the related concept of *to prepon* (the appropriate) apparently prescribing that what is said must conform to both audience and occasion. Illustrating *to prepon*, Gorgias praises in his *Epitaphios* the dead for having been "well-disposed toward the appropriate," while in his *Defense of Palamedes* (28) he has the defendant admit that what he is about to say is "inappropriate to one who has not been accused but suitable to one who has been accused." In the same speech, Gorgias strongly implies that the strategy of a legal defense depends largely on the speaker's audience. Specifically, he has the defendant state that while it is useful to employ appeals to pity and entreaties and the intercession of friends when the trial takes place before a mob, before noble and wise judges one must concentrate on the explanation of the truth (33).

A complement to the notion of *kairos*, *to prepon* points out that situations have formal characteristics, and demands that speaking as a response to a situation be suitable to those very characteristics. Both notions are concerned with the rhetor's response; but while the former is interested in the when, the latter is concerned with the what of speaking. *To prepon* requires that speech must take into account and be guided by the formal structure of the situation it addresses. Like *kairos*, *to prepon* constitutes not only a guide to what must be said but also a standard of the value of speech.[24] In distinction to *kairos*, which focuses on man's sense of time, *to prepon* emphasizes his sense of propriety.

Appropriateness refers to that quality which makes an expression be correlative to the formal aspects of the situation it addresses. When appropriate, speech is perfectly compatible with the audience and the occasion it affirms and simultaneously seeks to alter. An appropriate expression reveals the rhetor's rhetorical readiness and evokes the audience's gratitude; conversely, an inappropriate expression indicates a misreading on the rhetor's part and a mismeeting between rhetor and audience. If what is spoken is the result of a misreading on the part of the rhetor, it subsequently becomes obvious to us, even to him, that "this was not the right thing to say." If silence is called for and the response is speech, we have a rhetor misspeaking to an audience not ready to listen, or not ready to listen to what he has to say, or ready to listen but not to the things he is saying. If speech is needed and silence prevails instead, we have a rhetor who has misread the situation, a frustrated audience whose needs and expectations are not met, and a situation

---

[23]This view is expressed by Isocrates in *Against the Sophists* 293(13): "for it is not possible for speeches to be good if they do not partake of the opportune moments, and the appropriate and the novel." For a treatment of the moment as a criterion of the value of speech, see Gusdorf's *Speaking (La Parole)*, p. 85.

[24]Ibid.

that perpetuates itself.

Both timeliness and appropriateness are rhetorical motifs whose essence cannot be apprehended strictly cognitively and whose application cannot be learnt mechanically.[25] As George Kennedy states, "The two together constitute what may be called the artistic elements in rhetorical theory as opposed to the prescribed rules."[26] Unlike rigid scientific principles, the two are more a matter of feeling. Some of the factors contributing to one's sense of the timely and the appropriate are one's discretionary powers, the cultural norms in which he participates, his reading of the situation he wishes to address, his image of his audience, and his prediction of the potential effects of his words on his listeners. Timeliness and appropriateness are similar qualities in the sense that they render an expression more persuasive. What is said, then, must be both appropriate to time, or timely, and appropriate to the audience and the occasion. Untimely and appropriate speech cannot move an audience because it is untimely; similarly, timely and inappropriate speech cannot achieve its aims because it is inappropriate. If persuasion is to occur, both qualities must be present in the spoken word. In short, the right thing must be said at the right time; inversely, the right time becomes apparent precisely because the right thing has been spoken.

As pointed out earlier, these two qualities are vague in conceptualization and elastic in application. Their observance does not "confine reality within a dogmatic scheme but allow[s] it to rage in all its contradictions, in all its tragic intensity, in all its impartiality imposed by an intelligibility which will revive the joy of truth."[27] Because the rhetorician concerns himself with the particular and the pragmatic, his way is not that of an abstract absolutism created in the spirit of *a priori* truths; rather, it is that of a relativism of concrete rhetorical situations to which situationally derived truths are the only opportune and appropriate responses.

But the rhetorician is not confined to a single movement. After he captures the appropriate and places it temporally, he moves toward the suggestion of the possible. The starting point for the articulation of the possible is the ontological assumption that the main driving forces in man's life are his desires,[28] especially the desire to be other and to be elsewhere. Another relevant assumption is that the sphere of actuality always entails a lack, the absence of that which exists only in the future; more particularly, that actuality frustrates man when he dreams of being other and binds him to where he already is when he wants to be elsewhere.

Consideration of the possible affirms in man the desire to be at another place or at another time and takes him away from the world of actuality and transports him in that of potentiality. Moreover, it intensifies in him the

---

[25]Untersteiner stresses this point in *The Sophists,* p. 198.
[26]George Kennedy, *The Art of Persuasion in Greece,* (Princeton: Princeton Univ. Press, 1963), p. 67.
[27]Untersteiner, *The Sophists,* p. xvi.
[28]Hegel, p. 358.

awareness that actuality is hostile to what he wishes and, as such, denies its existence. Finally, it refines his wishes and shows him how to apply them, what to ask, and whom to reach.[29] To be sure, man walks on earth and his feet are a constant reminder of his connection to the ground. But at the same time, he looks at the horizon about him and perceives himself "not as he is, not where he is, but precisely as he is not and where he is not." Even though he functions daily in the world of actuality, he often finds himself concerned with his situation not as it is here-and-now but as it could be there-and-then. Thus, he participates at once in two worlds each of which opposes the other. For Georges Poulet, man finds himself in "Two realities which simultaneously exist at a distance and which reciprocally deny each other: the reality in which one lives and that in which one does not live, the place in which one has situated one's dream and the place where with horror one sees oneself surrendered to chance and ill luck."[30]

This is where the rhetorician steps in and helps him resolve his existential dilemma. By exploiting people's proclivity to perceive themselves in the future and their readiness to thrust themselves into unknown regions, the rhetorician tells them what they could be, brings out in them futuristic versions of themselves, and sets before them both goals and the directions which lead to those goals. All this he does by creating and presenting to them that which has the potential to be, but is not. Thus it is no paradox to say that rhetoric strives to create and labors to put forth, to propose that which is not.

The rhetorician concerns himself with the possible because he refuses to keep people in their actual situation. Granted, he must initially address them as they are and where they are. The earlier discussion about *kairos* and *to prepon* established that. But subsequently he tries to lift them from the vicissitudes of custom and habit and take them into a new place where new discoveries and new conquests can be made. Gorgias hints at this notion in the *Encomium to Helen* (5) when he states that "to tell the knowing what they know has credibility but brings no delight." Gorgias is stressing here that to speak about actualities to those who are already aware of them is nearly a purposeless act[31] whose most notable defect is that it fails to please the audience. But if by relying on actualities we fall short of our rhetorical ends, where should we turn? The *Encomium to Helen* suggests that the province of rhetoric is the possible, that which has not yet occurred to the audience. Following his own example, Gorgias argues that one of the causes of Helen's abduction is the might of *logos* (a presumably novel idea not previously entertained by those familiar with her story.)

---

[29]Georges Poulet, *The Interior Distance,* trans. Elliott Coleman (Ann Arbor: Univ. of Michigan Press, 1959), p. 239.

[30]Ibid., p. 240.

[31]Aristotle points out that "about those things which we know or have decided there is no further use in speaking about them" *Rhetoric* 1391b.

A special dimension of the possible, then, is afforded by the novel,[32] the unusual, that prior to which we have no awareness, the unprecedented. As a group, the Sophists are known to have been the first to say or do a number of things. Several fragments testify to their novel claims and practices: 80 A1 (51) and (52); 82 A1(1), A1a, A4(4); 84 A10; 85 A3; 86 A2. Xenophon tells us that Hippias told Socrates once: "I always try to say something new"[33] [86 A14 (6)] clarifying at the same time that he did so on matters which admit of subjective treatment (i.e., justice) and agreeing that on such subjects as arithmetic the novel has no place. Aristotle, pointing out one of the effects of the novel on audiences, refers to Prodicus, who thought that announcing that what one is about to say has never been heard before can literally awaken a drowsy audience (*Rhetoric* 1415b). Read together, the above fragments imply, as Aristotle remarks, that people are "admirers of things which are not part of their experience" (*Rhetoric* 1404b), and are drawn to them because they raise their curiosity and carry an element of surprise. New thoughts, new insights, and new ideas always attract our attention not only because we have not encountered them before but also because they offer us new ways to perceive ourselves and the world. On the other hand, things with which we are familiar condition our responses and restrict our actions.

The possible is the opposite of the actual. A derivative of the Heracleitan perspective, evoking the possible challenges the one and advances the manifold; it rejects permanence and favors change; it privileges becoming over being. Unlike the actual, the possible is not a given which can be known or verified; it exists in the future as something incomplete and dormant, something awaiting the proper conditions to be realized. Therefore, its evocation goes hand in hand with hope and modesty; hope because the speaker always awaits his listeners' contribution, which will bring the possible to completion and realization; and modesty because what the speaker says is always potentially dismissable. By voicing the possible, the rhetor discloses his vision of a new world to his listeners and invites them to join him there by honoring his disclosure and by adopting his suggestion. Essentially, he is asking them to abandon the shelter of their prudential heaven and opt for that which exists "by favor of human imagination and effort ."[34] Of course, the risk always exists that the audience may decline his invitation. But this is a risk he must face if he dares stand up and offer an alternative to the mundanity, the mediocrity, or misery of those he wishes to address.

The possible is an aspect of non-actuality claiming that, given the proper

---

[32]See n. 23.

[33]Ibid. As if he is echoing Hippias' comment, Gusdorf writes: "The great artist avoids imitating even himself. He continually undertakes the task of remaining vigilantly aware of the world of words, a task for ever unfinished because the world changes and is renewed, and living man with it" [*Speaking (La Parole)*, p. 75].

[34]Richard Weaver, *The Ethics of Rhetoric,* (Chicago: Henry Regnery, 1953), p. 20.

chance, it can turn into something actual. And even though it opposes the actual, it always seeks to become actualized. In and through the speech of the rhetor, the seed of the possible is planted in the ground of actuality. However, its roots do not begin to form until the audience fails to see "why not," until they cannot find any reason to frustrate or repudiate it. Granted, the rhetor must show them why they ought to adopt his possible; the tradition of rhetoric demands that propositions be justified. At the same time, he must go one step further and ask them to find reasons, their reasons, should they be inclined to say no. Thus, Gorgias asks in the *Encomium to Helen* (12): "What cause then prevents the conclusion that Helen . . . might have come under the influence of speech?" This rhetorical question pits the actual belief (Helen is blameworthy as a woman with loose morals) against the possible belief (she is not to blame because she fell under the might of speech). The same approach is taken by Thrasymachus, who asks in *The Constitution* (B1): "Why should anyone put off speaking [what] is in his mind, if [it has fallen] to him to be injured by the present situation and he thinks he is on to something that will put an end to such things?" In this instance, the possible Thrasymachus wishes to have his listeners adopt is speaking openly and with no hesitation, something which presumably will end their pain. In both cases, the rhetor is asking the audience to discover at least one reason why the conclusion suggested should not be the case. Should they fail, they ought to adopt what he says; should they succeed, they have grounds on which to reject what he advocates. In the former case, the possible is well on its way to actuality; but even in the latter, it has served a useful function: it has provided the challenge in response to which the listeners have reexamined their actual situation. That they may decide to affirm their previously held views is not that important. What is more important is that by doing so they have moved from accepting actuality uncritically, as it is and because it is, to accepting it deliberately, because it has withstood the challenge of a possible. To use Heidegger's language, they have moved closer to the realm of authenticity.

In this essay I have argued that the history of rhetoric dictates that the Sophists' views regarding the art of discourse need wider notice and further exploration. Extracting key ideas and terms from the preserved fragments of the Sophists, I have suggested a "sophistic" definition of rhetoric founded on and consistent with the notions of rhetoric as art, style as personal expression, the timely, the appropriate, and the possible. This definition posits that man is driven primarily by his desire to be other, the wish to move from the sphere of actuality to that of possibility. Moreover, it points out that as man becomes what he is not he encounters situations to which he often responds with language. It also suggests that if man's responses are to be effective, they must take into account the temporal and formal structure of the situations he addresses. As such, they must be guided by his sense of time and propriety, and must be formulated in ways consonant with himself. Finally, this definition stresses that the whole enterprise of symbolic expression falls within the region of art.

Since the time of the Sophists, the area over which this definition extends has been covered with rigor far greater than I can muster. Therefore, I do not claim to have introduced new ideas in the field of rhetorical theory. However, the contribution of this essay is threefold: (1) it establishes that the Sophists' rhetorical practices are founded upon a coherent notion of rhetoric, (2) it articulates that notion, and (3) it reinforces the often neglected idea that some of our contemporary concepts about rhetoric originated with the Sophists.

Sophistic Rhetoric: Oasis or Mirage?

by Edward Schiappa

Problematizing the Construct "Sophistic Rhetoric"

There has been a distinct "turn" in recent scholarship toward what is called most commonly "sophistic rhetoric." For a variety of writers, "sophistic rhetoric" represents a veritable oasis of ideas for contemporary theories of discourse, composition, and argumentation. Consider a few manifestations of a "sophistic turn": John Poulakos has developed a "sophistic definition of rhetoric" which he believes provides an important contribution to a contemporary understanding of discourse ("Towards"), and which he offers as a model of liberating rhetoric ("Critique"). Declaring himself a sophist, Jasper Neel advocates "sophistical rhetoric" as "a study of how to make choices and a study of how choices form character and make good citizens" (211). Roger Moss has made a "Case for Sophistry" as an antidote to the paralyzing influence of realism, and Sharon Crowley has made "A Plea for the Revival of Sophistry" to encourage a more sociopolitical engaged model of pedagogy. These examples can be multiplied, but I think they suffice to show that the concept of "sophistic rhetoric" has grown in popularity in a variety of ways.

The turn to "sophistic rhetorics" is, in many ways, attractive and productive. To those who see our understanding of the workings of discourse as inescapably rooted in ancient Greece, the turn to "sophistry" provides a valuable alternative to Platonic and Aristotelian pedagogical traditions. Nevertheless, I want to make the case that "sophistic rhetoric" is, for the most part, a mirage—something we see because we want and need to see it—which vaporizes once carefully scrutinized. My position is that we are unlikely to come up with a historically defensible definition of "sophistic rhetoric" that is nontrivial and uniquely valuable. Furthermore, I believe that the practice of reproducing incoherent historical concepts is pedagogically unsound, and hence alternatives should be considered. I close by suggesting specific alternative appropriations that allow us to retain the "best" contributions of "sophistic rhetoric" without engaging in anachronism.

Reprinted from *Rhetoric Review* 10 (1991): 5-18. Used by permission.

Who Were the Sophists?

The first problem with the notion of "sophistic rhetoric" is identifying what we mean by "sophistic." Most scholars take the word as meaning literally belonging to the sophists, and refer to the group of individuals of the fifth century BCE to whom Plato denotes as such.[1] The standard list, canonized by Diels and Kranz and adopted by scholars such as Poulakos ("Towards" 40), includes Gorgias, Protagoras, Hippias, Prodicus, Thrasymachus, Critias, and Antiphon. Unfortunately, canonized or not, the list is somewhat arbitrary and cannot be squared with the available ancient testimony.

The word "sophist" is in Greek *sophistês*, meaning a person of wisdom *(sophia)*. The term first appears in Pindar in the early fifth century and predates the appearance of the group of so-called "older" sophists of Diels-Kranz. The notion that there was a distinctive "sophistic rhetoric" seems to have originated in the writings of Plato, and it has been reified through a series of accounts that (mistakenly) take Plato seriously as a historian (see, e.g., Cope; Guthrie). But Plato's references to "sophists" include people normally not included in the standard list (Miccus, Proteus), and though he refers to four of the standard list as "sophists" (Protagoras, Gorgias, Prodicus, Hippias) he does not do so with the other three (Thrasymachus, Critias, Antiphon). When he uses the term *generically*, such as in his *Sophist*, it appears that he is often referring to fourth-century rivals rather than fifth-century sophists.[2] In both Plato's and Aristotle's writings there is evidence of different *kinds* of "sophists," which they sometimes take pains to distinguish and sometimes lump together (Classen). In other words, even in the corpus of texts that has most influenced our conception of "sophistic rhetoric," there is sufficient equivocation to warrant another look at the evidence.

Aristophanes' comedy *Clouds* is the only preplatonic text which survives that discusses "sophists" at length, and it provides a perspective quite different than that found in Plato. The main "sophist" lampooned is Socrates, and decades later the label "sophist" was still commonly applied to him despite Plato's protests (Nehamas, "Eristic"). Most of the play's action takes place at "Thinkery" *(phrontistêrion)* and the object of sophistic training is portrayed as to produce "persons of wisdom" *(sophistês)* or "thinkers" *(phrontistês)*. When Strepsiades comes to the Thinkery to learn how to avoid paying his debts, Socrates requires him to learn to reason analytically and "scientifically." Socrates' lesson concerning how to win a lawsuit is an exercise in the invention of creative arguments that has little in common with

---

[1] As the texts of writers such as Diogenes Laertius (CE 3rd century), and Philostratus (CE 2nd or 3rd century) demonstrate, later antiquity clearly recognized a specific profession of "sophist." What is at issue in this essay is the usefulness of such a label for describing a consistent position toward "rhetoric" in the fifth and fourth centuries BCE.

[2] It is noteworthy that Plato's *Sophist* never once uses the word "rhetoric" *(rhêtorikê)*.

the discussions of forensic rhetoric found in the fourth century. The play never once mentions "rhetoric" *(rhêtorikê)* or "oratory" *(rhêtoreia)*, yet there is a surprising variety of subjects explored at the Thinkery. The subjects include what are now called astronomy, surveying, geometry, and meteorology; all are treated as serious interests of the Thinkery's inhabitants. Throughout the play, Aristophanes portrays the process of learning to speak *(legein)* as a natural consequence of learning to engage in "sophisticated" reasoning.

As documented in detail by G. B. Kerferd, a wide variety of people occupying an assortment of professions were called sophists in ancient Greece, including poets (such as Homer and Hesiod), musicians and rhapsodes, diviners and seers, and an assortment of "wise men" we now would categorize as presocratic philosophers, mathematicians, and politicians. According to Kerferd, "the term *sophistês* is confined to those who in one way or another function as the Sages, the exponents of knowledge in early communities" ("The First" 8). In fact, the term "philosopher" was not used to demarcate a specific group of thinkers until well into the *fourth* century BCE (Havelock). As Martin Ostwald notes, "the Athenian public made no attempt to differentiate sophists from philosophers" (259). We are reading history backwards when we call presocratics such as Thales and Pythagoras "philosophers" since prior to Aristotle they would have been described as "sophists." Even in the fourth century, Isocrates and Plato called each other "sophists" and themselves "philosophers," making it purely a modern bias to label either definitively (cf. Quandahl).

Despite the ancient evidence suggesting that "sophist" was a label used to describe a variety of people, a common means of identifying a specific group of fifth-century sophists is by reference to their professionalism; that is, some distinguish sophists from nonsophists by whether or not they charged fees for their teaching (Kerferd, *SM* 25). The question then becomes: Why is this a useful litmus test? The "parasitical" behavior of some sophists was often cause for their approbation in ancient times (Blank); how could it possibly benefit us to limit the label of sophist in such a way? Surely we would not limit "sophistic" teaching to that which has been paid for! If, on the other hand, some *substantive* differences can be identified between the teachings of those who charged for their services and those who did not, then would not those doctrinal differences be more appropriate defining variables? One appeal of the "sophistic movement" that is often claimed is that it helped provide an education useful for a democracy. Accordingly, defining "sophist" as a "professional educator" has a certain egalitarian appeal. The evidentiary merits of such a view are dubious, however (see below), and even if true it would follow that those who offered their teachings for *free* would be even *more* useful for the democratic masses. In short, there seems to be no good reason why the charging of fees ought to be considered a *necessary* condition for being a sophist. Nor is the charging of fees a *sufficient* condition for being a sophist, since even Zeno and Plato charged fees, and few defenders of a "sophistic" perspective would want to include their doctrines.

In ancient as well as modern times, the label "sophist" is assigned rather inconsistently according to the biases of the writer. In ancient times, persons as diverse as Prometheus, Homer, Hesiod, Damon, Solon, Thales, Pythagoras, Anaxagoras, Empedocles, Zeno, Plato, Socrates, and Isocrates were called "sophists" (Blank; Kerferd *SM*). Aeschines, Eudoxus, and Protagoras are included in Philostratus' *Lives of the Sophists* as well as in Diogenes Laertius' *Lives of Eminent Philosophers*. In modern times, even the list of seven sophists listed by Diels-Kranz is far from universal. George Grote omits Critias and adds Polus, Euthydemus, and Dionysodorus (486); Kerferd adds Callicles and Socrates, as well as the authors of *Dissoi Logoi,* the *Anonymus Iamblichi*, and the *Hippocratic Corpus (SM)*; and W. K. C. Guthrie adds Antisthenes, Alcidamas, and Lycophron.

Whom we choose to call a "sophist" necessarily impacts upon how we describe "sophistic rhetoric." As Kerferd points out, the process of designating certain individuals as "sophists" necessarily influences what "sophistic" doctrine or curricula turn out to be (*SM* 35). If "sophist" includes the presocratic philosophers, Socrates, Plato, and Isocrates, then the resulting picture of "sophistic rhetoric" is considerably different than if a smaller group of people is so designated.

To summarize the argument thus far, it is clear that we cannot identify a defining characteristic of "the sophists" that allows us to narrow the group to a degree sufficient to adduce a common perspective or set of practices. Either we treat the term as broadly as did the ancient Greeks, in which case almost every serious thinker must be included, or we are forced to pick a trait that serves no useful function other than to confirm some preconceived preference. *Any* account of "sophistic rhetoric" will tend to beg the question because it will presuppose who should be called a "sophist"—a determination which must be made on doctrinal grounds. The circularity of the reasoning seems to be unavoidable, and is part of the reason "sophistic rhetoric" should be considered a mirage.

What is Sophistic Rhetoric?

Even if we were able to agree on who to call "the sophists," it does not follow necessarily that a clear notion of sophistic *rhetoric* would result. There are three senses of "rhetoric" which need to be distinguished at this point— rhetorical theory, practice, and ideology. Rhetorical *theory* is what George A. Kennedy refers to as "conceptual" or "meta" rhetoric, and is what scholars generally mean when they say that the sophists "taught rhetoric." Some, but not all, writers advocating "sophistic rhetoric" imply that there was a distinctly "sophistic" definition or theory of rhetoric attributable to the sophists. Unfortunately, there are good reasons for challenging any claim that there was ever such a thing as a distinct and explicit sophistic theory or definition of rhetoric. A host of philological sources claim that the Greek word for rhetoric *(rhêtorikê)* originates no earlier than Plato's writings, and it is possible that Plato himself coined the word.[3] *Rhêtorikê* appears nowhere in any document or fragment attributable to a fifth-century source, nor does it appear in the writings of Isocrates—the most famous teacher of oratory in the fourth century BCE.

If one cannot identify an *explicit* sophistic theory of rhetoric, one is left with ferreting out an *implicit* theory. But even this task is difficult—even if one treats the Diels-Kranz list of sophists as definitive. The pivotal theoretical term (or "keyword"[4]) found in the few surviving doctrinal fragments of the "sophists" is *logos*—one of the most equivocal terms in the Greek language. The implicit theory of language one finds in Protagoras and Gorgias (the two sophists we know the most about) have little in common: Gorgias treats persuasion as a matter of deception and questions the possibility of communication altogether, while Protagoras' fragments suggest that he viewed "making the weaker account the stronger" as a matter of improving a person's (or city's) objective condition.[5] In a recent critique of Poulakos' "sophistic definition of rhetoric," I argue that while it might be possible to identify the incipient rhetorical theory of *individual* fifth-century figures, the available ancient evidence renders suspect any generalization about a common "sophistic" theory of rhetoric ("Neo-Sophistic"; cf. Cole *Origins*).

It is equally difficult to identify anything like a common set of sophistic *rhetorical practices* (Cole, *Origins* 71-112). Some portrayals of "sophistic rhetoric" suggest that the speeches of the sophists shared certain stylistic characteristics. Roger Moss's "case for sophistry," for example, notes the "highly-wrought use of alliteration, assonance, rhyme and other parisonic devices, parallelisms of all kinds" that "define sophistry" (213). There are two problems with such portrayals. First, even working with the "standard" list of seven sophists, one finds little evidence of stylistic commonality. Most writers who take a "tropical" approach to "sophistic rhetoric" rely extensively on the example of Gorgias' highly poetic style.[6] But Gorgias was virtually unique among the public speakers of his time, a fact which undercuts any effort to equate his style with that of a general "sophistic" style. Accordingly, it would be more appropriate to espouse a "Gorgianic rhetoric" than a "sophistic" rhetoric. Second, stylistic accounts of "sophistic rhetoric" confuse cause and effect. As argued by Thomas Cole *(Origins)* and Robert J. Connors, the stylistic innovations found in surviving "sophistic" treatises are

---

[3] According to Werner Pilz, "*Rhêtorikê* findet sich nicht vor Plato" (15). Other sources concluding that Plato's *Gorgias* is the earliest extant use of the word "rhetoric" include Kroll (1039), Liddell and Scott (1569), Atkins (766), Hommel (1396), and Martin (2). For the argument that Plato coined the word *rhêtorike*, see Cole (*Origins* 2) and Schiappa ("Did Plato?").

[4] On "keywords" in classical rhetorical theory, see Welch (12-14).

[5] Sharon Crowley's "Plea for Sophistry" cites only Protagoras and Gorgias as examples of sophists, and her analysis acknowledges that the two perspectives conflict (327). Similarly, Renato Barilli's treatment of "the sophists" includes only Protagoras, Gorgias, and Isocrates. For Gorgias see Verdenius, Segal; for Protagoras see Cole ("Relativism"), and Schiappa (*Protagoras*). For a comparison of their perspectives on language, see Kerferd (*SM* 68-82).

[6] See, for example, Moss (213-17) and Kennedy (29-31).

a manifestation of the widespread changes associated with the shift from "oral" to "literate" modes of composition. Paradox, allusion, antithesis, and the like can be found in a wide variety of fifth-century texts by "sophists" *and nonsophists alike* (Solmsen, 83-125; see also Quandahl). Hence the appearance of these devices is not a sufficient criterion by which to differentiate between "sophistic" and nonsophistic discourse.

The third sense of "rhetoric" that one finds linked to "the sophists" is best described as an ideology. Describing "sophistical rhetoric" as "emancipatory," Poulakos suggests that "the Sophists' rhetorical lessons were subversive in that they aimed to disempower the powerful and empower the powerless," and that "sophistical rhetoric flourished as a radical critique of the Hellenic culture in the fifth century BC" ("Critique" 99). Similarly, Harold Barrett and others (Kennedy, 18-19; Müller) contend that the most useful aspect of sophistic teaching was that it aided participation in the democracy. Unfortunately, such idealistic accounts of "the sophists" cannot be squared with the historical evidence.

It is simply wishful thinking to describe the sophists collectively as populist-minded teachers wishing to aid the "hitherto voiceless and marginalized" (Poulakos, "Critique" 101). Whoever "the sophists" were, the ancient authorities are virtually unanimous in their assessment that the fees the sophists charged were very high (Blank). Ostwald contends that "only the wealthy" could afford to hire a sophist, and that their followers "consisted largely of ambitious young men of the upper classes" (237-42). Kerferd concludes that "what the Sophists were able to offer was in no sense a contribution to the education of the masses" (*SM* 17). The verdict, in ancient times as well as the present, is that the most appreciative audience was an aristocratic one and, indeed, most of the political leaders who managed to overcome a nonaristocratic birth were rather suspicious of the sophists (Blank 14-15).

We would do well not to over-romanticize the relationship between "the sophists" and Athenian democracy. True, Protagoras is credited with providing the first theoretical defense of democracy (Menzel), but it should not be forgotten that even the most advanced stage of Athenian democracy still limited citizenship to a minority of the adult male population, retained the institution of slavery, and was thoroughly misogynist (Cantarella; Keuls). Furthermore, there was by no means a consensus among "sophists" about the value of democracy (cf. Dupréel; Guthrie; Ostwald 229-50). Antiphon, Critias, and Socrates were all *"sophists"* who eventually were put to death for their *anti*-democratic teachings or activities.[7] Furthermore, some "sophists" explicitly championed the doctrine of *physis*, or "nature," over *nomos*, democratically derived custom-law:

---

[7] For Socrates see Stone; for Critas see Sprague (241-49); for Antiphon see Sprague (108-11, 127-28).

> For a price only the well-to-do could afford, sophists promised to provide the disenchanted younger generation with rhetorical and other training. . . . By and large, *nomos* identifies the conventions, traditions, and values of the democratic establishment, which the older generation tended to regard itself as guarding; arguments from *physis* were marshaled by an intelligentsia that took shape in the Periclean age and from the 430s attracted the allegiance of young aristocrats. (Ostwald 273)

In short, even if we stipulate the traditional list of sophists as "definitive," there is no consistent ideology which could be called a distinct "sophistic rhetoric."

I strongly suspect that the label sophistic-*anything* may be more misleading than useful. The attributes one finds common to all or most of the standard lists of sophists are also common to many other thinkers of the fifth century—such as their questioning of the dominant religious dogmas, their innovation in compositional style, and their roles as "teachers." When one finds an authentically unique contribution, such as Gorgias' account of the power of *logos*, the very uniqueness that makes the contribution noteworthy makes the label "sophistic" an over-generalization.

The Uses and Limits of Interpretation

One defense of the notion of "sophistic rhetoric" is to admit that it may be, in some sense, a "mirage," but to insist that it can be retained as a "useful fiction." After all, history is a form of story-telling that is *interpretive* and *rhetorical* through and through; the myth of a single, authoritative "objective" historical account has been exploded. Furthermore, "sophistic rhetoric" forms part of a useful narrative with which to explore certain recurring issues in the history of ideas. As Poulakos puts it, "because cultural conflicts and contradictions are still with us, because no utopia has yet been devised, and because rhetoric pervades so many human practices, the story of the Sophists is still relevant" ("Critique" 100). Specifically, as Susan C. Jarratt has argued, "sophistic rhetoric" provides a point of departure from "classical philosophy" that allows us to identify and deconstruct certain persistent "binary structures" (such as rhetoric/philosophy) that are prototypical of hierarchal strategies used to displace and marginalize people and ideas.

I am sympathetic toward such an argument. In fact, the sort of narrative that pits the provocative "revolutionary" sophists against the "establishment" figures of Plato and Aristotle is exactly what attracted me to study "the sophists" in the first place (cf. Pirsig). And clearly any theory of "history" that asserts that a single objective true account of an era or event is possible is no longer tenable (Novick). Are there any good reasons, therefore, to resist the turn to "sophistic rhetoric," even if such a notion is granted to be a fiction? I believe that there are, and consequently will proceed to defend three propositions: first, that there are limits to interpretive variability; second, that there are more useful constructs to study for political and social critique than "sophistic rhetoric"; and third, that "sophistic rhetoric" fails to overcome the binary oppositional structures it is credited with challenging.

Consider first the argument that "all history is interpretive; hence there is no problem maintaining the fiction of 'sophistic rhetoric.'" From "all history is interpretive," it simply does not follow that "all interpretations are equally useful." Those who defend a radical version of reader-response theory with respect to historical texts find themselves in a dilemma. If, on one hand, history is *merely* a matter of interpretation, and *all* readings are considered "equal," then the question becomes "Why trouble ourselves with the sophists at all?" If all we will ever find in "sophistic" texts is what our presuppositions tell us we'll find, then why bother? Why not instead simply formulate those presuppositions into a contemporary, postmodern theory of rhetoric, and wash our hands of dead Greeks altogether? So the first part of the dilemma is that if there is no way to escape the present by engaging ancient texts, then there is no apparent reason for considering "sophistic" texts.

If, on the other hand, we admit that ancient texts resist some interpretations more than others, then we are encouraged to accept that interpretations may be *evaluated* and *compared*. Consider the case of the writings of Friedrich Nietzsche, the writer most often credited with formulating the "there are no facts, only interpretation" position. Why couldn't I simply declare that *my* reading of Nietzsche revealed that he was "really" a Platonist? What is it about his texts that resists such a reading? Similarly, what is it about the texts of the fifth century BCE that prevent me from arguing that they articulate a "sophistic calculus"? Alexander Nehamas argues that even Nietzsche insists that some interpretations are better than others. The problem with some renditions of Nietzschean perspectivism "is that they have been too quick to equate possible with actual falsehood, interpretation with mere interpretation" (*Nietzsche* 67). Noting that Nietzsche sought to replace the standard Christian interpretation of morality with his own, Nehamas argues that those who equate interpretation with *mere* interpretation "presuppose that to consider a view an interpretation is to concede that it is false" (*Nietzsche* 66).

There are no magic formulas for knowing in advance the difference between a good and bad interpretation or a more or less defensible historical account. But some interpretations are more persuasive than others, and hence display a longer shelf life. Some interpretations even become "facts." As long as we treat "facts" as *temporarily reified interpretations* which are socially constructed and subject to deconstruction, it does no harm to say that "facts" exist and even help to explain the difference between more or less reliable historical accounts.

An example can illustrate the relationship between the process of reification/deconstruction and the social utility of "facts." Consider the statement "John F. Kennedy died in 1963." I think it is fair to call this statement a reliable fact to which most, if not all, readers would give their assent, and which is more persuasive than some alternatives ("JFK died in 1881") or the statement's contrary ("JFK did *not* die in 1963"). Nonetheless, it is certainly possible to imagine that our "fact" could someday be rejected by the vast majority of people. Aside from the phenomenon of "new" theories that challenge the statement (such as the discovery of a secret conspiracy), the *concepts* and *presuppositions* underlying the statement could be revised. Postmodern challenges to the concept of "self" or "personhood" might render the notion of "John F. Kennedy" problematic; our understanding of *death* might change in such a way as to require revision of the statement; and, alternative calender systems (or even a rejection of linear time!) could make "1963" obsolete. But until we are willing to pay the conceptual cost of rejecting present notions of identity, death, or time, "John F. Kennedy died in 1963" can be regarded as a reliable "fact."

Recent philosophers of science talk of facts and observations being "theory-bound." That is, even the simplest measurement or observation in science is made possible only through a host of conceptual commitments (Latour and Woolgar). A scientist rejects a "fact" only at the cost of giving up the conceptual apparatus producing it, which is why Thomas S. Kuhn says that scientists abandon one theory only when a suitable alternative is available that also can account for certain "facts." It is also the case that new theories sometimes have rendered old "facts" obsolete. Knowing that scientific "facts" are socially constructed, historically contingent, and theory-bound does not make them any less useful or reliable—it simply helps us to understand science as a human activity. Similarly, the more general statement that "all facts are interpretations" does not vitiate the utility of "facts." It simply helps us to understand the social processes that construct facts, and it points out that there is a conceptual cost to rejecting those that are well-established.

Accordingly, we can conclude that the interpretive, narrative, and rhetorical aspects of doing history do not require a cessation of efforts to evaluate competing historical accounts. Though historians must concede that any account is potentially subject to later revision, they need not abandon their efforts to produce accounts that make sense of the available socially constructed, historically contingent facts.

The price we pay for giving up "facts" altogether is that we must give up history as well. For the only difference between the genre of literature called "history" and various sorts of fiction is that the former has something to do with "facts." If history is *purely* fiction, then Ronald Reagan's history of the Vietnam War is as reliable as that of Stanley Karnow, and his account of the Iran-Contra Affair is as good as that of Bill Moyers.[8] I hope these examples challenge the often implicit assumption that radically relativizing history is an emancipatory move; "it ain't necessarily so." "Facts" figure crucially in the "power/knowledge" dynamic problematized by Michel Foucault. Eliminate *all* vestiges of the will-to-truth, and naught but the will-to-power remains. If

---

[8] For a compelling analysis of Reagan's abuse of "facts," see Green and MacColl.

power is all that writes history, then there is no basis for reclaiming marginalized histories, no basis for critiquing establishment narratives, and no basis for curing cultural amnesia about past genocide, misogyny, and racism. In the face of poststructuralist critiques of "facts," one historian of rhetoric recently reported "I feel almost paralyzed by the impossibility of writing history" (Crowley, "Octalog" 13). Her testimony suggests that—far from emancipation—cynicism toward "facts" can induce intellectual self-imprisonment.

"Sophistic rhetoric" has and can be used to critique various sociopolitical arrangements and modernist notions of disciplinarity (Takis Poulakos). Hence the sophists' "story" is sometimes revisited as a useful chapter in the history of ideas. Once again, however, such a turn can be as misleading as it is useful. From a host of perspectives—political, social, demographic, technological, economic, aesthetic, linguistic, etc.—contemporary American life has little in common with ancient Greece. At a superficial level, one can find similarities between contemporary sociopolitical or educational arrangements and virtually *any* culture. It is mostly what Martin Bernal calls "European cultural arrogance" that we regard ancient Greece as the "birthplace" of the most valuable elements of "western thought" (73). Citing mostly the testimony of the ancient Greeks themselves, Bernal argues that much of the philosophy, geometry, and even political theory we often credit the Greeks for devising actually had their origins in Egypt (see esp. 103-09). It was the racism of various nineteenth-century historians that replaced the ancient Greek's own account of their Egyptian and semitic heritage with what Bernal calls the "Aryan Model" of western intellectual history.

Far more useful "chapters" in intellectual history abound, and most of them offer far more textual and other sorts of "data" than do the ancient Greeks. We need not turn to Athens to find strategies of oppression and marginalization; we need only look around us. We need not turn to ancient Greece to understand how power/knowledge relationships are manifested through disciplinary arrangements; we need only consider the past two centuries of the relationship between capitalism and higher learning. In short, *we do not need the fiction of "sophistic rhetoric" as a way into pressing contemporary issues.* In a culture saturated by rhetoric, we need not seek refuge in a romanticized fictionalization of a place "long ago and far away."

There is an important sense in which the turn to "sophistic rhetoric" functions ideologically to support the status quo. By promoting an historical fiction, we legitimize political leaders who do the same. By suggesting that there is a sort of transmillennial "essence" of "sophistic rhetoric," we promote an outdated metaphysics that obfuscates our own contingency in history. Richard Rorty notes that historicist "writers tell us that the question 'What is it to be a human being?' should be replaced by questions like 'What is it to inhabit a rich twentieth-century democratic society?' . . . This historicist turn has helped free us, gradually but steadily, from theology and metaphysics—from the temptation to look for an escape from time and chance" (xiii).

Obviously, I am not saying that historians should ignore ancient Greece. My point is only that once we grant that "sophistic rhetoric" is largely a fiction we need not use it as a route to studying other topics. Instead we should skip the detour and move directly to the contemporary sites of social and political struggle. As James A. Berlin has put it:

> Rhetorics interpellate us, hail us, position us, subject us, put us in our places—and not in others. The places, the positions, the subjects, and subjectivities are not eternal and true, are not timeless and trusty. . . . *We need new rhetorics.* . . . We need rhetorics that allow new voices to be heard, new audiences to act, new actions to be taken, new actors for these actions, new ways of figuring the ways language figures us. (6-10)

"Sophistic rhetoric" also has been invoked as a means for transcending certain philosophical dualisms which poststructuralist and postmodernist critiques have called into question. Aside from the obvious reply that these contemporary critiques make such a "sophistic" turn superfluous, it is arguably the case that the notion of "sophistic rhetoric" *reproduces* such binary thinking. Even if some scholars have succeeded in *reversing* the verdict on the case of *Plato vs. Sophists*, they have not *transcended* the dualities implicit in the conflict. The postmodern challenge is not merely to reverse our evaluation of such pairs as rational/emotional, literal/figurative, truth/opinion, *physis/nomos*, and philosophy/sophistry, but to *deconstruct and replace* the pairs.[9] Hegel portrayed the presocratics as Objectivists (thesis), the sophists as Subjectivists (antithesis), and Plato/Aristotle as providing the proper Synthesis. We do not overcome such binary oppositions by preferring one over the other; we overcome them by moving beyond the Hegelian framework.

The Rhetoric of Definition

A basic assumption of this essay is that definitions are both normative and important. I assume that most readers will concede the point that there is no such thing as a "correct" definition of a word in any absolutist, metaphysical sense. One can either surrender to the conventional definition of a word—the most common or "dominant" definition—or one can defend an alternative. Accordingly, any discussion of a concept such as "sophistic rhetoric" unavoidably involves what can be called the rhetoric of definition— persuasion about how some facet of our experience *ought* to be labeled and defined. Scholars defending "sophistic rhetoric" typically must engage in some act of defining what the terms mean to them, or else rely on readers'

---

[9] See, for example, Jarratt's useful reworking of the *mythos/logos* pair into a fifth-century-inspired *mythos-nomos-logos* schema (31-61). Even though Jarratt's title refers to "the Sophists," she avoids most of the criticisms launched in this essay by grounding her claims with specific fifth-century texts (mostly those of Protagoras and Gorgias) and by demonstrating considerable historiographical reflexivity.

intuitions as to what the terms denote. Similarly, my efforts in this essay have been concerned with the meaning(s) of "sophistic rhetoric." What is at stake is how we as a group of specialized language-users ought to define and use the phrase "sophistic rhetoric"—or whether it should be used at all. The question is normative because "all those who argue in favor of some definition want it . . . to influence the use which would probably have been made of the concept had they not intervened" (Perelman and Olbrechts-Tyteca 213).

My argument is that a historically based definition of "sophistic rhetoric" derived from fifth-century Greece is improbable, and ahistorical definitions are misleading, unhelpful, or superfluous. The principle of Ockham's Razor suggests that "sophistic rhetoric" is expendable. If we want to empower certain contemporary discourses with identifying labels, then let us use labels that are more straight-forward: feminist rhetoric, oppositional discourse, and cultural critique are three examples.

Or, if borrow we must, then let us be explicit about the nature of our debts. If we find more inspiration in Isocrates' educational program than in Plato's, then let us invoke Isocrates rather than the label "sophistic." Kathleen E. Welch's recent book is a positive model in this regard: She self-reflexively describes her efforts as "appropriations" of classical discourse, and she focuses on the contributions of specific individuals (Gorgias, Isocrates, and Plato) rather than on an artificial grouping. Alternatively, if we need a specific rhetorical antidote to competing appropriations of classical texts, then at least labels such as "modern sophistic" or "neosophistic" acknowledge that it is we who have formulated the rhetoric, and that we are bracketing consideration of what "sophistic" rhetoric might or might not have been (Leff; Schiappa, "Neo-Sophistic").

Though most of my examples in this essay have been drawn from recent champions of "sophistic rhetoric," my argument "cuts both ways" in the dispute between those who praise or castigate the sophists. That is, if it is anachronistic to praise fifth-century "sophistic rhetoric," so too is it fallacious to condemn it. Those who would praise Plato's or Aristotle's treatment of rhetoric must do so on grounds other than by comparison with a hypothetical "sophistic rhetoric" if they want to avoid the charge of attacking a person of straw.

The dichotomy between "mirage" (a purely "subjective" phenomenon) and "oasis" (an "objective" phenomenon) is, in the final analysis, inappropriate. For "sophistic rhetoric" is better characterized as a "reservoir"— a human-made construct with many possible uses. The concerns I have expressed in this essay about "sophistic rhetoric" have more to do with the potential consequences of such a turn than the actual quality of the above scholars' work—in other words, I have less quarrel with the specific "uses" of "sophistic rhetoric" that have been made so far than with the process-related question of whether it is necessary or appropriate to rely on an historical construct that cannot be historically grounded. I believe that "sophistic rhetoric" is a construct that we can do without; a fiction, originally invented by Plato for his own ends. We no longer need to maintain the fiction for ours.[10]

---

[10]I am very grateful for the comments on an earlier draft of this essay by John T. Kirby, Janice M. Lauer, and James A. Berlin.

Works Cited

Atkins, J. W. H. "Rhetoric, Greek." *The Oxford Classical Dictionary.* Oxford: Clarendon, 1949.

Barilli, Renato. *Rhetoric.* Trans. Giuliana Menozzi. Minneapolis: U of Minnesota P, 1989.

Barrett, Harold. *The Sophists.* Novato, CA: Chandler, 1987.

Berlin, James A. "Polylog: Professing the New Rhetorics." *Rhetoric Review* 9 (1990): 5-35.

Bernal, Martin. *Black Athena: The Afroasiatic Roots of Classical Civilization.* New Brunswick, NJ: Rutgers UP, 1987.

Blank, David L. "Socratics vs Sophists on Payment for Teaching." *Classical Antiquity* 16 (1985): 1-49.

Cantarella, Eva. *Pandora's Daughters: The Role and Status of Women in Greek and Roman Antiquity.* Baltimore: John Hopkins UP, 1987.

Classen, C. J. "Aristotle's Picture of the Sophists." *The Sophists and their Legacy.* Ed. G. B. Kerferd. Wiesbaden: Steiner, 1981, 7-24.

Cole, A. Thomas. *The Origins of Greek Rhetoric.* Baltimore: John Hopkins UP, 1991.

____. "The Relativism of Protagoras." *Yale Classical Studies* 22 (1972): 19-45.

Connors, Robert J. "Greek Rhetoric and the Transition from Orality." *Philosophy and Rhetoric* 19 (1986): 38-65.

Cope, Edward M. "On the Sophistical Rhetoric." *Journal of Classical and Sacred Philology* 2 (1855): 129-69; 3 (1856): 34-80, 252-88.

Crowley, Sharon. "Octalog: The Politics of Historiography." *Rhetoric Review* 7 (1988): 5-49.

____. "A Plea for the Revival of Sophistry." *Rhetoric Review* 7 (1989): 318-34.

Diels, Herman, and Walther Kranz. *Die Fragmente der Vorsokratiker.* Vol. 2, 6th ed. Berlin: Weidmann, 1951/2.

Dupréel, Eugène. *Les Sophistes.* Neuchatel: Griffon, 1948.

Foucault, Michel. *Power/Knowledge.* New York: Pantheon, 1980.

Green, Mark, and Gail MacColl. *There He Goes Again: Ronald Reagan's Reign of Error.* New York: Pantheon, 1983.

Grote, George. *A History of Greece.* Vol. 8. 2nd ed. London: Murray, 1851.

Guthrie, W. K. C. *The Sophists.* Cambridge: Cambridge UP, 1971.

Havelock, Eric A. "The Linguistic Task of the Presocratics." *Language and Thought in Early Greek Philosophy.* Ed. Kevin Robb. La Salle, IL: Hegeler Institute. 1983. 7-82.

Hommel, H. "Rhetorik." *Der Kleine Pauly.* Vol. 4. München: Druckenmüller, 1972.

Jarratt, Susan C. *The Return of the Sophists: Classical Rhetoric Refigured.* Carbondale: Southern Illinois UP, 1991.

Kennedy, George A. *Classical Rhetoric and its Christian and Secular Tradition from Ancient to Modern Times.* Chapel Hill: U of North Carolina P, 1980.

Kerferd, G. B. "The First Greek Sophists." *Classical Review* 64 (1950): 8-10.

____. *The Sophistic Movement.* Cambridge: Cambridge UP, 1981.

Keuls, Eva C. *The Reign of the Phallus: Sexual Politics in Ancient Athens.* New York: Harper, 1985.

Kroll, Wilhelm. "Rhetorik." *Pauly's Real-Encyclopädie der classischen Altertumswissenschaft.* Supp. 7 (1940): 1039-138.

Kuhn, Thomas S. *The Structure of Scientific Revolutions*. 2nd ed. Chicago: U of Chicago P, 1970.

Latour, Bruno, and Steve Woolgar. *Laboratory Life: The Social Construction of Scientific Facts*. Beverly Hills: Sage, 1979.

Leff, Michael C. "Modern Sophistic and the Unity of Rhetoric." *The Rhetoric of the Human Sciences*. Eds. J. S. Nelson, A. Megill, and D. N. McCloskey. Madison: U of Wisconsin P, 1987. 19-37.

Liddell, H. G., and R. Scott. *A Greek-English Lexicon*. 9th ed. Oxford: Clarendon, 1940.

Martin, Josef. *Antike Rhetorik: Technik und Methode*. München: Beck, 1974.

Menzel, Adolf. "Protagoras, der älteste Theoretiker der Demokratie." *Zeitschrift für Politik* 3 (1910): 205-38.

Moss, Roger. "The Case for Sophistry." *Rhetoric Revalued*. Ed. Brian Vickers. Binghamton, NY: Center for Medieval and Early Renaissance Studies, 1982. 207-24.

Müller, Reimer. "Sophistique et démocratie." *Positions de la Sophistique*. Ed. Barbara Cassin. Paris: Vrin, 1986. 179-93.

Neel, Jasper. *Plato, Derrida, and Writing*. Carbondale: Southern Illinois UP, 1988.

Nehamas, Alexander. "Eristic, Antilogic, Sophistic, Dialectic: Plato's Demarcation of Philosophy from Sophistic." *History of Philosophy Quarterly* 7 (1990): 3-16.

____. *Nietzsche: Life as Literature*. Cambridge, MA: Harvard UP, 1985.

Novick, Peter. *That Noble Dream: The "Objectivity Question" and the American Historical Profession*. Cambridge: Cambridge UP, 1988.

Ostwald, Martin. *From Popular Sovereignty to the Sovereignty of Law: Law, Society, and Politics in Fifth-Century Athens*. Berkeley: U of California P, 1986.

Perelman, Chaïm, and Lucie Olbrechts-Tyteca. *The New Rhetoric*. Trans. J. Wilkinson and P. Weaver. Notre Dame, IN: Notre Dame UP, 1969.

Pilz, Werner. *Der Rhetor im attischen Staat*. Weida: Thomas, 1936.

Pirsig, Robert M. *Zen and the Art of Motorcycle Maintenance*. New York: Morrow, 1974.

Poulakos, John. "Sophistical Rhetoric as a Critique of Culture." *Argument and Critical Practice*. Ed. Joseph W. Wenzel. Annandale: Speech Communication Association,1987. 97-101.

____. "Towards a Sophistic Definition of Rhetoric." *Philosophy and Rhetoric* 16 (1983): 35-48.

Poulakos, Takis. "Intellectuals and the Public Sphere: The Case of the Older Sophists:" *Spheres of Argument*. Ed. Bruce E. Gronbeck. Annandale, VA: Speech Communication Association, 1989. 9-15.

Quandahl, Ellen. "What is Plato? Inference and Allusion in Plato's *Sophist*." *Rhetoric Review* 7 (1989): 338-48.

Rorty, Richard. *Contingency, irony, and solidarity*. Cambridge: Cambridge UP, 1989.

Schiappa, Edward. "Did Plato Coin *Rhêtorikê?*" *American Journal of Philology* 111 (1990): 457-70.

____. "Neo-Sophistic Rhetorical Criticism or the Historical Reconstruction of Sophistic Doctrines?" *Philosophy and Rhetoric* 23 (1990): 192-217.

____. *Protagoras and* Logos: *A Study in Greek Philosophy and Rhetoric*. Columbia: U of South Carolina P, 1991.

Segal, Charles P. "Gorgias and the Psychology of the Logos." *Harvard Studies in Classical Philology* 66 (1962): 99-155.

Solmsen, Friedrich. *Intellectual Experiments of the Greek Enlightenment*. Princeton: Princeton UP, 1975.

Sprague, Rosamond Kent. *The Older Sophists*. Columbia: U of South Carolina P, 1972.

Stone, I. F. *The Trial of Socrates*. New York: Little, 1988.

Verdenius, W. J. "Gorgias' Doctrine of Deception." *The Legacy of the Sophists*. Ed. G. B. Kerferd. Wiesbaden: Steiner, 1981. 116-28.

Welch, Kathleen. *The Contemporary Reception of Classical Rhetoric: Appropriations of Ancient Discourse*. Hillsdale, NJ: Erlbaum, 1990.

Section 3:
Platonic Rhetorical Theory

Plato's View of Rhetoric

by Edwin Black

Whether Plato had a consistent view of rhetoric and, if he did, what that view was have been subjects of considerable debate among commentators and critics of the dialogues. The interpretive controversy of twenty-three centuries has so encrusted his ideas that, though we seldom seem to see them in the same way, it must be even more seldom that we really see them at all. Of course, Plato is difficult to understand. He is complicated, variegated, audacious, and sometimes paradoxical. The apparent elusiveness of his view of rhetoric, alone, has engendered a vast accumulation of commentary, with few of the commentators in substantial agreement on the defining characteristics of that view. Indeed, the only uniformity which crystallizes from this diversity of interpretation is the judgment that Plato disapproved of rhetoric, and was, in fact, rhetoric's most effective historical opponent.[1]

Fortunately, we still have the dialogues, their durability so manifestly established that they could not be hurt by one more fresh look. The objective of the present investigation is to attempt that fresh look.

It is inevitable that any expositor will approach a work from a certain point of view. His frame of reference may be subconscious and unsystematized, but it will assuredly be present, shaping the bias of his interpretation by influencing the direction of his attention, selectively sharpening some and dulling others of his sensibilities, and molding the nuances of his judgment in a thousand imperceptible ways. The critical presuppositions of this study can be simply and dogmatically put. They are that Plato was both a subtle and disciplined thinker and a subtle and disciplined writer, that he would not have allowed patent inconsistency or contradiction into the constantly revised body of his work,[2] and that the dialogues, as speculative inquiries, must explain and justify themselves independent of any circumstances impinging

---

Reprinted from *The Quarterly Journal of Speech* 44 (1958): 361-374. Copyright by the Speech Communication Association. 1958. Reproduced by permission of the publisher.

[1] See e.g., Everett Lee Hunt, "Plato and Aristotle on Rhetoric and Rhetoricians," *Studies in Rhetoric and Public Speaking in Honor of James Albert Winans* (New York, 1925), esp. pp. 18-42.

[2] If the dialogues themselves are not evidence enough of a systematic perfection of literary and philosophical technique, we have also the testimony of Dionysius of Halicarnassus that Plato "curried and combed the locks of his dialogues" to the end of his days.

on their composition.[3]

Such are the premises from which the present examination of Plato's view of rhetoric will proceed. The dialogues in which the view itself receives its most elaborate and methodical treatment are the *Gorgias* and the *Phaedrus*. Plato's treatment of rhetoric is not confined exclusively to these two dialogues; on the contrary, his consideration of rhetoric bears relations with philosophical subjects treated throughout his extant writings. But these relations will develop and clarify as we explore the main body of Platonic rhetoric expounded in the *Gorgias* and the *Phaedrus*. The former is generally considered to have been the earlier written of the two and hence invites our scrutiny first.

The diversity of interpretations which have been placed on the *Gorgias* amply evidences its perplexity for Plato's literary interpreters.[4] It is curious that these interpreters, all excellently equipped for study in classical

---

[3] Some commentators undertake to "understand" the dialogues in terms of events which are thought to have affected Plato. See: Theodor Gomperz, *Greek Thinkers. A History of Ancient Philosophy*, trans. Laurie Magnus, II (New York, 1901); George Grote, *Plato, and the Other Companions of Sokrates*, II (London, 1867); William Hepworth Thompson, *The Gorgias of Plato* (London, 1894), esp. pp. xiv-xviii. Such psychologizing is fascinating to read, but of limited utility in the interpretation of the dialogues. Likewise, Richard Weaver's "reading" of the *Phaedrus* in "The Phaedrus and the Nature of Rhetoric," *The Ethics of Rhetoric* (Chicago, 1953), is an interesting performance, but is so deficient in evidence as to be irrelevant to the study of Plato.

[4] Thompson, after quoting Olympiodorus approvingly, paraphrases him: "The aim of the Gorgias is to discuss the principles which conduce to political well-being. It [the preceding paraphrastic sentence] explains, at least to a considerable extent, the later as well as the earlier discussions; whereas if we assume that the main end of the dialogue is to bring the art of rhetoric and its professors into discredit, we can assign no significant motive for the importance assigned to a character like Callicles, who heartily despises the profession of a Sophist and hates the schools and their pedantry." Pp. xii-xiii.

Thompson asserts that the *Gorgias* was "the public vindication" of the conviction, held by a Plato disillusioned by the execution of Socrates, that "it was hopeless to amend the laws and practices of the Greek communities by any of the ordinary and constitutional means." P. xxx.

Herman Bonitz's interpretation of the *Gorgias* is summed up in the statement, "Schwerlich kann dann noch ein Zweifel sein, dass die mit Kallikles verhandelte Frage: 'ist Philosophie im Platonische Sinne, oder ist politische Rhetorik in ihrem damaligen thatsächlichen Zustande eine würdige Lebensaufgabe? den Kern und Zweck des ganzen Dialogs bezeichnet," *Platonische Studien* (Vienna, 1858), p. 33.

Bonitz's position is, in its general characteristics, shared by E. M. Cope, *Plato's Gorgias*, 2nd ed. (London, 1883). See esp. Cope's introduction; and Werner Jaeger, *Paideia: The Ideals of Greek Culture*, trans. Gilbert Highet, III (Oxford, 1954), p. 50. Both Cope and Jaeger take the references to "rhetoric" in the *Gorgias* to refer to all the activities of Athenian society associated with oratory, especially the practices of the courts, the aspirations of the young, and the popular systems of education.

Gomperz interprets the *Gorgias* as a literary counterattack against Polycrates, who was supposed to have written a lampoon of Socrates after the latter's execution, II, p. 343.

Eduard Zeller interprets the *Gorgias* as containing a wholesale condemnation of rhetoric as an instrument of Sophistical ethics. *Plato and the Older Academy*, trans. Sarah Frances Alleyne and Alfred Goodwin (London, 1876), p. 190. This condemnation is unqualified in Zeller's view, although when, in the same book, Zeller deals with the treatment of rhetoric in the *Phaedrus* (p. 515), he does not seem even to recognize a logical difficulty in his interpretation, nor does he attempt to resolve the question of how Plato can be read as unqualifiedly condemning rhetoric in one place and writing of it constructively in another.

Walter Pater argues that Plato opposed rhetoric, and opposed it because it represented to him the abhorrent Heraclitean metaphysics. *Plato and Platonism* (London, 1920), esp. chap. 4.

philology, and all having reference to exactly the same document, cannot agree on its meaning. The cause of the confusion does not seem to lie in any obscurity of statement in the dialogue. Rather, we discover what troubles the commentators the moment we compare the *Gorgias* with the *Phaedrus*: the former, satirical, contentious, and refutative, the latter emerging with a constructive, affirmative judgment clothed in the most majestic poetry. The contrast is both striking and discomfiting. Have we here irreconcilably contradictory views of rhetoric expressed by the same author? The dilemma solicits resolution, and the commentators have responded by maintaining either that Plato changed his mind or that Plato did not mean by "rhetoric" in the *Gorgias* what he meant by "rhetoric" in the *Phaedrus*. The first position tacitly assumes that our author admitted a patent and obvious contradiction into his literature; the second position tacitly assumes that our author was inconsistent or, at the least, careless about his use of language. Since I hold that one should not adopt either of these assumptions in interpreting Plato except only as a last resort, after every more generous alternative has been vainly tested, I shall tentatively reject these possibilities.

One other difficulty besides the apparent difference in the moral attitude toward rhetoric expressed in the *Gorgias* and in the *Phaedrus* plagues the commentators. This other difficulty relates to the internal structure of each of the two dialogues, and presents itself to us in the form of two questions: What is the theme of the *Gorgias*? and What is the theme of the *Phaedrus*? If the *Gorgias* is concerned with ethics, why is so sizeable a portion of it devoted to the subject of rhetoric? If the *Phaedrus* is concerned with rhetoric, why is so much of the dialogue taken up with a consideration of love? Of course, these questions and those who ask them presuppose, without proof, that a literary work must have a single theme. One might reply to these questions by denying the assumption and asserting that in the *Gorgias* and the *Phaedrus* we have two dialogues with multiple themes. I shall not adopt this position at this stage of the analysis. The search for a single theme in a literary work can provide fruitful insights into the work. But the point is worth making that, after all, there is no binding fiat of literary activity nor any logical necessity demanding that a piece of writing, even a great piece of writing, and especially a dialectical inquiry, must have one and only one paraphrasable theme. The suggestion, once made, need not be pursued. It is enough to note for the present that determining the themes of the two dialogues is one of the major difficulties which commentators have found.

All major modern commentators on Plato's view of rhetoric, with the exceptions of Walter Pater, Paul Shorey, and possibly Werner Jaeger, design their interpretations of the *Gorgias* or the *Phaedrus* to deal with one or both of the difficulties mentioned. Troubled by the apparent inconsistency of the *Gorgias* and *Phaedrus*, they infer a change of heart and mind, and a concomitant modification of doctrine, by Plato. Or, troubled by an inability to assign a single theme to one or both of the dialogues, they redefine and expand the meanings of key terms to make the work fit themes which they wish to assign to it. Now, it follows that if these two difficulties can be

resolved with more parsimony of assumption and with stricter adherence to
the texts of the dialogues than has heretofore been the case, then the
interpretations of the commentators will have been circumvented, for the
problems which these interpretations were designed to resolve will have
evaporated. Further, if these two difficulties are to be resolved, their
resolution would involve a clear and accurate explication of Plato's view of
rhetoric, which is the object of this inquiry. With these observations before
us, we might begin the investigation of the *Gorgias* by determining what the
term "rhetoric" means there.

2.

The crucial passages in the *Gorgias* which deal directly with the
definition of "rhetoric" occur in what might be called the first act, i.e., the
conversation between Socrates and Gorgias. Pressed for a definition of
"rhetoric," Gorgias defines this term as meaning the art of that kind of
persuasion which is exercised before public assemblies and is concerned with
the just and the unjust. Having elicited this definition, Socrates goes on to
force from Gorgias the admission that sometimes rhetoric is used for unjust
purposes. Since Gorgias contends that the rhetorician has knowledge of the
just and unjust, or, at least, must have such knowledge before Gorgias will
call him a "rhetorician," Socrates claims to have discerned a contradiction in
Gorgias's position. It has been alleged by some commentators, Cope and
Shorey among them,[5] that Socrates is made to argue sophistically in this
portion of the dialogue. The main objection is that Socrates is incorrect in
assuming that if a person knew the just and unjust, then he could not act but
justly. As a matter of fact, there are strong reasons which Plato might have
adduced to support this contention.[6]

Suppose the case of a man who enjoyed committing murder and who
committed murder at every opportunity; yet, every time someone asked the
man if he knew that murder was wrong, he said that he did. Suppose further
that this man made no claims of acting under duress or compulsion, but chose
to commit murder freely and soberly. Should we not conclude, in the
presence of such evidence, that he did not really "believe" or "know" that
murder was wrong? In assuming, as he did, that the rhetorician who knows
the nature of justice and injustice will actually be just, Plato took the position
that to understand a moral rule necessarily involves obeying it, since part of
understanding the rule would be understanding its obligatory quality, i.e.,
understanding that it is a *rule*.

To dismiss the exchange between Gorgias and Socrates as a "conscious

---

[5] Cope, pp. xlii-xliii; Paul Shorey, "The Unity of Plato's Thought," *The Decennial Publications of the
University of Chicago*, First Series, VI (Chicago, 1904), p. 23.
[6] The assumption was evidently considered too obvious to require explanation. Cf. the concept of
phronesis in Aristotle's *Nicomachean Ethics*, esp. Book VI, chap. 12.

dialectical sport," as does Shorey,[7] is to ignore an important moral insight which Plato presented. Put in simpler terms, Plato's analysis of the Gorgian definition of "rhetoric" might run as follows:

If a person (the rhetorician) claims knowledge of the just, then it follows *as a necessary condition of having such knowledge* that the person will be just. What if Gorgias had refused to concede the point, and had instead contended that the rhetorician does not necessarily know the just? In that case, Socrates could contend that such a person could not possibly use rhetoric because, since part of the definition of rhetoric is that it is persuasion about the just and unjust, such a person could not know what rhetoric was and hence could not use it. So, Gorgias is obliged to concede that according to his definition of rhetoric, the rhetorician must have knowledge of the just and unjust. As a result of the arguments in the dialogue, we can see that Gorgias's definition implicatively claimed a moral feature for rhetoric which in fact rhetoric does not have. A logical consequence of the Gorgian definition is that there can be no such thing as morally bad rhetoric, or rhetoric which is unjust. Plato knew, as we know, that there is morally bad and unjust rhetorical discourse. It therefore follows that the Gorgian definition is false.

We must bear in mind that the definitions which Plato sought by the dialectical process were neither stipulative nor lexicographical definitions. They were what Richard Robinson calls "real definitions."[8] That is to say, when Plato sought a definition, he was not satisfied with a stipulation about how a term was to be used or with a report about how it was generally used; he sought, rather, a description of the nature of the thing designated by the term. Looked at in this way, we can understand how Plato could call a definition "false" in the sense that the definiendum was inaccurately described, while a lexicographical definition might be false only in an entirely different sense, and a stipulative definition could not be false at all.

It will assist our consideration of the *Gorgias* to amplify a bit more Plato's dialectical procedure. It is a procedure which is described in the *Phaedrus, Philebus, Cratylus, Sophist, Politicus,* and *Laws.*[9] Cornford gives the following account:

> The expert in Dialectic will guide and control the course of philosophical discussion by his knowledge of how to "divide by Kinds," not confusing one Form with another. He will discern clearly the hierarchy of Forms which constitutes reality and make out its articulate structure, with which the texture of philosophic discourse must correspond, if it is to express truth. The method is that method

---

[7] *Loc. cit.*
[8] Richard Robinson, *Definition* (Oxford, 1950), pp. 7, 8, 161, 162.
[9] *Phaedrus,* (section nos.) 265, 266, 270D; *Philebus* 16-18; *Cratylus,* 424C; *Sophist,* 226C, 235C, 253 ff.; *Politicus,* 285A ff.; *Laws,* 894AA, 936D, 965C.

of Collection and Division which was announced in the *Phaedrus* and has been illustrated in the *Sophist*. Finally, to discern this structure clearly is the same thing as "to know how to distinguish in what ways the several Kinds can or can not combine." In other words, the science will yield the knowledge needed to guide us to true affirmative and negative statements about the Forms, of which the whole texture of philosophic discourse should consist. . . .[10]

The meanings of common names and verbs are the Forms. Statements are not propositional forms but actual significant statements, existing while we utter them. The science of Dialectic does not study formal symbolic patterns to which our statements conform, nor yet these statements themselves. Nor does it study our thoughts or ways of reasoning, apart from the objects we think about. It is not "Logic" if Logic means the science either of *logoi* or *logismoi*. What it does study is the structure of the real world of Forms. Its technique of Collection and Division operates on that structure.[11]

. . . Dialectic is not Formal Logic, but the study of the structure of reality—in fact Ontology, for the Forms are the realities.[12]

The goal of Dialectic is not to establish propositions ascribing a predicate to all the individuals in a class. The objective is the definition of indivisible species—a Form—by genus and specific differences. What we define is not "all men" but the unique Form "Man."[13]

These cullings from Cornford's exposition should serve to clarify not only Plato's *modus operandi* in all the dialogues, but as well the way in which he deals with the Gorgian definition of rhetoric. When Plato sought the meaning of "rhetoric," he was seeking a series of true propositions about an existential class.

What does all of this imply for our analysis of the *Gorgias*? Primarily that all we have a right to infer from the first conversation between Socrates and Gorgias is that Gorgias's description of "rhetoric" has been overthrown. *Rhetoric in general has not been attacked.* Indeed, up to this point in the dialogue,[14] Plato has not written a single line about rhetoric, the Form. Plato's concern has been with Gorgias's description of rhetoric, and nothing else. Why has Plato given so much space to overthrowing a definition which he has put into the mouth of Gorgias? Of course, we cannot be certain of all his reasons, though we can be reasonably sure that they are not reducible to

---

[10]Francis Macdonald Cornford, *Plato's Theory of Knowledge* (London, 1935), pp. 263-264.
[11]*Ibid.*, p. 265.
[12]*Ibid.*, p. 266.
[13]*Ibid.*, p. 269.
[14]*Gorgias*, 461.

"conscious dialectical sport." The probability, suggested in somewhat different contexts by Cope, Bonitz, and Jaeger,[15] is that what Plato represents as Gorgias's view of rhetoric was widely held by influential and respected Sophists; it was a view with sufficient currency and respectability to seem to Plato to merit careful examination.

It is in the portion of the dialogue with Polus that Socrates is made to formulate the famous argument that rhetoric is not an art but is merely a knack like cookery, a counterfeit of a part of politics. This passage, like the one discussed above, has been widely interpreted as a wholesale condemnation of rhetoric. Such an interpretation is unwarranted by the text. We have, for example, within the passage itself clear indications that the "rhetoric" being dismissed as a knack is not *all* rhetoric. We find Socrates hesitating about making accusations against rhetoric with the comment, "I fear it may be somewhat rude to say the truth; for on Gorgias's account I am reluctant to speak out for fear he should suppose that I am satirizing his professional pursuits. At the same time whether this *is* the kind of rhetoric that Gorgias practises, I really don't know."[16] It is perfectly clear that Plato conceives of a rhetoric that is not open to this analysis since he suggests here that Gorgias might practice another kind of rhetoric. Later in the same dialogue, in the conversation between Socrates and Callicles, Socrates says, "So then it is to this [justice] that the genuine orator,[17] the man of science and virtue will have regard in applying to men's souls whatever words he addresses to them, and will conform all his actions; and if he give any gift he will give it, or if he take aught away he will take it, with his mind always fixed upon this, how to implant justice in the souls of his citizens and eradicate injustice, to engender self-control and extirpate self-indulgence, to engender all other virtue and remove all vice."[18]

It is impossible to maintain that Plato intended the *Gorgias* to be a total condemnation of all rhetoric as a "knack" and a "counterfeit of politics" when, in that very dialogue, he already sketches out some of the conditions of a rhetoric which would deserve the name of art. Obviously, the passage in which rhetoric is called a knack has been misinterpreted. The "rhetoric" referred to in the passage must be that which Gorgias has attempted to define. Plato's attack is limited only to a particular practice of rhetoric, and it is clear enough from the *Gorgias* alone that the attack was legitimate, deserved, and, given the Platonic theory of Forms, logically valid.

When we add to the evidence already adduced from the *Gorgias* the passage in the *Laws*[19] in which Plato, with a clear opportunity to condemn

---

[15]*Loc. cit.*
[16]*Gorgias*, 462D. Unless otherwise indicated all quotations are from Cope's translation.
[17]The phrase is rendered, "true and scientific rhetor," by Paul Shorey, *What Plato Said* (Chicago, 1933), p. 503.
[18]*Gorgias*, 504C.
[19]*Laws*, 938A.

rhetoric as unscientific, waives the question of whether rhetoric is an art or a knack, and the passages in the *Phaedrus*[20] which lay down the conditions for rhetoric to be an art, we are bound to the conclusion that Plato did not intend his condemnation to apply to *all* rhetoric. At the risk of being repetitious, I shall reiterate that all we have a right to infer from the text of the *Gorgias* is that Plato opposed only a particular view of rhetoric unsuccessfully defended in the dialogue by Gorgias, Polus, and Callicles, and probably actually defended by leading sophists and rhetoricians of Plato's time.

At this point the question might arise, if Plato wished to oppose the Gorgian view of rhetoric, why did he attack its definition rather than its practice? The answer to this question must be, as previously indicated, stated in terms of the objectives and methods of dialectic. Plato sought to know the true Form. In the *Gorgias* and the *Phaedrus* he was seeking the Form of rhetoric. That was his objective. His method, too, has been mentioned, as Ross has described it: "Plato has in the *Phaedrus* described dialectic as consisting in a joint use of collection and division. Of these operations, the first seems to be merely preliminary to the second. In the attempt to reach the definition of a specific term the first stage—the 'collection'—is the tentative choice of a wide genus under which the term to be defined seems to fall."[21]

With the dialectical procedure in mind we can understand why Plato approaches the subject of rhetoric in quite the way that he does in the *Gorgias* and also why that dialogue is a unified literary work with a single theme. Plato's attack was on the Gorgian view of rhetoric (which was probably a general Sophistical view of rhetoric). The attack focussed on the Gorgian definition, though "definition" in the distinctively Platonic sense. This definition could be expected to have two parts: the collection and the division. The *Gorgias* is a refutation of both parts of the Gorgian definition. We find in the first two parts of the dialogue, where Gorgias and then Polus are Socrates's prime antagonists, that Socrates aims to overthrow the "collective" definition. The burden of Socrates's argument in these sections is to establish that rhetoric does not belong to the genus, art-concerned-with-justice. The introduction of Callicles does not represent a change in theme; rather, it represents a shift in focus to the "divisive" definition. Against Callicles, Socrates might describe his own position thus:

"But even if we grant for the sake of argument this 'collective' definition which I have just refuted, I shall now demonstrate that even your 'divisive' definition is false."

This is what Socrates proceeds to do. The animus of the argument against Callicles is that Callicles's analysis of justice is wrong. Why did Plato trouble to refute a definition represented by Callicles in the dialogue? While the question is not central to the present study, the probability is that Callicles's

---

[20]E.g., *Phaedrus*, 263B.
[21]W. David Ross, *Plato's Theory of Ideas* (Oxford, 1951), pp. 116-117.

views were widely and influentially held in Plato's time, just as we know them to be held in our own time. We can further infer that, if the present view of the thematic unity of the *Gorgias* is correct, the opinions represented by Gorgias, Polus, and Callicles were probably held as a coherent theory by the people whom Plato intended to refute when he wrote the *Gorgias*.[22]

Before proceeding to a consideration of the *Phaedrus*, it might be well briefly to review. I have attempted to demonstrate the following points:

1. The *Gorgias* is a thematically unified dialogue having for its single main theme the refutation of the Gorgian definition of rhetoric.
2. The *Gorgias* is concerned with ethical questions because the definition being subjected to dialectical inquiry claims a moral characteristic for the definiendum; however, there are no issues raised in the *Gorgias* which are not demonstrably pertinent to the definition of "rhetoric" presented by Gorgias early in the dialogue.
3. The *Gorgias* is fundamentally a refutative rather than a constructive dialogue, as are other of the "Socratic" dialogues, i.e., dialogues written early in Plato's career, as the *Gorgias* evidently was.
4. Plato cannot be interpreted as having pronounced a general condemnation of rhetoric.

3.

With these points clear, I shall proceed to propose that the *Phaedrus* is the constructive complement of the *Gorgias* and that the two dialogues taken together constitute a consistent view of rhetoric. A. E. Taylor pronounces the judgment with which my proposal is consistent:

> In taking leave of the *Phaedrus*, we may note that while it supplements the *Gorgias* in its conclusions about the value of "style," it modifies nothing that was said in the earlier dialogue. The moral condemnation pronounced on the use of eloquent speech to pervert facts and produce false impressions remains the same. So does the verdict that the sort of thing professional teachers from Tisias to Thrasymachus profess to expound is not a science but a mere "trick" or "knack" (and therefore cannot be conveyed, as they profess to convey it, by "lessons"). In adding that a thorough knowledge of a subject-matter and a sound knowledge of the psychology of the public addressed furnished a really scientific basis for a worthy and effective style, Plato is saying nothing inconsistent with the results of the *Gorgias*. There is thus no sufficient ground for thinking that the teaching of the *Phaedrus* represents a later "development" from the more "Socratic" position of the *Gorgias*.[23]

---

[22]The important thing is that we not strain credulity by attributing to a philosophical genius reasons that are ill-defined, trivial, or plain silly.

[23]A. E. Taylor, *Plato, the Man and his Work* (New York, 1929), p. 319.

Since there is considerably less disagreement among students of Plato and among expert commentators about the interpretation of the *Phaedrus*, there is no need for a detailed examination of that dialogue here. Plato turns the collective and divisive resources of dialectic on "real" rhetoric, and his examination is clearly reported in the *Phaedrus*. The collective definition is: "Must not the art of rhetoric, taken as a whole, be a kind of influencing of the mind by means of words, not only in courts of law and other public gatherings, but in private places also?"[24] And further on: "The function of oratory is in fact to influence men's souls."[25]

Plato's divisive definition is explicated by his setting forth the conditions necessary to make speech-writing an art:

> The conditions to be fulfilled are these: first, you must know the truth about the subject that you speak or write about: that is to say, you must be able to isolate it in definition, and having so defined it you must next understand how to divide it into kinds, until you reach the limit of division; secondly, you must have a corresponding discernment of the nature of the soul, discover the type of speech appropriate to each nature, and order and arrange your discourse accordingly, addressing a variegated soul in a variegated style that ranges over the whole gamut of tones, and simple soul in a simple style. All this must be done if you are to become competent, within human limits, as a scientific practitioner of speech, whether you propose to expound or to persuade.[26]

In sum, Plato conceived a true art of rhetoric to be a consolidation of dialectic with psychogogia—applicable to all discourse, public and private,[27] persuasive and expository, which aims to influence men's souls. Dialectic was Plato's general scientific method; rhetoric is a special psychological application of it.[28] This definition of rhetoric is in one sense narrower, in another broader than the definition which Plato overthrew in the *Gorgias*. It is narrower in the sense that he does not admit the nature of justice and injustice to be a part of the "art" of rhetoric, but places it rather in the "art" of statesmanship. It is a broader definition in that Plato does assign to the art of rhetoric a specific province of its own, and a province which is not, as with the earlier sophists, confined to forensic and deliberative oratory, but extends to all discourse which influences men. Plato's position here is fully consonant with that of the *Gorgias*; indeed, the treatments of rhetoric in the two dialogues supplement one another.

---

[24]*Phaedrus*, 261A. Unless otherwise indicated, all quotations from the *Phaedrus* will be from R. Hackforth, *Plato's Phaedrus* (Cambridge, England, 1952).

[25]*Phaedrus*, 271C. The more famous rendering of this passage, "Oratory is the art of enchanting the soul . . . ," is by Benjamin Jowett, *The Dialogues of Plato* (New York, 1937), I.

[26]*Phaedrus*, 277BC.

[27]Cf. *Sophist*, 222C.

[28]See Shorey, *What Plato Said*, p. 52.

The question of the thematic unity of the *Phaedrus* too has puzzled commentators. It is evident from the dialogue itself that its main subject is rhetoric; on this point, there is virtually unanimous agreement. But the three speeches on love in the dialogue, occupying as they do such a large proportion of space and reaching, in the third speech, such a luminous intensity of poetic eloquence and philosophical insight, have suggested to some readers a formal defect in the dialogue's structure.[29] The speeches fasten the reader's attention on themselves; Socrates's second speech is the climax of the drama: all converse in the dialogue builds up to and then down from that section. How can we account for the unity of the dialogue? I believe that we can account for the speeches by observing that they operate on at least seven different levels of meaning, at least five of which are directly and clearly pertinent to a consideration of rhetoric. By my reference to "levels of meaning," I indicate only that there are at least seven different ways in which these speeches might legitimately be understood by a reader:

1. The three speeches are investigations of love, and are intended to convey Plato's ideas on that subject. As such, they are not directly and clearly pertinent to a consideration of rhetoric, though they still have great value taken exclusively in this non-rhetorical sense.

2. The speeches, culminating in Socrates's second speech, are intended to express Plato's counterpart of Sophistical education. It is clear that Socrates's second speech focuses on and advocates the development of the intellectual and moral qualities of the beloved by the lover. It would not be inaccurate to characterize Plato's ideal lover as a philosophical tutor; certainly he is given a primarily educative function with respect to the beloved. Since, in the *Gorgias*, Plato attacked some of the pretensions of rhetorical education as conducted by the Sophists, we might expect a more constructive treatment of education in the *Phaedrus*.[30] Even so, the speeches, read in this way, cannot be said to have an unqualifiedly clear and direct relevance to the subject of rhetoric. The remaining five "readings," however, do have such relevance.

3. The three speeches can be taken as specimens of rhetoric. In this way they serve a function to the theme of the dialogue so obvious that few commentators have even troubled to remark it directly. The speeches represent different kinds of persuasion, each superior to its predecessor, and the third represents the apogee of rhetorical discourse. The first speech, besides being subject to all the criticisms which Socrates makes of it, appeals exclusively to the prudential self-interest of the auditor. It is devoid of dialectic, and its disorder is evidence of its lack

---

[29]See, e.g. Shorey, p. 198.

[30]This interpretation is obliquely suggested by W. C. Helmbold and W. B. Holther, "The Unity of the Phaedrus," *University of California Publications in Classical Philology*, XIV, No. 9 (Berkeley and Los Angeles, 1952).

of adaptability to any possible person.[31] The second speech argues from grounds of definition and moral self-interest. It is better than the first because at least it is a kind of dialectic, though it is not "true" dialectic, as Socrates's later critique of it observes. The third speech is the perfection of the technique: the consummate amalgam of dialectic and psychogogia.

In exemplifying dialectic in a speech, Plato would not encounter any unusual literary problems. All of his dialogues illustrate dialectic in one way or another. But the exemplification of psychogogia certainly must have been a unique literary problem to Plato, a problem which he brilliantly resolved by choosing love as the subject of the speeches. Plato could not very well have exemplified the psychogogic aspect of rhetoric *only* by having Socrates's speeches adapted to Phaedrus. If Plato had done only that, his exemplification might not have been clearly made, and he uncharacteristically would have limited the applicability of his paradigm to the dramatic situation created in the dialogue. Plato's resolution of the problem is to have Socrates discourse directly on the soul, which the subject of love enables him to do. Since the theory of the soul presented in the speech is itself the product of dialectic, the speech becomes an explicit consolidation of dialectic and psychogogia and, as such, a paradigm of Platonic rhetoric in a philosophical as well as a literary sense.

4. The three speeches can be taken as considerations of a particular type of rhetoric: courtship. As such, the speeches can be interpreted as dealing with the objectives of the suitor and, implicatively, with the objectives available to rhetors in general. Plato rejects personal pleasure and reciprocal pleasure as worthy objectives, finally endorsing the love of wisdom as the aim worthy of fulfillment. Considered in this way, the third speech can be taken as a poetic restatement of the doctrine developed in the *Gorgias* that the true orator and statesman aims at the moral improvement of his audience. This reading would reveal that the speeches in the *Phaedrus* contain paradigms within paradigms, i.e., the speeches *qua* speeches are paradigms of artistic form, and their contents are also paradigmatic.

5. The three speeches can be taken as Plato's advice to audiences. In a view of rhetoric so concerned as Plato's with the sorts of things rhetors ought to say, we should rather expect a concomitant treatment of what audiences ought to attend to. The speeches of the *Phaedrus* can be read as functioning in that way. We must not neglect the care with which the character of Phaedrus is drawn in the dialogue. He is neither a witless foil for Socrates's ironies nor the representative of an antagonistic philosophical idea. Phaedrus is a lover of discourse, a

---

[31]Plato insisted that principles of organization be based on human psychology. See *Phaedrus* 277C.

young man who is impressionable, an auditor. Several times in the dialogue Socrates insinuates that the Lysian speech was composed to influence Phaedrus and that Socrates's own speeches have the same objective.[32] The three speeches, taken together, constitute a symposium on the subject of whether one ought to yield to the lover or the non-lover. Since, as was observed in the fourth "reading" above, the wooing of the lover would be a type of rhetoric in Plato's schematism, we might suppose him to have wished his readers to generalize from the particular case, wooing, to the general Form, rhetoric. Since these speeches are directed to Phaedrus, we might be expected to take him as the paradigm of audiences. Once the generalization is made, it becomes evident that the speeches deal with what sorts of arguments one should be influenced by, and to what sorts of speakers one ought to listen. In this light too, the speeches would be taken as a restatement of the *Gorgias's* doctrine about the proper objective of oratory, with the emphasis falling on the moral implications which this doctrine has for audiences.

6. The speeches can be taken as poetic discussions of the moral attitude which the speaker takes toward his speech. More than once in the dialogue Socrates describes Phaedrus and himself as "lovers of discourse." They would therefore belong to the genus "lover" according to the prescriptions of Platonic dialectic, and whatever is true of that genus would be true also of them with respect to discourse. Accordingly, the third speech would be read as saying that the true lover of discourse will strive to enhance the moral quality of the object of his love: his discourse.

It may seem odd to the modern reader to encounter the concept of a "love" of discourse, but we know from Plato's writings and from a multitude of other sources in antiquity that the Greeks did take a deep and critical pleasure in rhetorical discourse. Plato, then, was setting down the conditions for the expression of that love, holding, in effect, that the lover of discourse will imbue his discourse with moral elevation.

7. The three speeches can be taken as a consideration of benign and malign forms of "madness" or inspiration, with the third speech exemplifying poetic inspiration in form and erotic inspiration in content. Plato recognized the existence of four types of benign madness, two of which are discussed and exemplified in these speeches.[33] The relationship between poetic madness and Platonic rhetoric will be briefly examined below.

---

[32]E.g., *Phaedrus*, 237B, 257.

[33]For a fuller discussion of this subject see: Ivan M. Linforth, "Telestic Madness in Plato," *University of California Publications in Classical Philology*, XIII (Berkeley and Los Angeles, 1950).

These seven readings of the speeches may well not exhaust the possibilities, but the levels of possible interpretation are numerous enough to reveal the plurality of function of the speeches. Since Plato was a conscious literary artist, I believe that we must take this ambiguity as deliberate. Considering the fact that this ambiguity enables Plato to write on one level about an apparently disparate subject while, at other levels, still to maintain a unitary theme in the dialogue, we must judge that his ambiguity is actually a glorious tour de force. I hope at least to have established that the speeches in the *Phaedrus* represent a violation of the dialogue's thematic unity only when they are read in only one of several possible ways. The general inference which can be drawn is that there is no lack of thematic unity in either the *Gorgias* or the *Phaedrus*, nor are the positions taken in those two dialogues anything but fully consistent and logically complementary to one another.

4.

Plato is not so directly concerned with rhetoric in dialogues other than the two we have been considering, but even so, some of the darker corners of Platonic rhetoric are illuminated by his insights in other areas. This is especially true of his seminal contributions in the area of epistemology.

One recurrent distinction which Plato makes between knowledge or intelligence and true belief is particularly noteworthy for its implicative relevance to rhetorical theory. The pertinent section in the *Timaeus* is:

> If intelligence and true belief are two different kinds, then these things—Forms that we cannot perceive but only think of—certainly exist in themselves; but if, as some hold, true belief in no way differs from intelligence, then all things we perceive through the bodily senses must be taken as the most certain reality. Now we must affirm that they are two different things, for they are distinct in origin and unlike in nature. The one is produced in us by instruction, the other by persuasion; the one can always give a true account of itself, the other can give none; the one cannot be shaken by persuasion, whereas the other can be won over; and true belief, we must allow, is shared by all mankind, intelligence only by the gods and a small number of men.[34]

We find a restatement of this position in the *Theaetetus*,[35] and though the context in that dialogue is different, the important point is that Plato did draw a distinction between knowledge and conviction, and based this distinction on the method by which each was attained. Plato looked upon knowledge, the

---

[34]*Timaeus*, 51DE. Translation from Francis Macdonald Cornford, *Plato's Cosmology* (London, 1937).
[35]*Theaetetus*, 201A.

object of instruction, as accompanied by an unshakeable certitude which conviction, the object of persuasion, lacked. This deficiency of certitude was not affected by the truth-value of the conviction. "True belief," by which Plato meant a state of having been persuaded to accept a proposition that was in fact true, was still, despite its truth, more tenuously held than knowledge *(episteme)* or intelligence *(noesis)*, i.e., rational intuition.[36]

To Plato, belief or conviction *(pistis)* was one of four possible states of mind in an hierarchy of mental states.[37] The lowest of these states of mind is imagining *(eikasia)*, which Cornford describes as, "the wholly unenlightened state of mind which takes sensible appearances and current moral notions at their face value—the condition of the unreleased prisoners in the Cave allegory . . . who see only images of images."[38]

Above imagining is belief which, when true, is a sufficient guide to action, but which can be shaken by persuasion and is the objective of persuasion. Higher on the scale is thinking *(dianoia)* characteristic of mathematical procedure. It is reasoning from premise to conclusion in which the premises are taken axiomatically. The highest state of mind is intelligence or knowledge, in which the premises themselves are examined and the ultimate principle on which they depend is apprehended.

In the third speech of the *Phaedrus* and in the *Meno*,[39] Plato discussed an unusual mental phenomenon which he called "madness" or inspiration, by which one, possessing only true belief, utters profound truth. It is clear in these passages that Plato did not consider the profoundest insights to be exclusively the product of intelligence or knowledge. The poet, the statesman, and the orator might have moments of vivid revelation by which audiences can be inspired, but the source of this revelation is not in any state of mind. Rather, it is divinely inspired.[40] Its capacity to persuade is due to the epidemic quality of divine madness. Such inspirations have nothing to do with art. They are the gifts of God, and cannot be further explained.[41]

In these considerations we have perhaps the only instance in the formal history of rhetorical theory of an investigation of the epistemological character of rhetoric, and the relative strength with which any persuasively induced belief will be sustained measured against a broad psychological scale. Plato's conclusion was that no matter how fervent our conviction that a proposition is true, that conviction will always be less secure than the knowledge even of a more trivial proposition. The method by which a belief has come to be held makes all the difference.

Given the observation that belief or conviction is inferior to knowledge in

---

[36]Cornford, *The Republic of Plato* (Oxford, 1941), p. 223.
[37]*Republic*, 6.509 ff.
[38]Cornford, *Republic*, p. 222.
[39]*Meno*, 98B ff.
[40]This notion is developed in the *Ion*.
[41]See Hackforth, pp. 60-62.

certitude and persistence, and given also Plato's deep commitment to the pursuit and cultivation of knowledge, the question arises: What place, if any, would rhetorical persuasion have in Plato's doctrine of politics? What place could rhetoric have when the state itself is designed to serve philosophical ends, when its leaders are carefully selected and arduously trained philosophers, and its economy, educational system, family pattern, artistic enterprise —all of its institutions, including even the most personal and intimate—are arranged to serve the interests of abstract Justice? Where is there room for the flexibility of argument, the contingency of decision, and the inconstancy of commitment, all so characteristic of rhetorical activity, when the fabric of society is woven after the pattern of certain, immutable, universal Truth? Plato answers these questions, and defines with precision the place of rhetoric in the Platonic commonwealth.

In considering the social utility of rhetoric, Plato's emphasis falls on the function of persuasion as a means of social control. As such, its utility to the state is obvious, and Plato has not neglected it. Despite the ideological differences between the *Republic* and the *Laws*, a congruous view of the function of rhetoric is maintained. Its place is defined in the *Politicus*, where rhetoric is made subordinate to the art of statesmanship; but even though in a subordinated capacity, rhetorical persuasion is considered by Plato as the only means of social control besides coercion which the statesman can exercise.[42]

In the *Republic*, Plato not only states that rhetoric should be used by the Guardians, but explicitly condones the use even of willful deception in the best interests of the community.[43] The state is to be organized and governed after metaphysical principles, yet metaphysical knowledge cannot be apprehended by unmetaphysical minds. Hence, it is justifiable to simplify complex truths and to present them appealingly.

In the "second best state," rhetoric occupies the same place and discharges the same function as in the *Republic*. Here too, it is a means of social control to be used by the Legislator,[44] who may use even a benevolent lie to persuade.[45] Since Plato considered freedom of expression inimical to the best interests of the community, his condoning of deception is not general, but is always confined to the governing class. The *Laws* explicitly bans unrestricted forensic advocacy and shyster lawyers from the state,[46] but nowhere in his political writings do we find a general banishment of rhetoric.

In addition to social control, Plato attributes an educational value to rhetoric. Moral and metaphysical truths are to be rhetorically disseminated, not alone for the maintenance of political order, but so that they will be believed for their own sakes as well.[47] Young men who are without

---

[42] *Politicus*, 304.
[43] *Republic*, 3.388, 413, 459.
[44] *Laws*, 4.720-722; 10.885D.
[45] *Laws*, 2.663 ff.
[46] *Laws*, 11.937E.
[47] *Laws*, 2.664.

philosophy, and so are not yet equipped to attain true knowledge, would be attracted to the study of philosophy by "persuasion."[48]

5.

It may now be apparent that Plato did not despise rhetoric, but only the excesses of the sophists. He was far from blind to the practical need for social order and to the limitations of the popular mind, and he gave to rhetoric some functions for which, even today, no apologies need be offered. Certainly Plato was repelled by the Gorgian view of rhetoric: by the pretensions of its claims, the flaccidity of its formulation, and the easy virtue of its practice. But he was far too good a writer and clear a thinker to overstate his case or to extend it unreasonably.

It is undeniable that Plato's preoccupation with the moral character of rhetoric in his critique colored his positive formulations of rhetorical theory, so that he gives us not an account of rhetoric, but an account of a "true art" of rhetoric, not an account of the general social functions of rhetoric, but an account of its utility to the Ideal State. That there were actually theories and practices of rhetoric which did not fit his mold, no author has observed more brilliantly than he. But these other theories and practices were not "true" arts of rhetoric; they were "false" arts, knacks only. Plato did not deny their reality; what he denied was their moral efficacy.

From our perspective in history, we are able to perceive the irony that Plato, the arch-enemy of the Sophists, was actually closer to them in his rhetorical theory than was his successor, Aristotle. Plato's repudiation of Sophistical rhetoric was neither so complete nor so thorough as his student's, for though Plato rejected and refuted with finality the particular moral interpretation of rhetoric which the Sophists propounded, he did not reject the attempt to suffuse an investigation of rhetoric with a moral concern. It is on this very point that his great disciple departed from him.

Still, we must regard it as an open question whether Aristotle surpassed him by that particular departure. Can it be denied that so fearsomely potent a force as rhetoric participates in moral values? Is it the case that any instrument which affects human life is not subject to moral assessment? Aristotle affirmed the moral neutrality of rhetoric; Plato's answer to both these questions was an emphatic negative. When, in recent history, we find the clamorous spirit of fanaticism at large in the world, sustained by rhetorical discourse; when we contemplate the undiminished and undiminishing potentiality for savagery latent in all men, waiting to be triggered by suasive language; and when we observe the Sophists of our time, rationally discredited but thriving still, we may begin to suspect that, after all, Plato was even wiser than we had thought.

---

[48] *Euthydemus*, 274 ff.

The Axiological Foundations of Plato's Theory of Rhetoric

by Charles Kauffman

Stripped from its philosophical and social contexts, Plato's theory of rhetoric has been the subject of examination and dispute among scholars for centuries. In spite of the enormous volume of literature on the subject, most discussion has tended to focus on Plato's attitude toward rhetoric rather than on the substantive characteristics of the theory itself.[1] The views which have emerged have been extremely misleading. The first view, that Plato hated rhetoric, would have nothing to do with it, and any rhetoric that might be worthwhile was surely beyond human capabilities, has been historically influential.[2] The second view, perhaps more popular today, is that Plato developed a theory of rhetoric harnessed to the service of truth, to be used to better the lot of the individual and the state. Plato's attacks on rhetoric were only intended as the first step in a general program of reform.[3] This latter view of Platonic rhetoric is just as misleading, and more dangerous than the first because, in their haste to make an ally of Plato, rhetorical theorists have overlooked the totalitarian and repressive characteristics of Plato's rhetorical art.

Reprinted from *Central States Speech Journal* 33 (1982): 353-366. Used by permission.

[1] See, for example, Everett L. Hunt, "Plato on Rhetoric and Rhetoricians," *Quarterly Journal of Speech Education,* 6 (1920), 33-53; Edwin Black, "Plato's View of Rhetoric," *Quarterly Journal of Speech,* 44 (1958), 361-74; Rollin Quimby, "The Growth in Plato's Perception of Rhetoric," *Philosophy & Rhetoric,* 7 (1974), 71-79; Oscar Brownstein, "Plato's *Phaedrus*: Dialectic as the Genuine Art of Speaking," *Quarterly Journal of Speech,* 51 (1965), 392-98. David Kaufer comments on this phenomenon in his article, "The Influence of Plato's Developing Psychology on His Views of Rhetoric," *Quarterly Journal of Speech,* 64 (1978), 78.

[2] Among those taking the view that Plato had no use for rhetoric are: Everett L. Hunt, "Plato and Aristotle on Rhetoric and Rhetoricians," in *Studies in Rhetoric and Public Speaking in Honor of James Albert Winans* (New York: Russel and Russel, 1962), pp. 3-60; Robert Cushman, *Therepeia: Plato's Conception of Philosophy* (Chapel Hill, North Carolina: University of North Carolina Press, 1958); Adele Spitzer, "The Self-Reference of the *Gorgias,*" *Philosophy & Rhetoric,* 8 (1975), 1-14; Oscar Brownstein, "Plato's *Phaedrus*: Dialectic as the Genuine Art of Speaking." Argument has raged for centuries about Plato's actual views on rhetoric. It seems to me that those who argue that Plato did recognize some legitimate uses for rhetoric have much the stronger case and the passages cited in this paper should help to confirm this view.

[3] See, for example, Edwin Black, "Plato's View of Rhetoric"; Rollin Quimby, "The Growth in Plato's Perception of Rhetoric"; David Kaufer, "The Influence of Plato's Developing Psychology on His Views of Rhetoric." These essays are intended to respond to some of the essays cited in note 2. For an older view, see Eduard Zeller, *Plato and the Older Academy,* trans. Sarah Alleyne and Alfred Goodwin (London: Longmans, Green, & Co., 1876); Werner Jaeger, *Paideia: The Ideals of Greek Culture,* III, trans. Gilbert Highet (New York: Oxford Univ. Press, 1944), ch. 8; I. M. Crombie, *An Examination of Plato's Doctrines,* I (London: Routledge and Kegan Paul, 1962), pp. 196-99.

It is my contention that a re-examination of Plato's theory of rhetoric will reveal that Plato did, in fact, develop a theory that is entirely his own, a theory of rhetoric which embraces falsehood, deception, and censorship in its effort to inculcate "correct" thought and action. Plato's theory stands in opposition to other classical theories of rhetoric, at the head of a rhetorical tradition which survives even today. When placed in the social and political context in which it is intended to function, Plato's rhetoric becomes something few would find praiseworthy. In order to demonstrate these points, it will be necessary to examine Plato's theory of rhetoric and its relationship to other aspects of Plato's political philosophy.

An examination of the dialogues reveals four essential characteristics of Platonic rhetorical theory: (1) rhetoric is defined broadly to encompass all forms of persuasion through language; (2) rhetoric is tied to an a priori epistemology which determines its content; (3) rhetoric depends on a prior dialectic to discover its language and its content; and, (4) rhetoric functions to guarantee doctrinal conformity and social control. A look at each of these points in turn will help to establish a more complete picture of Platonic rhetorical theory.

Plato's Definition of Rhetoric

While there are frequent references to rhetoric in the dialogues, Plato defines the term only twice. The first instance occurs in the *Gorgias* 463a-465c, and this passage is responsible for much of the confusion about Plato's rhetoric.[4] In response to a question by Polus, Socrates describes rhetoric not as an art *(techné)* but as a kind of flattery *(kolakeia)*. While some have argued that Plato intends an absolute condemnation of rhetoric,[5] there is substantial evidence to indicate that the attack extends only to the way rhetoric was practiced by Gorgias and his contemporaries. Plato denies the name *techne* to any routine which cannot deliver an account *(logos)* of the principles by which it functions. What is condemned at *Gorgias* 465a is rhetoric as "*empeiria,*" practice without knowledge of principles. Such rhetoric is irrational because it can give no account of its methods or its effects.[6]

---

[4] All translations, unless otherwise noted, are from *The Collected Dialogues of Plato,* eds. Edith Hamilton and Huntington Cairns (Princeton, New Jersey: Princeton University Press, 1961). All references to the dialogues have been incorporated into the text.

[5] See, for example, Adele Spitzer, "The Self-Reference of the *Gorgias*"; Robert Cushman, *Therepeia, p.* 231; Werner Jaeger, *Paideia,* II ch. 6, III ch. 8. This argument is put in particularly interesting fashion by Paul Newell Campbell, "The *Gorgias:* Dramatic Form as Argument," *Central States Speech Journal,* 31 (1980), 1-16. Campbell's indictments of Plato's argument are telling. Nevertheless, it seems to me that Campbell errs when he dismisses those passages in which Plato refers to a "genuine" art of rhetoric because they refer only to an "ideal world" (p. 5). Plato's attempts to reform rhetoric are part of his attempt to reform the world and the reformed rhetoric that Plato speaks of in the *Gorgias* is intended to be a practical art in that reformed world.

[6] E. R. Dodds comments, "A *techné* differs from an *empeiria in* that it is based on a rational principle *(logos),* and can thus explain its procedure in every case." See Plato, *Gorgias,* text and commentary by E. R. Dodds (London: Oxford University Press, 1959), pp. 228-29.

This distinction is enough for Plato to condemn rhetoric as practiced but does suggest the possibility for a rhetorical *techné*.[7] Plato seems to establish the groundwork for a rhetorical *techne* at the *Gorgias* 503a-504d. Here Plato argues that rhetoric can be "something fine—an effort to perfect as far as possible the souls of its citizens" (503a). Such a rhetoric would attend to the souls of citizens in an attempt to impart justice and banish injustice. Plato supports this interpretation by noting at the close of the dialogue that rhetoric, like all other arts, should be employed to further the interests of justice (257c).

There are several noteworthy points made in these passages. First, rhetoric is linked with the care of the soul, establishment of justice, and the welfare of the state, which suggests that Plato thought of rhetoric as a practical instrument essential to the conduct of everyday affairs. Second, it is important to note the directionality of the rhetoric: it is delivered from the statesman to the citizen, but there is no indication of any reciprocal influence. Rhetoric is hierarchical, pronounced by the philosopher unto the masses. Third, there is the implicit suggestion that there are very few genuine rhetors qualified to practice the Platonic *techne*. When Callicles asks Socrates for examples of practitioners of the genuine art of rhetoric, Socrates can think of no one who meets the standards. Hence, it seems likely that there will be few practitioners of Platonic rhetoric.

In the *Phaedrus*, Plato again attempts to define rhetoric. And once again he dismisses the practice of his contemporaries as a "knack that has nothing to do with art" (260e). Instead, he offers his definition of the legitimate art of rhetoric. Socrates asks: "Must not the art of rhetoric, taken as a whole, be a kind of influencing of the mind by means of words, not only in the courts of law and other public gatherings, but in private places also? And must it not be the same art that is concerned with great issues and small, its right employment commanding no less respect when dealing with important matters than with unimportant" (261a-b).

Socrates' definition of rhetoric extends the art far beyond its traditional confines of the law courts and the assembly to the entire domain of influential discourse. As Socrates concludes, "So contending with words [*antilogike*] is a practice found not only in lawsuits and public harangues but, it seems, wherever men speak we find this single art, which enables people to make out everything to be like everything else, within the limits of possible comparison, and to expose the corresponding attempts of others who disguise what they are doing" (261d-e).

In equating rhetoric with persuasion, Plato does not depart significantly from the wisdom of his contemporaries. However, the scope and influence

---

[7] Most commentators support this view. See for example, *The Gorgias of Plato*, text and notes by W. H. Thompson (London: Whittaker 1971; rpt. New York: Arno Press, 1973), p. 124; Plato, *Gorgias*, text and notes by Terence Irwin (Oxford: Clarendon Press, 1979), note at 502; Dodds, pp. 328-30.

Plato assigns the art goes far beyond rhetorical theories of the day.[8] Wherever persuasive discourse was found, so one found rhetoric, and Plato saw it almost everywhere: in music (*Republic* 376e-377a), in legal statutes (*Laws* 723a), in the theatre (*Gorgias* 502c), in private discussions, and in public speeches. Plato thought that rhetoric exercised a pervasive influence throughout society and, because it was so influential, sought to limit its use to what he thought were acceptable purposes.

Rhetoric and Epistemology

Plato's definition of rhetoric explicitly states that the rhetorician must employ the art to improve the souls of citizens by making them more just. Plato censured the typical rhetors of his day because they had no concept of justice and, thus, could not impart it to audiences; this is the entire point of the conversation between Socrates and Gorgias (*Gorgias* 455a-461b). In order to impart justice, the rhetorician had to know the just, a requirement which demands that the rhetor be knowledgeable about things beyond the principles of rhetoric. Plato is at pains to explain the types of knowledge required of the rhetor.

According to Plato, there are two broad types of knowledge: *doxa,* or opinion resulting from sense data, and *episteme,* knowledge of the permanent and the real, knowledge of the forms. Two types of cognition are characteristic of *doxa: eikasia,* or images, which include "shadows, and then reflections in water and on surfaces . . . and everything of that kind" (*Republic* 509e-510a) and *pistis,* belief, which is comprised of the class of empirical things such as, "animals about us and all plants and the whole class of objects made by men" (*Republic* 510a). Taken together, *eikasia* and *pistis* form *doxa,* or what Cornford calls, "the many conventional notions of the multitude about morality. It is the physical and moral world as apprehended by those 'lovers of appearance' who do not recognize the absolute ideas which Plato calls real."[9] *Doxa* is a lower form of cognition than *episteme* because it ignores genuine reality, the intelligible forms, in favor of the world of the senses. If the soul is preoccupied with the senses and attends "the world of becoming and passing away, it [the soul] opines only and its edge is blunted, and it shifts its opinions hither and thither, and again seems as if it lacked reason" (*Republic* 508d).

The masters of *doxa* in the age of Plato were the Sophists, and Plato's concern was directed to the point that their rhetoric did not reflect any real learning whatsoever but dealt merely in appearances. Their rhetoric has the

---

[8] With the possible exception of Gorgias, who saw rhetoric as a transcendent art. See W. K. C. Guthrie, *The Sophists* (Cambridge: Cambridge University Press, 1971), p. 272.
[9] Francis Cornfield, *The Republic of Plato* (London: Oxford University Press, 1945), p. 221.

appearance of learning, deals with the appearance of justice, but knows nothing of real justice. When the Sophists speak about justice, they are themselves confused, and their rhetoric serves only to confound their audiences. Plato remarks, "Those who view many beautiful things but do not see the beautiful in itself and are unable to follow another's guidance to it . . . have opinions about all things but know nothing of the things they opine" (*Republic* 479e).

Opposed to the visible realm of appearance is the intelligible realm of the forms (*Republic* 511e). The intelligible also has two characteristic forms of cognition: thinking (*dianoia*) and knowledge (*episteme*). The intelligible is the only genuine reality; permanent and unchanging, it can be known only by the mind (*Republic* 510e). *Dianoia* is a lower state of mind than *epistemê* because it does not apprehend the intelligible in itself but instead is forced "to employ assumptions" and "images or likenesses" in its attempt to understand reality (*Republic* 511a). The highest form of knowledge, *episteme*, refers to "That which reason itself lays hold of by the power of dialectic, . . . making no use whatever of any object of sense . . ." (*Republic* 511b-c).

Episteme can only be said to exist when an individual can give an account of the essence of something *(Timaeus* 51d-e). In the *Gorgias,* rhetoricians are deficient in two respects: they know nothing of the principles of their art, nor do they know anything about justice. Hence, both their method and their content are suspect.

Plato's concern for *episteme* is not simply intellectual curiosity about the structure of the cosmos. Rather, he believes that genuine knowledge carries with it an ethical obligation to convey the truth to others, which is to say nothing more than that, for Plato, knowledge is normative. To appreciate why this is the case, one must understand the complex interrelationship between knowledge, the soul, and the state.

According to Plato, the soul is the repository of the rational, the spirited, and the appetitive elements of human character. Plato thinks of the rational part of the soul as "divine and immortal" (*Timaeus* 41a-d), the appetitive as base and harmful, and the spirited as an ally of either reason or appetite. He elaborates upon his concept of the soul at the *Republic* 580d-e: "One part, we say, is that with which man learns, one is that with which he feels anger. But the third part . . . [we called] the appetitive part because of the intensity of its appetites concerned with food and drink and love and their accompaniments. . . ." Each part of the soul seeks a different, and conflicting, end. The rational part of the soul seeks knowledge; the spirited element, which feels anger, honor, and the like, pursues honor and fame; while the appetitive part of the soul seeks gain (*Republic* 581a-b).

Because it is the duty of the soul to govern the body (*Republic* 353d), the outcome of the conflict is important because it determines the predispositions of the individual. As Plato says, "A bad soul will govern and manage things badly while the good soul will all these things do well" (*Republic* 353e). That which makes the soul good is knowledge. It is the natural function of the rational part of the soul, the reason loving part, to govern. It is often unable to exercise this function, however, because it is overcome by the appetites which "contaminate the soul with imperfection" by "interrupting, disturbing, distracting, and preventing us from getting a glimpse of the truth" (*Phaedo* 66d).

The Myth of the Charioteer, related in the *Phaedrus,* describes the efforts of reason, "the soul's pilot," to lead the soul to wisdom while appetite balks at every step of the journey (246a-249d). When appetite overcomes reason, the soul is defective and the individual is unjust. The proper relationship between the parts of the soul is described at the *Republic* 441e: "Does it not belong to the rational part of the soul to rule, being wise and exercising forethought in behalf of the entire soul, and to the principle of high spirit to be subject to this and its ally?" Therefore, the best soul is governed by the rational part, which through *episteme,* governs spirit and appetite.

Appetite and spirit are ill-suited to govern the soul because they pursue *doxa,* in pursuit of that which is easy over that which is true. When reason fails to overcome the appetites, the result is a "civil war" in the soul which causes injustice (*Republic* 444b). Plato compares this condition to a kind of disease within the soul; the soul, growing progressively weaker as it is taken over by appetite, becomes mired in *doxa,* and turns from *episteme.* The soul which accepts the rule of reason, by contrast, becomes just: "when the entire soul accepts the guidance of the wisdom-loving part and is not filled with inner dissension, the result for each part is that it in all other respects to its own task is just, and likewise that each enjoys its proper pleasures and the best pleasures and, so far as such a thing is possible, the truest" (*Republic* 586e-87a).

Because most people are unable to acquire knowledge, their souls are given over to injustice, their lives to unhappiness. Knowledge of being is necessary to nurture the soul and to produce happiness and justice within the individual. However, the attainment of such knowledge depends on the proper disposition of the soul, the ability to discipline the appetites, and the ability to look beyond the spell cast by appearances. This problem leads to one of the central concerns in Plato: how can this human fallibility be overcome and the individual made happy and just?

Plato's answer is that if the individual is unable to control the appetites within her or his soul, then the state must undertake the responsibility. The state has a compelling interest in the welfare of the individual soul because Plato recognizes a fundamental identity between the health of the soul and the health of the state. Plato views the state as an extension of the individual soul complete with the same parts and motivations. He notes in the *Republic* that "the same forms and qualities are to be found in each one of us that are in the state" (435e). Plato concludes, "Just too, then Glaucon, I presume we shall say a man is in the way in which a city was just" (*Republic* 441d). G. M. A. Grube argues: "He [Plato] has already established [in the *Republic*] three classes in the state and, since goodness in the individual is the same as in the state, he concludes that there must also be three parts of the soul. This parallel is not mere analogy to Plato, for he was deeply convinced of the close connexion between social and individual psychology."[10] Plato does not distinguish between individual and social welfare. What is good for the state will be good for the individual. Justice and happiness result when the soul is ruled by reason and comes to contemplate "the good in itself." In the state, justice and happiness arise when it is governed by lovers of wisdom.

The philosopher becomes a ruler not out of an urge for power but in order to perfect the community (*Republic* 519e). The philosopher alone has the wisdom necessary to manage affairs because he or she has not been corrupted by *doxa* and is, therefore, capable of recognizing the best interests of the state and its citizens. Plato warns of the consequences of any other type of government: "Unless . . . either philosophers become kings in our state or those whom we now call our kings and rulers take to the pursuit of philosophy seriously and adequately and there is a conjunction of these two things, political power and philosophical intelligence, while the motley horde of the natures who at present pursue either apart from the other are compulsorily excluded, there can be no cessation of troubles, dear Glaucon, for our states nor, I fancy, for the human race either . . . there is no other way of happiness either for private or public life" (*Republic* 473c-e).

The task of the philosopher is to rule with *episteme* in order to bring the ambitious and appetitive elements under control and to make them serve the interests of the state. Hence, the first duty of the philosopher king is to "take the city and the characters of men, as they might a tablet, and wipe it clean— no easy task" (*Republic* 501a). It is then the task of the philosopher to make over the city and its inhabitants, using superior knowledge to inculcate justice by regulating thought and action (*Republic* 501b; 587a). Until this happens, "there will be no surcease of trouble for the city or its citizens" (*Republic* 501e).

Justice within the state depends on just citizens. However, most people are incapable of *episteme* and are, consequently, unjust and unhappy (*Republic* 503b; 496b; 491a-b). R. K. Sprague has noted that, for Plato, good comes only from contact with the good, and if there can be no direct contact through mind, "then the contact may be indirect (as when the auxiliaries and artisans consent to be governed by the philosopher). . . ."[11] It is the duty of the philosopher, knowing justice, to establish laws and conventions in the state that will lead the ignorant to act as if they knew justice. For the purposes of the multitude, true opinion is all that is necessary to guide their everyday conduct (*Meno* 97a-c). For the ignorant, people accustomed to *doxa,* confused by the deceptive information revealed through the senses, Plato makes sure that the imitations they respond to are "likenesses" of the real so that the opinions of the multitude are "correct" (*Republic* 377a-e; 389b-c; 607d-e; *Laws* 659d-660a).

---

[10]G. M. A. Grube, *Plato's Thought* (London: Methuen, 1935), p. 130.
[11]R. K. Sprague, *Plato's Philosopher King* (Columbia, South Carolina: University of South Carolina Press, 1976), p. 93.

By this somewhat circuitous path, Plato delimited the role of rhetoric in society. Rhetoric is the instrument employed by the philosopher king in an attempt to make over the *polis* and its citizens *(Statesman* 304a).[12] Rhetoric is an imitative art which produces opinion *(doxa)* rather than knowledge *(episteme)*. When used by the philosopher king and based on genuine knowledge, rhetoric may be used with success to "produce the conviction that would be most beneficial to a city" *(Laws* 664a). Because imitations appeal to the irrational parts of the soul, rhetoric is capable of persuading all human beings, especially those accustomed to *doxa (Republic* 604d).[13] While most people may be incapable of responding to reason, all may respond to imitation through rhetoric. Hence, while rhetoric does not assist in the discovery of truth, when properly employed, it can persuade people to act as if they knew the truth *(Statesman* 304c).

Viewed in this light, Plato's statements that the rhetorician must know the truth and must understand the soul before speaking, take on special significance. Plato does not mean that the rhetorician should have some general understanding of topic and audience before speaking: his requirement is much stricter than that. Plato means that, before speaking, the rhetor must have knowledge *(episteme)* of the topic, the beliefs of the audience, and the requirements of their souls. The philosopher must be able to give a precise account of the principles and techniques by which a change of belief will be produced in the audience. While such knowledge is very difficult to attain, and there are very few in any state who will attain it, for the philosopher king, rhetoric itself will not prove to be a difficult art.[14] At the *Laws* 664a, Plato casually remarks that, "the youthful mind will be persuaded of anything, if one will take the trouble to persuade it." For Plato, the problem is a simple one of taxing the power of invention. To object to Platonic rhetoric on the grounds that its standards are impossible to meet misses the point. While it is true that *episteme* is difficult to attain, once it is, rhetoric is a rather simple task for the philosopher.

To recapitulate briefly, Plato attacked the sophists and rhetoricians of his day because their rhetoric was based on *doxa* and produced injustice and unhappiness in its audiences and in society. A genuine art of rhetoric, he believed, had to be based on higher knowledge, *episteme*, knowledge of the

---

[12]Jacob Klein renders these lines: "To which knowledge should one assign the task of persuading a multitude, a mob, not by teaching, but by telling stories? Young Socrates: 'The art of rhetoric.'" *(Plato's Trilogy* [Chicago: University of Chicago Press, 1977], p. 193). This passage seems to me to settle the question about Plato's views on rhetoric. In this passage, rhetoric, generalship, and judging are described as tools of the true statesman, though they are subservient to philosophy.

[13]On the nature of imitation see Richard McKeon, "Literary Criticism and the Concept of Imitation in Antiquity," *Modern Philology,* 34 (1936), 7; Iris Murdoch, *The Fire and the Sun* (Oxford: Clarendon Press, 1977), p. 5 and *passim.*

[14]Hunt, for example, argues that Plato's standards were impossible to meet. See, "Plato on Rhetoric and Rhetoricians," p. 47. Plato does not seem to consider his standards to be impossible to meet. In the *Phaedrus,* his recommendations are offered to ensure that speakers "attain such success as is within the grasp of mankind" (273e).

forms. A rhetoric based on *episteme* was essential because until the causes of injustice and unhappiness were known, they could not be eliminated. Because most citizens were too ignorant to attain *episteme,* they were condemned to depravity unless the philosopher intervened and guided the masses to correct thought and action (*Republic* 519-520).

Dialectic and Rhetoric

Some scholars have argued that, for Plato, dialectic is the genuine art of persuasion, the art by which the philosopher guides citizens toward the good.[15] This confuses the relationship between rhetoric and dialectic and leads to confusion about other aspects of Platonic philosophy as well. Rhetoric and dialectic are separate arts, and each has a different role to play. As a preliminary point it is worthwhile to consider this: if citizens are capable of dialectic, why is Plato so pessimistic about the intellectual capacities of the multitude? If it is impossible for the masses to be philosophical, then it seems odd to suggest that the masses should understand the method of the philosophers, dialectic.

Plato describes dialectic as "the study that would draw the soul away from the world of becoming to the world of being" (*Republic* 521d). Dialectic is an imitation of the higher processes of thought, which Plato conceives of as a kind of dialectic spoken silently in the mind (*Theatetus* 189e-190a; *Sophist* 263e). Dialectic takes nothing for granted: it examines all of its assumptions in an attempt to discover *episteme* (*Republic* 511b-c). "And the only person," Plato says, "to whom you would allow this mastery of dialectic is the pure and rightful lover of wisdom (*Sophist* 253d-e).

Thus, the dialectician has the power to define according to type (*Cratylus* 388b-389d) and to discern the inter-connections between forms *(Republic* 537c). Dialectic makes philosophy possible by allowing human beings direct access to intelligible reality. The Athenian Stranger explains this point to the Young Socrates in the *Statesman:* "we must train ourselves to give and to understand a *rational* account of every existent thing. For the existents which have no visible embodiment, the existents which are of the highest value and chief importance, are demonstrable only by reason and are not to be apprehended by any other means" (285d-286a). The "rational account" that Plato speaks of makes philosophy possible by allowing the mind to contemplate being. It is for this reason that Plato states, "To rob us of discourse would be to rob us of philosophy" (*Sophist* 260a).

Plato explicitly states that dialectic is not suited to everyone. In the *Sophist,* dialectic is reserved for the "pure and rightful lover of wisdom." In the *Republic,* Plato speaks of the unsuitability of dialectic for those confined

---

[15]See Brownstein, "Plato's *Phaedrus:* Dialectic as the Genuine Art of Speaking"; Cushman, *Therepeia,* p. 231; Spitzer, "The Self-Reference of the *Gorgias,*" p. 22.

to *doxa:* perceiving dialectic as an instrument of confutation, they attempt to prove fantastic conclusions to make "the worse seem the better reason." Hence, Plato concludes, "those permitted to take part in such discussions must have orderly and stable natures instead of the present practice of admitting to it any chance and unsuitable applicant" (*Republic* 539d).

Dialectic derives much of its power from Plato's notion that names imitate the properties of the thing they name. There are numerous passages in the dialogues which indicate that names should imitate their nominates.[16] This amounts to a natural theory of language which holds that words, because of their correspondence to their referents, have fixed and permanent meanings.[17] In his analysis of the *Theatetus,* F. M. Cornford concludes that: "the conclusion that Plato means us to draw is this: unless we recognize some class of knowable entities exempt from the Heraclitean flux and so capable of standing as the fixed meaning of words, no definition of knowledge is any more true than its contradictory. . . . Without the forms, as Parmenides said, there can be no discourse."[18] Names are "correct" if they closely resemble the thing they name and incorrect if they fail to do so. When names imitate well, they point to the intelligible; when they imitate poorly, they point to the visible realm of appearances. The best, and the most appropriate, names are names which are likenesses of the things they name.[19]

All of this is important because Plato holds that names influence one's perception of reality. Proper names assist the ignorant to live in harmony with the forms while improper names lead to confusion about reality. Language creates a world view which ensnares its users (*Cratylus* 439c). Through the power of dialectic, the philosopher can discover proper names and guide the thought of the community. Plato comments: "[T]he work of the legislator is to give names, and the dialectician must be his director if names are to be rightly given" (*Cratylus* 390d).

---

[16]See, for example, the *Timaeus* 29b-c, *Republic* 596a, and the *Phaedo* 103a.

[17]For an analysis of this theory of language see, C. K. Ogden and I. A. Richards, *The Meaning of Meaning* (New York: Harcourt, Brace & World, 1923), pp. 31-34.

[18]Francis Cornfield, *Plato's Theory of Knowledge* (New York: Harcourt, Brace, & Co., 1935), p. 99.

[19]I think this is the point of the *Cratylus,* although interpretations of the dialogue vary. In the dialogue, Plato attempts to refute the theory of Cratylus, that all names are properly given, and, therefore, that the nature of reality can be discovered through the study of names. It seems evident that Plato was concerned with the state of language as he found it. As handed down, Plato thought that language contained both correct and incorrect names. At 439c, Socrates assumes that the original name givers attempted to make names in the image of things but were mistaken about the nature of reality, and, consequently, named incorrectly. Thus, Socrates holds that one cannot discover the nature of being through the study of names. However, at the same time, Socrates seems to argue that, as far as possible, names should imitate the things they name. At 435c, Socrates argues, "I quite agree with you that words should as far as possible resemble things. . . . For I believe that if we could always, or almost always, use likenesses, which are perfectly appropriate, this would be the most perfect state of language. . . ." For concurring views see Raphael Demos, *The Philosophy of Plato* (New York: Octagon Books, 1966); Raphael Demos, "Plato's Philosophy of Language," *The Journal of Philosophy,* 61 (1964), 595-610; Gail Fine, "Plato on Naming," *The Philosophical Quarterly,* 27 (1977), 289-301. For opposing views see, J. L. Ackrill, "Demos on Plato," *The Journal of Philosophy,* 61 (1964), 610-13; and Richard Robinson, *Essays in Greek Philosophy* (London: Oxford University Press, 1969), chs. 2-3.

It is the function of the dialectician to discover the intelligible, to name its elements, to discover the relationships between the elements, and to ensure that language reflects this reality. Dialectic is, therefore, logically and temporally prior to rhetoric; it discovers the materials and the words to be used by the rhetorician. Dialectic is Plato's method for rhetorical invention. This is the point of the passages on dialectic which occur in the last section of the *Phaedrus*. There Plato argues that the rhetor must know the proper names of things (263b), must have infallible knowledge of the audience and of the subject (273d-e) if the speech is to "attain such success as is within the grasp of mankind" (*Phaedrus* 273e). Rhetoric depends on dialectic for its language, content, and methods. In spite of this dependency, dialectic cannot substitute for rhetoric because it is ill suited to persuading the multitudes. Dialectic and rhetoric are discrete and complementary arts, and both are necessary in the well governed state.

Rhetoric and Social Control

Rhetoric is Plato's method for bringing justice and happiness to the multitude and to the state by "persuading men to do what is right" (*Statesman* 303e). His theory, in spite of its lofty aims, is essentially a rhetoric of social control that is repressive and totalitarian in its outlook and application. This aspect of Plato's theory of rhetoric, more than any other, has been infrequently noted and often overlooked. Edwin Black is one of the few to note that Plato considered "freedom of expression inimical to the best interests of the community,"[20] yet he concluded, "When, in recent history, we find the clamorous spirit of fanaticism at large in the world, sustained by rhetorical discourse; when we contemplate the undiminished and undiminishing potentiality for savagery latent in all men, waiting to be triggered by suasive language; and when we observe the Sophists of our time, rationally discredited but thriving still, we may begin to suspect that, after all, Plato was even wiser than we had thought."[21] That a critic as perceptive as Professor Black celebrates a rhetoric which is ostensibly totalitarian is testimony to the seductiveness of Plato's writing.

At that, Professor Black is in very good company. Eduard Zeller has written that rhetoric is the instrument by which the "philosopher brings his principles to bear on the unphilosophic many" in order to establish "the rule of right and morality."[22] Rollin Quimby concludes that, "Rhetoric is the art by leaders who discern the truth guide toward the good."[23] Werner Jaeger argues

---

[20]Black, "Plato's View of Rhetoric," p. 373. I am indebted to Black's essay for its many insights about the social role of Platonic rhetoric.
[21]Black, p. 374.
[22]Zeller, *Plato and the Older Academy*, pp. 514-15.
[23]Quimby, "The Growth in Plato's Perception of Rhetoric," p. 78.

that Plato's rhetoric is a moral art concerned with inculcating the truth.[24] Ronald Levinson has argued that Plato's rhetoric "is the means to good and to truth."[25] These are able scholars, and their conclusions are not to be taken lightly; however, a re-examination of Plato's words about rhetoric and its uses will reveal a rhetorical theory that may be unworthy of such lofty praise.

In Western, democratic political systems, rhetoric has traditionally been employed to help human beings discover the political, legal, and ethical choices they confront as individuals living in society and to help people to make the best choice when they are confronted with several alternatives. For Plato, rhetoric served precisely the opposite function. In the *Statesman,* Plato argues that it is the function of rhetoric to "persuade the general mass of the population by telling them suitable stories rather than by giving them formal instruction' (*Statesman* 304c). The aim is to ensure that the entire community "treat[s] the topic in one single and selfsame lifelong tone, *alike in song, in story, and in discourse*" (*Laws* 664a).[26] The aim, of course, is absolute homogeneity of opinion in society. Later on in the *Laws,* Plato expounds on this principle: the goal is "to teach one's soul the habit of never so much as thinking to do one single act apart from one's fellows, of making life, to the very uttermost, an unbroken consort, society, and community of all with all" (942b-c). Plato views rhetoric as useful because it induces "us all to practice all justice freely, and without compulsion" (*Laws* 663d-e).

In order to assure uniformity of opinion and conduct within society, Plato strictly limits the use of rhetoric. First, he restricts the use of rhetoric to those who have knowledge of the intelligible (*Phaedrus* 273d-e; *Statesman* 303e-304d; *Gorgias* 504d; *Republic* 389d). As a practical manner, this means that there will be very few rhetoricians in any state and that all will be members of the philosophic ruling class, dedicated to the propagation of doctrine. The philosophers will employ rhetoric to control all aspects of community life: the masses are presumed to be incapable of making even the most basic decisions about their lives. Hence, rhetoric will be used to influence the selection of mates (*Republic* 414b-417b; *Statesman* 310b-c), the rearing of children (*Republic* 377b; *Statesman* 308e), the popular understanding of history, custom, and tradition (*Menexenus, passim; Republic* 392b), in short, to control all aspects of community life. Plato justifies this on the grounds that the masses, and even the rulers, do not necessarily know what is in their own

---

[24]Jaeger, *Paideia,* III, p. 195.

[25]Ronald Levinson, *In Defense of Plato* (Cambridge: Harvard University Press, 1953), p. 434.

[26]Emphasis mine. I am indebted to Popper for pointing out the authoritarian aspects of Platonic political philosophy. While Popper does not analyze Platonic rhetoric, he does mention that Plato's state would make extensive use of propaganda. I believe this analysis to be consistent with Popper's. See Sir Karl Popper, *The Open Society and Its Enemies,* I, 5th ed. (Princeton, New Jersey: Princeton University Press, 1966), esp. ch. 10. For similar views, see Warner Fite, *The Platonic Legend* (New York: Charles Scribner's Sons, 1934); for a more recent, shorter treatment, I. F. Stone, "Plato's Ideal Bedlam," *Harper's,* Jan. 1981, pp. 66-71. For a sympathetic treatment of Plato, responding to the charges made by Popper and Fite, see Levinson's *In Defense of Plato.*

best interests (*Republic* 414b). Therefore, the power to use rhetoric is reserved for the philosopher-statesman: "The kingly art controls [rhetoric] . . . according to its power to perceive the right occasions for undertaking and setting in motion the great enterprises of state. The other arts [generalship, judging and rhetoric] must do what they are told to do by the kingly art" (*Statesman* 305d).

When Plato limits the practice of rhetoric to the philosopher king, he implicitly denies the values of freedom of speech, the marketplace of ideas, and reasoned disagreement. All of these concepts lose their meaning when the practice of rhetoric is so sharply restricted. A state with one speaker is, by its very nature, totalitarian, and it is noteworthy that the authors who praise Plato (Black, Zeller, Quimby, Jaeger, and Levinson) all seem to recognize that, for Plato, the only legitimate rhetor is the philosopher king.

The second restriction that Plato places on rhetoric is that it must always be used to serve the ends of justice, which, for Plato, means that it must work to further the established order (*Gorgias* 504, 527; *Phaedrus* 270b; *Statesman* 304a; *Laws* 938a-b). When Plato says that rhetoric should inculcate justice, he means, by justice, something very different from what we do. For Plato, justice is a concept grounded in nature, a quality of being. Justice is, very simply, hierarchical order (*Republic* 443c-d).

Justice is nothing more than the "principle of doing one's own business" (*Republic* 433b). More specifically, it means that everyone must accept his/ her allotted role in life without complaint or question. The implications of Platonic justice are graphically explained in the *Statesman:*

> [The statesman] may purge the city for its better health by putting some of its citizens to death or banishing others. They may lessen the citizen body by sending off colonies like bees swarming off from a hive, or they may bring people in from other cities and naturalize them so as to increase the number of citizens. So long as they work on a reasoned scientific principle following essential justice and act to preserve and improve the life of the state so far as may be, we must call them real statesmen according to our standards of judgment . . . (293d).[27]

Plato's concept of justice places the welfare of the state above that of the individual so it turns out that what is just for the individual is that which perpetuates the state. Rhetoric serves justice insofar as it makes citizens conform to their allotted role in society.

---

[27]Jacob Klein comments that the ruler may kill or banish anyone, either according to law or without the sanction of law as long as his or her actions are based on knowledge and serve to inculcate justice (*Plato's Trilogy,* p. 183). It is clear that justice is the willing submission of individual judgment to the knowledge of the philosopher. The individual is expected to defer to the philosopher in all circumstances. For a comment on the implications of this philosophy, see Paul Shorey, *What Plato Said* (Chicago: University of Chicago Press, 1933), p. 314.

In order to make the populace receptive to the authoritarian measures taken by the philosopher king, the rhetor is allowed to lie, to censor, and to deceive. In fact, this becomes the norm for rhetorical conduct. Plato recognizes that the lie may be essential and sanctions its use in the *Republic:* "It seems likely that our rulers will have to make considerable use of falsehood and deception for the benefit of their subjects. We said, I believe, that the use of that sort of thing was in the category of medicine" (459c-d). And at the *Republic* 389b-c, Plato authorizes the use of the lie by the philosopher, "but for a layman to lie to rulers . . . we shall affirm to be a great sin." Plato gives an example of the kind of lies to be told at the *Republic* 415, where he invents one to convince the guardians to maintain an oppressive caste system which, among other things, requires parents to repudiate unfit children. The important point is the reason for the lie: it is done to benefit the state and only indirectly for the benefit of its subjects. If one assumes that it is proper for the king to "put to death" or "banish" unfit subjects, to regulate marriage and procreation, as Plato recommends in the *Statesman,* then lies may benefit the community, but they are only helpful to the individual when one makes the further assumption that the interests of the state are paramount. Even Ronald Levinson, Plato's most vociferous defender, is forced to admit that he finds these lies "distasteful."[28]

In order to make sure that political doctrine is treated in a "selfsame life-long tone," Plato authorizes considerable use of censorship. He starts with the tales that are told to children: "We must begin, then, it seems, by a censorship over our storymakers, and what they do well we must pass and what not, reject. And the stories on the accepted list we will induce nurses and mothers to tell to the children. . . ." (*Republic* 377b-c). This same kind of censorship is later extended to history, poetry, and oratory (*Republic* 392b, 380c). Plato regards certain ideas as dangerous, and those ideas are not to be spoken of in any context. As Plato commands, "This is my teaching, and I conceive you will persuade, or constrain, your national poets to teach it too. . . ." (*Laws* 661c).

Where lies and censorship fail, Plato authorizes deception. When Plato defines rhetoric as the art which persuades the masses by "telling them suitable stories," he links a series of passages in the *Republic* and the *Laws* which are concerned with the inspiration of right conduct through fables, stories, and the like. Rhetoric has no resemblance to Plato's high minded dialectic; there is no calm argument, impassioned case-making, or heated debate. Instead, people hear "fictions," composed for the sake of their salutary effects. These fictions are intended "to prepare the auditor of the legislator's actments to receive his prescription, that is to say, his law, in a spirit of friendliness and consequent docility" (*Laws* 723a).

Platonic rhetoric, whatever its form, is not concerned with choice-making,

---

[28]Levinson, *In Defense of Plato,* p. 435.

the evaluation of probability, or the construction of valid argument. Instead, it has as its sole aim the regulation of conduct by eliminating choice through lies, censorship, and deception. For this reason, Popper has called Plato the "pioneer of the propagandists."[29] The only legitimate use of rhetoric, within Plato's state, is for the dissemination of doctrine. All expression in the state, be it song, story, history, myth, panegyric, or oratory, is censored to serve the ends of the state. This kind of rhetoric, I assert, is unworthy of praise.

Conclusions

It is commonly asserted that Plato initiated a serious and philosophical consideration of rhetoric which culminated in the *Rhetoric* of Aristotle.[30] But in his *Rhetoric,* Aristotle largely repudiated his master. Aristotle thought human beings could be persuaded because they were rational; Plato thought the opposite. Aristotle viewed rhetoric as epistemic, at least insofar as it was useful in discovering the nature of the probable, while Plato thought rhetoric served only to communicate a priori knowledge discovered through dialectic. Where Aristotle saw rhetoric as a method that contributed to choice-making, Plato saw it as a method to eliminate choice, a method by which the statesman could persuade the multitude to conform to the dictates of doctrine. And where Aristotle saw rhetoric as a tool to be used by all members of society, Plato limited the practice of rhetoric to the philosopher king. The essential difference between the two rhetorics is evident in Aristotle's preoccupation with methods versus Plato's interest in results.

This brief overview is intended only to illustrate some of the differences between Aristotle and Plato in order to show that they stand at the heads of two radically different traditions in rhetoric. Where Aristotle's influence is seen most in rhetorical theory, Plato's influence has, over the centuries, been evident in the justifications for all sorts of shabby rhetorical practices. In our own time, Plato's influence is most evident in some of the technicians who run political campaigns. Apparently based on the assumption that the electorate is uninformed and uneducable, campaign rhetoric is structured to appeal to popular prejudices by creating "impressions" which sway the emotions. Commenting on the 1968 presidential campaign, Joe McGinniss

---

[29]Popper, *The Open Society and Its Enemies,* I, p. 199.

[30]See, for example, E. M. Cope, *An Introduction to Aristotle's Rhetoric* (London: MacMillan, 1867; rpt. New York: Georg Olms Verlag, 1970), pp. 6-7; Paul Shorey, "What Teachers of Speech May Learn from the Theory and Practice of the Greeks," *Quarterly Journal of Speech Education,* 8 (1922), 118; Gilbert Ryle, *Plato's Progress* (Cambridge: Cambridge University Press, 1965), pp. 260-62; and, more recently, George Kennedy, *Classical Rhetoric and Its Christian and Secular Tradition from Ancient to Modern Times* (Chapel Hill, North Carolina: University of North Carolina Press, 1980). Kennedy places Plato and Aristotle together as the seminal figures in what he call the "philosophical" tradition in rhetoric. Plato, he notes, exercized his influence primarily through Aristotle and his followers (pp. 59-60). While it is true that both Plato and Aristotle treated rhetoric philosophically, just as their philosophies differ, so do their theories of rhetoric.

wrote "[Raymond Price] began with the assumption that, 'the natural use of reason is to support prejudice, not to arrive at opinions.' Which led to the conclusion that rational arguments would 'only be effective if we can get the people to make the emotional leap, or what theologians call' (the) 'leap of faith' "[31] This elitist perspective is characteristic of Platonic rhetorical theory. It makes it necessary for the rhetor to "shape" the truth for the ignorant, lazy, uninformed masses. If the populace is unable to understand argument, unable to digest information and make probable deductions from it, then political rhetoric must lose its deliberative character.[32]

In order to understand classical and contemporary theories of rhetoric, it is important to identify theoretical statements which make Platonic assumptions. Platonic rhetoric is not simply an offshoot of Aristotelian theory or a celebration of the superiority of philosophy. Rather, it represents an entirely different way of conceptualizing the art and, concomitantly, implies different methods, goals, and strategies. It is because Platonic rhetoric tends toward repression that enlightened criticism is essential.

---

[31] Joe McGinniss, *The Selling of the President 1968* (New York: Pocket Books, 1970), p. 199.

[32] These assumptions are common in contemporary campaign theory. See, in addition to McGinniss, Dan Nimmo, *The Political Persuaders* (Englewood Cliffs, New Jersey: Prentice Hall, 1970), pp. 22, 118, 141, 193-99; and Murray Edelman, *The Symbolic Uses of Politics* (Chicago: University of Illinois Press, 1964), pp. 31, 73, 141. For a different perspective see Jeff Greenfield, *Playing to Win* (New York: Simon and Schuster, 1980).

Section 4:
Isocratean Rhetoric

The Rhetoric of Isocrates and Its Cultural Ideal

by Werner Jaeger

Greek literature of the fourth century reflects a widespread struggle to determine the character of true paideia; and within it Isocrates, the chief representative of rhetoric, personifies the classical opposition to Plato and his school. From this point on, the rivalry of philosophy and rhetoric, each claiming to be the better form of culture, runs like a leitmotiv throughout the history of ancient civilization. It is impossible to describe every phase of that rivalry: for one thing, it is rather repetitious, and the leaders of its opposing sides are not always very interesting personalities.[1] All the more important, therefore, is the conflict between Plato and Isocrates—the first battle in the centuries of war between philosophy and rhetoric. Later, that war was sometimes to degenerate into a mere academic squabble, in which neither side possessed any genuine vital force; but at its beginning the combatant parties represented the truly moving forces and needs of the Greek people. The field on which it was waged lay in the very centre of the political scene. That is what gives it the vivid colouring of a truly historical event, and the large sweep which keeps our interest in it permanently alive. In retrospect, we realize that in this conflict are symbolized the essential problems of that whole period of Greek history.

Today as of old, Isocrates has, like Plato, his admirers and exponents; and there is no doubt that since the Renaissance he has exercised a far greater influence on the educational methods of humanism than any other Greek or Roman teacher. Historically, it is perfectly correct to describe him (in the phrase used on the title-page of several modern books) as the father of 'humanistic culture'—inasmuch as the sophists cannot really claim that title, and from our own pedagogic methods and ideals a direct line runs back to him, as it does to Quintilian and Plutarch.[2] But that point of view, dictated as

---

Reprinted from *Paideia: The Ideals of Greek Culture*, Vol. III, by Werner Jaeger. Translated by Gilbert Highet. © 1944, 1971 by Oxford University Press, Inc. Used by permission.

[1] There is a full account of the history of this conflict in H. von Arnim's *Leben und Werke des Dion von Prusa* (Berlin 1898) pp. 4-114.

[2] See, for instance, a work by Drerup's pupil Burk, *Die Pädagogik des Isokrates als Grundlegung des humanistischen Bildungsideals* (Würzburg 1923), and in particular the two sections called *Das Nachleben der Pädagogik des Isokrates* (p. 199 f.) and *Isokrates und der Humanismus* (p. 211 f.). More recently Drerup himself has brought out four lectures entitled *Der Humanismus in seiner Geschichte, seinen Kulturwerten und seiner Vorbereitung im Unterrichtswessen der Griechen* (Paderborn 1934). British scholars like Burnet and Ernest Barker often call Isocrates the father of humanism.

it is by modern academic humanism, is vastly different from the attitude of this book—for our task here is to examine the whole development of Greek paideia and to study the complexities and antagonisms inherent in its problems and its meaning.[3] It is important to notice that what is often regarded by contemporary educators as the essence of humanism is mainly a continuation of the rhetorical strain in classical culture; while the history of humanism is a far broader and richer thing than that, for it contains all the manifold survivals of Greek paideia—including the world-wide influence exercised by Greek philosophy and science.[4] For this point of view, it is clear that an understanding of the true Greek paideia at once entails a criticism of modern academic humanism.[5] On the other hand, the position and character of philosophy and science within Greek civilization as a whole cannot be properly estimated until they are seen striving against other types of intellectual activity in order to be accepted as the true form of culture. Ultimately, both the rivals, philosophy and rhetoric, spring from poetry, the oldest Greek paideia; and they cannot be understood without reference to their origin in it.[6] But as the old rivalry for the primacy of culture gradually narrows to a dispute about the relative values of philosophy and rhetoric, it becomes clear enough that the ancient Hellenic partnership between gymnastic training and 'musical' culture has at last sunk to a much lower level.

To one who has just read Plato's *Protagoras* and *Gorgias* it seems obvious that the educational system of the sophists and rhetors was fundamentally an outworn ideal; and, if we compare it with the lofty claims advanced by philosophy—the claim that henceforth *all* education and *all* culture must be based on nothing but the knowledge of the highest values—it really was obsolete. And yet (as we have seen from our first glance over the

---

[3] Some critics have laid down that a historian of paideia must begin by giving his own definition of it. That is rather as if they expected a historian of philosophy to start either from Plato's definition of philosophy, or from Epicurus', or from Kant's or Hume's—all four being widely different. A history of paideia should describe as accurately as possible all the different meanings of Greek paideia, the various forms which it took, and the various spiritual levels at which it appeared, and should explain both their individual peculiarities and their historical connexions.

[4] On this see my essay, *Platos Stellung im Aufbau der griechischen Bildung* (Berlin 1928), which first appeared in *Die Antike*, vol. 4 (1928), nos. 1-2.

[5] From this point of view philosophy, and Greek philosophy in particular, has played a decisive role in the development of modern humanism, which would have had no impetus without it, and would not even have been able to expound its own aims. Actually, the study of the philosophical aspects of classical civilization has become more and more important not only in modern philosophy but in modern philology too, and has deeply influenced the purposes and methods of classical scholarship. But, seen from the same point of view, the history of humanism itself takes on a new appearance. Historians usually speak of two sharply contrasting periods—the Middle Ages and the Renaissance, scholasticism and humanism. But this simple pattern is shown to be an over-simplification as soon as we realize that the rebirth of Greek philosophy in the Middle Ages was really another great epoch in the uninterrupted influence of Greek paideia. That influence never died away entirely, but lived on continuously through mediaeval and modern history. *Non datur saltus in historia humanitatis.*

[6] It is impossible to appreciate the part played by philosophy within the organic structure of Greek civilization without being fully alive to its close connexion with the internal and external history of Greece.

later centuries of Greek history[7]) the older type of education, the method of the sophists and the rhetoricians, remained unconquerably active and alive beside its rival, and in fact continued to hold a leading place as one of the greatest influences on the spiritual life of Greece. Perhaps the savage scorn with which Plato attacks and persecutes it may be partly explained by the victor's feeling that he is at war with an enemy who is, as long as he remains within his own frontiers, unconquerable. It is difficult for us to understand the violence of his detestation, if we think of his attacks as directed solely against the great sophists of Socrates' generation, considered as embodiments of the type of culture which he loathed: Protagoras, Gorgias, Hippias, Prodicus. When he wrote his dialogues, these men were dead, and, in that rapid century, half forgotten. It needed all Plato's art to call the strong personalities of the famous sophists out of the shadows to life once more. When he made his caricatures of them (caricatures which in their way are quite as immortal as his idealized portrait of Socrates), a new generation had grown up; and he was attacking them, his contemporaries, as well as his predecessors. We need not go so far as to see, in the opponents whom he describes, mere masks for notable men of his own age; and yet, in his presentment of the sophists, there are many contemporary traits. And there is one absolutely certain fact: Plato never argues with dead men, with historical fossils.

Nothing shows how strong and vital sophistry and rhetoric were, at the time when he began his struggle against them, more clearly than the personality of Isocrates, who actually entered on his career after *Protagoras* and *Gorgias* were written.[8] It is particularly interesting that from the very outset he contested the claims of Plato and the Socratic circle, and defended sophistic education against their attacks. This means that he was writing from the firm conviction that such criticisms did not seriously shake his position. He was really a genuine sophist: indeed, it was he who brought the sophistic movement in education to its culminating point. Biographical tradition represents him as the pupil of Protagoras, of Prodicus, and especially of Gorgias; and archaeologists of the Hellenistic age found proof of the third of these connexions in his tombstone, which bore a figure they identified as Gorgias, pointing to a celestial globe.[9] Another tradition asserted that Isocrates had studied with the great rhetor in Thessaly—doubtless during the last phase of the Peloponnesian war.[10] Plato too, in his *Meno*, mentions that some part of Gorgias' career as a teacher was passed in Thessaly[11]: an

---

[7] See note 1.

[8] Plato wrote *Protagoras* and *Gorgias* as early as the first decade of the fourth century. Isocrates cannot have founded his school before 390, because in his extant orations we can trace his work as a hired writer of forensic speeches down to that date at least; perhaps it lasted even into the 'eighties.

[9] The facts of Isocrates' life are thoroughly examined by Blass in the second section of *Die attische Beredsamkeit* (2nd ed., Leipzig 1892); see p. 11 of that book for the traditions about his teachers. On the tombstone, see pseudo-Plutarch, *vit. X orat.* 838d; the author of those biographies took his archaeological and antiquarian data from a work by the Hellenistic epigraphist Diodorus.

[10] It is impossible to set a definite date for Isocrates' stay in Thessaly, but it must have been either just before or just after 410.

[11] Plato, *Meno* 70b; and cf. Isoc. *Antid.* 155.

interesting proof of the fact that the new culture was penetrating even the frontier lands of Greece. Isocrates' first great book, the *Panegyricus*, which brought him fame almost overnight, closely resembles Gorgias' *Olympicus*; and the fact that he deliberately chose to compete with such a celebrated author in treating the same theme—a call to the Greeks to achieve national unity—is, according to Greek usage, a proof that he considered himself Gorgias' pupil. And the chief evidence for the fact is the dominant position he assigns to rhetoric—that is, to the most concrete, the least purely theoretical, type of sophistic culture. Throughout his life he aimed, like Gorgias, at teaching the art or craft of speaking (*logôn technê*);[12] but he preferred to apply the title 'sophist' only to theorists, whatever their special interests might be. He used it, among others, for Socrates and his pupils, who had done so much to discredit the name. His own ideal he called 'philosophy.' Thus, he completely inverted the meanings given by Plato to the two words. Today, when Plato's definition of 'philosophy' has been universally accepted for centuries, Isocrates' procedure appears to have been a mere whim. But really it was not. In his time, those concepts were still developing, and had not yet finally hardened into their ultimate shapes. It was not Plato, but Isocrates, who followed the general idiom in calling Socrates and his pupils 'sophists' quite as much as Protagoras or Hippias; and in using 'philosophy' to mean intellectual culture in general,[13] which is the sense it has in Thucydides, for example. He could well have said (as Pericles says in Thucydides[14]) that the characteristic mark of the whole Athenian state was its interest in things of the mind, *philosophein*, and he does actually say something of the kind in the *Panegyricus*. Athens, he writes, invented culture (*philosophia*)—and he is obviously thinking of the whole community rather than of the small group of sharp-witted dialecticians gathered round Plato or Socrates.[15] What he was aiming at was universal culture, contrasted with one definite creed or one particular method of attaining knowledge, as preached by the Platonists. Thus, in the opposing claims made by both sides to ownership of the title 'philosophy,' and in the widely different meanings given to the word by the opponents, there is symbolized the rivalry of

---

[12]He calls it *ê tôn logôn meletê*, or *paideia*, or *epimeleia*. Blass, on p. 107 of the work cited in note 9, suggests that he avoids calling it a *technê*: probably to avoid being confused with the writers of technai, or rhetorical handbooks. But passages like *Soph.* 9-10 and *Antid.* 178 are enough to show that he held his *philosophia* to be a *technê*.

[13]It is unnecessary to prove this point by enumerating all the relevant passages. In *Antid.* 270 he claims the title *philosophia* for his own work alone, and says that other teachers (e.g. dialecticians, mathematicians, and rhetorical 'technographers') have no right to use it. He is less exclusive in his earlier works, where he speaks freely of the *philosophia* of the professional disputers or eristics (*Hel.* 6) and of teachers of rhetoric like Polycrates (*Bus.* 1); and in *Soph.* 1 he uses it as a general description of all the branches of higher education and culture which are characterized in that work.

[14]Thuc. 2.40.1.

[15]*Paneg.* 47. The word *katadeizai* describes the act of the founder of a cult. In this place the word *philosophia* does *not* mean 'philosophy.'

rhetoric and science for leadership in the realm of education and culture.[16]

Isocrates, then, was the post-war representative of the sophistic and rhetorical culture which had flourished in the Periclean period. But he was much more. To think of him as nothing more than that is to ignore the best and most characteristic aspects of his personality. The particular way in which he distributes the emphasis, magnifying the importance of rhetoric and of practical politics, and pushing mere sophistry and theory into the background, shows his fine perception of the Athenian attitude to the new culture. It had, during his boyhood and youth, achieved an astonishing success in his native city of Athens; but it had also been violently opposed. Although he was far from being the first Athenian to declare himself its pupil and its champion, it was not really naturalized in Athens until he gave it a truly Athenian dress. In Plato the rhetors and sophists who argue with Socrates are always at a disadvantage, simply because they are foreigners, and do not understand the real problems of Athens and the Athenians. They always seem to be outsiders, as they enter the close, compact Athenian society, bringing with them their knowledge, 'imported ready-made', as it were.[17] Of course they all speak the same international language, in which they can be understood by every educated man. But it never has the Athenian overtones. They lack the casual grace and the social ease without which they cannot achieve full success in the Athenian world. Their wide culture and their fabulous technical skill are admiringly welcomed, but in a deeper sense they remain ineffectual—at least for the time. Before it could become effective, the new element had to coalesce with the very special way of life which characterized the incomparable state of Athens; and none but an Athenian could bring about the coalition—an Athenian who, like Isocrates, was fully alive to the nature of his city and of the crisis which then confronted it. It was a full generation after its first appearance in Athens that rhetoric was naturalized there, under the influence of the tremendous events of the war and the post-war years—events which wrought a deep change in the very nature of rhetoric. At the same time it was profoundly affected by the moral reformation initiated by Socrates,[18] and by the great social crises which had shaken the Athenian state throughout Isocrates' youth and early manhood. The new generation, heir to the Periclean

---

[16]Blass (p. 28 of the book quoted in note 9) points out that in Isocrates' time the word 'philosophy' still meant 'culture,' so that there is nothing silly about his claim to 'teach philosophy'; however, he says it is arrogant of Isocrates to pretend to be the only representative of true philosophy—i.e. true culture. Still, Plato and all the other schools and teachers made the same claim: see Plato *ep.* 7. 326a, *Rep.* 490a, etc.

[17]Plato, *Prot.* 313 c f.

[18]It is difficult to tell how much historical truth there is in that passage of Plato's *Phaedrus* where Socrates is made to prophesy a great future for Isocrates. Perhaps the two had met at some time, and there is no more in it than that. It can hardly mean that Isocrates was Socrates' friend, still less his pupil. And yet his works show many traces of the influence of Socratic ideas. The fullest examination of them is H. Gomperz' *Isokrates und die Sokratik* (*Wiener Studien* 27, 1905, p. 163, and 28, 1906, p. 1). He assumes, correctly, that Isocrates got his knowledge of these ideas from books about Socrates; and this is supported by the fact that he did not begin to talk about them till the years between 390 and 380, when he himself first entered the field of educational theory. Still, I think Gomperz exaggerates the influence of Antisthenes upon Isocrates.

system, found tasks of enormous difficulty confronting it. It was rhetoric, and not philosophy in the Platonic sense, that seemed to Isocrates to be the intellectual form which could best express the political and ethical ideas of his age, and make them part of the intellectual equipment of all contemporary Athenians. With this new conception of its purposes, Isocrates' rhetorical teaching emerged as part of the great post-war educational movement of Athens, into which all the efforts of his day to reform and rejuvenate the Athenian state were inevitably destined to flow.

The factors which brought this about were very various. Despite his mastery of language and of style, Isocrates was not a born orator. And yet, by its very nature, the Athenian democracy still held that no man could be an effective political force unless he were a master of oratory. He says himself that physically he had a weak constitution. His voice was not nearly powerful enough to reach large audiences; and he had an invincible fear of making a public appearance. Crowds terrified him.[19] In speaking without embarrassment of this agoraphobia, Isocrates was not merely offering an excuse for his complete abstention from all political activity; besides that, he felt that his strange condition was a very personal feature of his character, rooted far in its depths. As with Socrates, his refusal to enter politics was not a sign of lack of interest, but the result of a profound intellectual and spiritual conflict—a conflict which both hampered his activity and at the same time enlarged his understanding of the part he must play in the contemporary political crisis. Like the Platonic Socrates, he was convinced that he must initiate the much-needed reformation in some other way than by entering an active career as an orator in the assemblies and the law courts. Thus, he felt that the personal disabilities which made him unfit for normal political life summoned him to a higher vocation. His weakness was his destiny. But whereas Socrates, with his incessant questioning and examining, became an explorer in the sphere of morality, and found himself at last standing before the closed gates of a new world of knowledge, the more practical Isocrates, although for the time being he was deeply impressed by the personality of his great contemporary, and constantly strove to rival the lofty standard he set, felt nevertheless that his special gifts and his natural dislike for the mob predestined him to become within a small circle the teacher of a new type of political action.[20]

Even the age in which he lived seemed to make this course inevitable. In the calm and concentration of his retirement, he wished to educate statesmen who could give new direction to the efforts of the misguided masses and to the politics of the Greek states, which had long been revolving hopelessly in a closed circle. He set out to inspire every pupil with a passion for the new

---

[19]For the facts of Isocrates' life, see Blass (cited in note 9) p. 8 f.; Jebb, *Attic Orators* (London 1876) 11, p. 1 f.; and Münscher's exhaustive article in Pauly-Wissowa's *Realenzyklopädie der klass. Altertumswiss.* 9.2150 f. On his weak voice and his timidity, see *Phil.* 81, *Panath.* 10.

[20]In *Phil.* 81-82 he admits his physical and psychical weakness, but nevertheless claims to be far ahead of others in phronésis and paideia.

aims which occupied his own mind. There was within him a political visionary whose thought moved in the same direction as that of the practical statesmen, and was led like them by such aspirations as Power, Glory, Prosperity, Progress. Gradually his experience led him to modify his aims; but from the very beginning he held that they could not be fulfilled by the outworn methods of the Periclean age—competitive diplomacy and exhausting wars between the separate Greek city-states. In that his thought is wholly a product of the weakness of Athens after the Peloponnesian war. Dreamer that he was, in his visions of the future he overleapt that weakness. He believed that Athens could play a leading part in Greek affairs only in peaceful agreement with Sparta and the other Greek states, with entire equality between victors and vanquished; for then the intellectual superiority of Athens to her coarser rivals would assure that she acquired the balance of power.[21] Only such establishment of equality among the Greek states and their devotion to one great national purpose could arrest the dissolution of Greece, and therewith the total annihilation of the small separate states—which hitherto had striven only to destroy one another, although none of them had ever acquired a real superiority over all the rest, with the supreme power which would impose a lasting peace on the entire nation. To save Greece, a common national purpose must be found. And, after the bitter experiences of the Peloponnesian war, Isocrates considered that the essential duty of true statesmanship was to find it. True, there was an urgent preliminary: the political life of the Greek state had to be purged of its deep corruption, and of the cause of that corruption—the poisonous mutual hatreds of the separate states and parties. It was exactly that selfish hatred of each for his neighbour which, according to Thucydides' tragic description, had during the Peloponnesian war served as a justification for every kind of monstrous crime, and had destroyed the foundations of all established moral codes.[22] But Isocrates did not, like the Platonic Socrates, believe that the sorely needed reformation could be achieved by the creation of a new moral world, a state as it were within each man's soul.[23] He held that the *nation*, the idea of Greece, was the point round which the new elements in the spiritual renaissance were to crystallize. Plato had accused rhetoric of being able only to teach men how to convince an audience, without pointing out any ideal to be pursued: and therefore of being only a practical means to provide intellectual instruments by which to achieve immoral ends.[24] That weakness in the pretensions of rhetoric was undeniable; and, at a time when the conscience of the best of the Greeks was constantly becoming more sensitive, it was a real danger for the art. In the adoption of the Panhellenic ideal, Isocrates saw the way to solve

---

[21] That is the role which he assigns to Athens in the *Panegyricus*. Even after the collapse of the second naval confederacy, he continued to maintain the spiritual leadership of Athens—for instance in the *Antidosis* and the *Panathenaicus*. But he later (as in the *Peace* speech and *Philip*) abandoned the claim that Athens should likewise wield the political hegemony of Greece.

[22] Thuc. 3.82.

[23] Plato, *Rep.* 591e; see *Paideia* II, 353 f.

[24] See *Paideia* II, 131 f.

this problem also. The essential was to find a mean, as it were, between the moral indifference which had previously characterized rhetorical education, and the Platonic resolution of all politics into morality, which from a practical point of view was certain to lead away from all politics.[25] The new rhetoric had to find an ideal which could be ethically interpreted and which at the same time could be translated into practical political action. This ideal was a new moral code for Greece. It gave rhetoric an inexhaustible theme; in it the ultimate topic of all higher eloquence seemed to have been discovered once and for all. In an age when the old beliefs were losing their binding force and the long-established structure of the city-state was breaking up (the structure in which, till then, the individual had felt his own moral foundations securely embodied), the new dream of national achievement appeared to be a mighty inspiration. It gave life a new meaning.

In that critical time, therefore, Isocrates was, by his own choice of rhetoric as a career, driven to formulate the new ideals which we have described. It is entirely probable that he had been directly impelled towards them by Gorgias, whose *Olympicus* set forth the theme that was to be the centre of Isocrates' life-work. That happens often enough: in his last years a great master formulates an ideal, inspires his pupil with admiration for it, and through it shapes and directs his pupil's entire career. If Isocrates wanted to become a politician without being an orator, if he wished to assert himself as an educator and a rhetorical teacher against the competition of Socratic philosophy and of the earlier type of rhetoric, and to make head against their criticisms, he had found the only possible method of doing so in his concentration on the new ideal. That explains the doggedness with which he followed it to the end. His weaknesses make it easy enough to criticize him; but it is hard to find a man who fulfilled his self-imposed task more completely than Isocrates, and who was better suited to his own conception of his mission. That conception gave rhetoric the realistic content which it had long been accused of lacking.[26] Through it the teacher of rhetoric at last achieved the dignity which put him on a level with the philosopher and made him independent of machine politicians—which actually gave him a higher rank than they possessed, inasmuch as he represented a higher interest than that of any separate state. The defects in Isocrates' own nature—not only his physical weakness, but the faults in his intellect and his character—and even the defects of rhetoric itself were, through his programme, almost converted into virtues; or so it seemed. The rhetor, the political pamphleteer and ideologist, has never since found himself in such a favourable situation or commanded such a widespread influence throughout an entire nation; and if his influence lacked something in richness, power, and genius, Isocrates partially compensated for that by an exceptionally long life of determined

---

[25] In the speech *Against the sophists*, Isocrates draws a contrast between these two extreme types of contemporary paideia.
[26] Cf. Plato, *Gorg.* 449d, 451a, 453b-e, 455d. Later he repeated the charge in *Phaedrus*.

industry. Of course his determination does not affect the quality of his work; but still it was a vital element in the success of his mission, which, like that of the teacher, depended on his relation to living men.

For centuries past, historians have seen in Isocrates nothing more than a moralist, and have conceived him too exclusively as a writer and publicist, too little as a teacher. They did not fully realize that all his published writings, like those of Plato and Aristotle, were ancillary to the educational programme of his school. But the modern view of his career now does full justice to the political content of his books, and understands all their significance in the history of the fourth century. They were of course intended to produce an effect even outside the circle of his own pupils, and through them he often influenced men who had never heard him teach. But at the same time his political speeches were models of the new type of eloquence which he taught in his school. Later, in the *Antidosis*, he himself exemplified to a wider public the special character of his teaching, in a selection of passages taken from his most celebrated speeches. These speeches were intended to be models not only of content but of form,[27] for in his teaching the two elements were inseparable. Whenever we try to re-create from the orations—which are our only evidence—the real character of the culture which he taught, we must always remember that dual purpose. Fortunately for us, he often expressed his views of his art and of his educational ideals; he often seized an opportunity to break off the thread of his argument, and to explain what he was saying, how he was saying it, and why. Indeed, at the beginning of his career he published several programme-works which clearly defined his position with reference to the other educational authorities of his time. We must start with them, if we are to comprehend the full extent of his activity, the true character of his paideia.

He had been a 'speech-writer', which in many respects corresponded to the profession of a barrister today; but we know nothing of the time when he abandoned that vocation for that of a teacher of rhetoric, or the reasons which led him to do so. Like Lysias, Isaeus, and Demosthenes, he had taken it up in order to make money—for his father's property had been largely destroyed by the war.[28] At a later time he was reluctant to mention that period of his career, although (as Aristotle humorously pointed out) volumes and volumes of the legal speeches he had written lay in the bookshops.[29] Only a few of them survive: his pupils, who had charge of editing his works after his death, had no more interest in preserving them than the master himself.[30] We can

---

[27]Isocrates' 'speeches' were never delivered as such. Their oratorical form is a pure fiction.
[28]On his work as a logographer, see Dion. Hal. *de Isocr.* 18, and Cicero, *Brutus* 28 (whose source is Aristotle's *synagôgê technôn*). He mentions the destruction of his father's property, in *Antid.* 161.
[29]Cf. Dion. Hal. *de Isocr.* 18.
[30]According to Dion. Hal. *de Isocr.* 18, Isocrates' stepson Aphareus said, in his speech against Megacleides, that his stepfather had *never* written forensic speeches; but that can only mean never since he became the head of a school. His pupil Cephisodorus admitted that there were some such speeches by him in existence, but said only a few were authentic.

For the sophists, R was a persuasion technique
For Plato, R was a means to higher moral good.
For Isocrates, R was the mechanism for bringing about political utopia.

trace them no later than 390 or so.[31] Therefore, the foundation of Isocrates' school roughly coincided with that of Plato's.[32] In his introductory speech *Against the sophists*, it is clear that he has Plato's 'prospectuses', *Gorgias* and *Protagoras*, before him, and is deliberately trying to set up his own ideal of paideia in contrast to theirs.[32a] That takes us back to the same period. The incomparable value of that speech for us lies in the vividness with which it re-creates, blow upon blow, the first battle of the generation-long cultural war between the two great schools of education. And it is no less interesting for us to trace in it the immediate impression which Plato made on many of his contemporaries at his first appearance. Accustomed as we are to estimate his importance by the influence of his philosophy on more than twenty centuries of human history, we naturally imagine that he exercised the same powerful influence on the men of his own time. For that view Isocrates is a useful corrective.

He begins by saying that the representatives of paideia have a bad reputation, and he traces it to the excessive hopes which their self-advertisement excites among the public.[33] Thereby he steps forth to oppose the exaggerated estimates of the power of education that were customary in his day. And, as a matter of fact, there must have been something very bizarre in the revolutionary change from Socrates' loudly expressed doubts whether such a thing as education really existed, to the passionate educational conviction of Plato's earlier dialogues. Here as elsewhere, Isocrates represents the happy mean. He himself, of course, wants to be a teacher too; but he 'very well understands' the laymen who would rather do nothing about education at all than believe the enormous promises of professing

---

[31] The *Trapeziticus* and *Aegineticus* can be dated roughly to 390.

[32] There is no confirmation for the statement of pseudo-Plutarch, *vit. X orat.* 837b that Isocrates first had a school in Chios (*scholês de hêgeito ôs tines phasin, peôton epi Chiou*). And *epi Chiou* is an uncommon way to say *en Chiôi*. What we should expect, following *epi*, is the name of the archon in whose time Isocrates began to teach; but if *Chiou* is a corruption of that name, it is difficult to emend. None of the archons in the 'nineties or early 'eighties has a name like *chiou*. If it were <*Musti*>*chidou* that would take us down to 386-385, which is a very late date for the foundation of Isocrates' school.

[32a] Isocrates himself, in *Antid.* 193, says that the speech *Against the sophists* belongs to the beginning of his teaching career. There is a list of the many works which deal with his relation to Plato, in Münscher's article in Pauly-Wissowa 9.2171. Unfortunately, many of them are obsolete, since the assumption on which they are based is false—the assumption that Plato's chief dialogue on rhetoric, *Phaedrus*, was written in his youth or middle life. Münscher's article, which is otherwise an admirable introduction to the subject, still goes on the same assumption. Modern scholars have revised their views on this point. (About the late date of *Phaedrus*, see p. 330, n. 5 f.) On the other hand, I think it is impossible to follow Wilamowitz (*Platon* 11, 108) and avoid the conclusion that *Against the sophists* attacks Plato just as violently as the other Socratics. It assumes knowledge of Plato's *Protagoras*, *Gorgias*, and perhaps *Meno* too (see my discussion of the problem on pp. 56 and 66). Münscher's belief, that when Isocrates wrote the speech he still 'felt himself in agreement with Plato' in everything essential, cannot be backed up by anything in the speech, and is actually contradicted by every line of it. The sole basis for that belief is the early dating of *Phaedrus*, in which Plato is clearly more friendly to Isocrates than to rhetors like Lysias. The assumption that it was written before or soon after *Against the sophists* would compel us to make a forced interpretation of that speech as expressing friendship for Plato.

[33] Isocr. *Soph.* 1.

philosophers.[34] How is it possible, he asks, to put any trust in their yearning for truth, when they themselves arouse so many false hopes? Isocrates names no names, but every word of his polemic is aimed straight at the Socratics, whom here and elsewhere he contemptuously calls 'disputers'.[35] In *Protagoras* and *Gorgias* Plato had presented dialectic as an art far superior to the long-winded orations of rhetoricians. His opponent makes short work of dialectic: he couples it with eristic—namely, argument for argument's sake. True philosophy always endeavoured to keep itself free from eristic,[36] although the methods of Plato's Socrates often seem to have much in common with it; and in fact there is a good deal of it in the earlier dialogues like *Protagoras* and *Gorgias*.[37] No wonder then that Isocrates does not see dialectic in the same favourable light as the Socratics, who thought it was a perfect panacea for all spiritual ills. The infallible knowledge of values (*phronêsis*) which they promise as the result of their teaching must appear to ordinary reasonable people to be something too great for mankind to attain.[38] Homer, who knew so well the frontiers that separate men from gods, claims that only the gods have such unerring insight, and he is right. What mortal man has the audacity to promise to give his disciples infallible knowledge (*epistêmê*) of everything they ought to do or leave undone, and to lead them through that knowledge to supreme happiness (*eudaimonia*)?[39]

In this criticism Isocrates has collected in a small space all the features which make Platonism repulsive to ordinary common sense: the peculiar technique of controversy by question-and-answer, the almost mythical importance which it attributes to phronésis (or knowledge of true values) as a special organ of reason, the apparently exaggerated intellectualism which holds knowledge to be the cure for everything, and the quasi-religious

---

[34]Of course the word 'philosopher' is not confined to those representatives of paideia whom we should call philosophers to-day—the Socratic circle. It includes all sorts of professed teachers of culture (see *Soph.* 11 and 18). But it does include philosophers in the strict sense, as we can see from *Soph.* 2, where Isocrates ridicules their claim to teach 'truth'. That is aimed at *all* the Socratics, not merely (as some have held) at Antisthenes' book *Truth*.

[35]*Soph.* 1: *hoi peri tas eridas diatribontes hoi prospoioutai tên alêtheian zêtein*; *Antid.* 261: *hoi en tois eristikois logois dunasteuontas*. In the latter passage the 'disputers' are put in the same class as teachers of geometry and astronomy—both subjects which were taught in Plato's Academy. Münscher's illogical assumption that in the later speech on the Antidosis Isocrates means his readers to think chiefly of Plato when he mentions disputers, but does not in the speech on the sophists, is based on the early dating of *Phaedrus* and the inference that Isocrates and the young Plato where friendly (see note 32a).

[36]Most probably it was because Plato found his dialectic being confused with eristic, as in Isocrates' attacks on it, that he distinguished Socrates so sharply and clearly from the eristics in *Euthydemus*. In *Rep.* 499a he repeats his complaint that no one knows the true philosopher, and he tries to vindicate him from confusion with mere disputers. There he describes him as a man who finds no pleasure in clever but useless arguments, and seeks 'knowledge for its own sake.'

[37]At several points Protagoras refuses to agree with the logical conclusions reached by Socrates, and he obviously thinks his opponent is trying to trap him. Plato describes this in a perfectly objective way, and thereby shows how easy it was for Socrates' dialectic to be called eristic. In the same way Callicles (Plato, *Gorg.* 482 f.) objects to Socrates' trick of giving different meanings to the same concept in the same argument. On this, see *Paideia* 11, 138.

[38]*Soph.* 2.

[39]*Soph.* 2-4.

enthusiasm with which 'blessedness' is foretold to the philosopher. Obviously Isocrates is aiming some of his sharpest shafts at the terminological peculiarities of the new philosophical method: he tracks them down with the subtle instinct of the stylist for everything which seems odd or ludicrous to the average educated man; and by contrasting the Universal Virtue (*pasa aretê*), which is the putative aim of the Socratic knowledge of that which is 'good in itself',[40] with the trifling fees for which the philosophers sell their wisdom, he really makes the man in the street doubt whether what the young student learns from the philosopher is worth very much more than he pays for it.

He adds that the philosophers themselves cannot believe very strongly in the perfect virtue which they say they wish to release in the souls of their pupils, because the regulations of their school betray a far-reaching distrust of its members. They demand that the fees be paid into an Athenian bank in advance, before the pupil can be admitted.[41] They are justified, no doubt, in looking out for their own interests; but how can their attitude be reconciled with their claim to educate men to attain justice and self-mastery? This argument seems to us to be pitched rather too low; but it is not without wit. In *Gorgias* Plato had argued with just the same malice against the rhetors, who complain about the misuse their pupils make of the art of oratory, without seeing that they are accusing themselves—for if it were true that rhetoric improved its students, it would be impossible for those who had really learnt it to misuse it as they do.[42] Actually, the amoral character of rhetoric was the principal charge against it. In several different contexts, Isocrates supports the view represented by Gorgias in Plato's dialogue: the view that the teacher imparts to his pupil the art of rhetoric in order that he may use it rightly, and is not to blame if the pupil misuses it.[43] That is, he does not accept Plato's criticism, and maintains that Gorgias is wholly in the right. But he goes beyond that, and attacks the philosophers for distrusting their own pupils. That makes it probable that when he was writing the speech *Against the sophists* as an inaugural address, he knew Plato's *Gorgias* and deliberately set out to answer it.[44]

---

[40]Plato contrasts 'universal virtue' and 'special virtues' like justice, courage, self-control, etc. Sometimes he calls the former 'virtue in itself' (*autê hê aretê*)—a kind of expression new and strange to his contemporaries. In c. 20 also, Isocrates emphasizes the ethical element in the paideia of the 'disputers'; they assert that virtue can be taught (21), which Isocrates and all the sophists violently deny. See Plato's *Protagoras*.

[41]*Soph.* 5.

[42]Cf. Plato, *Gorg.* 456e-457c, 460d-461a.

[43]In *Antid.* 215 f., Isocrates tries to defend teachers of rhetoric against the charge that their pupils learn evil from them. See also *Nic.* 2 f.

[44]This is the most probable view of the dates at which the two works were written. *Gorgias* is now generally believed, on convincing grounds, to have been written between 395 and 390 B.C.; but Isocrates had scarcely opened his school at that time, since we can trace his work as a logographer down to 390. Therefore the speech *Against the sophists*, which gives his programme, was written in the 'eighties. Some scholars have attempted to fix the chronological relationship between *Against the sophists* and Plato's *Gorgias* by what appear to be allusions in Plato's dialogue to Isocrates' speech. But even if Plato speaks of a *psychê stochastikê* (*Gorg.* 463a) and Isocrates of a *psychê doxastikê* (*Soph.* 17), that does not prove that Plato is imitating Isocrates. Also, *doxastikê* is a Platonic phrase. Plato despises mere *doxa*, while here as elsewhere Isocrates insists that man's nature does not allow

Plato's dialogue must have seemed particularly offensive to him as a
pupil of Gorgias, and he must have felt himself arraigned in the person of his
master: for as we have shown, it was not only Gorgias himself but rhetoric in
all its branches that Plato had impugned. All the typical doctrines of the
'eristics' which Isocrates ridicules in his inaugural speech *Against the
sophists* had already been clearly enunciated in *Gorgias*, where they were
analyzed with special reference to their significance for the new Platonic
system of paideia.[45] (*Paideia* II, 126 f.) Plato and the Socratics are among the
foremost of the opponents whom Isocrates attacks, and since he attacks them
with special violence and completeness, it is clear that he fully understands
the danger that threatens his ideal from their teaching. His invective is
entirely realistic. He never makes it a theoretical refutation of his opponents'
position, for he knows that if he did he would lose his case. The terrain he
chooses is that of ordinary common sense. He appeals to the instincts of the
man in the street—who, without comprehending the philosophers' technical
secrets, sees that those who would lead their followers to wisdom and
happiness have nothing themselves and get nothing from their students.[46]
Their poverty did not harmonize with the traditional Greek concept of
eudaimonia, perfect happiness, and other sophists—Antiphon, for instance—
had already derided Socrates for exalting it.[46a] The man in the street sees that
those who expose the contradictions in people's speeches do not notice the
contradictions in their own acts; and that, although they profess to teach their
pupils how to make the right decision on every problem of the future, they
cannot say anything at all or give any correct advice about the present.[47] And
when he further observes that the mob, whose conduct is based on nothing
more than Opinion (*doxa*), find it easier to agree with one another and to hit
the right course of action than those who pretend to be in full possession of
Knowledge (*epistêmê*), he is bound to end by despising the study of
philosophy—concluding it to be empty chatter, mere hair-splitting, and
certainly not 'the care of the soul' (*psychêis epimeleia*).[48]

This last point above all makes it certain that Isocrates is aiming his
attacks at Plato and at the rest of the Socratics—Antisthenes in particular. He
has deliberately—and in a way justifiably—mixed up their features into a

---

him to engage in more than *doxa* and *doxazein*. The very fact that he is replying to Plato shows that
he depends on Plato's formulation of the problem. But the main argument is that given in the text
(page 56 f.): the information about Plato's fundamental concepts and their logical interrelation (e.g.
pasa aretê :: *eudaimouia*, *epistêmê* :: *doxa*, *aretê* :: *epistêmê*) which is contained in *Against the
sophists* is so full that it could have been derived from no other early Platonic work but *Gorgias*, the
only work of Plato's youth in which he gives a fairly systematic exposition of his thought.
[45]It would anyhow be difficult to name any of Plato's early works which more convincingly and
completely expounds all those characteristic features of his philosophy which are referred to by
Isocrates, and makes their underlying connexions so clear.
[46]*Soph.* 6.
[46a]Xen. *Mem.* 1.6.1 f.
[47]*Soph.* 7.
[48]*Soph.* 8.

composite portrait of 'the pupil of Socrates' which they all claimed to be.[48a]
Nevertheless he knows very well that the pupils of Socrates are bitterly
hostile to one another, and he converts their strife into another argument
against professional philosophers—the favourite argument of common sense
in every age. It was Antisthenes in particular who imitated his master's
poverty and independence; while the abstract and theoretical aspects of
Isocrates' portrait are principally drawn from Plato, and the description of
philosophy as hair-splitting is obviously pointed at Plato's elaboration of
dialectic into the art of logic.[48b] That was, as Isocrates rightly saw, a step into
the sphere of theory and pure form. So he measures this new art of
discovering contradictions—the art which attempts to conquer Opinion by
Knowledge[49]—against the old Socratic aim of 'caring for the soul,'[50] and
throws doubt on its ability to achieve that aim. Thereby he concludes his
criticism precisely at the point where (as history shows) the real problem lies.
And so, in the argument which we here witness between Plato and Isocrates,
there is unfolded part of the long series of conflicts through which the ideal
of culture has been developed—a dialectic process which still retains a deep
and permanent value, independently of the small personal details of the
dispute.

The second group of opponents attacked by Isocrates are described by
him as teachers of politics.[51] They do not, like the philosophers, search for the
truth. They simply practise their techné—their craft, in the old sense of the
word,[52] whereby it implied no trace of moral responsibility. In *Gorgias*, Plato
had asserted that true rhetoric ought, like the craft of the doctor, to entail such
moral responsibility.[53] Isocrates could not deny Plato's claim; and the moral
factor is especially prominent in his treatment of the third group of his
opponents, the teachers of forensic oratory. But he did not assert its validity
simply in order to exalt Plato. His criticism of those who teach the craft of
making political speeches introduces us to a type of education which was the
absolute opposite of philosophy—the art of extempore speechmaking. As
typical of the specialist in this subject we must think of Isocrates' own

---

[48a]Perhaps the charge of asking pupils for contemptibly small fees is more appropriate to Antisthenes
than to Plato, who probably took no fees at all. But we know far too little of these matters to judge
with certainty. Even in the Academy, pupils probably had to pay a small sum—for instance, their share
of the symposium. This was not meant to be the salary of their teacher, but Isocrates may have chosen
to describe it as if it were, and to imply that Plato was underbidding his competitors. He attacks Plato
and Antisthenes again in *Helen* 1: see note 85. On the fees of the Socratics, see Diog. Laert. 2.62, 65,
80, and 6.14.

[48b]The charge that dialectic is hair-splitting recurs in *Antid.* 262, where it is admittedly an attack on
Plato. Why should it not be an attack on Plato here too?

[49]This description of the art of discovering contradictions, 'elenctic', is aimed at Socrates and Plato. See
the parallel in *Helen* 4, where the Socratic technical term *elegchein* is particularly derided.

[50]See *Paideia* 11, 39, which explains how the purpose of all Socrates' educational activity can be
described as 'caring for the soul' (*psychês epimeleia*).

[51]*Soph.* 9: *hoi tous politikous logous hypischnoumenoi.*

[52]Isocrates' phrasing clearly shows that he is putting the word techné (as used by these teachers of
rhetoric) inside quotation-marks, so to speak. The same thing applies to the passages where he parodies
the terminology of the Socratics.

[53]See *Paideia* 11, 131, and *passim.*

fellow-student in the school of Gorgias, Alcidamas[54]—who like him published several model speeches, but whose forte was improvisation (*autoschebiazein*). One of his speeches, which has been preserved, is significantly aimed against rhetors like Isocrates, who can write well enough but are incapable of seizing the critical moment to say the words demanded by the immediate situation.[55] There can be no doubt that the constant practice of this technique was invaluable training for the student who intended to be an active public speaker, even although the actual teaching often degenerated into mere routine instruction, and grossly neglected the higher claims of art. This class of his opponents Isocrates charges with lack of taste: they have, he affirms, no aesthetic sense.[56] In practice, their type of rhetoric turns out to be nothing more than a collection of formal devices which the pupil gets off by heart and can bring into play at any moment. It enlarges neither his intellect nor his experience, but merely teaches him the patterns of speechmaking as abstract forms to be learnt by rote, as the elementary teacher teaches little children the alphabet.[57] This method is a fine example of the contemporary trend towards mechanizing both education and life itself as far as possible. Isocrates seizes the opportunity to distinguish his own artistry from this empty commercialized technique, and to clear himself from the charge which he might well have incurred through his distaste for the subtleties of philosophical education—the charge of being narrow-mindedly practical. What he is looking for is the middle way between highflown theory and vulgar penny-chasing technical adroitness; and he finds it in artistically disciplined Form.[58] In this he introduces a third principle. Here again we find that he explains himself and his ideal by contrast with another point of view. But by thus waging war on two fronts, he shows that his conflict with philosophical education, important as it is, expresses only half of his own ideal. He is just as far removed in the other direction from rhetoric in the accepted sense. For, in the sphere of rhetoric as well as in that of philosophy, Isocrates' paideia was something perfectly new.

More than any other sphere of life, the art of oratory resists the effort of systematic reason to reduce all individual facts to a number of established *schemata*, basic forms. In the realm of logic Plato calls these basic forms the Ideas. As we have seen, he took this three-dimensional mode of describing them from contemporary medical science, and applied it to the analysis of Being. In rhetoric we can see the same process in operation at the same time, though we cannot definitely say that it was directly influenced by Plato's use of the term *idea*. Medicine and rhetoric were by their very nature the spheres in which this conception of basic forms or Ideas could be developed—for

---

[54]See J. Vahlen, *Gesammelte Schriften* 1, p. 117 f.; and before him, C. Reinhardt, *De Isocratis aemulis* (Bonn 1873).
[55]This speech is best explained as Alcidamas' reply to the attack on him made by Isocrates in the speech *Against the sophists*.
[56]*Soph.* 9.
[57]*Soph.* 10.
[58]*Soph.* 12 f.

medicine reduces a number of apparently different physiological events to a few fundamental types; and rhetoric likewise simplifies what seem to be separate and distinct political or legal situations. The essence of both skills is to analyze the individual case into its general aspects, so as to make it easier to treat in practice. The comparison of these general patterns to the letters of the alphabet (*stoicheia*)—which we find in Isocrates here, and later in Plato— was obvious enough. The act of reading is just the same as that of political or forensic or medical diagnosis: a large number of variously assembled shapes are reduced to a limited number of basic 'elements', and thus the meaning of each of the apparently manifold shapes is recognized.[59] In science too, the 'elements' which make up physical nature were first called by that name in the same period, and the same analogy, drawn from language and the letters of the alphabet, lies behind it.[60] Isocrates of course does not by any means reject the doctrine of a rhetorical system of Ideas. In fact, his writings show that he largely adopted that doctrine, and that he took as the foundation of his own teaching the mastery of the basic forms of oratory. But oratory which knew no more than these forms would be as sounding brass and a tinkling cymbal. The letters of the alphabet, immovable and unchangeable, are the most complete contrast to the fluid and manifold situations of human life, whose full and rich complexity can be brought under no rigid rule.[61] Perfect eloquence must be the individual expression of a single critical moment, a *kairos*, and its highest law is that it should be wholly appropriate. Only by observing these two rules can it succeed in being new and original.[62]

In a word, oratory is imaginative literary creation. Though it dare not dispense with technical skill, it must not stop short at that.[63] Just as the sophists had believed themselves to be the true successors of the poets, whose special art they had transferred into prose, so Isocrates too feels that he is continuing the poets' work, and taking over the function which until a short time before him they had fulfilled in the life of his nation. His comparison between rhetoric and poetry is far more than a passing epigram. Throughout his speeches the influence of this point of view can be traced. The panegyric on a great man is adapted from the hymn, while the hortative speech follows the model of the protreptic elegy and the didactic epic. And, in these types, Isocrates copies even the order of his ideas from the well-established traditional order which was a rule in each of the corresponding poetic genera. More than that: the position and prestige of the orator are determined by this parallel with the poet. The new vocation must support itself on an old and firmly-established one, and take its standards therefrom. The less Isocrates hopes or wishes to succeed as a practical statesman, the more he needs the

---

[59]Plato compares his 'ideas' to letters of the alphabet in *Cratylus, Theaetetus, The Statesman,* and *The Laws.*
[60]This was first done in Plato's *Timaeus* 48b, 56b, 57c: see H. Diels' *Elementum.*
[61]*Soph.* 12.
[62]Cf. *Soph.* 13, on the *kairos* and *to prepon.*
[63]*Soph.* 12.

prestige of poetry to set off his spiritual aims; and even in the educational spirit by which his rhetoric is inspired, he is deliberately emulating what the Greeks conceived to be the educational function of the poets of old. Later, indeed, he compares his work with that of the sculptor (as Pindar had done) and proudly puts himself on a level with Phidias;[64] but that is more to illustrate the fact that there are still some who, despite the loftiness of his art, consider the rhetor's profession to be something second-rate. The classical Greeks had always tended to depreciate the sculptor's trade a little, as resembling the work of a common artisan—and that although the word *sculptor* could be applied to every worker in stone, from the ordinary mason to the creator of the Parthenon. But later, as the prestige of the plastic arts and their great masters gradually rose in the post-classical centuries, the comparison of oratory to sculpture and painting seems to become commoner. However, the dynastic succession of rhetoric to poetry remained the true image of the spiritual process in which rhetoric arose as a new cultural force: all late Greek poetry is simply the offspring of rhetoric.[65]

Naturally, Isocrates' view of the educational value of rhetoric is defined by this conception of its true character. Being an act of creation, oratory in its highest ranges cannot possibly be taught like a school subject. And yet he holds that it can be employed to educate young men: because of his own peculiar view of the relation between the three factors which, according to the pedagogic theories of the sophists, are the foundation of all education. They are: (1) talent, (2) study, and (3) practice. The current enthusiasm for education and culture had helped to create and disseminate exaggerated views of their powers;[66] but that enthusiasm had been succeeded by a certain disillusionment—due partly to Socrates' far-reaching criticisms of the limitations and pretensions of education,[67] and partly to the discovery that many a young man whom the sophists had educated was no better than those who had never enjoyed such advantages.[68] Isocrates explains the exact value of education with great care. He asserts that natural talent is the principal factor, and admits that great gifts, untrained, often achieve more than mere training without ability—if indeed it is possible to speak of training when there is nothing there to train. The element second in importance is experience, practice.[69] It would appear that until then professional rhetors had theoretically recognized the trinity—talent, study, practice—but had in their own courses pushed study and training into the foreground. Isocrates modestly relegates training (*paideusis*) to the third rank. It can, he says, achieve much if it is helped by talent and experience. It makes speakers more clearly conscious of their art, stimulates their inventive faculty, and saves

---

[64]In *Antid.* 2 Isocrates compares himself to the sculptor Phidias and the painters Zeuxis and Parrhasius—the greatest artists in Greece. So does Plato in *The Republic:* see *Paideia* II, 258 f.

[65]Plato too, in *Gorg.* 502c, implies that poetry is a kind of rhetoric.

[66]*Soph.* 1.

[67]See *Paideia* 11, 59 f.

[68]*Soph.* 1 and 8.

[69]*Soph.* 14.

them much vague and unsuccessful searching. Even a less gifted pupil can be improved and intellectually developed by training, although he can never be made into a distinguished orator or writer.[70]

Rhetorical training, says Isocrates, can teach insight into the 'ideas' or basic patterns out of which every speech is built. He appears to mean that this phase of it, hitherto the only one which had been cultivated, was capable of far profounder development; and we would gladly hear more of his new doctrine of ideas, to be able to compare it with that of the older rhetors. But the real difficulty of the subject does not lie in that aspect of it—all the less so because it is taught so thoroughly. It lies in the right choice, commixture, and placing of the 'ideas' on each subject, in the selection of the correct moment, in the good taste and appropriateness with which the speech is decorated with enthymemes, and in the rhythmic and musical disposition of the words.[71] To do all that correctly needs a powerful and sensitive mind. This, the highest stage of training, assumes in the pupil full knowledge of the 'ideas' of speech and skill in their employment; from the teacher it requires the ability to expound everything which can be rationally taught, and beyond that—i.e. in everything which cannot be taught—it demands that he should make himself a model for his pupils: so that those who can form themselves by imitating him may at once achieve a richer and more graceful style than any others.[72]

Plato, in *The Republic*, later declared that the highest culture could be attained only if certain qualities which are rarely found together were to coincide. Similarly, Isocrates asserts that it is impossible for the teacher to succeed unless all the factors which we have mentioned are brought into play at once.[73] Here the general Greek idea, that education is the process by which the whole man is shaped, is enunciated independently of Plato, and variously expounded in such imagery as 'model' or 'pattern' (*paradeigma*), 'stamp' (*ektupoun*), 'imitate' (*mimeisthai*).[74] The real problem is how this process of 'shaping' can be converted from a beautiful image into a practical reality— that is, what is to be the *method* of forming the human character, and ultimately what is the *nature* of the human intellect. Plato seeks to form the soul through knowledge of the Ideas as absolute norms of the Good, the Just, the Beautiful, etc., and thus eventually to develop it into an intelligible cosmos which contains all being within itself. No such universe of knowledge exists for Isocrates. For him, rhetorical training is worked out simply by Opinion, not by Knowledge. But he frequently claims that the intellect possesses an aesthetic and practical faculty which, without claiming absolute

---

[70] *Soph.* 15.
[71] *Soph.* 16.
[72] *Soph.* 17.
[73] *Soph.* 18. Plato also speaks of the 'coincidence' of power and intellect in *Rep.* 473d, and *Laws* 712a. But also, without using the word, he sets up an ideal of many-sided talent (Rep. 485b f.)—the *philosophos physis*, which is a coincidence of qualities that can exist together but seldom do. This way of formulating ideals is characteristic of the literature of paideia.
[74] *Soph.* 18.

knowledge, can still choose the right means and the right end.[75] His whole conception of culture is based on that aesthetic power. Plato's dialectic guides the young student step by step towards the Ideas; but that still leaves it to him to employ them in his life and conduct, and the way in which he employs them cannot be rationally explained. In the same way Isocrates can describe only the elements and the separate stages of the educational act. The formative process itself remains a mystery. Nature can neither be wholly banished from it, nor be put wholly in control of it. Therefore, everything in education depends on the proper cooperation of nature and art. If we once decide that Isocrates' incompleteness (as Plato would call it) and his reliance on mere Opinion (which Plato called the vital force of all rhetoric) were imposed on him by his subject, then we must conclude that his resolute self-limitation, and his deliberate renunciation of everything 'higher', everything which he felt to be obscure and doubtful, were a sort of constitutional weakness converted by him into a strength. This, in the sphere of culture, is the same thing that assured Isocrates' own personal success: he has made a virtue of necessity. He recognizes the empirical character of rhetoric; and, whether or not it is right to call it a true techné or art—Plato in *Gorgias* had claimed that it was not—Isocrates holds fast to its empiricism. Therein he clings to the principle of *imitation* established by his predecessors—the principle which in the future was to play such an enormous part in rhetoric and (as literature came more and more under the influence of rhetoric) in every branch of literature. Here we know more of his method of teaching than we do of his attitude to the rhetorical doctrine of ideas; for all his great speeches were meant to be models in which his pupils could study the precepts of his art.

He spends little time on the third group of educators, the writers of forensic speeches. Obviously he considers them his weakest opponents—although Plato attacked them a good many years later in *Phaedrus*, and therefore thought them fairly important even then. It is clear that Isocrates believes their rivalry far less dangerous than that of the new philosophical culture, in which he recognizes the real threat to his own ideals. The forensic speechmakers were out to make money, and their product was meant for practical use. We know their technique from the sample speeches published by Antiphon, Lysias, Isaeus, Demosthenes, and even Isocrates himself at the outset of his career. This type of literature is one of the most remarkable plants in the garden of Greek literature—and a native Attic vegetable at that. The Athenian mania for litigation, so delightfully satirized by the comedians, is the obverse of the firm legality of the Athenian state: of that foundation in Law of which its citizens were so proud. It produced a universal interest in *agones*—lawsuits and prosecutions. The model speeches written by the logographers served both as advertisements for their authors, as patterns for

[75]Cf. *Soph.* 17, on the *psychê doxastikê*.

their pupils to copy, and as interesting reading-matter for the public.[76] Here too Isocrates manifests the more sensitive taste of the younger generation. Ironically he recommends that the logographers should leave it to the enemies of rhetoric (already numerous enough) to display this, its least attractive side, instead of proudly dragging it out into the glare of publicity; and he adds that anything that can be learnt in rhetoric is just as valuable in other spheres as in legal disputes. We need not question the sincerity of this attitude. It explains quite clearly why Isocrates abandoned the profession. He felt that the speechwriter was morally far below the philosopher.[77] Clearly he is thinking not only of the men who write speeches for use in law courts, but of all kinds of rhetors, since he includes them all under the name of 'teachers of political oratory.'[78] Doubtless the subjects investigated in philosophical education are not worth the trouble, and the arguers who 'wallow' in debates would get into serious danger if they applied their conclusions to real facts (here Isocrates is quoting Callicles in Plato's *Gorgias*, and taking his side too), but at least the fact that the rhetors talk about a better subject, politics, must not keep us from recognizing that in practice they generally misuse it and become interfering and ambitious busybodies. Thus Isocrates follows Plato in his criticism of the political orators, though he does not accept his positive conclusions. He does not believe that virtue can be taught, any more than the aesthetic sense. Plato refuses to grant the name of *techné* to any kind of education which does not teach virtue; and Isocrates frankly thinks it impossible to create such education. Nevertheless, he is inclined to concede that education of a political tendency might have some ethical influence if it were practised in the manner he recommends, not in the amoral way represented by earlier rhetoricians.[79]

The striking thing about Isocrates' conception of Plato's paideia, as set forth in his speech *Against the sophists*, is that he entirely overlooks the political content of his opponent's theories. From Plato's early dialogues he must have got the same impression as they made, until a short time ago, on most modern readers—that their author's sole concern was moral reformation, an ideal which is somehow strangely connected with dialectic reasoning. The superiority of rhetoric, as Isocrates conceives it, is that it is entirely political culture. All that it has to do to attain spiritual leadership in the state is to find a new approach to life and its problems. The older type of rhetoric missed many important opportunities because it was content to serve day-to-day

---

[76]Isocrates thinks that, if these model speeches are meant to be specimens of the teaching technique used by their writers, they come under the definition of paideia just as much as his own political rhetoric and its products. After all, that kind of literature represents a formal educational principle which is valuable and interesting in itself. However, since its content has comparatively little importance, it has not been exhaustively treated here. In this, I have accepted the estimate of Plato and Isocrates. General and legal historians will of course take a different view.

[77] *Soph.* 19-20.

[78] *Soph.* 20.

[79] *Soph.* 21.

politics as an instrument, instead of rising above it. From this we can see that Isocrates believed he could inspire the political life of his nation with a higher moral creed. Unfortunately only a fragment of the speech on the sophists now survives, without the principal section, which doubtless explained his new ideal. Isocrates must have changed his attitude to Plato's cultural plans as soon as he understood the political aspect of his philosophy. Actually, he had already been warned by Plato's *Gorgias* that Socrates was the only real statesman of his age, because he alone tried to make his fellow-citizens better.[80] That might well be interpreted as pure paradox—especially by Isocrates, who held that the moving impulse of all contemporary writers was to struggle for originality at all costs, hunting out hitherto unheard-of-paradoxes on every subject, and who feared (with justice) that he could not rival Plato and the other philosophers in that exercise. But later, in his *Philip*, he reviews Plato's life-work not long after his death, and treats him as a very great political theorist, whose theories could unfortunately never be put into practice.[81] When did he first change his view of Plato's character and philosophy?

We can find the answer in his *Helen*. *Helen* is a model encomium, addressed to a mythical personage, and paradoxically praising her although she was generally reviled. The exact date of its composition is unknown, but it was obviously written soon after the speech *Against the sophists*—namely, while Isocrates' school was yet new. A lower limit for its date is fixed by the singular form which Isocrates, towards the end, gives to the praise of his heroine: it was she, he says, who first brought about national unity among the Greeks, in the war against Troy that resulted from her abduction.[82] Thus he makes Helen a mythical symbol of the political aspirations which he expressed more fully soon after that, in the *Panegyricus* (380)—of the great struggle to unite the Greek states in a national crusade against the barbarians. In this first decade Isocrates is still moving in the paths beaten out by Gorgias. The relation between his *Panegyricus* and Gorgias' *Olympicus* is the same as that between his *Helen* and Gorgias' *Defence of Helen*. The little speech is (as he says[83]) a first-fruits offering suitable for a man of paideia. It is interesting because of its renewed polemics against the Socratic school and its cultural ideal.[84] Here again, as in the speech on the sophists, he blends the features of Plato and Antisthenes in a composite portrait. His attack is aimed, not at one particular person, but at the entire tendency of the new movement.

---

[80]See *Paideia* II, 150.
[81]*Phil.* 12.
[82]*Hel.* 67.
[83]*Hel.* 66.
[84]This attack on the 'disputers' occupies the whole of the introduction to *Helen*, and has nothing to do with the rest of the speech. It will be enough for our purpose, therefore, to discuss the introduction alone. Aristotle (*Rhet.* 3.14.1414b26) says that the prooemium need have no connexion with the main part of an epideictic speech, and cites Isocrates' *Helen* as an example. He compares the introduction to an encomium with the loosely attached prelude (*proaulion*) to a flute-solo.

Isocrates says he cannot interpret their utterances as anything more than attempts at paradoxical wit, when some of them (Antisthenes) teach that it is impossible to make a false statement, or to make two contradictory assertions about the same thing, while others (Plato) try to prove that courage, wisdom and justice are one and the same, and that none of these qualities is implanted in us by nature, but that they are all attained by one and the same knowledge (epistêmê).[85] Here Isocrates really does distinguish the Socratics from those who are mere arguers, who teach nobody, but only try to make difficulties for others. He objects that all of them try to refute others (elegchein), although they themselves have long since been refuted,[86] and that their paradoxes are thrown into the shade by those of their predecessors the sophists: for instance, by Gorgias' statement that no existing thing exists, or Zeno's, that the same thing is both possible and impossible, or Melissus', that the apparently infinite multitude of things is really one.[87]

With this pettifogging, Isocrates contrasts the simple effort to find out what is true: which he conceives to be the effort to get experience of reality and to educate oneself for political action. Philosophers are always chasing the phantom of pure knowledge, but no one can use their results. Is it not better to spend one's time on the things which people really need, even if we cannot achieve exact knowledge, but only approximate opinions about them? He reduces his own attitude towards Plato's ideal of scientific accuracy and thoroughness to the formula that the smallest advance in our knowledge of really important things is better than the greatest intellectual mastery of unimportant trifles which are irrelevant to our life.[88] As a good psychologist, he evidently understands how much young men love dialectical disputation—for at their age, they have no interest in serious private or public problems, and the more futile a game, the more they enjoy it.[89] But those who profess to teach them deserve reproach for allowing them to be charmed by it. They incur thereby the same guilt of which they accuse forensic orators—they corrupt the youth.[90] They do not shrink from preaching the absurd doctrine that the life of beggars and exiles, deprived of all political rights and duties, is happier than that of others—namely, of the full citizens who remain peacefully in their native land. (This is clearly an allusion to the ethical individualism and cosmopolitanism of the radical wing in the Socratic school—Antisthenes, Aristippus, and their followers.[91] He finds the other philosophers to be even more ridiculous: those who think that their moral paradoxes really contribute something to the spiritual upbuilding of the state.

---

[85]Hel. 1. It is easy enough to identify Isocrates' two unnamed opponents. On Antisthenes see Arist. Met. Δ 29.1024b33, with the commentary of Alexander of Aphrodisias on it, and Plato, Soph. 251b.
[86]Hel. 4.
[87]Hel. 2-3.
[88]Hel. 5.
[89]Hel. 6.
[90]Hel. 7.
[91]Hel. 8.

This can only be a hit at Plato, who held that Socrates' moral evangel was true political science.[92] If we are right in this identification, it was as early as the 'eighties, soon after he wrote his speech *Against the sophists*, that Isocrates changed his views of Plato's cultural ideal, and recognized that it too had political implications. Only he felt that its concentration on individual morality and on dialectical quibbles—which seemed to him the distinguishing tendency of Plato's educational system—was absolutely irreconcilable with the universally useful purpose which it professed to serve.

Thus, as Isocrates and Plato appear to approach nearer and nearer to each other in the practical aim of their cultural theories, Isocrates' disapproval for Plato's abstract 'roundabout way'[93] becomes more and more pronounced. He knows only the direct route. There is in his system none of the inward tension that exists in the mind of Plato between the urgent will to action and the long philosophical preparation for action. True, he stands far enough away from the politics of his day and the activity of contemporary statesmen to understand Plato's objection to them. But, as a man who keeps to the middle way, he cannot appreciate the bold ethical claims of the Socratic system, which creates a gulf between the state and the individual. He does not look to Utopia for the improvement of political life. He embodies the rooted hatred of the propertied and cultured bourgeoisie both for the mad eccentricities of mob-rule and for the tyranny of individuals, and he has a strong admiration for respectability. But he has none of Plato's uncompromising passion for reformation, no thought of introducing such a terrific intensity into everyday life. Therefore, he does not realize the enormous educational power which lies in Plato's thought: he judges its value exclusively by its immediate utility for the particular political question which interests him. This is the internal condition of Greece, and the future relations of the Greek states to one another, after the great war. The Peloponnesian war had clearly demonstrated that the existing regime could not be permanent, and that the whole Greek world had to be rebuilt. When he wrote *Helen*, Isocrates was already at work on his great manifesto, the *Panegyricus*. Its purpose was to show the world that his school was able to state, in a new language, new ideals—not only for the moral life of the individual, but for the entire nation of the Hellenes.

---

[92]*Hel.* 9.
[93]See *Paideia* II, 280 and III, 193.

Isocrates' Ideal of Rhetoric:
Criteria of Evaluation*

by Erika Rummel

In Isocrates' lifetime Athens became an arena for competing sophists who sought to attract pupils by displaying their rhetorical prowess and promising to make a competent speaker of anyone who hired their services.[1] Their claims did not go unprotested. Plato subjected the sophists to sharp criticism in his dialogues and concluded that they made no valid contribution toward rhetorical perfection because they lacked true knowledge of the soul and excelled only in technical expertise.[2] This was a philosopher's challenge—the layman had other qualms about the teachers of rhetoric. His misgivings are represented in the comedy which attacks the sophists' instruction for being morally irresponsible, removed from the needs of daily life and unsuitable for mature men.[3] Midway between the philosopher's arguments and the layman's objections we find the views expressed by Isocrates, a professional teacher with philosophical aspirations, but also sharing the layman's bourgeois ethics and his taste for practicality.

Isocrates' rhetorical ideal is as complex as his creed. He denied that rhetoric was a science which followed strict rules; he expected the accomplished speaker to please as well as benefit his audience; he demanded from him a practical and worldwise handling of his subject, yet also insisted that he maintain a high level of integrity.[4] His demands are a mixture of epistemological theories, literary preferences, moral principles and practical

---

Reprinted from *Classical Journal* 75 (1979): 25-35. Used by permission.

*Translations of longer passages are taken from the Loeb edition of Isocrates' works.

[1] Cf. Plato, *Gorgias* 449B for this unqualified claim.

[2] Cf. *Phaedrus* 271A: "Anyone who seriously teaches the art of rhetoric will first describe the soul with perfect accuracy."

[3] Strepsiades in Aristophanes' play goes to the sophists to learn how to defraud his creditors (*Clouds* 112f). The activities of the sophists were frequently described as *adoleschia* and *leptologia* (e.g. Eupolis fr. 352-3; Alexis fr. 180, Aristophanes fr. 490, Hermippus fr. 22). For the view that sophistic quibbling is a young man's fancy see Aristophanes, *Knights* 1373ff.

[4] General accounts of Isocrates' views on rhetoric can be found in A. Burk, *Die Paedagogik des Isokrates* (Wuerzberg 1923); W. Steidle, "Redekunst und Bildung bei Isokrates," *Hermes* 80 (1952) 257-296; E. Mikkola, *Isokrates: Seine Anschauungen und Gedanken im Lichte seiner Schriften* (Helsinki 1954); G. Heilbrunn, *An examination of Isocrates' Rhetoric*, Diss. Chicago 1967, concentrates on Isocrates' style which he claims obfuscates content; H. Gillis, "The ethical Basis of Isocratean Rhetoric," *La Parola del Passato* 24 (1969) 321-348 emphasizes Isocrates' moral commitments.

considerations. The rationale behind this bewildering array of determinants becomes clear, however, if we follow the guidelines set by Isocrates himself.

Relativism determines the general direction of Isocrates' educational theory: he proceeds toward excellence on the basis of *doxa*. Operating on this premise he consistently uses three criteria to assess the merit of a rhetorical composition. He judges the value of a speech by its style, content and purpose. While his considerations for style are rooted in his love for ornate language, his views on content and purpose are ethically oriented. In fact, Isocrates' idea of rhetorical perfection is closely related to his concept of moral excellence. The perfect orator must therefore combine both ideals in his person.

The Basis: Relativism

If we consider Isocrates' aims and methods in rhetorical instruction we find that his approach is influenced by the epistemological scepticism made prominent by Protagoras and Gorgias.[5] Like them Isocrates believed that human knowledge was limited and that knowing the right course of action in each case was "one of the impossibilities" of life.[6] Advancing his views on this subject, he commented on the relationship between *episteme*, knowledge, and *doxa*, opinion:

> "It is not in the nature of man to attain an *episteme* by the possession of which we can know positively what we should do or what we should say; in the next resort I hold that man to be wise who is able by his *doxais* to arrive in most cases at the best course."[7]

Applying this epistemology to rhetoric, Isocrates concluded that in this field as in all other human endeavours *kairos*, the feeling for the right word at the right time, was not a matter of *episteme*.[8] He realized however that this view, taken to the extreme, would prevent judgment even in the smallest matters of daily life. He therefore retreated into conceding a certain value to informed opinion and allowing that man, by observing cause and effect relationships, could arrive at a reasonably accurate assessment of a given situation. Unlike Plato he therefore accepted and in fact established *doxa* as a criterion of judgment.

Since Isocrates did not accept the idea of absolute knowledge, he attacked teachers who either claimed to have *episteme* or professed to impart such knowledge to students in the field of rhetoric. He criticized them for implying

---

[5] On the relativism of the older sophists see W.K.C. Guthrie, *History of Greek Philosophy* (Cambridge 1969), vol. III, 164-175.
[6] *Soph.* 2.
[7] *Ant.* 271.
[8] "We cannot grasp *kairoi* by means of knowledge—to determine them for each and every case is not a matter of science." (*Ant.* 184).

that rhetoric was a *tetagmene techné*, a science with definite rules for the composition of a speech.[9] Such a simplistic approach to the subject required from the student only a mechanical reproduction of pre-cast notions and did not allow for imagination and creativity which Isocrates considered essential for the attainment of rhetorical excellence. Rehearsing topics which a student was likely to encounter in his career merely provided him with materials, not with the tools to handle them. Isocrates, for his part, placed emphasis on the development of skills and stressed the importance of judgment, taste and versatility. He explained that it was certainly necessary for the student of rhetoric to have a stock of phrases and to practise them, but that such exercises were only preliminaries, stepping-stones on the way to rhetorical perfection.[10]

Isocrates' description of the process of education is marked with the terminology of relativism. "Appropriate," "suitable" and "fitting" are epithets frequently used to describe his rhetorical ideal.[11] *Kairos*, right timing and choice of words, becomes the all-important catchphrase: "good rhetoric is difficult to learn because it requires imagination and awareness of *kairos*"; "one must aim at *kairos*" in one's speech; it takes much study and exercise until students are able to gauge their speeches according to *kairoi*.[12] Lists of topics and examples are useful to the orator but his skill is demonstrated in their suitable application. Facts and figures are a source common to all orators but the good craftsman will have "the ability to make use of them, *en kairo*" and to conceive the right sentiments about them.[13]

An examination of Isocrates' own treatment of "facts" will illustrate the significance of this statement: in the *Panegyricus* he recounts the story of Adrastus and Athens' intervention on his behalf, relating that the Athenians achieved their goal by military force. In the *Panathenaicus* he offers a variation on the same episode. This time the Athenians are said to have engaged in negotiations and to have arrived at a peaceful settlement with the Thebans.[14] Isocrates considers his treatment of the topic exemplary and draws attention to the discrepancy in the two accounts ("let no one suppose that I fail to realize that I am giving a different version of the same events"). He invites the reader's praise for his discreet handling of the situation and concludes on a self-congratulatory note: "I know that on this topic I have written well and expediently."[15]

---

[9] *Soph.* 12.

[10]This criticism is set out in the *Sophists* 12-18.

[11]Consider the expressions used in *Soph.* 16: "appropriate elements," "suitable arrangement," "fitting thought"; compare *Ant.* 10: "not without reason or fitness, but with due appropriateness"; *Phil.* 110: "pertinent and in keeping with the context." On the significance of these terms for Isocrates' educational theory see H. Wersdoerfer, *Die philosophia des Isokrates im Spiegel ihrer Terminologie*, Diss. Bonn 1940, especially 18-33, 56-71.

[12]*Hel.* 11, *Panath.* 34, *Ant.* 184.

[13]*Paneg.* 9.

[14]*Paneg.* 55f, *Panath.* 168ff.

[15]*Panath.* 172.

Isocrates' practice illustrates his belief that ideas and arguments are right if they are appropriate, that their value is relative to a given situation and that a rhetorical composition must be judged on this basis. Since these elements are not subject to rules, the teacher's role is limited to *epimelos epistatesai*—the success of the student will depend on his talent, industry and experience.[16]

Isocrates' de-emphasis of rules and his restraint in describing the effectiveness of rhetorical instruction in producing a competent speaker gives him a more professional image than the common breed of sophists who advertised their services in the manner of hawkers and towncryers and displayed their skills like jugglers in a circus. Yet neither party can lay claim to philosophical integrity. Isocrates used relativism to support his cautious nature and his feelings of ambivalence, the sophists employed it to dazzle the unskilled.

Criteria of Evaluation:
Purpose, Style and Content of the Ideal Speech

Epistemological scepticism forms the basis of Isocrates' approach to rhetoric. To evaluate the quality of a composition he employs three criteria: purpose, style and content. If we reduce his remarks to the essentials we can assign a pair of alternatives to each criterion. The purpose of a speech is either pleasure or profit; the style is unadorned or elaborate; the subject trifling or important. Isocrates combines these criteria in his definition of ideal rhetoric in the *Panegyricus*. The highest kind of oratory is that

> "which is concerned with the greatest affairs and, while best displaying the ability of those who speak, brings most profit to those who hear it."[17]

The ideal speech therefore meets three demands: it is composed in a lofty style which will be a credit to the orator; it deals with a worthy subject; and it benefits the audience. This particular combination of criteria recurs in the *Antidosis* where Isocrates defends his profession and promotes his rhetorical ideal. Again he lists as determinants of a good composition purpose, style and content. First he expresses disapproval of certain forms of rhetoric "because they profit no one", next he demands that the subject be "great and honourable, devoted to the welfare of man and our common good", and finally he requires that the orator demonstrate his "dexterity and love of language".[18]

In the *Panathenaicus* he adopts a similar platform, urging his audience to develop a taste for speeches which are composed

---

[16]*Ant.* 186 and ff. For Isocrates' views on the respective roles of teacher and student in the educational process see E. Rummel, "The effective teacher and the successful student," *Classical News & Views* 21 (1977) 92-96.

[17]*Paneg.* 4.

[18]*Ant.* 269, 276, 296.

"for instruction and with finished style, to prefer them to others which are written for display or for the law-courts; . . . speeches that aim at the truth to those which seek to lead astray the opinions of the hearers; discourses which rebuke our faults and admonish us to those which are spoken for our pleasure and gratification."[19]

In this characterization of the good speech Isocrates touches on style, yet rejects the idea of *epideixis* as an aim in itself. The orator must have a higher purpose than the mere gratification of his listeners, he must aim at their improvement as well. The best kind of oratory is not concerned with private matters, but deals with the conduct of public affairs.

A student whose literary criticism Isocrates invites,[20] dutifully applies his master's criteria to the *Panathenaicus*. He praises it as being

"packed with history and philosophy (content); full of embellishments and fictions (style); not the kind which, used with evil intent, are wont to injure one's fellow citizens, but the kind which, used by cultivated minds, are able to benefit or delight one's audience (purpose)."[21]

This rather flattering description is related by Isocrates with more pride than modesty. Needless to say, he regarded his own speeches as models of rhetorical perfection, worthy in subject, pleasing in style and beneficial in content.

When we examine Isocrates' views on each of these criteria separately, we find a certain ranking among them. Generally, form is subordinated to content. Content is closely related to purpose, for only a worthy subject can profit the audience. How successful the orator is in fulfilling his purpose is measured in practical terms—his words ought to have an impact on his audience, his ideas should carry beyond the last applause. The profit which the good orator promises his readers is defined in moral terms and the equation of virtue with advantage is proclaimed with almost Socratic zeal.

Style

Isocrates expected the accomplished orator to be, among other things, a good craftsman and to offer his audience a carefully finished product. He himself took pride in "the hours he had devoted to his speech"[22] and showed no appreciation for extempore speaking. In his opinion the good orator ought to smooth out and polish his speech until the arguments are well-ordered, the sentence structure harmonious and the phrases agreeable and melodious. Plain

---

[19]*Panath.* 271.
[20]Compare *Phil.* 7 and 23. For the practice of soliciting criticism and conducting discussions on works in progress see R. Johnson, "Isocrates' methods of teaching," *AJP* 80 (1959) 31 f.
[21]*Panath.* 246.
[22]*Paneg.* 14, compare *Panath.* 2.

language and a straightforward presentation of thought held no appeal for
Isocrates who expected the ideal orator to present a sophisticated image and
to offer an elaborate composition.[23]

Style was important to Isocrates because he believed that it played a
supportive role in persuading the audience, that rhythm and harmony had the
power of *psychagogia*. Although rhythmic and melodious expressions are
more typically associated with poetry, the orator too can make use of them
and imitate the devices of the poets as far as his genre allows. The most
effective speech is the one that is "poetic and imaginative", "similar to works
composed in metre and set to music." The good orator therefore challenges
the poet and enters into his domain:

> "We must see if it is possible in prose to eulogize good men in no
> worse fashion than the encomiasts do who employ song and verse."[24]

For this idea Isocrates is indebted to his teacher Gorgias who first
introduced a poetic element into rhetorical prose and whose speeches were
famous for their pompous and ornate diction. This trend is continued by
Isocrates, though in a more moderate fashion. His euphony, rhythm and
elaborate period structure are in the Gorgian tradition, but he approaches
poetic diction without repeating the excesses of his master.[25]

Despite his concern for the formal appearance of an oration, Isocrates
was prepared to sacrifice form to content and to neglect stylistic principles if
the context required it. Thus he justified a digression in the *Panathenaicus* in
the following manner:

> "I thought that I should be applauded by the most cultivated of
> my hearers if I could show that I was more concerned, when
> discoursing on the subject of virtue, about doing justice to the theme
> than about the symmetry of the speech."[26]

It appears therefore that style, though an important aspect in judging the
quality of a speech, occupied a lower rank in the hierarchy of Isocrates'
criteria than content and subject matter.

Content

In the *Helen* Isocrates draws a general distinction between grand and
lowly subjects. In the latter category he places epideictic speeches on trifling
and insignificant topics such as "praise of bumblebees or salt", paradoxical

---

[23]Cf. *Ant.* 47, *Panath.* 271f, *Soph.* 16. He singled out court oratory as being disagreeably plain—see
Panath. 1, *Paneg.* 11.
[24]*Ant.* 47, *Euag.* 11.
[25]For Isocrates' indebtedness to Gorgias and the general characteristics of his style see G. Kennedy, *The
Art of Persuasion in Greece* (Princeton 1963) 64ff., J.F. Dobson, *The Greek Orators* (New York 1967)
129ff.
[26]*Panath.* 86.

subjects like eulogies of poverty and exile, philosophical speculation and eristic disputation.[27] Anyone, he contends, can lower himself to the level of these compositions, but it is doubtful if the orator who addresses himself to ignoble topics can also do justice to worthy themes such as the right course of action for a city or the right conduct for an individual, in short topics dealing with "great and noble themes".[28]

Most of Isocrates' own speeches are indeed on subjects of general importance and deal with noble themes such as Athens' position in the Greek world, peaceful coexistence of city-states, the nature of education, the responsibilities of the ruler toward his subjects. Yet, Isocrates too may be accused of writing *peri tapeinon* in his encomia, in particular those in praise of Helen and Busiris. In fact he concedes that the *Busiris* is not "serious and does not call for a dignified style".[29] Nevertheless he strives to give even this oration a grave character: flaunting tradition he makes Busiris a moral hero, one of the "founders of noble pursuits," and snubs other authors for dwelling on the less edifying aspects of Busiris' career.[30]

In the *Helen*, too, he expresses a specific interest in the moral potential of his topic. For instance, he dwells on Helen's physical beauty and divine parentage, but immediately puts these qualities in perspective contending that Paris chose Helen "not with a view to pleasure" but because he realized that he would gain a noble ancestor for his children.[31] He also takes the opportunity to praise another suitor of Helen, Theseus, and to elaborate on his virtues, his excellence of mind, qualities of leadership, equitable disposition and sense of justice. He excuses this digression with the argument that no greater praise could be accorded to Helen than to show that she was admired by a man of excellence.[32] This is, of course, only a formal justification—the true reason for Isocrates' digression is his preoccupation with ethics and his emphasis on the didactic element of a speech.

The eulogy of Euagoras has the same moralizing tone. Indeed Isocrates terms it a "protreptic speech" rather than an encomium and states specifically that he chose his topic so "that the younger generation might with greater emulation strive for virtue" and imitate the qualities portrayed in his discourse.[33] By giving his eulogy an ethical dimension Isocrates succeeds in adding a measure of dignity to an otherwise perfunctory composition.

---

[27]*Hel.* 13; the whole section of *Hel.* 1-13 is concerned with the question of content.

[28]*Panath.* 11.

[29]*Bus.* 9.

[30]Isocrates disregards traditional mythology and proclaims that the gods and their offsprings "are by nature endorsed with all the virtues and have become for all mankind guides and teachers of the most noble pursuits" (*Bus.* 41). He criticizes other authors who do not provide this kind of moral censorship (*Bus.* 38-43).

[31]*Hel.* 42. He also introduces a political motif, using his topic to support Panhellenism. For this element see G. Kennedy, "Isocrates' Encomium of Helen: A Panhellenic Document," *TAPA* 89 (1958) 77-83.

[32]*Hel.* 22.

[33]*Euag.* 5. In *Euagoras* 76 Isocrates calls the oration a *paraklesis*; for his protreptic purpose see also J. Sykutris, "Isocrates' Euagoras," *Hermes* 62 (1927) 24-53.

The subject matter of an oration is closely related to its purpose, for arguments are proposed with a certain goal in mind and presented in a manner that will serve the ends of the author.

Purpose

Discussing the desired effects of a speech Isocrates praises the speaker who pursues a practical goal in his discourse. He contrasts him to the orator who simply wishes to impress his audience with his skills or please them with gratifying words. Rejecting *epideixis* as an aim in itself, Isocrates lauds the man "who wishes to accomplish something as well."[34] This remark occurs in the *Panegyricus*, a most unlikely platform for condemning epideictic speeches, since Panegyric orations were, by tradition, display pieces delivered on the occasion of public festivals. Isocrates' statement makes it clear that he is using an old theme for a new purpose. He fully expects his message to be translated into action and his words to be realized in deed. He therefore concludes this speech with another appeal to his audience to carry out his advice and an exhortation to fellow-orators to follow his example and to compose speeches with a view to making a practical impact. The orator's ideas ought to be such that "if carried out . . . they will be a credit to the speaker as a source of great blessings."[35] It is therefore important that an oration is timely and that the moment of action has not passed—in short, that the orator's words are not merely of academic interest but "foreshadow the future."[36]

Isocrates' remarks on this subject are rooted in his ideal of the all-round man. He found this ideal realized in the person of his favourite pupil Timotheus who, having passed through Isocrates' school, became a prominent general and politician.[37] Homer's "speaker of words and doer of deeds" is also Isocrates' hero. He wants the good orator to be as effective as he is accomplished and mocks the onesidedness of rhetoricians who are versed in the art of discourse only—who can spot contradictions in argument, but not inconsistencies in deed.[38] He criticizes teachers who aim only at perfection in rhetoric. In his opinion the sophists ought not only to teach political theory, but also "give a practical demonstration of their knowledge."[39] Now, Isocrates could hardly lay claim to this achievement himself, as he shied away from public life and considered himself unsuitable for a political career,[40] yet he displayed an air of superiority. He argued that he had compensated for his shortcomings by urging on others and by having sought out a champion for

---

[34] *Paneg.* 17, compare *Peace* 5.
[35] *Paneg.* 189.
[36] *Paneg.* 5, 171; compare *Phil.* 7.
[37] See his eulogy of Timotheus in *Ant.* 107-138.
[38] *Soph.* 7.
[39] *Hel.* 9.
[40] *Phil.* 81f., *Panath.* 9f.

his ideas "who was able to speak as well as act." He had therefore done his duty by proxy.[41]

The practical goal of every symbouleutic speech is the profit or advantage of the audience. Claims that the orator's proposals are advantageous therefore occur regularly in the *exordia* of political speeches and constitute an integral part of their argumentation.[42] However, Isocrates differed from the majority of political advisors in his ethically oriented definition of advantage. He emphasized that it was by morally correct counsel that the orator benefitted his audience most. He stressed this point in his own speeches, particularly in the *Peace* and the *Areopagiticus*[43] where he defended his proposals not only as being expedient, but also as representing the just course of action. He emphasized this aspect of his writings in the *Antidosis* where he reviewed his career as orator and claimed that "all his speeches tended toward virtue and justice."[44] In the same speech he defined the nature of advantage thus:

> "Those are better off now and will receive the advantage in the future at the hands of the gods who are the most righteous and the most faithful in their devotions and those receive the better portion at the hands of men who are the most conscientious in their dealings with their associates."[45]

Morally correct advice profits not only the orator's audience but also the speaker himself. Isocrates believes that the good orator derives personal benefits from his skills through the good impression which his *ethos* makes on his audience and the climate of goodwill which it creates.[46] Apart from this popularity and the practical advantages associated with it, the good orator is rewarded by fame. He is "held in high esteem in every society and at all times."[47] His work brings him immortality, an ambition which Isocrates himself expresses in the *Antidosis*:

> "I hoped that this would serve as an image of my ideas . . . and that I would leave behind a monument after my death, more noble than statues of bronze."[48]

At a time when the sophists were denounced as self-seeking and commercially minded, Isocrates could not propound the idea of self-interest without qualifications. He therefore compared moral with rhetorical

---

[41]*Phil.* 13. Disillusioned with Athenian politics ("to address a crowd is to address no one at all"—*Phil.* 12) Isocrates turned to Philip in whom he saw the strong leader needed at the time.

[42]Cf. Anaximenes 29.4, Aristotle *Rhet.* 1451b 13; on the common nature of this claim see J. Martin, *Antike Rhetorik* (Munich 1974) 171ff.

[43]Cf. *Peace* 136-171; for a picture of the just society see *Areop.* 31-35.

[44]*Ant.* 67.

[45]*Ant.* 282.

[46]Cf. *Ant.* 122; good character earns *eunoia*; also compare *Peace* 139f. where justice is said to produce *eunoia* in one's associates.

[47]*Ant.* 48.

[48]*Ant.* 7, compare *Euag.* 73. This idea is of course a commonplace in poetry through the ages.

excellence, explaining that they engendered similar benefits and that it would be strange if the public "blamed men who were ambitious to speak well, but applauded men who desired to act rightly." There was no reason to reject any practical advantages connected with either pursuit or to condemn "any means by which one may gain advantage without losing sight of virtue."[49] And since Isocrates defined advantage as being in accord with virtue, he did not consider self-interest an ignoble aim in rhetoric.

The Equation of Rhetorical Excellence
with Moral Goodness

Isocrates frequently suggests a proximity of the ideals of moral and rhetorical excellence. We find this view rooted in his ideas on the effect of words on the soul. Isocrates assigned a double role to speech, contending that it affected not only the hearer but also the speaker himself, shaping the views of the audience by persuasion and moulding the orator's character by habituation.

Isocrates' ideas on this subject represent a psychological theory of literature which was being formulated at the time.[50] An awareness of the interaction between *logos* and *psyche* had of course existed before and the image of words as charms or drugs has a long tradition in Greek literature. The effect of words was perceived either as negative, beguiling the soul and leading it astray, or as therapeutic, curing the soul of its ills and correcting its faults.[51]

Isocrates employs the positive notion of words as drugs, healing the soul and freeing it from evil. He expresses this idea in the *Peace* asserting that "there exists no better *pharmakon* for souls when they are ignorant of the truth and filled with base desires than *logos* to boldly rebuke its sins."[52] He uses a similar idea elsewhere, likening education to medicine and comparing its effects on the soul to that of *pharmaka* on the body.[53]

The healing and corrective power of the word does not only affect the audience who listens to the orator's counsel, but also the orator himself. Isocrates believed that the man who dwelt on morally correct advice became accustomed to the ideals which he proclaimed and would therefore practise them in his own life. Consequently he advised Nicocles to speak of noble and

---

[49] *Nic.* 2.
[50] On this development see Ch. Segal, "Gorgias and the Psychology of the Logos," *HSPh* 66 (1962) 99-155.
[51] The quasi-magical effects of words were already acknowledged by Homer who called them *thelkteria* (*Od.* 1.337, compare Pindar, *Pyth.* 4.217, Gorgias *Hel.* 8-10 etc.). Hesiod (*Theog.* 27f.) emphasized the deceptive quality of the word, but words were also likened to drugs. Thus the sophist Antiphon set up a "clinic" in Athens to heal "depressed people by means of words"! (fr. A6 D.-K.) On the whole motif in literature see L. P. Entralgo, *The Therapy of the Word in Classical Antiquity* (New Haven 1970); J. de Romilly, *Magic and Rhetoric in Ancient Greece* (Cambridge 1975).
[52] *Peace* 39f.
[53] *Bus.* 22.

honourable topics "that your thoughts may through habit become to be like your words."[54] He repeated this idea in the *Antidosis* where he claimed that the orator who spoke on edifying subjects and praised great men "habituated himself to contemplate and appraise such examples." A discourse therefore not only directed the views of the audience but also influenced the orator's life. Approached with "a love of wisdom and a love of honour" the art of rhetoric would teach the acolyte both "how to think right and how to speak well."[55]

The mental connection between rhetorical and moral excellence is carried over into Isocrates' language and vocabulary, so that he shows a preference for terms which can operate equally well in either sphere of reference.[56] A passage in his address to Nicocles affords a particularly striking example of this fusion of ideas. Its terminology is equally meaningful in ethics as in literary criticism.

> "Try to be *asteios* as well as *semnos* . . . yet no admonition is so difficult to carry out as this; for you will find that for the most part those who affect dignity are *psychrous* while those who desire to be urbane are *tapeinous*. But you should try to combine both *ideais* and avoid the danger that attaches to each."[57]

The passage refers to conduct, but if read out of context may well be taken as pertaining to style. The young king is being counselled to be neither vulgar nor aloof (*tapeinos, psychros*), for it is easy to fall into these extremes when one attempts to be urbane and dignified (*asteios, semnos*). The adjectives *psychros, tapeinos* and *semnos*[58] are commonly used to characterize style and the term *idea* (in this passage: life style) is familiar in the meaning of "elements of speech."[59]

Isocrates' preference for words with a double meaning suggests that in his mind he equated the good orator with the good man. And the use of words which are equally applicable to moral advice and to literary criticism prompts such an association in the reader's mind. A similar effect is produced by a juxtaposition of the two ideals in context.

In the *Sophists*, for instance, Isocrates states that the education which he proposes leads to an improvement in both areas. In fact, his instruction will direct the student "toward probity more often than toward rhetorical skill."[60] In the *Antidosis* a similar interchange of themes takes place. Isocrates asserts that speech helps us to distinguish between "good and bad, just and unjust"

---

[54]*Ad Nic.* 38.
[55]*Ant.* 277, compare Aristotle *E.N.* 1103 a 17, Anon. Iambl. 5.2.
[56]This has also been observed by Wersdoerfer, *op. cit.* 127.
[57]*Ad Nic.* 34.
[58]*Psychros*: Aristotle *Rhet.* 1406a 18; *tapeinos*: ibid. 1408a 19; *asteios*: Anaximenes 2.2.
[59]*Idea* is used in the sense of "element of a speech" by Aristotle *Rhet.* 1379a 13, Anaximenes 2.1, 3.8.
[60]*Soph.* 21.

and that to speak well is a sign of *psyche agathe*.[61] In other words, speech can function as the basis of judgment. Isocrates states specifically that the power of judgment acquired through rhetorical practice rests on "a principle applicable to all other matter," in particular to human conduct and the questions "what kind of reputation you should set your heart on and which kind of honour you should be content with."[62] Of course it does not automatically follow that the good orator is also a good man, but at least he has been given the tools to work with. Isocrates concedes that the study of rhetoric cannot "implant sobriety and justice in depraved souls" but he assures his readers that it "can help more than any other discipline to stimulate and form these qualities."[63] Interweaving these topics Isocrates manages to obscure the dividing line between moral and rhetorical ideals and invites the reader to accept his claim that *eu phronein* and *eu legein* are both products of rhetorical instruction.[64]

The central position of this idea in Isocrates' theories determines the ranking among the criteria by which he judges the merits of a speech. We have seen that rules of composition must yield to ethical considerations, that the subject of a speech is ennobled or debased depending on its moral direction. Motivation therefore becomes the predominant factor in evaluating an orator's performance. Thus Isocrates' ideal, though many-faceted is yet clearly structured: given that any judgment must be based on *doxa*, the ideal speech is characterized by a moral purpose, a subject which can suitably convey this purpose and act as its carrier, and by a style that lends support to the arguments by giving them esthetic appeal.

In his definition of rhetorical excellence Isocrates emerges as an eclectic who takes from the sophistic movement his epistemological scepticism, from Gorgias his notion of poetic style, from tradition his staid morality, from the common man his emphasis on practical success. What raises Isocrates above the crowd of unscrupulous teachers of rhetoric is his willingness to assume moral responsibility and to consider the ethics of persuasion. His conscientious approach to rhetoric and his understanding of the powers as well as the limitations of the instructor also make him a respectable figure among the sophists of his time. It is perhaps this element of moral concern that earned him a place among the *hetairoi* of Socrates and prompted Plato to concede him a *philosophia tis*.[65]

---

[61]*Ant.* 254f., compare ibid. 271.
[62]*Ep.* 6.8-9.
[63]*Soph.* 21, compare *Ant.* 274f.
[64]See above note 55.
[65]*Phaedrus* 279 A-B. Although the remark carries the notion of an unfulfilled prophesy and speaks of potential rather than realization it does at any rate concede special status to Isocrates among the speech-writers.

Section 5:
Aristotelian Rhetorical Theory

The Intention of Aristotle's 'Rhetoric'

by Carnes Lord

At a time when Thomas Hobbes had decided that Aristotle was »the worst teacher that ever was«, he could still say: »but his rhetorique and discourse of animals was rare«[1]. It may be doubted whether many today would agree with this judgment. In spite of the fact that the authority of Aristotle carries greater weight in the contemporary study of rhetoric than in any other current academic discipline, his 'Rhetoric' is little read today by non-specialists, and it has been neglected to a remarkable degree by those interested in Aristotle's thought generally or in the history of moral and political ideas in antiquity[2]. This neglect certainly has something to do with the low estate of rhetoric in the contemporary world. Yet it also derives in part from a very generally shared view of the 'Rhetoric' as a compendium of rhetorical materials and techniques loosely framed by a theory of the nature of rhetoric which is in the last analysis unrealistic or incoherent or both. To the extent that the 'Rhetoric' is regarded as a practical handbook of rhetorical techniques, it is seen as beneath philosophic concern; to the extent that it is regarded as theory, it is measured against the Platonic discussions of rhetoric or against Aristotle's own ethical and political works and found wanting.

This view has not gone entirely unchallenged. William Grimaldi has insisted on the necessity of treating the 'Rhetoric' as 'philosophy' and as an integral part of Aristotle's larger theoretical or philosophic enterprise. For him, »the object of Aristotle's treatise on rhetoric is ultimately an analysis of the nature of human discourse in all areas of knowledge«; and he believes that Aristotle succeeds in reconciling apparent tensions within the theory of

Reprinted from *Hermes* 109 (1981): 326-339. Used by permission of Franz Steiner Verlag, Stuttgart, publishers.

[1] John Aubrey, *Brief Lives*, ed. A. Clark (Oxford 1898) I, 357.

[2] No modern work has yet replaced the monumental if diffuse commentary of E. M. Cope, *The 'Rhetoric' of Aristotle* (Cambridge 1877). But a new edition of the 'Rhetoric', based on a thorough reexamination of the manuscript tradition, has recently appeared (R. Kassel, *Aristotelis Ars Rhetorica* [Berlin 1976], with 'Der Text der aristotelischen Rhetorik' [Berlin 1971]); and there are other signs that the situation may now be changing. See particularly A. Hellwig, *Untersuchungen zur Theorie der Rhetorik bei Platon und Aristoteles*, Hypomnemata 38 (Göttingen 1973), with the bibliography given there (11-17); also J. De Romilly, *Magic and Rhetoric in Ancient Greece* (Cambridge, Mass. 1975) 47-75. The standard history of Greek rhetoric and rhetorical theory is that of George Kennedy, *The Art of Persuasion in Greece* (Princeton 1963). For the place of Aristotle in recent discussions of rhetoric see, for example, *Contemporary Theories of Rhetoric*, ed. Richard L. Johannesen (New York 1971), especially 18-49.

rhetoric itself and between the theory and its practical applications[3]. But apart from the fact that Grimaldi makes larger claims for this interpretation than his narrowly focused study (which is concerned almost entirely with Aristotle's understanding of the enthymeme and related technical questions) can readily support, he does not succeed in clarifying the sense in which the 'Rhetoric' can or must be understood as a work of philosophy in any tolerably precise meaning of that term. As a result, he never adequately accounts for the peculiarly hybrid character of the 'Rhetoric' as at once a theoretical treatise and a practical handbook, and he tends to lose sight of the fact that rhetoric as a whole is treated by Aristotle himself not as a form of philosophy or science strictly speaking but as an 'art' (technê) or 'capacity' (dynamis) directed to the satisfaction of certain human needs. Above all, he loses sight of the fact that rhetoric for Aristotle is not a pursuit of purely theoretical interest but rather one of the highest practical importance for the governance of republican political orders.

Why did Aristotle write a 'Rhetoric'? This question is so elementary that it is rarely asked; yet the answer is by no means self-evident. It is not sufficient to say that the subject interested him. Aristotle was not in the habit of producing technical treatises or handbooks. Of the extant or attested works of the Aristotelian corpus which can be said with some assurance to be genuine, only the 'Rhetoric' and the 'Poetics' can claim to be concerned with 'arts' in some commonly accepted sense of the term. It cannot be accidental that rhetoric and poetry are precisely the arts or pursuits that had been criticized by Plato as the most powerful and dangerous intellectual competitors of philosophy in the education of political men. Regardless of the exact nature of Aristotle's relationship to Plato's attacks on rhetoric in the 'Gorgias' and the 'Phaedrus' and on poetry in the 'Republic', it seems highly probable that his preoccupation with these two arts reflects a view of their practical significance which is not very different from the view of Plato. The fact that Aristotle undertook to teach rhetoric while still a member of the Platonic Academy cannot be plausibly explained with reference merely to a personal rivalry with Isocrates[4]. It almost certainly reflected a recognition by Plato and his pupil of the strength of the influence of the rhetorically-dominated education championed by Isocrates and the sophists and the dangers it posed both for philosophy and for politics, and of the need to provide an alternative education in rhetoric for political men that would be less subject to these dangers[5].

---

[3] William M. A. Grimaldi, "Studies in the Philosophy of Aristotle's 'Rhetoric'", Hermes Einzelschriften 25 (Wiesbaden 1972) 1, 15-17 and passim. See also Antonio Russo, La filosofia della retorica in Aristotele (Naples 1962).

[4] Aristotle is supposed to have justified his lectures on this subject with the remark (parodying a line of Euripides): »It is base to remain silent and let Isocrates speak.« See Diogenes Laertius V. 3, Cicero 'De Oratore' III. 35, 141, Quintilian III. 1, 14.

[5] The fullest source for Aristotle's early rhetorical teaching is the hostile account of Philodemus' 'On Rhetoric' (Volumina Rhetorica, ed. S. Sudhaus [Leipzig 1896] II, 50-64). Aristotle's lectures on rhetoric are said to have been given in the afternoon along with others that were intended for the

If Aristotle's preoccupation with rhetoric in his early years was in some measure practically motivated, does it not make sense to assume that the same is true of the definitive version of his rhetorical doctrines composed during his final period in Athens? Or had Aristotle's reaction against his intellectual heritage proceeded by then to the point that he had become indifferent to these Platonic quarrels—or, indeed, had in the decisive respects joined the enemy camp? The latter, at any rate, is the widely accepted interpretation of the 'Rhetoric' first proposed by Friedrich Solmsen in the wake of Werner Jaeger's hypothetical reconstruction of Aristotle's intellectual development[6]. More precisely, Solmsen argues that the 'Rhetoric' actually represents an amalgam of writings from both periods of Aristotle's activity in Athens, though with a preponderance of material from the later period—and that the fact of amalgamation sufficiently explains the apparent doctrinal inconsistencies which have troubled many readers of Aristotle's treatise.

I agree with Grimaldi against Solmsen that Aristotle's treatise is fundamentally coherent in doctrine and unified in structure. Yet I believe that the only way to show this in convincing fashion is by acknowledging rather than denying the existence of the anomalies and apparent inconsistencies in Aristotle's argument, and by showing that they are consistent with the intention informing the work as a whole. I shall suggest that Aristotle's argument can only be properly understood by assuming that the 'Rhetoric' is above all a practical book guided by a practical intention, or that the 'Rhetoric' is concerned less to elaborate a satisfactory theory of the nature of rhetoric than to effect a transformation of contemporary attitudes toward rhetoric. And I shall try to show that this transformation, so far from involving a radical break with the Platonic analysis of rhetoric, rather presupposes the essential correctness of that analysis.

I.

The Socrates of Plato's 'Gorgias' had criticized rhetoric on two grounds: it is not a true 'art' based on knowledge and capable of giving a reasoned account of its own operation, but merely a certain facility deriving from familiarity and experience—a 'knack' (*tribê*); and it is not directed toward improving those with whom it deals, but merely toward pleasing or flattering them to the ultimate advantage of the speaker. Rhetoric and sophistry are sham arts which together tend or attempt to usurp the place of the true art of

---

public as distinguished from students of the school (Quintilian III. 1, 14; cf. Aulus Gellius XX. 5 and W. Wieland, "Aristoteles als Rhetoriker und die exoterischen Schriften," *Hermes* 86 [1958] 323-346). See generally A.-H. Chroust, *Aristotle* (London 1973) I. 105-116.

[6] F. Solmsen, *Die Entwicklung der aristotelischen Logik und Rhetorik* (Berlin 1929). Kennedy (82-83) accepts Solmsen's general thesis as 'certain'; but consider the detailed criticisms of R. Tessmer, "Untersuchungen zur aristotelischen Rhetorik" (Diss. Berlin 1957). Older discussions of the composition of the 'Rhetoric' have been collected in *Rhetorika: Schriften zur aristotelischen und hellenistischen Rhetorik*, ed. R. Stark (Hildesheim 1968).

politics[7]. In the 'Phaedrus', however, Plato had appeared to be open to the possibility of an improved rhetoric which would not be exposed to such objections. A true art of rhetoric, Plato there suggests, would be one based on genuine knowledge of the matters it is concerned with rather than mere familiarity with 'the probable' (*to eikos*) as understood by the ignorant multitude; in addition, it would have available a knowledge of the human soul which would enable it to persuade more effectively, and perhaps also to serve as an instrument of moral improvement rather than of mere flattery[8].

The very fact that Aristotle appears to acknowledge that rhetoric is or can be an art in the strict sense of the term is frequently taken as showing that he has already broken with the Platonic view in the decisive respect. How one ought to read the account of rhetoric provided by Socrates in the context of the highly polemical discussion of the 'Gorgias' is not a question that can be taken up here[9]; but it is too often forgotten that the Plato of the 'Phaedrus' appears much more inclined to entertain the claim of rhetoric or of the right kind of rhetoric to be considered an art[10]. As regards the second of Plato's criticisms, it is usually held that one of Aristotle's primary concerns in the 'Rhetoric' is to vindicate rhetoric as a morally and politically respectable pursuit. »Rhetoric is a counterpart to dialectic«, Aristotle tells us at the very beginning of the book. Rhetoric is evidently not, as Plato had seemed to suggest, a 'counterpart' to sophistry[11]: not an unscrupulous appeal to the passions and the uninformed opinions of the mass but the reasoned presentation of reasonable arguments appears to be the core of rhetoric as Aristotle understands it. Characteristically, Aristotle rejects the definition of rhetoric as the 'artificer of persuasion' that was associated with Isocrates and the sophists. For Aristotle, the proper 'function' (*ergon*) of an art of rhetoric is not to persuade but to »see the available means of persuasion in each instance« (*idein ta hyparchonta pithana peri hekaston*, 1355b 10-11). Rhetoric

---

[7] 'Gorgias' 463a-465e.

[8] 'Phaedrus' 269a-274b (the suggestion that rhetoric can inculcate 'virtue' occurs at 270b 7-9). On Plato's view generally see Hellwig 24-42, 72-105.

[9] Consider the interpretation offered by Quintilian (II. 15, 23-32).

[10] At the same time, it should perhaps not be too quickly assumed that rhetoric is simply an art for Aristotle. According to Quintilian (II. 17, 14 = Aristotle fr. 69 Rose), Aristotle argued against the view that rhetoric is an art in the dialogue 'On Rhetoric or Gryllos', which was apparently composed at the time that he was lecturing on rhetoric in the Academy (see the account of Chroust, II. 29-42). In the 'Rhetoric' itself, Aristotle limits himself to the remark that »it is possible to examine the cause of people succeeding through familiarity or chance« in speaking persuasively, »and all would agree this is the work of an art« (1354a 9-11). But he does not say that the causes of persuasive speech are uniformly susceptible to being taught as an art, and it is conceivable that the most effective causes of persuasive speech are in fact not susceptible to being so taught. In the third book, we discover that of the parts of rhetoric 'delivery' (*hypokrisis*) has »very great power« in spite of the fact that »being skilled in delivery belongs to nature and is lacking in artfulness« (1404a 15-16); and that while metaphor is the »most powerful« of the elements of style, metaphorical invention »cannot be learned from another« or is a natural talent (1405a 4-10; cf. 'Poetics' 1459a 5-8). One should at least consider the possibility that rhetoric for Aristotle is finally less an art properly speaking than a non-teachable 'knack' which derives from natural talent and 'experience' or familiarity rather than knowledge. Cf. Plato 'Phaedrus' 269d, Cicero 'De Oratore' II, 57, 232, Quintilian II. 17, 1-15, 19.

[11] 'Gorgias' 465c 4-5. At 465d 7-e1, Plato calls rhetoric the 'counterpart' (*antistrophos*) to cookery.

is to be viewed, it seems, less as a practical art than as a kind of science. What is crucial is to attain a proper understanding of the possibilities of persuasion in a given situation; whether the speech constructed in accordance with this understanding has any effect on its audience is an incidental consideration from the point of view of rhetorical art strictly speaking.

However, Aristotle's argument is not without its ambiguities. In fact, it is precisely on this fundamental point that the 'Rhetoric' is regularly charged with contradiction and incoherence. It is above all in the first chapter of the 'Rhetoric' that Aristotle stands forth as a defender of the respectability of rhetoric, in theory if not in practice. He begins by upbraiding the authors of previous handbooks of rhetoric for their failure to discuss the only truly artful part of rhetoric: »For proofs are the only artful thing (*entechnon*), the rest is supplementary; but they say nothing about enthymemes, the body of the proof, and instead concern themselves with what is outside the matter at hand; for slander and pity and anger and such passions of the soul do not concern the matter at hand, but rather the judge« (1354a 13-18).

Current rhetoricians, in their concentration on swaying their audience by appealing to the passions, have failed entirely to grasp the proper objects of the rhetorical art, and they have acted in a way that can only be described as morally and politically reprehensible. A forensic rhetoric that appeals directly to the passions of the judges is prohibited in well-governed states, and rightly so, according to Aristotle: »One ought not to pervert the judge by inducing him to feel anger or pity or fear—this is as if one were to make crooked the measure one intended to use« (1354a 21-26). The primary concern of the orator should rather be the truth of the matter under consideration, or probabilities which approach strict or scientific truth as closely as possible given the uncertainties inherent in the matters with which rhetoric deals. »For the true and what is similar to the true belong to the same capacity to see, and at the same time men are by nature sufficiently directed to the true and for the most part hit on the truth« (1355a 14-17). While the orator should be able to prove both sides of an issue, it remains the case that »the things that are true and naturally better are more susceptible to reasoned argument (*eusyllogistotera*) and more persuasive, generally speaking« (1355a 36-37).

As Aristotle proceeds, however, this picture is, to say the least, substantially qualified. In the second chapter, where he undertakes to define rhetoric again »as if from the beginning« (1355b 23-24) and to set forth the elements of the rhetorical art in a systematic way, we learn that there are three types of 'artful proofs' (*entechnoi pisteis*): those connected with the 'character' of the speaker, those involved in »disposing the hearer in a certain way« by affecting his passions, and those provided in the speech itself »through demonstrating or appearing to demonstrate«. Proofs from the character of the speaker, like the demonstrative proofs or enthymemes referred to previously, had been neglected by professional rhetoricians, Aristotle notes, in spite of the fact that »character affords, so to speak, the most decisive proof«. As for proofs from passion, Aristotle remarks only that »it is with a view to this alone that the current authors of handbooks undertake to treat the subject« (1356a 1-20). Arguments—arguments on the facts of the matter alone—are then evidently not enough. Rhetoric must indeed appeal to the passions. Indeed, rhetoric must be able to appeal to the passions in more serious and systematic fashion than had previously been the case. For as we learn in the second book of the 'Rhetoric', the study of the passions, far from being a merely ancillary element of rhetorical education, is central to it. Aristotle follows the lead of the Plato of the 'Phaedrus' in anchoring rhetoric to a systematic—though not fully theoretical—study of psychology[12].

Nor is this all. If Aristotle's concession to the passions permits one to wonder whether for him men are indeed »by nature sufficiently directed to the true«, it will later appear that the orator's audience is of such a kind as to be »incapable of surveying many things at once or of reasoning at length«, so that he is compelled for practical purposes to base his arguments immediately on »matters of common opinion« (*endoxa*, 1357a 2-13). Indeed, »the whole business of rhetoric looks toward opinion« (*holês ousês pros doxan tês pragmateias tês peri tên rhêtorikên*, 1404a 1-2): not truth but opinion—and opinion in the first instance of ordinary men or 'the many'—is the element of rhetoric. And precisely because truth or right cannot always prevail against opinion by its intrinsic persuasive force, rhetoric must admit to its arsenal, as it appears, not only arguments that are genuine conclusions from probable premises but also arguments that are only 'apparent'—that is, actually false—conclusions from such premises (1400b 34ff.; cf. 1356a 1-4, 35 - b 4). It is with every sign of repugnance that Aristotle introduces into the 'Rhetoric' the subject of 'apparent enthymemes' or rhetorical fallacies: men were justly disgusted with Protagoras' claim to be able to »make the weaker argument the stronger«, we are told, for an argument of this kind is »a lie, not a true but an apparent probability, and exists in no other art but rhetoric and eristic« (1402a 22-28). Yet he introduces it nonetheless; and if he intends expertise in proofs of this kind to be used only to expose the fallacies of less scrupulous opponents[13], it must be said that this intention is hardly communicated in an emphatic manner. In the last analysis, it would seem, rhetoric for Aristotle has at least as much in common with eristic or sophistry as it does with dialectic.

II.

What precisely is the relationship between rhetoric, dialectic and sophistry? Aristotle's most extended treatment of this question—the answer to which is by no means as clear as seems to be generally assumed—occurs at

---

[12]Aristotle's reliance on Plato in this respect is emphasized in the detailed discussion of Hellwig (178-250). That the psychological knowledge required of the student of rhetoric is not theoretical or scientific in the strict sense is, however, relatively clear: the definitions of the passions in the 'Rhetoric' are 'dialectical' definitions which are not derived from a scientific account of soul and its relation to body (compare *Rhet.* 1378a 30-32 and ff. with *De An.* 403a 16-b 16).

[13]As is assumed, for example, by Grimaldi (94-95).

several places in the first few chapters of Book I. Near the end of the first chapter, Aristotle argues that it belongs to rhetoric »to see the persuasive and the apparently persuasive, just as it is within the scope of dialectic to see the syllogism and the apparent syllogism; for sophistry is not in the capacity but in the intention [*proairesei*], the difference being that here one will be an orator whether according to the knowledge or according to the intention, while there one is a sophist according to the intention, but a dialectician not according to the intention but according to the capacity« (1355b 16-21).

Both rhetoric and dialectic properly incorporate a knowledge of forms of fallacious reasoning (the apparent enthymeme and the apparent syllogism respectively). The orator and the dialectician both possess the capacity or the knowledge to employ such reasoning; indeed, it is the ability to »prove opposites« which most clearly distinguishes rhetoric and dialectic from other arts or sciences (1355a 29-36). In the case of dialectic, the deliberate use of fallacious reasoning is sophistry, and the dialectician who so employs it by that fact is or becomes a sophist. As Aristotle makes clear elsewhere, the concern of the dialectician as dialectician is the (probable) truth. To the extent that a dialectician departs from this concern—or example, from a desire for intellectual victory—his 'intention' is no longer that of a dialectician properly speaking but rather of a sophist[14].

What, then, of the case of rhetoric? Is Aristotle's point merely the semantic one that there is no specific term to designate the sophistical orator? Is it really the case that Aristotle recognizes »a spurious fallacious branch of rhetoric, corresponding to the theory of fallacies . . . in dialectics«[15]? This would make sense if it were the case that for Aristotle »rhetorical discourse is discourse directed toward knowing« or toward »the demonstration of the true«[16]. But such a view cannot be sustained. Aristotle never loses sight of the fact that rhetoric is directed toward persuasion, or that the audience it must persuade is one that is not simply open to rational argument or to the truth. »Human nature is enslaved in many ways«[17]. For Aristotle, the human concern for the truth is obstructed or obscured by passion and by the opinions that are bred by passion. It is for this reason that the orator who employs apparent enthymemes does not cease to be an orator properly speaking. The use of fallacious reasoning is not a conspicuous part of Aristotle's art of rhetoric, but it is a part of it nevertheless. This is why Aristotle can say at a later point in Book I: »Rhetoric is composed of the science of analytic on the one hand and on the other of political science insofar as it is concerned with character, and it resembles in part dialectic and in part sophistical arguments« (1359b 9-12). Rhetoric is the 'counterpart' at once of dialectic and of sophistry.

---

[14]Consider 'Topics' 101a 25-b 4, 'Soph. El.' 165a 19-31.
[15]E. M. Cope, *An Introduction to Aristotle's 'Rhetoric'* (Cambridge 1867) 148.
[16]Grimaldi 85.
[17]'Metaph.' 982b 29-30.

[What is the ground of the difference between rhetoric and dialectic? Aristotle reveals it by implication in the passage just cited: while dialectic is genuinely universal in its subject matter, rhetoric is for practical purposes limited to the subject of politics. It is limited to the subject of politics precisely because its primary purpose is the practical one of persuading men in law courts and public assemblies. This practical purpose also determines the other salient characteristics of rhetoric. To paraphrase the interpretation of Aristotle's view that is provided by Alexander of Aphrodisias: rhetoric is political, expository and concerned with particulars, while dialectic is universal, conversational and concerned with general questions[18]. Rhetoric is the method of communication of political men. More precisely, it is the method of communication of the political elite with the political mass, 'the many'; its character is determined above all by the requirements of persuading the mass. Dialectic, on the other hand, is the method of communication of philosophers. According to Aristotle, dialectic has three uses: for intellectual training, for conversing, and for investigating the principles of the sciences[19]. One may say that dialectic is the method of communication of philosophers both with one another and with the political elite[20].

Such a view of the character and purpose of rhetoric, while not explicitly developed by Aristotle anywhere in the 'Rhetoric', appears nevertheless to be assumed by him throughout. It will have been noticed that the sophistic aspect of rhetoric is adumbrated, if not fully stated, in a passage within the first chapter. A careful reading of that chapter can leave little doubt, I think, that the view of rhetoric implied in it is essentially congruent with the view assumed throughout the rest of the 'Rhetoric'[21]. Aristotle does not maintain for long the sanguine notion that the average juror constitutes a standard of objective judgment with which the orator should not be allowed to tamper. It is rather the case that »it is easier to find one or a few sensible men who are capable of legislating and judging than many«, and that friendship, enmity and private interest frequently affect jurors or assemblymen in such a way that »they are no longer capable of discerning sufficiently what is true, but

---

[18] Alexander, 'In Top.' I pr. (CAG II² 5, 7-16 Wallies). Alexander's distinctions are not intended to be sharp ones: the orator is »particularly concerned with politics« (peri tên politikên mallon, 5, 11-12) but is not in principle restricted to politics, and may deal with subjects such as medicine, philosophy and music (4, 11-15).

[19] 'Topics' 101a 25-b 4.

[20] Aristotle indicates that the second use of dialectic applies to conversations with 'the many' ('Topics' 101a 30-34; cf. 'Rhet.' 1355a 26-29); but he appears to understand this term in contradistinction to the philosophic elite (»the wise« - cf. 'Topics' 100b 21-23) rather than to the political elite. The distinction between a 'demonstrative' class (the philosophic elite), a 'dialectical' class (the political and theological elite) and a 'rhetorical' class (the people) is prominent in Islamic Aristotelianism; see, for example, Averroes, Decisive Treatise 19-21; Müller (Medieval Political Philosophy, ed. R. Lerner and M. Mahdi [Ithaca 1972] 180-181).

[21] It may be added that Solmsen's view (213 ff.) that the first chapter is a survival of Aristotle's youthful lectures on rhetoric is in any case instrinsically implausible: Aristotle's revision of an introduction can be expected to have been the first order of business in any reworking of old material. Cf. Hellwig 107-108, who attempts to account for the 'ideal' view of rhetoric presented in this chapter as a 'Gedankenexperiment'.

their judgment is clouded by private pleasure or pain« (1354a 31-b 11). Somewhat later, Aristotle undertakes to defend the utility of rhetoric on the grounds that, »the true and the just things being by nature stronger (*kreittô*) than their opposites«, it is a matter of blame for their supporters if they do not prevail. But this is to suggest that the true and just things are not always stronger than their opposites in fact, or that there are indeed circumstances under which rhetoric must be able to »make the weaker argument the stronger«. Furthermore, it is not knowledge in the strict sense but 'common matters' (*ta koina*) which must serve as the basis for persuasion, for there are men whom it is impossible to instruct through an argument that accords with knowledge or science; these men are, it would seem, most men, or 'the many' (1355a 21-29). To repeat, rhetoric must take its bearings from probability as ordinary men conceive it, or from common opinion.

In chapter 1, Aristotle defines the function of rhetoric as »seeing the available means of persuasion in each instance«. This definition is criticized by Quintilian on the ground that it »embraces nothing other than invention, which, without delivery [*elocutio*], does not constitute oratory [*oratio*]«[22]. Aristotle himself was not unaware of this difficulty. In the third book of the 'Rhetoric', he does justice, if reluctantly, to the importance of style (*lexis*) in oratory and of delivery (*hypokrisis*) as a subdivision of style. As he puts it there, delivery in particular is rightly considered a vulgar matter: »the just thing is for the contest to be joined on the basis of the facts alone, so that everything apart from demonstration is superfluous; all the same, this has great power . . . on account of the depravity of the audience«. Because »the whole business of rhetoric looks toward opinion« or toward appearances (*pros doxan*), delivery must be made a concern of the student of rhetoric—not as a matter of right, but as a necessity (1403b 35 - 4a 8). Aristotle indicates that the importance of delivery for oratory is a relatively late development, connected with the political corruption caused, as it seems, by the gradual democratization of Greek or Athenian political life—that is, by the increasing predominance in politics of 'the many' at the expense of the educated elite[23]. Yet he does not for that reason deny delivery, or style generally, a place in the art of rhetoric as such. It is finally the 'necessity' of persuasion and nothing else which defines for Aristotle the nature of rhetoric.

The fact that the definition of rhetoric provided by Aristotle in the first

---

[22]Quintilian II. 15, 13.

[23]That the text at 'Rhet.' 1403b 34-35 indeed speaks of »the depravity of the regimes [*politeiôn*]« (the reading of the mss.) and not »the depravity of the citizens [*politôn*]« (the conjecture of Spengel, adopted by Ross) has been argued by M. Lossau, *mochthêria tôn politeiôn* und *hypokrisis*. *Zu Arist.* '*Rhet.*' 3, 1, 1403b 33 f., *RhM* 114 (1971) 146-158. It has sometimes failed to be recognized (as, for example, in the translations of J. H. Freese and of Dufour and Wartelle) that Aristotle's remark at 1403b 18-22 refers not to the argument of the 'Rhetoric' itself but to an actual historical development: in the beginning—that is, prior to the rise of extreme democracy and the coincidental development by Gorgias of a rhetorical style heavily dependent on poetry (1404a 20-28)—what was sought in oratory in the first place was »what comes first by nature, the facts themselves and how persuasiveness can be derived from them«.

several chapters of the 'Rhetoric' does not appear to leave room for the material treated in its third book has led some to argue that this book did not originally form part of the 'Rhetoric' but constituted a separate treatise[24]. It is true that Aristotle nowhere specifically indicates in the first two books of the 'Rhetoric' that he will later treat the matters discussed in the third. Yet is it so clear that the early definitions of rhetoric are in fact meant to exclude the two subdivisions of the art—style and order—discussed in the third book, as Quintilian as well as contemporary commentators seem generally to assume? Propriety of style certainly appears to be an integral element of »the available means of persuasion« by the fact that it supports or enhances the persuasiveness of the three kinds of proofs discussed in the earlier books (1408a 10-36; consider particularly 19-20 *pithanoi de to pragma kai hê oikeia lexis*).

III.

Yet all of this only begs the fundamental question. The interpretation I have offered only sharpens the tension between different elements of Aristotle's argument; what must now be done is to account for this tension. Why is Aristotle's presentation of his view of the nature of rhetoric so incompletely stated and so productive of confusion and misunderstanding?

Without wishing wholly to deny the possibility of compositional anomalies, I believe the argument of the 'Rhetoric' develops as it does fundamentally because Aristotle so intended it. I believe, in other words, that Aristotle's presentation is governed by a conscious desire to emphasize what one may call the highminded view of rhetoric, while deemphasizing as far as possible or dissociating himself from those aspects of rhetoric which he considered low and potentially dangerous, yet necessary for effective persuasion. Aristotle chooses to emphasize the logical or intellectual component of rhetoric not merely because it had been largely neglected by his predecessors, but also because he regarded such an emphasis as intellectually and politically salutary. Aristotle's initial comparison of rhetoric to dialectic is misleading or provisional not only through its silence regarding the sophistic element in rhetoric, but also through its obfuscation of the connection between rhetoric and politics. Yet the provisional assimilation of rhetoric to dialectic serves the important purpose of conferring on rhetoric a dignity capable of engaging the attention of men of intellectual and moral seriousness, and of ensuring that such men are encouraged to view rhetoric, not as an instrument of personal aggrandizement in the sophistic manner, but rather as an instrument of responsible and prudent statesmanship.

It is above all in his handling of the question of the relation between rhetoric and politics that Aristotle reveals his intention. As he gradually

---

[24]There is also some external evidence for this view: the catalogue of Aristotelian works preserved in Diogenes Laertius (V. 22ff.) seems to list our 'Rhetoric' as a work in two books, and also mentions a separate treatise 'On Style' in two books. Yet whatever the history of the third book, its authenticity and its essential congruence with the teaching of the earlier books seem no longer seriously disputed. See, for example, M. Dufour and A. Wartelle, *Aristote: 'Rhétorique'* III (Paris 1972) 5-22.

makes clear in the course of the first four chapters, the assimilation of rhetoric to dialectic is intended both to dignify rhetoric and to limit it. As soon as it emerges that rhetoric is at least as concerned with the 'proofs' deriving from the orator's character and the passions of his audience as with the facts themselves and the proofs deriving from them, Aristotle informs us that »rhetoric is a sort of offshoot of dialectic and of the study of characters, which may justly be called political science (*politikê*)«. He then adds: »It is for this reason that rhetoric and those laying claim to it adopt the dress (*hypoduetai hypo to schêma*) of political science, partly through want of education, partly through boastfulness, partly through other all-too-human causes« (1356a 25-30)[25]. This assertion becomes less surprising as we discover that rhetoric and politics have much more in common than a concern with human character and passion. For in spite of the fact that rhetoric and dialectic are initially presented as arts or pursuits uniquely lacking a specific subject matter, Aristotle makes clear that rhetoric differs from dialectic above all by its concern with political matters. That rhetoric is susceptible of being confused with political science or of usurping the place of political science is, from Aristotle's point of view, a fact of the highest importance. When Aristotle undertakes at the end of the 'Nicomachean Ethics' to lay the foundations for a science of politics, he remarks that such a science has never been elaborated or transmitted by political men, while the sophists who claim to teach it are in fact ignorant of what it is and what sorts of things it is concerned with, for otherwise »they would not have treated it as identical with rhetoric or subordinate to it, and they would not have supposed it is easy to legislate by making collections of the most renowned laws«[26]. Rhetoric as taught by the sophists is a serious and dangerous rival of political science as taught by Aristotle. Worse, by encouraging the supposition that the exercise of political responsibility is easy or requires little substantive knowledge beyond rhetorical expertise itself, rhetoric as taught by the sophists tends to make men oblivious of the very need for a science of politics.

It is in the context of this rivalry between rhetoric and political science that one must consider Aristotle's attempted resolution of the problem of the source and character of the knowledge proper to rhetorical art[27]. Fundamental to this attempt is the distinction—original with Aristotle himself, according to his own emphatic assertion (1358a 2-3)—between the 'common' and the 'specific' topics which together supply material for all rhetorical syllogisms. The common topics or 'commonplaces' belong to no single art or science; the specific topics fall within the sphere of a specific art or science such as physics or politics. The orator as orator must have a familiarity with specific topics; yet it seems he will not, and need not, possess genuine knowledge of the matters dealt with by these topics. At the same time, »in proportion as one

---

[25]The verbal and substantive echo of Plato's 'Gorgias' (464c 7-d 1 *hypodusa . . . hypedu*) has often been remarked.
[26]'Eth. Nic.' 1180b 35-81a 17.
[27]Cf. Hellwig 79-82.

is better at selecting these, he will inadvertently practice a science other than dialectic and rhetoric, for if he encounters first principles it will no longer be dialectic or rhetoric but the science which has the principles« (1358a 23-26). Somewhat later, in the course of his discussion of the subjects generally treated in deliberative rhetoric, Aristotle makes the following statement: »There is no need at present to seek to enumerate singly or accurately or to grasp in their specifics the things men are accustomed to consult about, or again to define these matters as far as possible in accordance with the truth, since this belongs not to the rhetorical art but to one that is wiser and more genuine (*emphronesteras kai mallon alêthinê*), and since much more has been granted it even now than belongs among its proper objects of study ... But in proportion as one attempts to establish this or dialectic, not as capacities but as sciences, he will inadvertently destroy their nature in thus altering them by turning them into sciences whose objects are definite things and not only arguments« (1359b 2-16).

This statement is intended to correct the fundamental sophistic error of identifying or subordinating political science to rhetoric. Not political science but rhetoric is to be the subordinate art; it is to be subordinate because it is essentially incomplete or requires supplementation by genuine knowledge of political things. Aristotle's art of rhetoric is designed to counter the tendency of sophistic rhetoric or of rhetoric simply to emancipate itself from the tutelage of political science and to absorb and finally destroy political science. Aristotle assimilates rhetoric to dialectic or to logic in order to emphasize its purely instrumental role and its substantive incompleteness, and thereby to make rhetoric safe for politics.

The ultimate intention of the 'Rhetoric' is, then, not so much to transform the practice of rhetoric as to transform the theoretical or conceptual understanding of rhetoric by political men. Aristotle is concerned above all to show rhetoric can become an instrument of political prudence or of a political science which educates to prudence. Indeed, Aristotle's art of rhetoric can afford to incorporate sophistic or morally questionable elements precisely because it is finally in the service of a political science which is centrally concerned with the education of political men in moral virtue and in that variety of prudence which is inseparable from moral virtue. In this fundamental respect, Aristotle remains, I believe, an authentic expounder of the Platonic view of the nature of rhetoric. For the fundamental issue between the sophistic and the philosophic conception of rhetoric concerns not so much the morality of rhetoric as the claim of rhetoric to the status of an autonomous art or science. If Plato and Aristotle disagree in their view of the character of that science of politics to which rhetoric must be subordinated, they are in fundamental agreement on the need for such subordination[28].

[28]The author wishes to thank the National Endowment for the Humanities and the White Burkett Miller Center of Public Affairs of the University of Virginia for generous support in the preparation of this paper.

The Place of the Enthymeme in Rhetorical Theory*

by James H. McBurney

I.

Some Introductory Considerations

Aristotle has defined rhetoric as "the faculty of discovering in the particular case what are the available means of persuasion."[1] Interpreting this definition for our purposes we may say that rhetoric is the art of discovering and using in those situations in which speaking and writing play a part, what are the most desirable means of oral and written persuasion. The term persuasion is here used in the broad sense to mean the influencing of human behavior through the use of written and oral symbols. The theory of rhetoric may be understood as the science which underlies this art, and to consist of a more or less organized system of concepts and principles, mostly philosophical and methodological in nature. These concepts and principles have been studied by countless scholars for many centuries as generalizations from examples of speaking and writing designed to improve practice in these arts.

Classical rhetoricians commonly divided their subject into five parts which they called *inventio, dispositio, elocutio, memoria,* and *pronuntiatio. Inventio,* the phase with which we shall be primarily concerned here, is the art of exploring the material to discover the lines of reasoning suitable for discussion in any given case. It includes the study of kinds and methods of reasoning, refutation, and fallacies; and is that part of rhetoric most closely related to logic. Says Clark, "In the practice of rhetoric *inventio* was thus the solidest and most important element. It included all of what today we might call 'working up the case.'"[2]

The enthymeme is a concept developed in this field of *inventio* and has

---

Reprinted from *Speech Monographs* 3 (1936): 49-74. Copyright by the Speech Communication Association. 1936. Reproduced by permission of the publisher.

*This is an abstract of a dissertation submitted in partial fulfillment of the requirements for the degree of Doctor of Philosophy in the University of Michigan. This research was done under the direction of Professors J. M. O'Neill and N. E. Nelson in the University of Michigan and continued under the provisions of a post-doctoral fellowship in Teachers College, Columbia University.

[1] Cooper, Lane, *The Rhetoric of Aristotle*, New York: D. Appleton and Company, 1932, 7. References to *The Rhetoric*, unless otherwise indicated, are taken from Professor Cooper's translation.

[2] See Clark, D. L., *Rhetoric and Poetry in the Renaissance*, New York, Columbia University Press, 1922, 27-28.

specific reference to the problem of reasoning in speaking and writing. Ever since Aristotle the term "enthymeme" has been associated in some manner or other with the syllogism, the concept adduced by Aristotle to explain the nature of all reasoning and proof.[3] For Aristotle the enthymeme was the focal concept or element of all reasoned discourse. He speaks of it as "the very body and substance of persuasion."[4] Lane Cooper asks,

> How for example shall we know what our author (Aristotle) means by the term Enthymeme? This question goes to the very heart of the *Rhetoric* since Aristotle tells us that enthymemes are the essential instruments of oratorical persuasion.[5]

J. Barthelemy Saint-Hilaire says of the Aristotelian enthymeme in an appendix on the subject included with his French translation of the *Rhetoric:*

> ... it occupies in the art of speaking essentially the place that the syllogism holds in logic. If one does not know how to make Enthymemes, he can hardly flatter himself as being an orator.[6]

It is the purpose of this study to determine the place of the enthymeme in rhetorical theory. In the way of a justification of the inquiry, if such is necessary, I invite your attention to three propositions: (1) Contemporary rhetorical theory is essentially Aristotelian; (2) the enthymeme is the focal concept in the rhetoric of Aristotle; and (3) the enthymeme is seriously misunderstood today. For good or evil, depending upon one's point of view, our ideas about reasoned discourse in speaking and writing remain essentially Aristotelian. Even those who complain against the Aristotelian influence in this field, and seek new canons for these arts, will recognize the importance of this influence and should welcome interpretations. We have Aristotle's own word for the central place of the enthymeme in his rhetorical system. The respects in which this concept has been misunderstood, while the system of which it is a part remained relatively intact, will be developed as our study progresses. Suffice it to say here that the prevailing conception of the enthymeme as an elided syllogism is not the sense in which Aristotle used this term. As Saint-Hilaire puts it:

> Aristotle attached great importance to the use of the Enthymeme, without which the art of rhetoric seemed to him almost impossible. Today the Enthymeme is relegated to a very secondary position; and

---

[3] While the term "enthymeme" was used before Aristotle by Isocrates and others to indicate rather loosely and generally the thoughts or sentiments with which a speaker embellishes his work, as a definitive logical and rhetorical concept in the sense in which we are investigating the term it originated with Aristotle. See Octave Navarre, *Essai Sur La Rhétorique Grecque Avant Aristote*, Paris, 1900, 255; Mansel, H. L., *Artis Logicae Rudimenta from the Text of Aldrich* (third ed.) Oxford, 1856, Appendix, note F, "On the Enthymeme," 216.

[4] *Rhetoric* I, 1.

[5] *Op. cit.*, xxv.

[6] Saint-Hilaire, J. Barthelemy, *Rhétorique d'Aristote*, Paris, 1870, Tome Second, 348.

this difference enables us to see the enormous interval which separates the point of view of the ancients from ours.[7]

II.

The Enthymeme in Aristotle

The works of Aristotle which set forth his logical and rhetorical system are *Categoriae, De Interpretatione, Analytica Priora, Analytica Posteriora, Topica, De Sophisticis Elenchis,* and *Rhetorica.* Aristotle is attempting in these treatises to set forth a system by which truth and certainty, in respect to human knowledge, may be ascertained and demonstrated verbally; by which truth may be sought through discourse; and by which people may be convinced and persuaded.

A. *The Enthymeme as a part of Aristotle's Logical and Rhetorical System as a Whole:* The diagram on the following page may be helpful in following the discussion in this section. It is of first importance to notice the fundamental distinction which Aristotle makes between two great provinces of knowing, that of scientific knowledge or apodeictic certainty and that of reasoning in the realm of probabilities or opinion. As Professor John Dewey puts it:

> All philosophies of the classic type have made a fixed and fundamental distinction between two realms of existence. One of these corresponds to the religious and supernatural world of popular tradition, which in its metaphysical rendering became the world of highest and ultimate reality. . . . Over against this absolute and noumenal reality which could be apprehended only by the systematic discipline of philosophy itself stood the ordinary empirical, relatively real, phenomenal world of everyday experience. It was with this world that the practical affairs and utilities of men were connected. It was to this imperfect and perishing world that matter of fact, positivistic science referred.[8]

Aristotle distinguishes three separate but related methodologies for knowing and persuading, scientific demonstration, dialectic, and rhetoric. Scientific demonstration is developed in the *Prior* and *Posterior Analytics* as the method of discovering and demonstrating truth; dialectic is explained in the *Topics* as a method of discovering what is probable truth through special forms of dialogue; and rhetoric is understood as the method of discovering what are the available means of persuasion. Both dialectic and rhetoric are differentiated from scientific demonstration in the fact that they deal with

---

[7] *Op. cit.,* 376.
[8] Dewey, John, *Reconstruction in Philosophy,* New York: Henry Holt and Company, 1920, 22-23.

probabilities and do not attempt apodeictic proof in the sense that it appears in scientific demonstration.

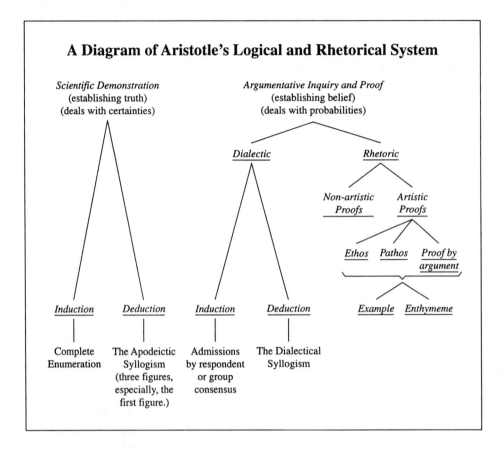

A Diagram of Aristotle's Logical and Rhetorical System

Special forms of the syllogism are explained as the methodological instrument in each of these fields and the distinction between induction and deduction introduced in each case. In the *Prior Analytics* Aristotle analyzes the several figures and modes of the syllogism, explaining the first figure as the means of scientific demonstration *par excellence*. It is the only figure in which the syllogism is perfect without conversion or reduction; it is the only figure in which every variety of conclusion can be proved; and the only one in which the universal affirmative can be proved—the great aim of scientific research.[9] While Aristotle repeatedly contrasts deduction and induction, he does take the position that induction can be reduced to the syllogism.[10] He

---

[9] See *Prior Analytics* (in *The Works of Aristotle*, vol. I, translated into the English under the editorship of W. D. Ross), Oxford: Clarendon Press, 1928, I, 4-7; also I, 14, 79ᵃ. All references to the *Prior Analytics*, *Posterior Analytics*, and *Topics* in this study are to the Ross edition, vol. I, *The Works of Aristotle*.

[10] *Prior Analytics* II, 23, 68ᵇ.

believes further that induction "proceeds through an enumeration of all the cases." In another connection Aristotle discusses induction as an intuitive process or an act of intellectual insight by which the particulars of our experience suggest to us the principles which they exemplify.[11]

The peculiar characteristic of scientific reasoning consists in its investigation of *causes* understood as *rationes essendi*, or the *reasons for the being of a fact* as distinguished from *rationes cognoscendi* or *reasons for acknowledging its being*.[12] Aristotle states:

> We suppose ourselves to possess unqualified scientific knowledge of a thing, as opposed to knowing it in the accidental way in which the sophist knows, when we think that we know the cause on which the fact depends, as the cause of that fact and of no other, and, further, that the fact could not be other than it is.[13]

> Assuming then that my thesis as to the nature of scientific knowledge is correct, the premises of demonstrated knowledge must be true, primary, immediate, better known than and prior to the conclusion, which is further related to them as effect to cause. . . . The premises must be the causes of the conclusion, better known than it, and prior to it; its causes, since we possess scientific knowledge of a thing only when we know its cause. . . .

> Where demonstration is possible, one who can give no account which includes the cause has no scientific knowledge.[13]

Dialectic constituted the art of discussion by question and answer, of attacking and defending a given thesis from principles of probability, such as the opinions of men in general, or of the majority, or of certain eminent authorities. For this purpose, Aristotle collected *topics*, or general principles of probability from which appropriate premises might be drawn. Nearly two hundred such topics are listed in his work of this name. Aristotle explains that so far as the forms and rules of the syllogism are concerned, these are alike applicable to both demonstration and dialectic. "In both the formal conditions are the same, and the conclusion will certainly be true, if the premises are true; in both the axioms of deductive reasoning are assumed," says Grote.[14] Mansel points out that Aristotle would at least regard logical or formal accuracy as "salutary" in dialectical discussion.[15]

Concerning the method of dialectic it is important to notice that Aristotle specifically recognizes its function as an agency for inquiry and investigation.

---

[11]*Posterior Analytics* II, 19, 100[b].

[12]See Joseph, H. W. B., *An Introduction to Logic* (Second edition revised), Oxford, 1916, 305.

[13]*Posterior Analytics* I, 2, 71[b] and I, 6, 74[b]. On this point see also Mansel's *Aldrich, op. cit.*, note K. "On the Demonstrative Syllogism," 241-242; Grote, George, *Aristotle* (ed. Alexander Bain and G. C. Robertson), London, 1872, vol. I, 315; and Joseph, H. W. B., *op cit.*, 398-399.

[14]Grote, George, *op. cit.*, 383.

[15]Mansel, H. L., *op. cit.*, 213.

Its purposes are listed as "intellectual training, casual encounters, and the philosophical sciences."[16] He adds that "it has a further use in relation to the ultimate bases of the principles used in the several sciences . . . for dialectic is a process of criticism wherein lies the path to the principles of all inquiries."[16] He distinguishes between dialectic as a competition and "those who discuss things together in the spirit of inquiry,"[17] and urges the importance of co-operative effort toward consensus. He states:

> The principle that a man who hinders the common business is a bad partner, clearly applies to argument as well; for in arguments as well there is a common aim in view, except with mere contestants, for these cannot both reach the same goal; for more than one cannot possibly win.[18]

Without pausing to recapitulate at this juncture, we now turn to rhetoric, which, like dialectic, is differentiated from scientific demonstration in the fact that it draws its premises from probabilities. Rhetoric is concerned primarily with long, continuous discourse both spoken and written rather than the short question and answer method of dialectic. Cope emphasizes the additional point that while theoretically rhetoric is as universal as dialectic in the field of probabilities, practically it is limited for the most part to a particular class of phenomena with which its two most important branches, the deliberative and the judicial, almost exclusively deal, namely human actions, characters, motives, and feelings; and so it becomes closely associated with the study of Politics (including Ethics) which treats of moral, social, and political phenomena, of man as an individual and as a member of society.[19]

Aristotle distinguishes two great types of rhetorical proof, *artistic* and *non-artistic*; the non-artistic proofs, roughly comparable to what contemporary writers in argumentation call 'evidence,' are explained as "such as are not supplied by our own efforts, but existed beforehand, such as witnesses, admissions under torture, written contracts, and the like."[20] "By 'artistic' proofs [means of persuasion] are meant those that may be furnished by the method of Rhetoric through our own efforts."[20] Three modes of persuasion are explained in connection with artistic proof. "The first kind reside in the character [*ethos*] of the speaker; the second consist in producing a certain [the right] attitude in the hearer; the third appertain to the argument proper, in so far as it actually or seemingly demonstrates."[20]

In rhetoric, as well as scientific demonstration and dialectic, induction and deduction are introduced as the methods of reasoning. Here, however, the term "example" is assigned to induction and the term "enthymeme" to

---

[16]*Topics* I, 2, 101ᵃ and 101ᵇ.
[17]*Ibid.* VIII, 5, 159ᵃ.
[18]*Ibid.* VIII, 11, 161ᵃ.
[19]Cope, E. M., *An Introduction to Aristotle's Rhetoric*, London: Macmillan and Co., 1867, 9.
[20]*Rhetoric* I, 2, 1355ᵇ and 1356ᵃ.

deduction. Aristotle states:

> 'Enthymeme' is the name I give to a rhetorical syllogism, 'example' to a rhetorical induction. Whenever men in speaking effect persuasion through proofs, they do so either with examples or enthymemes; they use nothing else. Accordingly, since all demonstration (as we have shown in the *Analytics*) is effected either by syllogism [that is, deductively] or by induction, it follows that induction and syllogism [deduction] must be identified respectively with example and enthymeme.[21]

In the following section we shall investigate the relations of the enthymeme to the various types of rhetorical persuasion and to the syllogisms of scientific demonstration and dialectic. Thus far, it has been our purpose to present a broad perspective of the logical and rhetorical system of which the enthymeme is a part. This larger view will be found helpful, if not indispensable, in interpreting the enthymeme. The diagram on page 172 may be taken as a summary of the present section.

B. *An examination of the Aristotelian passages in which the Enthymeme is given special treatment:* The several passages in which the enthymeme is given special treatment in Aristotle's works present six points for investigation as follows: (1) The passages in which Aristotle explains that the materials of the enthymeme are probabilities (*eikota*) and signs (*sêmeia*); (2) the passages in which Aristotle declares example to be a form of the enthymeme; (3) the passages in which he discusses the relationship of the enthymeme to the topics or *topoi*; (4) those in which we may see the relation of the enthymeme to *ethos* and *pathos*; (5) the passages in which demonstrative and refutative enthymemes are distinguished; and (6) the passages relating to the suppression of a proposition in the enthymeme.

1. *The Enthymeme and Probabilities (eikota) and signs (sêmeia):* The passages with which we are here concerned are those in the *Prior Analytics* II, 27, and the *Rhetoric* I, 2. While these passages are admittedly difficult to interpret,[22] it is my conclusion that Aristotle meant by probabilities (*eikota*) what we have previously referred to as *rationes essendi*, and by signs (*sêmeia*), *rationes cognoscendi*. We may say again that by a *ratio essendi* we mean an argument which attempts to account for the fact or principle maintained, supposing its truth granted: it assigns a cause or *a reason for the being of a fact*. The *ratio cognoscendi*, on the other hand, is *a reason for acknowledging the being of a fact;* it attempts to supply a reason which will establish the existence of a fact without any effort to explain what has caused

---

[21]*Rhetoric* I, 2, 1356ᵇ; see also *Prior Analytics* II, 23, and *Posterior Analytics* I, 1, and I, 18; also II, 19.
[22]See Ernest Havet, *De La Rhétorique D'Aristote*, Paris, 1843, 64.

it. When Aristotle defines an enthymeme as "a syllogism starting from probabilities or signs," this, then, is the distinction he appears to have in mind.

The greatest difficulty arises in understanding what Aristotle means by a probability or *eikos*. His discussion is obscure and he does not give us a complete example. From the description given, however, we can collect the following information concerning an *eikos*: (1) It is a generally approved proposition or *ôs epi to polu*;[23] (2) It is "already probable" as distinguished from a sign which "affects to be, would be if it could," *bouletai einai*;[24] (3) as the probable it bears the same relation to that of which it is probable as a universal statement to a particular; (4) it is dichotomized with sign; and (5) examples are "the envious hate" and "love attends the objects of affection."

In other words *eikos* is a proposition expressing a general principle of probability which when applied in argument does not attempt to prove the existence of a fact, but rather (assuming its existence) attempts to account for the fact. It is a *ôs epi to polu* (meaning "to happen generally and fall short of necessity") *already probable*, whose application to *particular phenomena* accounts for their probability. By supplementing the fragmentary examples which Aristotle gives us of *eikos* we can see that when one concludes that Orestes loves his mother, because "love (usually) attends the objects of affection," the argument does not attempt to prove (to give a sign) that Orestes actually does love his mother; but rather (assuming it probable that he loves his mother) attempts to account for or explain this phenomenon. Similarly with the other proposition Aristotle cites, "the envious hate"—if one concludes that John hates by virtue of the *eikos*, "the envious hate," it has not been proved that John actually does hate; but rather, assuming that he hates, it has suggested a possible cause of his hating.

Aristotle fortunately is much clearer in his definition of signs. He distinguishes three types and gives us examples of each, the certain sign in the first figure, the fallible sign in the second figure, and the "example" in the third figure.[25] He states, "a sign affects to be, would be if it could, a demonstrative proposition necessary or probable: for anything that accompanies an existing thing or fact, or precedes or follows anything that happens or comes into being, is a sign either of its existence or of its having happened." This statement is in itself an excellent definition of a *ratio cognoscendi*, and that this is in fact what Aristotle means by *sêmeion* we can conclude with considerable assurance from his three examples. His example of a certain sign (*tekmêrion*) which "bears toward the statement it is to prove the relation of a universal to a particular" and which appears in the first figure, viz. that a

---

[23] See *Prior Analytics* I, 13, 32ᵇ; also Freidrich Solmsen, "Die Entwicklung Der Aristotelischen Logik und Rhetorik" (in *Neue Philologische Untersuchungen*), Berlin, 1929, 13-14.
[24] See Cope, E. M., *op. cit.*, 161.
[25] It may be noted here that Aristotle reduces "example," or what he has previously discussed as rhetorical induction, to a form of the enthymeme just as he explains scientific induction in terms of the syllogism.

woman is with child, because she has milk, is clearly a *ratio cognoscendi* (even if the physiology is bad). The having of milk is proof of the fact that a woman *is* with child (or has recently given birth to a child), but it can hardly be construed to be the *cause* of the pregnancy or the child. The same can be said of the other examples of sign given in the *Prior Analytics* and the *Rhetoric*. Those in the second figure, concluding from the observation that a woman is pale that she is pregnant, and that a man has a fever because he breathes hard, are just as clearly cases of *rationes cognoscendi*. In these instances both "paleness" and "hard breathing" are plainly signs as distinguished from causes. The cases cited of "example" in the third figure are also good instances of signs as we have interpreted the term.

Even in the absence of conclusive affirmative evidence that Aristotle means to define *eikos* as a *ratio essendi* (and I think the evidence is fairly conclusive here), we can be reasonably safe in implying from his clear definition of sign as a *ratio cognoscendi*, that he meant so to define *eikos*; and especially is this true, since the same distinction is made in the case of the scientific syllogism as we have previously noticed.[26] An enthymeme, then, may be defined as a syllogism, drawn from probable causes, signs (certain and fallible) and examples. As a syllogism drawn from these materials, it is important to add here, the enthymeme starts from probable premises (probable in a *material sense*) and lacks *formal validity* in certain of the types explained. We shall have more to say about this later. It may also be well to notice here that the interpretation we have placed on *eikota* and *sêmeia* has an important bearing on the contemporary division of argument into antecedent probability, sign, and example.

2. *Example as a form of Enthymeme:* The second group of passages which help us to understand the enthymeme are those which explain "example" as a species of enthymeme. We have already noticed that Aristotle usually contrasts enthymeme and example, comparing the former to the syllogism and the latter to induction. We have also noted that in the *Prior Analytics* Aristotle takes the position that induction can be reduced to syllogistic form. Thus, he is altogether consistent in likewise reducing example to an enthymematic form. The passages bearing on this point are *Prior Analytics* II, 24, and *Rhetoric* II, 25. The most complete discussion of example as a form of argument without direct reference to its relation to the enthymeme is *Rhetoric* II, 20. Here Aristotle distinguishes two kinds of example, "one consisting in the mention of actual past facts, the other in the invention of facts by the speaker. Of the latter, again, there are two varieties, the illustrative parallel and the fable." The cases of example which Aristotle

---

[26]For authorities on this point see especially Richard Whately, *Elements of Rhetoric* (Reprinted from seventh edition), Louisville, Ky.: Morton and Griswold, 1854, 47; also Douglas Macleane, *Reason, Thought, and Language*, London: Oxford University Press, 1906, 418-419.

cites in this connection are instances of what we today understand as analogical reasoning. The reasoning in these cases, as is always true of analogy if analyzed completely, consists in generalizing from one or more instances and then making a deduction concerning the case in question. Aristotle says here, "Enthymemes based upon Example are those which proceed by induction from one or more similar cases, arrive at a general proposition, and then argue deductively to a particular inference."[27] In actual speaking, I might add, this "general rule" of which Aristotle speaks is rarely stated, thus giving the appearance of arguing directly from one particular case to another particular case. Aristotle recognizes this point when he states:

> Clearly then to argue by example is neither like reasoning from part to whole, nor like reasoning from whole to part, but rather reasoning from part to part, when both particulars are subordinate to the same term and one of them is known. It differs from induction, because induction starting from all the particular cases proves that the major term belongs to the middle, and does not apply the syllogistic conclusion to the minor term, whereas argument by example does make this application and does not draw its proof from all the particular cases.[28]

3. *The Enthymeme and Topics:* The passages in which Aristotle discusses the relation of the enthymeme to the *topoi* or topics are especially helpful in clarifying the relations between dialectical and rhetorical reasoning on the one hand and scientific demonstration on the other. *Topoi*, understood roughly as sources or places from which arguments may be obtained, is a conception which appears all through classical and mediaeval rhetoric. While the several lists of topics given in the *Rhetoric* are difficult to interpret,[29] it appears that Aristotle meant to distinguish three kinds of topics as indicated in the following diagram:

---

[27] *Rhetoric* II, 25, 1402[b].
[28] *Prior Analytics* II, 24, 69[a].
[29] Friedrich Solmsen, in his "Die Entwicklung Der Aristotelischen Logik und Rhetorik," *op. cit.*, argues that Aristotle's logical thought underwent a change or development and that this change may be seen in two conflicting enthymematic theories in the *Rhetoric*. The two theories which he finds conflicting are the enthymeme defined as a syllogism drawn from causes and signs, and the enthymeme developed in relation to the topics in *Rhetoric* II, 22-24. This latter topical treatment Solmsen believes to be a remnant of Aristotle's earlier logical theory; the enthymeme as a syllogism he holds to be indicative of a later development in Aristotle's logical thought. Without arguing the point here, I wish merely to say that while this development in Aristotle's logical theory does appear to have taken place, I do not find it impossible to reconcile the allegedly inconsistent theories of the enthymeme in the *Rhetoric*. I have attempted in this section to unify the references to the enthymeme in relation to the topics and the passages in which it is defined as a syllogism drawn from probable causes and signs. See also in this connection Stocks, J. L., "The composition of Aristotle's Logical Works," in the *Classical Quarterly*, vol. 27, 1933, 115-124.

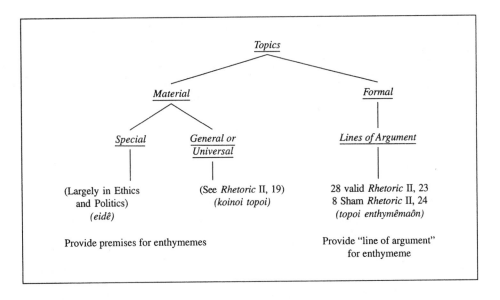

It is the distinction between special and general topics which helps to explain the relationships between the various specialized fields of knowledge and that of rhetoric and dialectic. Aristotle makes the point that the special topics may be looked upon as substantive items or propositions peculiar to the special discipline to which they belong; the general topics on the other hand, are general principles of probability, understood in a propositional sense, with application in all fields of knowledge. While he states that arguments drawn from the general topics are typically rhetorical (or dialectical, as the case may be) because of this universal application, he nevertheless makes the point that "enthymemes are mostly formed from these particular and special topics."[30] This seemingly paradoxical position may be explained as follows. Aristotle recognizes the autonomy of the various special disciplines and makes no claim that their subject matter is rhetorical or dialectical data *per se*. At the same time he feels strongly that so far as possible the speaker and the writer should draw their premises from the special data of whatever field they are discussing.[31] His conviction on this last point is evidenced, as every student of the *Rhetoric* knows, in his long treatment of politics and ethics in the *Rhetoric*, the two special disciplines with which the speaker is chiefly concerned. In other words, while rhetoric as a science is concerned generically with those broad principles of probability which can be adduced to lend cogency to an argument in any field, and, as a methodological science, cannot be expected to be conversant with the special topics of the various substantive fields with which it deals, nevertheless it is important that any speaker be as thoroughly informed as possible in the

---

[30]*Rhetoric* I, 2, 1358ᵃ.
[31]See *ibid.* II, 22, 1396ᵃ and 1396ᵇ.

particular substantive area in which he chooses to speak; and especially is it important that a skilled speaker "have a thorough and detailed knowledge of the special sciences which mainly concern the art of rhetoric—that is, Ethics and Politics, above all, since they have to do with the conduct of men as individuals, and with men in groups."[32]

The topics as "lines of argument" we interpret as *methods of reasoning* rather than material propositions. Aristotle makes his transition to this list from a few concluding remarks which he has been making about special and general topics as follows:

> Here, then, we have one principle, and the first for selecting enthymemes; and it refers to the choice of *materials* for them. Let us now pass on to their *elementary forms:* and by "elementary form" I mean the same thing as a class to which an enthymeme belongs.[33]

I think there is little question that we do have a list of methods of reasoning or types of inference in the topics discussed in *Rhetoric* II, 23-24. Aristotle appears to have intended that this long enumeration of lines of argument be correlated, roughly at least, with the causes, signs and examples which he discusses in another connection. The latter may be viewed as a careful, scientific statement of the kinds of enthymematic argument; the former, as a more or less random list of some of the more usual arguments from cause, sign, and example encountered in speaking and writing.[34]

In summary, then, we may say that whereas the speaker goes to the special or general topics for his premises, he may call upon these "lines of argument" for his mode of reasoning. The premises and the line of argument selected will together constitute an enthymeme. If the enthymeme combines these elements in such a way as to constitute a *ratio essendi*, it is then an *eikos*; if it combines them in such a way as to constitute a *ratio cognoscendi*, it is then an argument from sign, which may, as we have seen, appear in the first, second, or third figure of the syllogism.

4. *The Enthymeme and Ethos and Pathos:* A very common, and perhaps the usual interpretation of the *Rhetoric* is that enthymeme and example are the instruments of "rhetorical demonstration," and as such, are to be contrasted with those appeals which are evinced through the personality of the speaker (*ethos*) and those which make an emotional appeal (*pathos*). I wish to raise the question here: Does Aristotle mean to bring out this contrast to the extent of excluding the enthymeme from the realm of *ethos* and *pathos*?

---

[32] *Ibid.* II, 22, 1395^b.

[33] *Ibid.* II, 22, 1396^b. See also on this point Edward Poste, *Aristotle on Fallacies or the Sophistici Elenchi*, London, 1866, Appendix D, 204-207, especially 206.

[34] See Chaignet, A. E., *La Rhétorique et Son Histoire*, Paris, 1888, 134-5. See also Eng. Thionville, *De La Théorie des Lieux Communs dans les Topiques d'Aristote et des Principales modifications qu'elle a subies jusqu'à nos jours*, Paris, 1855.

The answer to this question is of considerable importance because upon it hinges the relationship of logical and non-logical or emotional factors in speaking and writing. Are we to consider the logical structure of an argument something that is separate and distinct from the so-called emotional appeals? In other words, what part if any does the enthymeme play in that mode of persuasion which depends upon the personal character of the speaker and that which attempts to affect the emotional state of the listener?

To begin with we must recognize that the enthymeme is a rhetorical device and as such is dependent, so to speak, upon language symbols, i.e., terms and propositions in significant combinations. Persuasion arising from the personality of the speaker and other kindred factors (except as it finds its expression in terms and propositions) is therefore clearly outside the realm of the enthymeme. But what about the personality appeal and attempts to influence the emotional state of the listener (or reader) which are expressed in words and sentences? Here we have the real question: Is the enthymeme the controlling unit of expression in such persuasion, or is it a purely "logical" instrument of proof?

A careful analysis of Aristotle's system will reveal the superficiality of attempting to separate the enthymeme from these "non-logical" methods of persuasion. I submit that in Aristotle's rhetorical system the enthymeme is the element or unit of all persuasive discourse. The admission of "emotionally loaded" terms and propositions is in fact one of the important characteristics of the enthymeme; the premises which compose an enthymeme are usually nothing more than the beliefs of the audience which are used as causes and signs to secure the acceptance of other propositions. These premises, as we have seen, are drawn from the general and special topics or *topoi*. It is organized around lists of these topics that Aristotle gives us his semi-popular discussion of ethics and politics, virtues, vices, and emotions. In other words, Aristotle presents what he has to say about both ethical and pathetical persuasion in the form of topics, and we are explicitly told that these topics are the sources to which we may turn for the propositions to compose our enthymemes.[35]

The order of treatment or sequence of the *Rhetoric* sustains the position here taken on the enthymeme in relation to *ethos* and *pathos*. Aristotle begins the *Rhetoric* by proclaiming the enthymeme to be the body and substance of all persuasion. In I, 2 he distinguishes among the three forms of artistic persuasion and explains the enthymeme in terms of causes and signs. He concludes the same chapter by explaining his topics or *topoi* as the places to which we turn for the premises of our enthymemes. Then in I, 3 he distinguishes the three great divisions of oratory, political, forensic or judicial, and epideictic or ceremonial, and states that he will organize his discussion

---

[35]See *Rhetoric* I, 2, 1356[a]; I, 9, 1366[a]; II, 12, 1388[b].

of topics around this division of the kinds of oratory. This he does and he concludes I, 3 just before taking up this discussion by saying,

> It is evident from what has been said that it is these three subjects, more than any others, about which the orator must be able to have propositions at his command. Now the propositions of Rhetoric are Complete Proofs, Probabilities, and Signs. Every kind of syllogism is composed of propositions, and the enthymeme is a particular kind of syllogism composed of the aforesaid propositions.

From I, 4 to I, 9 Aristotle gives the reader some practical politics designed to help the political orator in the selection of his enthymemes. In I, 9 he gives a discussion of virtues and vices designed to help the speaker in epideictic oratory. In I, 10 he turns to the topics of forensic oratory, stating: "We have next to treat of Accusation and Defense, and to enumerate and describe the ingredients of the syllogisms used therein." This discussion continues to I, 15 where we then are given a discussion of non-artistic proofs, with which Book I is closed.

Aristotle begins Book II by pointing out the importance of ethical and pathetical persuasion in the three types of oratory and from II, 1 to II, 19 gives us some practical psychology concerning human motives and emotions. It is with this that Aristotle concludes his discussion of special topics begun in I, 4. Having concluded his discussion of special topics, he devotes II, 19 to general topics. It will be remembered that the distinction between special and general topics in relation to the enthymeme was made in I, 3.

Upon concluding this discussion of the special and general topics from which the premises of our enthymemes must be drawn, he then in II, 20 takes up the study of the enthymeme in its various forms and concludes Book II in Chapter 26 with this material. Book III, of course, is devoted to style and delivery.

This view of the *Rhetoric* makes the organization of the work entirely logical and understandable. Aristotle first introduces us to the enthymeme as the element of rhetorical persuasion and gives us some preliminary definitions and classifications; second, he discusses the topics from which enthymemes are to be drawn, explaining that ethical, pathetical, and logical persuasion will be projected through these enthymemes depending upon our choice of propositions; and third the enthymeme is carefully analyzed in its several forms. Books I and II treat *inventio* and Book III considers mainly *elocutio*, to a limited extent, *pronunciatio* and *dispositio*, with little or no mention being made of *memoria*. My point is that if we view the enthymeme as the "body and substance of rhetorical persuasion" as Aristotle tells us to, we have no difficulty in understanding the organization of the *Rhetoric*. On the other hand, if the enthymeme is to be considered the instrument solely of logical proof with ethical and pathetical persuasion existing outside this concept, it is exceedingly difficult to understand the organization of the *Rhetoric*. There seems to me, however, to be no justification for this latter position except as we accept superficial impressions which might be gotten from a failure really to analyze and understand Aristotle's system of rhetorical invention.

5. *Demonstrative and Refutative Enthymemes:* Aristotle distinguishes between demonstrative and refutative enthymemes in *Rhetoric* II, 22 and 25. He discusses the two methods of refutation, "counter-syllogism" and refutation by "bringing an objection," and explains that refutative enthymemes are constructed from the same topics from which demonstrative enthymemes are built. Of special interest here, however, is his discussion of refutation in relation to *probable causes* and *signs*.[36] The point is clearly brought out that an argument drawn from probabilities cannot be refuted by showing that the conclusion is not necessary and that formal defects in an enthymematic argument do not necessarily destroy its claim to cogency. The *probable* nature of the enthymeme and its *formal* inconclusiveness are emphasized. One does not properly refute an enthymeme which reasons from a probable cause by showing that its premises are merely probable, because it is impossible to make these premises anything other than probable and probability is all that is claimed for the conclusion. Likewise to show that an argument from sign (in the second or third figures) is formally deficient does not necessarily refute the enthymeme; such an enthymeme "knows that it is formally deficient," so to speak, and it does not contemplate apodeictic certainty for its conclusion.

Perhaps no other passages in Aristotle bring out more forcibly the point that several forms of the enthymeme are *formally deficient* than these explanations dealing with the refutation of enthymemes. This is an exceedingly important point that is almost universally overlooked. Many rhetorical arguments which are perfectly legitimate in reasoned discourse and which may establish high degrees of probability, are formally deficient; i.e., they cannot be thrown into a formally valid syllogism. Many enthymemes which are wholly acceptable from the standpoint of cogent speech are formally deficient from the point of view of the apodeictic syllogism. As Mansel puts it:

> In the *Prior Analytics* II, 27 Aristotle admits a sign in the second figure. . . . The *logical* value of two affirmative premises in the second figure is absolute zero. . . . For rhetorical purposes, however, the second figure is admissible; an accumulation of Enthymemes, all *logically* worthless, may amount to a *moral* certainty.[37]

6. *A Consideration of the Suppression of a Proposition in the Enthymeme:* We know from our examination of Aristotle's works thus far that the identification of the enthymeme with probable causes and signs is a necessary part of the definition of this concept. A cursory examination of the *Rhetoric*, to say nothing of almost any sample of reasoned discourse, will show that the

---

[36]*Rhetoric* II, 25, 1403ᵃ.
[37]Mansel, H. L., *op. cit.*, 214.

enthymeme very often appears with one (or more) of the propositions of a complete syllogism suppressed. The only question raised here, therefore, is whether or not the omission of one or more of the propositions of a complete syllogism is *necessary* in the enthymeme. This question assumes considerable importance because of the almost universal tendency among recent writers to define the enthymeme as an elided syllogism and to make this elision the only differentiation between the syllogism and the enthymeme. Hamilton points out that "the enthymeme was used by the oldest commentators on Aristotle in the modern signification, as a syllogism of one suppressed premise."[38] Jebb states:

> A misapprehension of Aristotle's meaning had, as early as the first century B.C., led to the conception of the enthymeme as not merely a syllogism of a particular subject matter, but also a syllogism of which one premise is suppressed.[39]

Most of those who object to the contemporary notion of the enthymeme merely as a truncated syllogism hold that the characteristic thing about the enthymeme is its identification with probable causes and signs, and that the omission of a proposition is purely accidental. De Quincey enunciates this position as follows:

> The enthymeme differs from the syllogism, not in the accident of suppressing one of its propositions; either may do this or neither; the difference is essential, and in the nature of the matter; that of the syllogism proper being certain and apodeictic; that of the enthymeme simply probable, and drawn from the province of opinion.[40]

The commentator who has contended for this conception most vehemently and argued the point most convincingly is Sir William Hamilton. He contends (1) that the enthymeme as a syllogism of a defective enouncement constitutes no special form of reasoning; (2) that Aristotle does not consider a syllogism of such a character as such a special form; and (3) that admitting the validity of the distinction, the restriction of the enthymeme to a syllogism of one suppressed premise cannot be competently maintained.[41]

There appears to be no place in Aristotle's writings where he defines the enthymeme as an elided syllogism, nor is there any satisfactory evidence that

---

[38] Hamilton, Sir William, *Discussions on Philosophy*, 154.

[39] Jebb, R. C., *Attic Orators*, London: Macmillan and Co., 1876, vol. II, 291.

[40] De Quincey, Thomas, *Essays on Style, Rhetoric and Language* (edited by Fred N. Scott, Allyn and Bacon), Boston, 1893, 145-146.

[41] See Sir William Hamilton, *Lectures on Metaphysics and Logic*, New York: Sheldon and Co., 1876, vol. II, 276-278; *ibid.*, *Discussions on Philosophy*, 151-154; *ibid.*, "Recent Publications on Logical Science," in *The Edinburgh Review*, CXV, April, 1833, 221-222. See also Cope, E. M., *An Introduction to Aristotle's Rhetoric, op. cit.*, 102-103, especially the footnote; H. L. Mansel's *Aldrich, op. cit.*, 211-212; Joseph, H. W. B., *Introduction to Logic, op. cit.*, 350-351; Jacobi Facciolati, *Orationes XII* (Acrases and Patavii, 1729), 227; Chaignet, A. E., *La Rhétorique et Son Histoire, op. cit.*, 113-114.

he so understood it. In his discussion of *maxims* and in many other places, Aristotle recognizes the enthymeme with one or more of its propositions suppressed; as a matter of fact, I think we can safely interpret Aristotle to mean that the enthymeme *usually* lacks one or more of the propositions of a complete syllogism. On the other hand, it seems equally clear that there is no justification in interpreting him to mean that this is a necessary characteristic of the enthymeme. A syllogism drawn from probable causes and signs is an enthymeme without regard to the omission of a proposition.

From this study of the enthymeme as a part of Aristotle's logical and rhetorical system as a whole and our examination of the Aristotelian passages in which the enthymeme is given special treatment, I think that we can draw the following conclusions concerning the enthymeme in Aristotle: (1) The enthymeme is the syllogism of rhetoric, occupying in rhetoric essentially the same place that the syllogism occupies in logic; (2) the premises of the enthymeme are probable causes and signs; (3) these premises are drawn from topics varying in specificity and exactness from the particular facts of a given substantive field to the most general principles of probability; (4) these premises may be phrased in language designed to affect the emotional state of the listener, to develop in the audience a confidence in the speaker, or to establish a conclusion as being a probable truth; (5) the inferential process is formally deficient in several of the enthymematic types, and many enthymemes cannot therefore be stated in valid syllogisms; (6) the rhetorical example may be reduced to an enthymematic form just as scientific induction may be stated syllogistically; and (7) the enthymeme often (but not necessarily) appears with one or more of its three propositions suppressed.

For Aristotle the enthymeme is the element of reasoned discourse, constructive or refutative, demonstrative or "sham"; its persuasive force may be ethical, pathetical, or logical. In any case it draws its premises and line of argument from topics which combine to enunciate a *ratio essendi* or *ratio cognoscendi*; these take the form of probable causes, signs, and examples, and are usually expressed by a proposition with a reason, although they may appear in the complete syllogistic form.

III.

The Enthymeme After Aristotle

We know from our examination of the enthymeme in Aristotle that there have been substantial deviations from the Aristotelian meaning of this concept in the many centuries which separate contemporary rhetorical invention from that of Aristotle. These changes assume considerable importance in view of the central place which the enthymeme occupies in Aristotle's system and the persistence of Aristotle's system as the essential basis of contemporary rhetorical theory. In this section, therefore, we shall attempt to see where, when, and why these changes took place.

A. *The Stoics:* The more important philosophical school following

Aristotle, at least from the point of view of this study, is that of the Stoics. The accuracy with which Aristotle's successor, Theophrastus, and the other early leaders of the Peripatetic school "passed on" Aristotle's teaching, and the availability of reliable Aristotelian manuscripts even to these early students of the school appears to be questionable.[42] In any event the early Stoic philosophers, Zeno (c. 336 B.C.), Cleanthes (331-232 B.C.) and Chrysippus, head of the stoic school from 232-206 B.C., either because they lacked ready access to Aristotle's writings or because they sought to develop an original logical and rhetorical system, do not appear to have maintained the enthymematic conception. The extant fragments of these writers reveal no reference to the enthymeme[43] despite the fact that they are known to have written treatises on rhetoric. Such information as we have concerning these treatises seem to indicate that the stoics were concerned with establishing truth rather than probability and devoted themselves, even as rhetoricians, to the subtleties of the logical syllogism.[44] While this predilection for logic can doubtless be explained by the very nature of the stoic philosophic creed, it seems certain that rhetorical invention suffered by their disposition to replace the enthymeme with the logical syllogism.

The most renowned rhetorician in the stoic school was Hermagoras (c. 110 B.C.) who, confining himself almost entirely to invention as opposed to style, elaborated on the basis of previous treatises a system of rhetoric which remained a standard work throughout the Graeco-Roman period. The rhetorical system of Hermagoras we must glean from a few fragments and the many references to him by later rhetoricians, especially Cicero and Quintilian, who are known to have been influenced profoundly by his work.[45] The influence of Hermagoras on Cicero, as reflected in Cicero's early work *De Inventione* (c. 85 B.C.), is in my opinion a factor of great importance in explaining the subsequent tendency to confuse the enthymeme and the logical syllogism. We shall examine the *De Inventione* with this point in mind.

B. *The Roman Doctrine:* Cicero divides argument into induction and ratiocination in the *De Inventione* and then subdivides ratiocination (deduc-

---

[42]See Shute, Richard, *An Essay on the History of the Process by Which the Aristotelian Writings Arrived at Their Present Form*, Oxford: Clarendon Press, 1888, 19-45.

[43]Arnim, Joannes ab, *Stoicorum Veterum Fragmenta* (Lipsiae MCMV) four volumes; see also Pearson, Alfred C., *The Fragments of Zeno and Cleanthes*, London: C. J. Clay and Sons, 1891.

[44]Arnold, E. Vernon, *Roman Stoicism*, Cambridge: University Press, 1911, 73; Sandys, J. E., *A History of Classical Scholarship* (Second ed.), Cambridge: University Press, 1906, 149; Davidson, William L., *The Stoic Creed*, Edinburgh: T. and T. Clark, 1907, 63; Zellar, E., *The Stoics, Epicureans, and Sceptics* (tr. by O. J. Reichel, Longmans, Green and Co.), London, 1870, 118-119; Stock, St. George, *Stoicism*, London: Archibald Constable and Co., 1908, 31-34. See also Laertius, Diogenes, *Lives of Eminent Philosophers* (tr. by R. D. Hicks, in Loeb Class. Lib.), London: William Heinemann and New York: G. P. Putnam's Sons, 1925, VII, 42-43; Ciceronis, M. Tulle, *De Finibus Bonorum et Malorum, Libi Quinque* (tr. by James S. Reid), Cambridge: University Press, 1885, IV, III, 7-10; Dionysius of Halicarnassus, *On Literary Composition* (tr. by W. Rhys Roberts), 95-97.

[45]See Thiele, George, *Hermagoras: ein Beitrag zur Geschichte der Rhetorik*, Strassburg, 1893, for an attempted reconstruction of the rhetoric of Hermagoras.

tion) into five parts, *propositio, propositionis approbatio, assumptio, assumptionis approbatio,* and *complexio.* These five parts are related to the syllogism in the following manner: (1) Proposition (Major premise of syllogism); (2) Proof of Proposition; (3) Assumption (Minor premise of syllogism); (4) Proof of assumption; and (5) Summation (Conclusion of syllogism).[46] Thiele argues at some length that Cicero's five-part ratiocination (*epicheirema*), and the explanation which he gives of it, represents an attempt to accommodate the logical syllogism to the needs of rhetoric which fails to recognize the enthymeme and seriously perverts the purposes and methods of rhetorical invention.[47] Thiele traces this influence to Hermagoras.

Briefly, the chief objection to the logical syllogism as a rhetorical instrument lies in its apodeictic nature and formal rigidity. The materials with which the speaker and writer must constantly deal, and the type of reasoning in which they must engage, strongly militate against the application of the demonstrative forms of the logical syllogism. If an argument is considered unacceptable rhetorically because it falls short of material certainty or fails to achieve formal validity, the inevitable result must be a tremendous limitation of the lines of reasoning open to the speaker, to say nothing of the unfortunate effects on the style of the discourse. Cicero himself decries this mixing of logic and rhetoric in his later work *De Oratore,*[48] and Quintilian makes a point of it in his *Institutio Oratoria.*[48]

Both Cicero and Quintilian deal with the enthymeme; Cicero refers to it in his short work *Topica,* where he assigns a very special type of matter to this concept and appears not to have the Aristotelian meaning;[49] Quintilian observes the confusion which surrounds the enthymeme in his day and reviews some of the different meanings assigned to it.[50] While Quintilian does not take a final position on the form of the enthymeme, he appears to favor the idea that it is an elided syllogism. His discussion of the kinds and methods of rhetorical argument is comprehensive and generally Aristotelian although some departures traceable mainly to Cicero are noticeable.[51]

C. *The Mediaeval Doctrine:* Of first importance so far as rhetorical invention is concerned in the middle ages is the influence of Cicero's *De*

---

[46]Cicero's *De Inventione* (included with Cicero's *Orations,* tr. by C. D. Yonge, vol. IV, Bohn Class. Lib.), London, 1852, 241-380.

[47]Thiele, George, *op. cit.,* 131-137.

[48]Cicero's *De Oratore* II, 28; Quintilian's *Institutio Oratoria* V, 32.

[49]Cicero, *Topica* (included with Cicero's *Orations,* tr. by C. D. Yonge, vol. IV, Bohn Class. Lib.), London, 1852, 458-486. See also Saint-Hilaire, J. Barthelemy, *op. cit.,* 368.

[50]Quintilian's *Institutio Oratoria* V, 8, 9, and 10; V, 14.

[51]The enthymeme is treated by a number of the later Greek rhetoricians, Hermogenes (c. 170 A.D.), Apsines, Minucianus, Neocles and others in the second, third, and fourth centuries. Hermogenes assigns a wholly new meaning to the concept and the others make no contribution of note. While Hermogenes was followed by some later writers, for example, Georgius Trapezuntius in his *Rhetorica* (c. 1470), I shall not attempt to discuss the point here. See the several volumes of Leonardi Spengel's *Rhetores Graeci,* Lipsiae, 1885, and Christianus Walz, *Rhetores Graeci,* London and Lutetiae, 1832, for these later Greek rhetoricians.

Inventione throughout this period. This work, together with the *Rhetorica ad Herennium* (c. 85 B.C.),[52] is followed very closely by nearly every mediaeval rhetorician: As might be expected the confusion between the enthymeme and the syllogism which we found to exist in Cicero's epicheirematic conception is thereby transmitted to the middle ages. Unfortunately Aristotle's *Rhetoric*, Cicero's *De Oratore*, and Quintilian's *Institutio Oratoria* were almost wholly unknown during this period and were not recovered until the fifteenth century.

Examples of the influence of the *De Inventione* with respect to the applications of the syllogism in the field of rhetorical invention may be seen in the work of the fourth and fifth century writers, Fortunatianus, Victorinus, Julius Victor, and Cassiodorus.[53] All of these writers define the enthymeme as an "incomplete syllogism" and the epicheirema as a "broader following up of the rhetorical syllogism, differing by its breadth and extensiveness from dialectical syllogisms."

Two other important influences may be noted in the middle ages, that of Christian rhetoric with its beginnings in St. Augustine's (354-430) *De Doctrina Christiana*, and the writings of Boethius (c. 480-525). Rhetoric applied to the art of preaching constituted a strong current through this entire period. As Caplan puts it:

> Were the modern student, fortified by a knowledge of Aristotle's *Rhetoric*, to contend that the rhetorical enthymeme, not the syllogism, is proper to the art of rhetoric, the mediaeval preacher would perhaps reply that sacred eloquence differs from secular in that its subject matter lies not in the realm of opinion and probability, but in truth and divine science; that it is as sound a procedure to use a dialectical method in the demonstration of truth as in the investigation of it; and further, that in Aristotle and Cicero and Quintilian he had precedents for the policy of adapting to rhetorical purposes the methods of the allied arts of dialectic.[54]

Suffice to say here that the emphasis of these mediaeval "arts of preaching," in so far as they were concerned with the form of argument, was on the dialectical or logical syllogism. Furthermore, both the translations of Aristotle's *Organon* by Boethius and his own original writings carried

---

[52]The authorship of the *Rhetorica ad Herennium*, long attributed to Cicero, is unknown. The work resembles the *De Inventione* very closely, and was widely used as a text and reference. The author of the *Ad Herennium* explains a five step ratiocinative form which resembles that of the *De Inventione* superficially, but is in fact closer to the Aristotelian conception; like Cicero, he calls this form an *epicheirema*. The five parts are: *propositio, ratio, rationi confirmatio, exornatio,* and *complexio.* Cicero's epicheirema is the form which was almost universally cited by mediaeval rhetoricians, however. It should be noted that the *Ad Herennium* exerted a strong influence during the latter part of the middle ages and the early renaissance.

[53]See Halm, Carolus, *Rhetoris Latini Minores*, Lipsiae, 1863, 118-119, 242-243, 408-413, 498-500.

[54]Caplan, Harry, "Classical Rhetoric and the Mediaeval Theory of Preaching," in *Classical Philology*, vol. 28, No. 2, April, 1933; 87.

forward the conception of the enthymeme as an elided syllogism. Boethius translates the controversial passage concerning the enthymeme in the *Prior Analytics* II, 27, *"Enthymema ergo est syllogismus imperfectus ex elcotibus et signis"*;[55] and states in his *De Differentiis Topicis*, "The enthymeme is an imperfect syllogism, that is, a form of speech in which a hurried conclusion is arrived at before all the propositions have been established. . . ."[56] Sir William Hamilton and others point out that *atelês* (imperfectus) as found in this and other similar versions of the *Analytics* "is a manifest interpolation made to accommodate the Aristotelic to the common doctrine of the enthymeme."

With the authority of Aristotle thus apparently given to the conception of the enthymeme as an elided syllogism by his chief interpreter for the middle ages, it is not surprising that this doctrine persisted. Isidore of Seville (c. 570-636), following Cassiodorus almost word for word, discusses the enthymeme as "an incomplete syllogism" and the epicheirema as "a broader syllogism also in use among the rhetoricians,"[57] and Alcuin (735-804) adds nothing in his dialogues on rhetoric and dialectic. With the revival of Aristotle's logical works in the scholastic period we find much fuller discussions of syllogistic doctrine in such writers as Hugh of St. Victor, John of Salisbury, and Vincent of Beauvais, but little development is seen in the theory of the enthymeme. The concept is identified with probabilities somewhat more confidently and realistically, but it remains "the incomplete syllogism of the rhetoricians." Erasmus and Melancthon later discuss the enthymeme in much the same way.

In the sixteenth century, following the recovery of Aristotle's *Rhetoric*,[58] there appeared a large number of commentaries and reworkings of this treatise done chiefly by Italians. The first English work of any consequence, that of Leonard Cox (1530), remained largely in the mediaeval tradition and did little with invention. By the middle of the seventeenth century, however, Aristotle's *Rhetoric* was well known in England and Whately's *Elements of Rhetoric* and *Elements of Logic*, appearing at the turn of the eighteenth century, display a scholarly grasp of the best classical tradition. Whately's influence in the field of rhetorical invention is prominent in American writers, especially Henry Day and later writers on rhetoric and argumentation. Throughout this development to this day, however, the momentum gained by the conception of the enthymeme as an elided syllogism during the many centuries preceding has been sufficient to sustain this conception with but scattered dissent. While the rhetorical trilogy, antecedent probability, sign, and example, the basis of most contemporary classifications of argument,

---

[55] See Migne, *Patralogia Latina*, vol. 64, col. 711.
[56] *Ibid.*, vol. 64, col. 1184; see also col. 1050.
[57] Halm, Carolus, *op. cit.*, 511-512.
[58] The complete manuscript of Quintilian's *Institutio Oratoria* was found at St. Gaul by Poggio in 1416, Cicero's *De Oratore* and *Brutus*, at Lodi in 1421, and Aristotle's *Rhetoric* was published in the Latin version by George of Trebizond as early as 1478 and in the Greek in 1508; see Clark, D. L., *op. cit.*, 66.

preserves Aristotle's conception of the materials of the enthymeme with considerable accuracy, the formal relation of these arguments to the syllogism is very generally misunderstood.

IV.
The Place of the Enthymeme
in Contemporary Rhetorical Theory

The necessary limitations of this abstract will not permit me to discuss this subject in any detail. I do think that we can conclude with considerable assurance from the investigations here reported that to the extent that syllogistic logic is accepted as the basis of apodeictic proof, and Aristotle's system of rhetorical invention is retained as the essential basis of our theory of argument in speaking and writing, these interpretations of the enthymeme should be given serious consideration. On the other hand, to the degree that the syllogism is repudiated as an adequate concept in logical theory, there is at least a presumption established against the enthymeme which should lead to further investigations of its adequacy. Needless to say, however, a correct version of the enthymeme will be the necessary starting point of any significant attempt to evaluate this concept and the theory of argument of which it is a part.

Objections to the syllogism and its rhetorical applications have been raised as far back as Francis Bacon, John Locke, and George Campbell. These have continued to appear sporadically with growing frequency in recent years. The arguments of such writers as John Dewey, F. C. S. Schiller, Alfred Sidgwick, and Boris B. Bogoslovsky, while not generally rhetorical in the traditional sense, should be considered. I have argued in another connection that the conception of the enthymeme here set forth adapts the syllogism to the problems of ordinary speaking and writing in such a way as to remove, at least in part, what I understand to be some of the more important objections of these writers.

Aristotle's System of Topics

by Richard C. Huseman

In the first chapter of the *Rhetoric* Aristotle calls attention to the rhetorical concept of invention in this way:

> Of the modes of persuasion some belong strictly to the art of rhetoric and some do not. By the latter I mean such things are not supplied by the speaker but are there at the outset—witnesses, evidence given under torture, written contracts, and so on. By the former I mean such as we can ourselves construct by means of the principles of rhetoric. The one kind has merely to be used, the other has to be invented.[1]

This process, called invention, is an extremely important concept in the history of rhetorical theory.

Invention, however, as a rhetorical term is not very meaningful and perhaps confusing. The invention of a speech or argument is not really an invention in the scientific sense of the word. The invention of a speech is not to invent or discover that which is new. Rhetorical invention is rather the process of drawing forth from the mind materials that are pertinent to the purpose of the speech.

How is this process carried on? One assumes that a speaker has a subject in mind. One may also assume that he has in mind or has within reach, so that he can quickly draw upon it or pass it in review, sufficient knowledge for his speech. How does he proceed? This is a question which concerned many classical rhetoricians. *Inventio* was a subject of extended and important sections of their treatises, and lists of *topoi* (or topics), which were aids to invention, were carefully compiled.

The word *topos* has been defined in various ways. Jebb speaks of it as the "place in which a thing is to be looked for in the memory."[2] Cooper describes its meaning rather figuratively in regarding it "as a place or region in the whole realm of science, or as a pigeon-hole in the mind of the speaker."[3] Cope has a similar viewpoint:

Reprinted from the *Southern Speech Journal* 30 (1965): 243-252. Used by permission.

[1] Aristotle *Rhetoric* 1355b 35-40, in Vol. XI of *The Works of Aristotle. Translated into English under the Editorship of W. D. Ross* (12 vols.; Oxford: Clarendon Press, 1928). In this article, all references to all works of Aristotle will be from this edition of *The Works of Aristotle.*

[2] Richard C. Jebb, *The Rhetoric of Aristotle* (Cambridge: University Press, 1909), p. 143.

[3] Lane Cooper, *The Rhetoric of Aristotle* (New York, 1932), p. xxiv.

[A topic is] . . . a 'place' or 'region,' the place where you may look for something you want with the certainty of finding it, or a store which may be drawn upon to meet an occasional requirement: and in its application to rhetoric means a 'head' . . . or 'genus' or general conception, which includes under it a large stock of special arguments of the same kind.[4]

One of the most complete systems of topics in all of classical rhetoric is found in Aristotle's *Rhetoric*.

The purpose of this article is (1) to distinguish between the *topoi* of Aristotle and the *topoi* of his predecessors, (2) to examine the *eidē* or special topics in Aristotle's system, and (3) to examine the *koinoi topoi* or general topics in Aristotle's system.

I

In order to see clearly how the term *"topos"* is applied in Aristotle's *Rhetoric*, it is useful to distinguish between the *topoi* of Aristotle and the *topoi* of his predecessors. What was the nature of *topoi* as used by Antiphon, Protagoras, and other predecessors of Aristotle? Solmsen points out that "the *topoi* had before Aristotle been ready-made arguments or commonplaces 'into which they expected the speeches of both parties to fall most frequently.'"[5] A speaker by learning these ready-made or special arguments could deliver a speech without really knowing much about the art of preparing a speech. These special arguments were closely related to subject matter and could not be used in just any speech. Aristotle compares this type of instruction to a procedure by which instead of learning the art of making shoes the apprentice receives a great number of ready-made shoes without any suggestion on how to make them. Aristotle has the following to say regarding the use of *topoi* by his predecessors:

> . . . they used to suppose that they trained people by imparting to them not the art but its products, as though anyone professing that he would impart a form of knowledge to obviate any pain in the feet, were then not to teach a man the art of shoe-making, or the sources whence he can acquire anything of the kind, but were to present him with several kinds of shoes of all sorts: for he has helped him to meet his need, but has not imparted an art to him.[6]

The Aristotelian *topoi*, as distinguished from the *topoi* of the earlier

---

[4] E. M. Cope, *An Introduction to Aristotle's Rhetoric* (London and Cambridge: MacMillan and Co., 1867), p. 125.

[5] Friedrich Solmsen, "The Aristotelian Tradition in Ancient Rhetoric," *The American Journal of Philology,* LXII (1941), 40.

[6] Aristotle *On Sophistical Refutations* 184a 2-9 (Ross, Vol. I).

rhetoricians, are not to be looked at as only substitutes for research and investigation, but also as aids in invention or, as Jebb and Cope rnaintain, aids to the memory.[7] The essential change or addition in Aristotle's system is the "form" of the argument, which is perfectly independent of any particular subject matter or content.

As will be shown, the *Rhetoric* is not only a handbook containing arguments for specific kinds of oratory; the Aristotelian *topoi* can be guides in the invention of arguments to be used in any speaking situation.

Aristotle distinguishes between two kinds or classes of *topoi*, the *eidē* or special topics and the *koinoi topoi* or general topics. The general topics are those "that apply equally to questions of right conduct, natural science, politics, and many other things that have nothing to do with one another."[8] The special topics, on the other hand, "are based on such propositions as apply only to particular groups or classes of things."[9] Aristotle continues by saying:

> Thus there are propositions about natural science on which it is impossible to base any enthymeme or syllogism about ethics, and other propositions about ethics on which nothing can be based about natural science.[10]

Grimaldi recognizes the essential difference between the *eidē* and the *koinoi topoi* as a distinction between the following:

> ... a difference between what I would call *material topics*, or sources of information upon the subject matter to be discussed and to be employed by the enthymeme, and *formal topics*, or the sources for modes of argumentation: Inferential forms most suited for the enthymeme.[11]

It is clear, then, that the topics of Aristotle can be divided into two classes: those that are related to the content and those related to the form of rhetorical argument.

II

Aristotle begins his discussion of the topics with the *eidē* or special topics. In Aristotle's system, the *eidē* may be called "special lines of Argument."

But there are also those special Lines of Argument which are based

---

[7] Jebb, *op. cit.,* p. 143. Cope, *op. cit.,* p. 124.
[8] Aristotle *Rhetoric* 1358a 12-13 (Ross, Vol. XI).
[9] Aristotle *Rhetoric* 1358a 17-18 (Ross, Vol. XI).
[10] Aristotle *Rhetoric* 1358a 18-20 (Ross, Vol. XI).
[11] W. M. A. Grimaldi, *The Enthymeme in Aristotle* (Unpublished Ph.D. dissertation, Princeton University, 1953), p. 122.

on such propositions as apply only to particular groups or classes of things.[12]

Much of Books I and II of the *Rhetoric* are concerned with a discussion of special topics, essentially those of ethics and politics since rhetoric is concerned with those subjects about which men deliberate.[13] Aristotle seems to divide his discussion of *eidē* to correspond to the three modes of proof, *logos, ethos,* and *pathos*. The discussion of the *eidē* of *logos* is in Book I, and these *eidē* are further divided according to their connection with the three types of oratory: deliberative, forensic, and epideictic.[14] The *eidē* concerning *pathos* appear in Book II with an analysis of the emotions and character. For a discussion of the *eidē* of *ethos* Aristotle refers to his previous discussion of goodness, for "the way to establish your own goodness is the same as the way to establish that of others."[15]

These *eidē*, one will notice, are propositional in form. They are not enthymemes, but are propositions upon which we may base enthymemes. In addition, they are propositions concerning a specific subject.

An example of the Aristotelian approach to the discussion of a special line of argument is found in his introduction to the topic of "good":

> Now the political or deliberative orator's aim is utility: deliberation seeks to determine not ends but the means to ends, i.e. what it is most useful to do. Further, utility is a good thing. We ought therefore to assure ourselves of the main facts about Goodness and Utility in general.[16]

Aristotle then presents a full description of those things which are "good":

> The following is a more detailed list of things that must be good. Happiness . . . Also justice, courage, temperance, magnanimity, magnificence. . . . Further, health, beauty, and the like. . . . Wealth, again: for it is the excellence of possession, and also productive of many other good things. Friends and friendship: for a friend is desirable in himself and also productive of many other good things. So, too, honour and reputation, as being pleasant, and productive of many other good things, and usually accompanied by the presence of the good things that cause them to be bestowed. . . .[17]

Aristotle concludes his list by saying, "the above are pretty well all the things admittedly good."[18] Thus the orator, if he were looking for materials and

---

[12] Aristotle *Rhetoric* 1358a 17 (Ross, Vol. XI).
[13] Aristotle *Rhetoric* 1357a 1-8 (Ross, Vol. XI).
[14] Aristotle *Rhetoric* 1359a 26-30 (Ross, Vol. XI).
[15] Aristotle *Rhetoric* 1378a 17-18 (Ross, Vol. XI).
[16] Aristotle *Rhetoric* 1362a 22-25 (Ross, Vol. XI).
[17] Aristotle *Rhetoric* 1362b 11-23 (Ross, Vol. XI).
[18] Aristotle *Rhetoric* 1362b 29-30 (Ross, Vol. XI).

arguments, may use this discussion to suggest or prompt appropriate enthymemes.

As Aristotle discusses these special lines of argument he points out those which are considered best for the three types of oratory:

> We have now considered the materials to be used in supporting or opposing a political measure, in pronuncing eulogies or censures, and for prosecution and defence in law courts. We have considered the received opinions on which we may base our argument so as to convince our hearers—those opinions with which our enthymemes deal, and out of which they are built, in each of the three kinds of oratory, according to what may be called the special needs of each.[19]

In reference to the use of the special lines of development, Aristotle suggests that following the selection of arguments about the questions we are to handle "we must try to think out arguments of the same type for special needs as they emerge."[20] Aristotle asserts that the orator must keep his eyes on the facts of the particular subject in composing his enthymemes and gather in as many of them as he can.

> For the more actual facts we have at our command, the more easily we prove our case; and the more closely they bear on the subject, the more they will seem to belong to that speech only instead of being commonplaces.[21]

Although Aristotle desires the orator to be exacting and detailed in looking to the facts of his case, he has a word of caution. He says: "People fail to notice that the more correctly they handle their particular subject the further they are getting away from pure rhetoric or dialectic."[22] The domain of rhetoric must of necessity be general.

> The better the selection one makes of propositions suitable for special Lines of Argument, the nearer one comes, unconsciously, to setting up a science that is distinct from dialectic and rhetoric. One may succeed in stating the required principles, but one's science will be no longer dialectic or rhetoric, but the science to which the principles thus discovered belong.[23]

Aristotle's meaning is clear from his statement that scientific demonstration proceeds from the *archai* or first principles of the particular science involved, while dialectic and rhetoric reason proceed from common opinion.[24] It is clear that Aristotle's discussions of the *eidē* or special topics are discussions of

[19] Aristotle *Rhetoric* 1377b 15-20 (Ross, Vol. XI).
[20] Aristotle *Rhetoric* 1396b 5-7 (Ross, Vol. XI).
[21] Aristotle *Rhetoric* 1396b 10-12 (Ross, Vol. XI).
[22] Aristotle *Rhetoric* 1358a 8-9 (Ross, Vol. XI).
[23] Aristotle *Rhetoric* 1358a 23-25 (Ross, Vol. XI).

common opinion, not the first principles of a science. For example, in the
Rhetoric, Aristotle gives the following account of happiness.

> We may define happiness as prosperity combined with virtue; or as
> independence of life; or as the secure enjoyment of the maximum of
> pleasure; or as a good condition of property and body, together with
> the power of guarding one's property and body and making use of
> them. That happiness is one or more of these things, pretty well
> everybody agrees.[25]

This definition is quite different from the more technical and fundamental
definition of happiness as "activity of the soul in accordance with virtue,"[26]
which appears in the *Ethics*.

The special topics, in addition to being used only for certain subjects, are
propositions based on common opinion upon which a speaker may build his
enthymemes. The special topics supply the material basis of the enthymeme.

III

Lines of arguments may also be composed from materials of a more
general nature, or as Aristotle indicates from materials which "will not increase our understanding of any particular class of things."[27] Thus, these lines
of argument are those in which the emphasis is still on the word argument,
but no "special subject matter" is involved. Aristotle continues by saying: "By
special Lines of Argument I mean the propositions peculiar to each several
class of things, by general those common to all classes alike."[28]

It is evident that in reference to the general lines of argument Aristotle
meant that these lines would be used by all orators regardless of their special
fields.

> I mean that the proper subjects of dialectical and rhetorical syllogisms
> are the things with which we say the regular or universal Lines of
> Argument are concerned, that is to say those lines of argument that
> apply equally to questions of right conduct, natural science, politics,
> and many other things that have nothing to do with one another.[29]

Aristotle illustrates the use of the general topic when he says:

> Take, for instance, the line of argument concerned with 'the more or
> less'. On this line of argument it is equally easy to base a syllogism

---

[24] Aristotle *Topics* 100a 25-31 (Ross, Vol. I).
[25] Aristotle *Rhetoric* 1360b 14-18 (Ross, Vol. XI).
[26] Aristotle *Nicomachean Ethics* 1098a 16-17 (Ross, Vol. IX).
[27] Aristotle *Rhetoric* 1358a 21 (Ross, Vol. XI).
[28] Aristotle *Rhetoric* 1358a 30 (Ross, Vol. XI).
[29] Aristotle *Rhetoric* 1392a 4-6 (Ross, Vol. XI).

or enthymeme about any of what nevertheless are essentially disconnected subjects—right conduct, natural science, or anything else whatever.[30]

In his discussion of the *koinoi topoi* or general topics, Aristotle lists twenty-eight valid forms of argument and nine spurious or invalid forms. Consistent with Aristotle's purpose to give guides for invention, this list is probably not to be looked at as exhaustive, but as an indication of the more important argumentative forms that an orator will need to use. The important thing to notice about these general topics is that they are argumentative forms. As Grimaldi points out:

> No matter how you analyze them they assume a form of reasoning and lead the mind from one thing to another. And in their simplest expression they would resolve themselves into the proposition: if one, then the other.[31]

The general topics, then, are either implicitly or explicitly stated enthymemes.[32] Take, for example, Aristotle's first argumentative form, based upon a consideration of opposites.[33] His example of this argumentative form, "temperance is beneficial; for licentiousness is hurtful," is stated in enthymematic form and can be thrown into valid syllogistic form containing two premises and a conclusion. These general topics, then, are guides to the form of argument. It is in presenting these general topics, which can be used in all types of oratory, that Aristotle makes his contribution to the concept of *topoi* held by his predecessors, i.e. that *topoi* can only be used for certain speeches.

An analysis of Aristotle's system of topics would not be complete without a discussion of the universals which Cope calls the *koinoi topoi* and lists as four in number.[34] The author agrees with Grimaldi that when Aristotle discusses these "universals" they seem to be three, not four, in number. For example, Aristotle states:

> All orators, besides their special lines of argument, are bound to use, for instance, the topic of the Possible and Impossible; and to try to show that a thing has happened, or will happen in the future. Again the topic of Size is common to all oratory; all of us have to argue that things are bigger or smaller than they seem, whether we are making political speeches, speeches of eulogy or attack, or prosecuting or defending in the law courts.[35]

---

[30]Aristotle *Rhetoric* 1392a 7-8 (Ross, Vol. XI).
[31]Grimaldi, *op. cit.*, pp. 126.
[32]Grimaldi, *op. cit.*, pp. 126-127.
[33]Aristotle *Rhetoric* 1397a 7-11 (Ross, Vol. XI).
[34]Cope, *op. cit.*, p. 126
[35]Aristotle *Rhetoric* 1391b 28-1392a 1 (Ross, Vol. XI).

The universals listed here seem to be (1) Possibility—Impossibility, (2) Past and Future Fact, and (3) Amplification—Depreciation. The same seems to be true when Aristotle states at the end of his discussion: "Enough has now been said about these questions of possibility and the reverse, of past or future fact, and of the relative greatness or smallness of things."[36] As Grimaldi points out, Cope's topic of Degree is simply one aspect of the topic of Amplification—Depreciation.[37]

Grimaldi also argues that these "universals" are not true topics. His evidence for this claim is the following. First, Aristotle never calls these three universals topics in his discussion of them, although his translators and commentators do.[38] Second, Aristotle states specifically that the universal of Amplification—Depreciation is not a topic, and this position applies equally well to the other two.[39] Third, the nature of these universals is different from either the general or the special topics.[40]

If Grimaldi's analysis is accepted, what can be said about these universals? They seem to function as subject headings under which a number of general topics fall. The topics falling under these subject headings do not have specific material content, but are argumentative forms. These universals, then, can be looked at as a means of categorizing certain of the most important argumentative forms with which the orator is concerned.

The important function of the general topics is that they are lines of argument that can be used for all kinds of oratory and are argumentative forms. The topics, or universals, of Possibility—Impossibility, Past and Future Fact, and Amplification—Depreciation serve as "heads" under which many of the general lines of argument may be classified and thus aid the memory of the orator.

Conclusion

Having considered the special and the general lines of argument, in summary let us consider the relationship between these two kinds of topics. Aristotle shows a relationship when he states:

> For arguments about the Greatness and Smallness of things, [general line of argument] . . . what we have already said will show the line to take. In discussing deliberative oratory we have spoken about the relative greatness of various goods, [special line of argument] and about the greater and lesser in general. Since therefore in each type of oratory the object under discussion is some kind of good—it is

---

[36] Aristotle *Rhetoric* 1393a 19-21 (Ross, Vol. XI).
[37] Grimaldi, *op. cit.*, p. 129.
[38] Grimaldi, *op. cit.*, p. 133.
[39] Grimaldi, *op. cit.*, p. 133.
[40] Grimaldi, *op. cit.*, p. 131.

clear that every oratory must obtain the materials of amplification through these channels.[41]

The general topics are guides to argumentative forms, for which the special topics supply the material basis. The following table shows Aristotle's system of topics, and perhaps enables one to identify more clearly the kinds of topics.

Thus, it may be concluded that rhetorical topics in the theory of Aristotle are material and formal aids in the invention of arguments for speech-making. The special topics suggest material or content; they are typically used in only certain kinds of oratory. The general topics suggest form for rhetorical argument and are not restricted to any particular kind of oratory.

Aristotle's System of Topics

SPECIAL (Material) TOPICS

DELIBERATIVE	FORENSIC	EPIDEICTIC
Goodness	Justice	Virtue
Utility	Injustice	Vice
etc.	etc.	etc.

GENERAL (Formal) TOPICS

1. opposites	15. inward thoughts and outward show
2. inflections	16. proportional results
3. correlative terms	17. identical results
4. more and less	18. altered choices
5. time	19. attributed motives
6. definition	20. incentives and deterrents
7. opponent's utterance	21. conflicting facts
8. ambiguous terms	22. incredible occurrences
9. division	23. explaining circumstances
10. induction	24. cause to effect
11. existing decisions	25. course or action
12. from parts to whole	26. actions compared
13. simple consequences	27. previous mistakes
14. criss-cross	28. meaning of names

---

[41]Aristotle *Rhetoric* 1393a 10-15 (Ross, Vol. XI).

Section 6:
Post-Aristotelian Rhetorical Theory

Theophrastus (c.370-c.285 B.C.)

by George A. Kennedy

The extant works of Theophrastus are the *Characters,* two works on botany, a number of short scientific treatises, and some notes on metaphysics. These represent, however, only a small fraction of his total output. Diogenes Laertius (5.42 ff., esp. 47-49) gives a list of writings including some which may have dealt with rhetoric and a number which certainly did. The titles show an interest in invention—*On enthymemes,* for example, and two books of *Epicheiremes,*[14] which term replaced enthymeme as the name for the basic rhetorical argument. There was also work in the field of arrangement, style, and delivery; an *Art of rhetoric* in one book; works on commonplaces and topics; collections of *theses,* which may have been used as rhetorical exercises; and a treatise *On the ludicrous,* which may have influenced later rhetorical discussions of humor (e.g. Cicero, *De oratore* 2.217 ff.). Theophrastus lectured to as many as two thousand at once and gave practical attention to the technique of speaking (Diogenes Laertius 5.37), anointing and dressing himself with care and indulging in gestures (Athenaeus 1.21a-b).

Theophrastus' influence on rhetoric was greatest in the areas of style and delivery; in both cases he developed theories at which Aristotle had pointed. Of his lost rhetorical works we know best the treatise *On style* because Cicero made repeated use of it. In *Orator* (79) he says:

"The language will be pure and good Latin, it will be clearly and distinctly stated, attention will be given to what is fitting; one thing will be lacking which Theophrastus numbers fourth among the virtues of a speech, ornamentation which is pleasant and abundant."[15]

Theophrastus' four virtues had been taken up also in *De oratore* (3.37 ff.) and made the basis of the discussion of style in that work; that is, each of the virtues was discussed in order and other topics subordinated to it. The long discussion in Quintilian (8.1-11.1) is basically similar. Since accounts of style generally do concentrate on the four virtues and since Cicero attributes them to Theophrastus, it seems highly likely that Theophrastus' *On style (Peri*

Reprinted from *The Art of Persuasion in Ancient Greece.* Copyright © 1963 by Princeton University Press, renewed 1991. Reprinted by permission of Princeton University Press.

[14]Cf. W. Kroll, "Das Epicheirema," SBW 216.2 (1936) 16 f.

[15]"Sermo purus erit et Latinus, dilucide planeque dicetur, quid deceat circumspicietur. Unum aberit quod quartum numerat Theophrastus in orationis laudibus: ornatum illud suave et affluens." Probably some of what immediately follows is also from Theophrastus, but it is difficult to sort it out clearly.

Lexeôs) followed the same pattern.[16] It is not surprising that it should, since the virtue of style is a key phrase in the third book of Aristotle's *Rhetoric* (1404b1). Only one virtue is there recognized, namely clarity, though propriety is appended as also necessary. Aristotle subsequently discusses other qualities including ornamentation or weight (*ogkos*) (1407b26 ff.) and propriety (*to prepon*) (1408a10 ff.), and he includes also a discussion of Hellenism (1407a19 ff.) which, as we have seen,[17] was really an earlier discussion of clarity, but might be taken to refer to good Greek. Thus the four virtues of Theophrastus may be found, more or less, in Aristotle. Qualities of style had also been discussed by Plato, Isocrates, Theodectes, and others and can be seen in the *Rhetorica ad Alexandrum* (1438a22). What Theophrastus did was to organize the material into a set of clear and teachable categories. In so doing he departed from the logic and unity of treatment which Aristotle's demand for clarity had made, but it must be confessed that the third book of the *Rhetoric* as it stands does not carry through that doctrine with any clarity itself, and a rigorous application could only result in a kind of extreme Atticism. Was a teacher to discuss figures solely in terms of the clarity they imparted to the context? This could hardly be done in an age which tended more and more toward an elaborate literary style almost divorced from the context. Theophrastus gave Hellenistic rhetoricians a usable system which preserved the essential requirements of good style and did not overemphasize adornment.

Purity (*hellênismos, purus et Latinus)*, the first of Theophrastus' virtues, refers mostly to the correct form of a word. Cicero says (*De oratore* 3.40), "we shall preserve case and tense and gender and number. . . ." The brevity of the discussion in Cicero results partly from his opposition to extreme Atticism, which, under Stoic influence, stressed this virtue above others.[18]

Clarity (*to saphes, dilucide planeque*) is basically the clarity described by Aristotle. Cicero says (*De oratore* 3.49), "by speaking good Latin, with common words which clearly indicate what we wish to signify and declare, without ambiguous work or language, without an excessive number of words, nor with too elaborated metaphors, nor with the sentence structure broken up, without the tenses altered nor the persons confused nor the order disturbed. . . ."

The third virtue, propriety (*to prepon, decorum*) discusses the adaptation

---

[16]Cf. Johannes Stroux, *De Theophrasti virtutibus dicendi,* Leipzig, 1912. The fragments (and also a great deal that does not come from Theophrastus) are available in August Mayer, *Theophrasti peri lexeôs libri fragmenta,* Leipzig, 1910, cf. esp. the *conspectus fragmentorum,* 226 f. G. M. A. Grube's attempt to refute some of Stroux' conclusions seems to me unsuccessful, for it does not recognize the general acceptance of the virtues nor Cicero's clear turn to an earlier rhetoric, cf. "Theophrastus as a literary critic," TAPA 83 (1952) 180 ff. Cf. also Alain Michel, *Rhétorique et philosophie chez Cicéron,* Paris, 1960, 327 ff.

[17]Cf. supra pp. 104 ff.

[18]Cf. G. L. Hendrickson, "The *De analogia* of Julius Caesar: its occasion, nature, and date, with additional fragments," CP 1 (1906) 97 ff., esp. 105 ff. There was of course some feeling that grammar was "elementary," cf. Stroux, *op.cit.* supra n. 16, 13.

of the style to the circumstances of the speech, the character of the speaker, the sympathies of the audience, and the kind of speech. Frigidity was defined as an overshooting of the proper expression (Demetrius, *On style* 114). Some of the material included in the discussion can be seen in Aristotle (1408a10 ff. and 1413b3 ff.) and Cicero (*De oratore* 3.210-212). Cicero and Quintilian both discuss ornamentation *before* propriety, but it is likely that Cicero reversed Theophrastus' order since he calls *ornatus* Theophrastus' *fourth* virtue (*Orator* 79) and since it comes after propriety in the list of virtues adopted by the Stoics (Diogenes Laertius 7.59).[19]

The fourth and final virtue was ornamentation (*ornatus*). Theophrastus may have used the term *kataskeuê*, which the Stoics adopted (Diogenes Laertius 7.59); Cicero's *suave* and *adfluens* indicates a subdivision into the two qualities of *to hêdu* or "sweetness" and *to megaloprepes* or "distinction."[20] According to Dionysius of Halicarnassus (*Isocrates* 3) Theophrastus said that style becomes great, lofty, and unusual (*mega, semnon, peritton*) through choice of words, harmony, and the use of figures. Dionysius and Quintilian make the distinction between choice of diction and composition a basic one for their whole theory of style, but this should not be attributed to Theophrastus since it is neither in Aristotle nor in Cicero. An indication of the content of Theophrastus' separate parts of ornamentation can be seen in Aristotle's discussion of the several types of words—proper, rare, coined, compound, and metaphorical—of periodicity and prose rhythm, and of the Gorgianic figures. It may have been in this section that Theophrastus remarked (Quintilian 10.1.27) that the reading of the poets confers the most advantage to the orator. He also divided words into those beautiful by nature and those paltry and mean (Dionysius of Halicarnassus, *On composition* 16) and defined the beauty of a word as inherent in its sound or in its appearance or in its value in our minds (Demetrius, *On style* 173); he agreed with Aristotle (1408b2) in disliking overly bold metaphors (*On the sublime* 32.3, cf. Cicero, *Ad familiares* 16.17) and discussed in some detail (Cicero, *Orator* 173) prose rhythm, recommending the paean (*Orator* 194 and 218), rejecting the dactyl, iamb, and trochee (Quintilian 9.4.88), and preferring a general and varied rhythmical quality (Demetrius, *On style* 41 and Cicero, *De oratore* 3.184 ff. and *Orator* 228). We have his definition of an antithesis (Dionysius of Halicarnassus, *Lysias* 14) as threefold: when opposites are predicated of the same thing or the same thing of opposites or opposites of opposites (cf. Aristotle, *Rhetoric* 1409b36). The granting of a separate section to the *schêmata* or figures is important.[21] Heretofore they had been treated almost incidentally, but from now on they play an increasingly important role in the

---

[19]Cf. Stroux 60 ff.

[20]Cf. Stroux 25 ff. and 37 n. 2; Friedrich Solmsen, "Demetrios *peri hermêneias* und sein peripatetisches Quellenmaterial," *Hermes* 66 (1931) 241 ff.; Kroll 1073. For evidence that Theophrastus used the term *megaloprepes* cf. Demetrius, *On style* 41.

[21]The early history of figures is more fully discussed below in connexion with Demetrius.

theory of style. Theophrastus is probably responsible for elevating the subject to a level equal to diction and thus encouraging the process of identification of figures which led to the almost interminable lists in later rhetorical handbooks. Devices of stylistic amplification were also discussed; we have a fragment preserved in the *Laurentian epitome*[22] which attributes to Theophrastus six kinds of amplification, some of them suggestive of categories in Quintilian (8.4.3 ff.).[23] In Aristotle *(Rhetoric* 1368a10 ff.) they had been treated as part of the subject matter of epideictic oratory. Quintilian's discussion of maxims *(gnômai, sententiae)* as a device of style (8.5) probably also goes back to Theophrastus since Cicero, immediately after listing the four Theophrastan virtues, demands that the orator provide *acutae crebraeque sententiae* (*Orator* 79, cf. Gregory of Corinth in Walz 7.1154).[24] The maxim was a form of proof to Aristotle *(Rhetoric* 1394a1 ff.), but in the *Rhetorica ad Herennium* (4.24 f.) it has become simply a figure of speech.

Cicero's *De oratore* and to a lesser extent *Orator* are anachronisms in rhetorical theory because they leap back over nearly three centuries to the broader and more philosophical concept of rhetoric found in Aristotle and his pupil. Cicero's action greatly enriched the tradition. He was in turn followed by Quintilian and others. In the Hellenistic period the Stoics followed the approach of Theophrastus to style, but there occurred at some point an adaptation of the system which is found in the *Ad Herennium* (4.17 ff.). There three qualities *(res)* of style are required: *elegantia, compositio, dignitas. Elegantia* is divided into *latinitas* and *explanatio* (clarity), which gives us the first two of the Theophrastan virtues. *Compositio* is part of Theophrastus' ornamentation and so, it turns out is *dignitas,* which consists of figures of diction and of thought (4.18). Propriety, so necessary a feature to the Peripatetics, is completely omitted.

A second subject of later stylistic theory, the characters or kinds of style, was probably given some impetus by Theophrastus' discussion of styles as applied to diction and genre.[25] Concepts of different kinds of style, all good

---

[22]This is available at the end of the Oxford Classical Text of "Longinus," p. "F." Cf. Grube, *op.cit.* supra n. 16, 177.

[23]Cf. Mayer, *op.cit.* supra n. 16, 142; J. Cousin, *Etudes sur Quintilien* 1, Paris, 1935, 427; Grube, *op.cit.* supra n. 16, 174.

[24]Cf. Mayer, *op.cit.* supra n. 16, 143, and Cousin, *op.cit.* supra n. 23,435.

[25]Cf. George A. Kennedy, "Theophrastus and stylistic distinctions," HSCP 62 (1957) 93 ff. Objections to attributing the characters to Theophrastus have come primarily from G. L. Hendrickson, "The peripatetic mean of style and the three stylistic characters," AJP 25 (1904) 125 ff. and "The origin and meaning of the ancient characters of style," AJP 26 (1905) 249 ff.; Stroux, *op.cit.* supra n.16, 88 ff.; Theodor Herrle, *Quaestiones rhetoricae ad elocutionem pertinentes,* Leipzig, 1912, 18 ff.; Solmsen, *op.cit.* supra n. 4, 183; G. M. A. Grube, "Thrasymachus, Theophrastus, and Dionysius of Halicarnassus," AJP 73 (1952) 251 ff. and *op.cit.* supra n. 16, 179. Grube admits that Theophrastus discussed kinds of diction, but not three styles in a wider sense. For other discussions cf. W. Schmid, "Zur antiken Stillehre," RhM 49 (1894) 133 ff.; L. Radermacher, "Theophrast *peri lexeôs,"* RhM 54 (1899) 374 ff.; W. Kroll, "Randbemerkungen," RhM 62 (1907) 86 ff. (a reply to Hendrickson); Christian Jensen, *Philodemus über die Gedichte, fünftes Buch,* Berlin, 1923, 170 ff. and "Herakleides von Pontos bei Philodem und Horaz," SBB (1936) 303 ff.; Kroll 1074; Franz Quadlbauer, "Die *genera dicendi* bis Plinius d.J.," WS 71 (1958) 63 ff.

in their own way but appropriate for different subjects, objects, or speakers, are really basic to any literary sensitivity. There was thus from the earliest time in Greece a notion of a grand style,[26] and Plato (*Republic* 397b4 ff.) distinguished two kinds of poetic style which corresponded roughly to dramatic and narrative with the addition of a "mixed" style. This way of viewing style as a concomitant of genre was readily applicable to kinds of oratory and is employed by Isocrates (e.g. *Panegyricus* 11). In the twelfth chapter of the third book of the *Rhetoric* Aristotle developed this concept into a brief outline of a demegoric, dicanic, and epideictic style. He also perceived (*Poetics* 1459a8 ff. and 1460b8 ff.) styles in poetry varying with the diction. The two categories are not specifically mingled, though the discussion of kinds of oratory does make some mention of diction (1414a22 ff.). If Theophrastus developed the topic he did nothing more unusual than he did in developing the topic of the virtues of styles or of delivery.

Since the third book of Cicero's *De oratore* is heavily indebted to Theophrastus' *On style*, the presence of the theory of the three styles in Cicero's work is some indication that they may have been found in Theophrastus. In 3.210 ff. Cicero takes up the virtue of propriety and discusses it in terms of what style to use on what occasion: various judicial speeches, deliberative speeches, or laudations require various kinds of style. The full, the plain, or the middle kind should be chosen on the basis of what is appropriate. The three styles are thus associated with kinds of oratory, as Aristotle had done, in the context of a discussion of one of Theophrastus' four virtues. We have more explicit testimony from Quintilian (3.8.61 f.), who says that Theophrastus wished the diction in deliberative oratory to be free of all affectation. In other words, Theophrastus described certain styles as appropriate to certain kinds of oratory (cf. also Quintilian 3.7.1). In so doing he applied the styles of diction as outlined in the *Poetics* to the types of oratory as outlined in the *Rhetoric*, thus combining two distinctions of his master. It would seem most logical for this discussion to have been a part of propriety, but there is no proof that Theophrastus did not allude to the kinds of oratory at more than one place in the work.

Theophrastus further instanced certain authors as examples of certain styles of diction. According to Dionysius of Halicarnassus (*Demosthenes* 3), he gave Thrasymachus as an example of a *mixed* style. Different styles are based on diction in Dionysius' discussion, but are associated with kinds of oratory, and the examples given, Gorgias, Lysias, and Thucydides in chapter two, Plato and Isocrates in chapter three, might well have been those chosen by Theophrastus.[27] We know (Cicero, *Orator* 39) that Theophrastus discussed

---

[26]Cf. Quadlbauer, *op.cit.* supra n. 25, 55 ff.

[27]Dionysius of Halicarnassus' discussion in *Lysias* 6, as Grube has shown, "Thrasymachus, Theophrastus ..." *cit.* supra n. 25, 255 ff., is not concerned with composition, but with the subjects of different kinds of oratory. It is thus related to the contents of the twelfth chapter of the third book of the *Rhetoric* (esp. 1414a11 ff.) and was probably discussed by Theophrastus under the topic of the appropriate.

the style of Thucydides and also of Herodotus. It seems quite possible that Theophrastus illustrated his remarks on literary style with the styles of artists in which both Cicero (*De oratore* 3.26) and Quintilian (12.10.3 ff.) follow him.[28]

The references indicate that Theophrastus' theory of the three styles was based on diction and associated with genre. The middle style was essentially a mixed one, that is, something half-way between the grand and the plain. In adapting this system to their own purposes, later rhetoricians did not preserve the pure categories nor did they agree on standardized models of each style. Demosthenes, Isocrates, and Lysias are often instanced, but there is a tendency to see an illustration in any triad of speakers, as when Polybius applied the system to the three philosophers Carneades, Critolaus, and Diogenes (Aulus Gellius 6.14.8 ff.). The work *On style* attributed to Demetrius deals with four styles: plain (*ischnos*), grand (*megaloprepês*), elegant (*glaphuros*), and forceful (*deinos*). These are all based on diction and subject, which is roughly similar to genre, but also each has a characteristic composition, and the styles can be mixed, so that a single author may use them all or even use more than one at the same time. Each style has a corresponding faulty version. Clearly such a system is not based directly on Theophrastus but is probably a product of the same kind of desire to describe and categorize varieties of style. The *Ad Herennium* reverts to three styles, grand, middle, and plain (4.11), and though the author speaks of composition, he seems to regard the diction, or the diction and the figures (4.16), as the basic difference. A modern reader of his examples would probably stress the difference in subject matter. We are told to vary and interchange the types of style (16). Cicero's account in *De oratore* is brief and associated with the kinds of oratory; in the *Orator* he gives a fuller account, differentiating the styles on the basis of diction, composition, and subject (20 f.). His discussion of specific orators, which follows, is complicated by his desire to refute the extreme Atticists who preferred Lysias to Demosthenes. Dionysius of Halicarnassus' *On composition* (21) distinguishes an austere, intermediate, and smooth style of composition, his essay on Demosthenes notes three styles of diction. As Grube points out Isocrates is an example of the smooth style in composition, of the middle style in diction.[29] Quintilian (12.10.58) conflates these two schemes into the plain (*ischnos*), the grand and forcible (*hadros*), and a third which some call middle, others florid (*anthêros*). He does not find any set of three categories satisfactory (11.10.66). A set of types found in some late rhetoricians is austere (Thucydides, Antiphon), middle (Demosthenes, Hyperides), plain (Lysias, Isocrates).[30]

It seems safe to say, then, that no one system of stylistic classifications

---

[28]Cf. Kennedy, *op.cit.* supra n. 25, 99 ff.

[29]G. M. A. Grube, *A Greek critic: Demetrius on style,* Toronto, 1961, 24.

[30]Trypho in Spengel 3.201, cf. Mayer, *op.cit.* supra n. 16, 5 f. In general the names of styles reflect body types, cf. Quadlbauer, *op. cit.* supra n. 25, 65 ff.

was standardized, probably because rhetoricians found it convenient to apply the terms to writers of various periods and to approach the subject from different points of view, depending on whether they wanted to stress diction, composition, or thought. The categories were also applied to delivery. What the rhetoricians do generally agree about, though there are exceptions even to this, is that there should be three categories and that one should be a mean between the others and that they may be exemplified by certain, but varying, authors.

Theophrastus' second most influential rhetorical work was in the field of delivery.[31] Aristotle (Rhetoric 1403b20 ff.) had pointed out the need for the study of delivery and said that it was a matter of management of the voice to express the emotions. These he, of course, regarded as an integral part of rhetoric, though the subject of delivery itself he labels vulgar because it was the business of actors. As subdivisions of delivery he suggests the three qualities of volume, pitch, and rhythm. Theophrastus wrote a work in one book entitled Peri hypokriseôs (Diogenes Laertius 5.48), which could be translated On delivery, and he may have discussed the subject in his handbook or elsewhere.[32] Athanasius,[33] after telling the famous story that Demosthenes said delivery was the first, the second, and the third thing in rhetoric, continues:

> "Theophrastus the philosopher says that delivery is the greatest factor an orator has for persuasion, referring delivery to first principles and the passions of the soul and the knowledge of these so that the movement of the body and the tone of the voice may be in accordance with the whole science of delivery."

The passage suggests that Theophrastus related the subject to the psychological perception which Plato demanded of rhetoric and which Aristotle tried to attain in his treatment of proof and of such parts of style as metaphor. Second, it indicates a division of the subject into the topics of voice, which we may guess to have been treated according to Aristotle's three categories, and action or gesture. Cicero (De oratore 3.221) quotes a story from Theophrastus about an actor whose fixed gaze was equivalent to turning his back on the audience. Third, it implies that a high degree of accuracy is attainable in fitting the correct tone and gesture to the word and content.

The treatment of delivery in the extant first-century B.C. writings shows

---

[31]On Theophrastus' discussion of delivery cf. F. Striller, "De Stoicorum studiis rhetoricis," Breslauer philologische Abhandlung 1 (1886) 35; Armin Krumbacher, Die Stimmbildung der Redner im Altertum bis auf die Zeit Quintilians, Paderborn, 1920, 32 ff.; Kroll 1075 f.; Solmsen, op.cit. supra n. 4, 45 f.; Caplan, op.cit. supra n. 3, 189 ff. with notes; see also Robert P. Sonkowsky, "An aspect of delivery in ancient rhetorical theory," TAPA 90 (1959) 256 ff., who discusses especially the organic relation between delivery and composition involved in associating delivery with the ethical and emotional aspects of a speech.

[32]I. Kayser, "Theophrast und Eustathios peri hypokriseôs," Philologus 69 (1910) 327 ff. casts some doubt on whether this work was really concerned with rhetoric.

[33]Cf. Hugo Rabe, Prolegomenon sylloge, Leipzig, 1931, 177, also Walz 6.35 f.

the same general categories. Cicero (*De oratore* 3.213 ff. and *Orator* 55 ff.) divides the subject into voice and gesture and says that each emotion has its own facial expression, sound, and gesture. The *Ad Herennium* has the most systematic version (3.19 ff.). It divides delivery into the figure of the voice and the movement of the body. The former has three subdivisions: *magnitudo, firmitudo, mollitudo*. Despite the terminology these present Aristotle's three categories. *Magnitudo* is volume, *firmitudo* means rhythm (for there are objections to sudden piercing exclamations and approval of long unbroken periods), and *mollitudo* refers to the tone of the voice. Tone is of three types: *sermo* or conversation, *contentio* or debate, *amplificatio* or amplification. There is a resemblance in the descriptions to the doctrine of the three styles, plain, middle, and grand. Gesture is discussed in terms of subdivisions of the three types of tone. The whole subject of delivery received very detailed attention in the late Hellenistic period and, as in other areas of rhetoric, rules took on the force of law. Our fullest account is in Quintilian, who demands four qualities (11.3.30) that are identical to the four virtues of style established by Theophrastus. This does not mean that Theophrastus made the same requirement, but it shows how delivery was stamped with Theophrastus' attitude toward rhetoric.

Stasis*

by Otto Alvin Loeb Dieter

As a rhetorical concept *stasis* may be almost as ancient as the physical *ta atoma*, or the concept of atoms, but modern rhetoricians seem to have been less successful in understanding and utilizing stasis than have modern scientists in exploiting the atom. However, I believe we may say that we have made some progress since Piderit[1] published his dissertation on Hermagoras more than a century ago. German, French, and English scholars[2] have made

---

Reprinted from *Speech Monographs* 17 (1950): 345-369. Copyright by the Speech Communication Association. 1950. Reproduced by permission of the publisher.

*I wish to express appreciation to all my colleagues and friends who have encouraged me in this study. Some have discussed difficult points of interpretation and others have given aid with the manuscript; I am especially grateful to Professors Revilo Pendleton Oliver and John Lewis Heller of the Department of Classics, and to Professors Richard Murphy, Wayland Maxfield Parrish, and Karl R. Wallace of the Department of Speech, University of Illinois.

[1] Piderit, G., *De Hermagore rhetore* (Hersfeld, 1839).

[2] The Germans:

Volkmann, Richard. *Hermagoras, oder Elemente der Rhetorik* (Stettin, 1865).

____, *Die Rhetorik der Griechen und Roemer* (Leipzig, 1885).

____, *Rhetorik der Griechen und Roemer* von Dr. Richard Volkmann. Dritte Auflage besorgt von Casper Hammer (Muenchen, 1901).

Thiele, Georg, *Hermagoras, Ein Beitrag zur Geschichte der Rhetorik* (Strassburg, 1893).

Jaeneke, Walther, *De Statuum Doctrina ab Hermogene tradita* (Leipzig, 1904).

Radermacher, L., *Hermagoras,* Pauly-Wissowa, *R. E.,* VIII.

Weidner, Richard, *Ciceros Verhaeltnis zur griechisch-roemischen Schulrhetorik seiner Zeit* (Erlangen, 1925).

Martin, Josef, *Grillius, Ein Beitrag zur Geschichte der Rhetorik* (Paderborn, 1927).

Throm, Hermann, *Die Thesis, Ein Beitrag zu ihrer Entstehung und Geschichte* (Paderborn, 1932).

Stroux, Johannes, *Summum Ius Summa Iniuria in Festschrift Paul Speiser-Sarasin* (Basil, 1926).

____, "Aus der Status-Lehre," *Philologus,* lxxxv, 1930.

____, *Roemische Rechtswissenschaft und Rhetorik* (Potsdam, 1949).

Kroll, Wilhelm, *Das Epicheirema.* Sitzungsbericht der Akademie der Wissenschaften in Wien, Phil.-hist. Klasse, Vol. 216, 2, 1937.

____, *Rhetorik* (Stuttgart, 1937).

Solmsen, Friedrich, *Die Entwickelung der Aristotelischen Logik und Rhetorik* (Berlin, 1929).

____, "The Aristotelian Tradition in Ancient Rhetoric," *American Journal of Philology,* 1941, pp. 35-50, and 169-190.

The French:

Laurand, L., *De M. T. Ciceronis studiis rhetoricis* (Paris, 1907).

____, *Manuel des Etudes Grecques et Latines* (Paris, 1929).

Cousin, Jean, *Etudes sur Quintilien* (Paris, 1936).

The English:

Cope, E. M., *An Introduction to Aristotle's Rhetoric* (London, 1867), pp. 397-400.

Sandys, J. E., *The Rhetoric of Aristotle with a Commentary* (Cambridge, 1877), I, pp. 250-251; III, pp. 179, 198, 199.

____, *M. Tulli Ciceronis Ad M. Brutum Orator* (Cambridge, 1885), p. 132.

significant contributions. Americans have in the main investigated the concept as described in some one rhetorical treatise and have sought in particular to establish an adequate English translation of the term. H. M. Hubbell's recent translation of Cicero's *De Inventione* sheds no new light on our problem. What Harry Caplan will give us on stasis in his forthcoming translation of the *Ad Herennium* remains still to be seen. We are hardly warranted, however, in expecting from any one edition, or from any translation of one rhetorical treatise, a comprehensive treatment of a concept which has played so important a role in rhetoric for so many centuries. Stasis requires and demands a comprehensive study of its own. To investigate its origin is in itself a large problem; to trace its ramifications in detail would be to write long chapters in the history of rhetoric.

In examining earlier attempts to define stasis, we seem now to recognize certain shortcomings and to notice certain peculiarities either in the scope of the investigations or in the methods of research which have no doubt influenced and perhaps also vitiated the conclusions. As such shortcomings we would list the following:

1. An apparent failure to deal adequately with the Greek term *stasis* itself. After briefly citing five etymologies mentioned by a Fifth-Century commentator on Hermogenes and declaring them all to be wrong, one worse than the other, Volkmann proceeds immediately to tell his readers what the concept involves, "leaving aside the literal meaning of the term."[3] By so doing Volkman misled himself as well as those who followed him. In his 1885 revision, he derives his entire conception and interpretation of *stasis* from the late Latin description *"quod in ea causa consistit"*;[4] he abandons all etymological explanations as unsatisfactory, gives no account of the Greek word, and discusses the concept as though it might as well have been termed *Qameç-chatuph* or *Begatkepat*. Might not this have been a mistake? In spite of the objection which some might raise, namely, that terms are significant by convention only and may be assigned to things arbitrarily and without any 'reason,' it would still seem not wholly unreasonable that the Greeks had meaning for their word. Rarely, if ever, does it happen that an existing word is arbitrarily used to denote an object unrelated by analogy or by metaphor to its basic and recognized denotation.

2. Similarly, it would seem that little effort has been made to relate the stasis-concept to Greek thought and culture. That Roman surveyors defined *status* as *uniuscuiusque altitudo*,[5] that Ptolemy (II A.D.) in his *Tetrabiblos*[6] used the term *stasis* to designate the four phases, or aspects, of the moon, that

---

[3] Volkmann, R., *Hermagoras*, p. 16: *"Sehen wir ab von der Wortbedeutung des Ausdrucks...."*
[4] Volkmann, R., *Die Rhetorik*, p. 38.
[5] *Die Schriften der Roemischen Feldmesser*, Bluhme, F., Lachmann, K., u. Rudorff, A. F. ed., (Berlin, 1848-52), I, p. 373, 2.
[6] Ptolemy, *Tetrabiblos*, edited and translated into English by F. E. Robbins, L.C.L., Harvard, 1915, p. 73.

Aristoxenus,[7] a pupil of Aristotle, described a *tasis,* i.e., a melodic pitch, or a vocal tone as a *monē kai stasis* of the voice, and that one of the few extant lines of a Seventh or Sixth Century (B.C.) Greek lyric poet, Alcaeus, reads: "I cannot understand the *stasis* of the winds"[8]—these and similar facts seem never to be mentioned in the discussions of the possible meaning of the rhetorical term. Instead there would seem to be a sort of a tacit belief, a kind of an unexpressed understanding among those who know, that the rhetorical *stasis* is wholly unique, separate, and distinct, not related to any other thing, that it sprang full bloom from one man's mind, and that his reason for designating it *stasis* was wholly esoteric and past all finding out.

3. As a third rather interesting characteristic of all previous investigations, one might mention the apparent presumption that *stasis* is Stoic in origin. Since, as Quintilian (III, vi, 3) informs us, some rhetoricians credited Naucrates with having invented the theory of *stasis,* and since Naucrates very probably lived in the Third Century, B.C., and since this was the time of the older Stoics, it seems simply to have been taken for granted that the doctrine must be Stoic in origin. But surely not everyone living in the Third Century, B.C., was a Stoic, and surely even the Stoics inherited some things from their predecessors.[9]

4. In 1904 Walter Jaeneke finally provided evidence that Plato, Aristotle, and the Peripatetic school had supplied some of the materials and terms utilized in the details of the stasis-theory. But not even Jaeneke seems to have considered the advisability of a more intensive and comprehensive investigation; he confined his research to Aristotle's *Rhetoric* and the *Organon;* and Lehnert,[10] who reviewed Jaeneke's dissertation in 1905, was very well satisfied with it and gave not the faintest suggestion that the rest of the Aristotelian corpus also might profitably be consulted.

5. Finally, a critical reader of the extant studies on the origin and meaning of stasis might observe that very little use has been made of the one rhetorical treatise which is most highly commended by critical students. Most scholars from Susemihl to Stroux agree that the brief treatise long ascribed to St. Augustine, but since 1905 commonly recognized as the Pseudo-Augustinian rhetoric,[11] is our most reliable source of pure Hermagorean rhetoric.[12] This rhetoric contains a very interesting explanation of *status.* Volkmann quoted it in Latin without comment;[13] Jean Cousin made but slight use of it;[14]

---

[7] *The Harmonics of Aristoxenus* by Henry S. Macran, (Oxford, 1902), pp. 104 and 174.

[8] *ALKAIOY MELE, The Fragments of the Lyrical Poems of Alcaeus,* Edited by Edgar Lobel, (Oxford, 1927), p. 47.

[9] Kroll, W., *Rhetorik,* 26, p. 43.

[10] Lehnert, G., in *Berliner Philologische Wochenschrift,* 16 September, 1905, pp. 1173-1176.

[11] Zurek, J., *De S. Aurelii Augustini praeceptis rhetoricis.* Dissertationes philol. Vindobonenses, VIII, 1905.

[12] Radermacher, L., *Hermagoras,* in Pauly Real-Encyclopädie, 1913, VIII, p. 693.

[13] Volkmann, R., *Die Rhetorik,* p. 106.

[14] Cousin, Jean, *Etudes,* p. 177.

later, a German scholar published his wholly negative conclusion that no clear meaning could be derived from it.[15] Yet, his failure to discover a good meaning does not overthrow the presumption that the text does make sense. The particular passage is the opening sentence in Section 12.[16] It advances a unique explanation why that which some rhetoricians designated as the *Quaestio* has by others been called *status,* namely: *ab ea videlicet quod in ea et exordium quaestionis et summa consisteret,* that is to say, "from the fact, obviously, that the beginning as well as the 'summa' of the question consists in it." The author sensed that the remark required an explanation and straightway supplied it. His explanation is very clear in itself, but it is rather difficult to see how it explains the original statement. The question arises: Whence did Pseudo-Augustine obtain this statement? Was it written in Latin or in Greek? What was the original version of the text? What did it mean? Meagre as this evidence is and difficult as it may be to interpret, it deserves more careful and serious consideration.

In this study, I have, accordingly, tried to avoid such shortcomings of research. I have attempted to examine the original meanings of *stasis* and to interpret it historically in the light of concepts logically related to it. In this way, I hope to lay the foundation for a more correct understanding of the concept.

I.

To begin with, *stasis* is not an untranslatable term. The complaint that there is no equivalent for it in a modern language is never voiced except by English scholars. Every student of Indo-Germanic philology knows that *stasis,* as well as *status,* comes from the root STA, *to stand.* It is a short root, admirably well suited for heavy duty. In ancient Greek its verbal forms have been made to serve in as many different senses as does the verb *to stand* in modern English; as an example illustrating an additional peculiarly Greek use of the verb in a causative meaning, we may cite Aristotle, 16b20, "The speaker *stops* the *dianoia"* (Cf. also, 100a1, 230a4, 247b10-18, and 407a33).

The noun *stasis* has likewise found a variety of uses. The stall in which the horses stood was to the Greeks a *hippostasis;* they spoke of the *stasis* of the wind, the *stasis* of the water, the *stasis* of the air, the *stasis* of the bowel, and of the *stasis* of politics. Plato *(Cratylus,* 426d) clearly explains *stasis* as the *apophasis* of *ienai,* i.e., the negative of the verb *to go,* the opposite of walking, going, or moving, that is to say, as a standing still. Aristotle likewise in his *Progression of Animals* speaks of the origin of the movement *(kinēsis)* of each of these parts and also of their *stasis* (706b23). In general, the Greek

---

[15]*KOINE NOESIS* in one of the standard philological journals; I have been unable to relocate it and would appreciate assistance.
[16]Halm, Karl F., *Rhetores Latini Minores,* (Leipzig, 1863), p. 144.

term seems to have been used very much as it is used by modern physicians who commonly speak of hemostasis, renal stasis, intestinal stasis, stasibasiphobia, etc.,[17] and are therefore somewhat surprised to hear that the term is causing rhetoricians trouble. Truly, stasis doesn't need to be translated into English by rhetoricians: it has already become a perfectly good modern English word, defined by Webster as meaning "a standing still." It is Greek in origin, to be sure, but like kinesis and crisis and many others, it has been received into modern terminologies. Originally and basically, *stasis* is synonymous with *ēremia* (Heraclitus A 6), i.e., a rest; it equals the English stasis, a standstill, or a standing still, the German *Stillstand*,[18] or, as Plato said (*Cratylus* 426d), the apophasis of *ienai*, and (*Sophist* 251d) the opposite of motion of any kind.

II.

When we look for stasis in ancient thought and culture, we seem to find it everywhere. *Kinēsis* and *stasis* are generally accepted contraries in Greek thought and first principles applicable to most if not to all things (*Sophist* 251d; Aristotle, 1004b29; 1013b17-25; in Latin, Varro, *De Lingua Latina*, V, ii, *motus et status*). Since kinesis is a broad concept, explained by Aristotle (251a9; 1065b5; 1066a2ff.) as the actualization of any potentiality as such, stasis must also be interpreted broadly as the opposite of any such actualization. By observation Aristotle establishes that many such actualizations take place in this world, e.g., "Air changes into water and water back into air, an animal comes to be, a child grows, stones are made into an altar and bricks into a house, a white thing gets black, a body falls, a man forgets or acquires knowledge, and he walks from Athens to Thebes."[19] Associated with each such actualization there is a corresponding stasis. Since there is also such an actualization as an *amphisbētēsis*—Aristotle's standard expression for argument, or debate—there must also somehow be associated with it a stasis and likewise with every practice, for (1222a29) every *praxis* is an actualization.

Actualizations occur, or take place in four and only four categories, viz., *Being, Quantity, Quality,* and *Place*. Actualizations in Being are called *metabolai*, i.e., 'changes'; opposite 'changes' are progressions toward and away from, or into and out of positive *Existence,* or *Being (ousia)*. Actualizations in *Quantity, Quality,* and *Place* are styled *kinēseis,* i.e., 'motions' or 'movements'; and contrary 'motions' are progressions from A to B and from B to A, when A and B are contraries such as, for example, up and down, back

---

[17]Medical Dictionaries, e.g., Gould's or Dorland's, (Philadelphia, 1943).

[18]*Die Fragmente der Vorsokratiker* von Hermann Diels, I, 145, 29. *Wortindex* verfasst von Walther Kraus, (Berlin, 1937), p. 401: *Stasis, Stillstand, syn. ēremia, Herakl, A6.*

[19]Barrett, William, *Aristotle's Analysis of Movement: Its Significance for its Time,* Columbia University Dissertation, (New York, 1938), p. 12.

and front, right and left. "One movement is contrary to another, only if the terminal points of the former are spatially contrary to those of the latter. If, e.g., A is above and B below, or A right and B left, or A front and B back, then a movement from A to B is contrary to a movement from B to A." (336a18; H. H. Joachim, Aristotle *On Coming-To-Be and Passing-Away*, Oxford, 1922, p. 257). Vertical motion is not contrary to horizontal motion: (262a12, Ross,[20] p. 712) they are different genera, or kinds, of motion. Between opposite 'changes' as well as between contrary 'motions' of the same specific kind of one and the self-same subject there must needs always be stasis. For the purposes of this investigation, it will be well for us to note particularly (224b30) "that a 'change' may start *ek tou metaxy*, i.e., from an intermediate between contraries, because for the purpose of change the intermediate can be treated as opposed to either extreme, so that it may be regarded as a kind of a contrary to them and they to it." Likewise, it will be well for us to bear in mind (229b14-21) "that movements to something between such opposites as have anything between them are to be regarded in a sense as movements towards one or the other opposite; for the movement either way—from a state between to either opposite or from either opposite to a state between—makes the state between function as the opposite from which it is receding or toward which it is approaching as the case may be. . . . For in a sense that which is between *(to gar meson)* is so called in contrast with either extreme." *(Cornford,*[21] II, p. 69ff.) Emulating the method used by Aristotle himself (89b34) we might at this time establish by observation that rhetoricians in their praxis actually *amphisbētein,* argue, or debate, 'changes' as well as 'contrary motions,' and hence must necessarily also be concerned with *staseis.*

The further one reads Aristotle's physical science the better one understands stasis. The things with which physical science deals are the things which are 'constituted by nature'; these are the things which have the principle of *kinēsis* and *stasis* in themselves (192-b14). The matters with which the productive sciences, or the arts, concern themselves, e.g., bedsteads and garments and all other things manufactured, or 'made,' are not 'constituted' by nature; the principle of *kinēsis and stasis* is not in them, but in their producer, or maker. The efficient cause, however, of anything is that in which this principle is found, be it the seed, the doctor, the advisor, or in general, the agent (195-a23)

For a more particularized understanding of the physical concept, we must turn to Aristotle's doctrine of motion as set forth in Books V-VIII of his *Physics*. In 228b7 we learn that stasis is that which disrupts, or severs motion and robs it of its continuity. In 261-b18 we are told that in contrary motions,

---

[20]Ross, W. D., *Aristotle's Physics* (Oxford, 1936). Cf. also Cherniss, Harold Frederik, *Aristotle's Criticism of Presocratic Philosophy* (Baltimore, 1935).
[21]Wicksteed, Philip H. and Cornford, Francis M., *Aristotle, The Physics.* L.C.L. Harvard, 1929 and 1934.

one motion may be considered the contrary of the other as well as the contrary of the intervening stasis, but that no motion can ever exist simultaneously either with the stasis or with its contrary motion. All 'two-way' motions must occur consecutively.

Lastly, in Book VIII, 8ff. we find the following illuminating information:

1. 261b27. The only infinite movement in this world that can possibly be single and continuous is circular movement. For everything that is moved locally is moved either in a circle or on a straight line, or in a compound of the two, so that if one of the two simple movements is discontinuous, so is the composite. Now it is clear that that which moves in a straight line does not move continuously; for it turns back on itself and therefore moves with contrary movements: up and down, forward and backwards, or left and right (Cf. Ross, p. 446).

2. 262a12. That rectilinear movement cannot be continuous is most clearly shown by the fact that when it turns back, it must necessarily stand still *(anankaion stēnai)*.

3. 262a17. That it must necessarily come to a stop *(hoti d' anankē histasthai)* is clear not only from observation, but also by argument. For there are three things, beginning, middle, and end, and the middle is beginning relatively to the end and end relatively to the beginning *(pros ekateron amphō estin)*; it is one in number but two in definition (Cf. Ross, p. 446-447).

4. *"all' ou pasa stasis ēremia estin, all' hē meta kinēsin,"* wrote Simplicius, *(Commentaria in Aristotelem,* IX, p. 264), i.e., "not every stasis is a rest, but that only which is after movement." We note that in the opposite or contrary movements from A to B and B to A, the stasis at B is not a rest in Simplicius' definition of the term: it does not occur 'after movement', but 'between movements'. Movement that is interrupted by stasis (whether it be movement on a straight line, or on a line bent back at some sharp angle (1016a14), is not one, but two movements, (264a21) and like the *meson* in which it occurs, this stasis is not a part of either movement, but a 'thing-in-between' and as such functionally (229b15) the contrary, or opposite, of both. The stasis does not indeed terminate motion though it is the terminal point of the first movement, for it is disturbed and counter motion begins before it has attained duration. Likewise, stasis is not a motion, though in a sense it is the point, or moment, of change. Since what a thing is, is determined by the function which it performs (390a10), stasis at B is neither an *ēremēsis* nor a *kinēsis,* but the station in which the mobile stands and turns. Since nothing can be at rest 'in a moment' any more than it can be in motion, this stasis is nothing permanent, but a transitory state, a temporary standing in conflict, undecided and wavering, between contrary impulses: ultimately, it must follow one or the other and become either an *ēremēsis,* or the movement contrary to the movement after which it has occurred *(kinēsis enantia kinēsei).*

We conclude that the stasis of Aristotle's physical science is the unavoidable and indispensable concomitant of all opposite and contrary rectilinear motions. It is the event which must necessarily occur in-between opposite movements of one subject on a straight line as well as in-between contrary movements of a subject on a line deflected at an angle of more than 90 degrees. It is immobility, or station, which disrupts continuity, divides motion into two movements, and separates the two from one another; it is both an end and a beginning of motion, both a stop and a start, the turning, or the transitional standing at the moment of reversal of movement, single in number, but dual in function and in definition. Because it lacks duration, it is neither a rest, nor a motion, but an opposite, or contrary, of both: a dichotomic, bi-functional entity and concept comparable and analogous to the moment in time which we conceptualize whenever we make a particular 'now' the dividing point between time-past and time-to-come (222a10).

III.

What light does this Aristotelian doctrine of kinesis and stasis shed on the rhetorical stasis as presented by Pseudo-Augustine?

1. Let us recall that there is no such thing as motion in the abstract; without a thing being moved (200b32) there can be no kinesis of any kind, either simple or compound, no opposite or contrary movements either back and forth, this way and that way, or up and down, no *amphisbētēsis* either, nor any antagonistic motions between which stasis could occur. The terms are abstractions which the mind makes for theoretical purposes (100a12); actually there is no *kinēsis* apart from a *pragma*, no *noēsis* apart from a *noēton*, no *amphisbētēsis* apart from an *amphisbētēma*, no *zētēsis* apart from a *zētēma*, etc. The abstractions never occur, never exist, never have being, except as individual, particular, concrete actualities: every *kinēsis* is some particular, specific motion, or movement, of some one thing by another; every *amphisbētēsis* is an actual individual two-way movement in thought and speech of some one specific thing by opposite or contrary-minded speakers. And what of *stasis?* Can it 'stand alone,' or be of and by itself? Just as every kinesis is a motion of a specific thing so every stasis is an individual event, a real occurrence involving specific things, surrounded and supported by specific things which collectively are referred to as its *peristasis* and individually are designated as its *peristaseis,* or circumstances. The things which surround, envelop, or are involved in the opposite, or contrary movements are the things likewise which are involved in the intervening stasis. Any doctrine, theory, or system of rhetorical *amphisbētēseis* or *staseis* must therefore take its beginning from and be founded in the *peristaseis.* "Everything depends on the circumstances." This explains the important role which *peristaseis (circumstantiae)* play in Pseudo-Augustine's presentation of the rhetorical status.

2. Like all productive sciences, or arts, rhetoric, too, is in part *Noēsis* and in part *Poiēsis* (1032b15). *Noēsis* may also be termed Deliberation, Analysis,

or Zetesis, i.e., deliberate examination, investigation, or analysis (1112b20). "In all our inquiries we are asking whether there is a middle *(ei esti meson)* or what the middle is *(ti esti to meson):* for the middle *(to meson)* is the cause *(to aition)* and it is the cause that we are seeking in all our inquiries (90a5)." Since rhetors serve their clients by 'handling' or 'managing' their *amphis-bēteseis* for them, rhetors must in the zetetic phase of their rhetorical function also seek the *stasis* which is the *meson* of the *amphisbētēsis*. This *meson* is the 'thing sought in the investigation,' or the *zētēma* in the zetesis.

3. If we would think and speak of an *antiphasis* (17a33), i.e., a pair of contradictories, or a set of contrary statements, as an *amphisbētēsis,* i.e., a two-way movement, or motion, in thought and speech this way and that way, backward and forward, or upward and downward (261b27), we must also recognize the logical postulate that there must be a *stasis* within it. Without a *stasis* there can be no such *amphisbētēsis*. The *meson,* or middle[22] of every such *amphisbētēsis* must necessarily be a *stasis.* If we conceive of the movements in thought and speech which constitute an *amphisbētēsis* as opposite or contrary movements in the vertical dimensions, or upward and downward, the *meson,* or *stasis,* is the beginning of the later as well as the end of the earlier movement (262a21), or the finishing point as regarded from below as well as the starting point as regarded from above (262b28-263a1ff), or as Pseudo-Augustine expressed himself, *"in ea et exordium quaestionis et summa consisteret."* The thought may be paraphrased thus: This which some rhetoricians style *Zetema,* or *Quaestio,* because it is the *meson,* or *media,* i.e., the thing sought in the rhetorical *zētēsis,* has by others been designated as *stasis,* or *status,* for the obvious reason that it is the *meson,* or *media,* of the *amphisbētēsis* being investigated and as such must be a *stasis;* that it is both a *meson* and a *stasis* is indicated by the fact that both the beginning and the end or the "peak" of the *amphisbētēsis,* as well as of the *zētēsis,* stands still, or consists in it.

4. Applying Aristotle's terminology to Pseudo-Augustinean rhetoric we might say: In every complete *amphisbētēsis* there are three things: beginning, middle, and end. The middle is end relative to the beginning and beginning relative to the end; it is numerically one, but dual in function. In terms of vertical dimensions, the middle *stasis* is the point of reversal, that in which both the end of the prior upward motion and the beginning of the subsequent downward motion co-exist, consist, or stand still together. Between all oppo-site, or contrary, motions, movements, functions, or actions, there must needs always be stasis.[23] The *stasis,* or the *meson,* is the *aition,* or the proximate

---

[22]Thonssen, Lester and Baird, A. Craig, *Speech Criticism* (New York, 1948), p. 93: "The concept of the status, or the location of a center of argument." These authors are the first writers in centuries expressly to reassociate *stasis* with the *meson.* If we consider the movement of debate as a continuum, *stasis* is the *meson,* or *metaxy,* the *media,* middle, or 'in-between,' i.e., the center of the argument.
[23]Caisson, Stanley, *Progress and Catastrophe* (New York, 1937), p. 208. Mayo, Elton, *The Social Problems of an Industrial Civilization* (Boston, 1945), p. xiii.

cause, of any both-way movement, and hence also of an *amphisbētēsis*. Since in rhetorical *noēsis* we investigate an *amphisbētēsis* to find its middle, or its cause, the 'thing sought in the *zētēsis*,' i.e., the *zētēma* and the *stasis* of the *amphisbētēsis* are identical and the terms may well be used synonymously and interchangeably.

Our conclusion is that the *status* described in Pseudo-Augustine's *Vorlage* is the *stasis* of earlier Greek rhetoric, a Peripatetic adaptation to rhetoric of the *stasis* of Aristotelian physics and is, therefore, to be understood as a metaphoric use of a clear and precise term of physical science.

IV.

Rhetoricians found Aristotle's physical philosophy, specifically his theory of motion of which stasis is an integral part, eminently useful for their purposes.

A. It provided the condition for a scientific theory of rhetoric. If in this world *panta rhei aei,* that is to say, everything always is only in continuous flux and change, it would indeed seem to be poorly suited and ill-adapted for logical and rhetorical purposes. If in passing from the Lyceum to the marketplace, Koriscos not only changes his incidental relationships, but also his essential identity (219b22), any course of action which implied personal responsibility and accountability, though it might be practically useful and expedient, must, strictly speaking, be considered pseudo-scientific, at best, a kind of 'as if' procedure. The rhetoric which had been developed in harmony with the philosophy of eternal change was sophistic rhetoric: unreal, superficial, illogical, and unscientific, designed only to achieve "persuasion" by any means, and wholly inadequate in the mode of logical proof (1354a).

The world of Aristotle's physical philosophy, in contrast, provided the necessary basis and prerequisities for scientific thinking and speaking, logic and rhetoric. It was a world in which, in addition to circular motions, or movements, there were also rectilinear motions, or movements "on a straight line." There is not only *metabolē* and *kinēsis* in this world, but also *stasis*. Since all subjects of whatever kind of motion are more concrete and more comprehensible in stasis than they are in motion, it was the concept of stasis that appealed particularly to the rhetoricians. In the long struggle of rhetoric with philosophy, as reflected, for example, in the comic fragments of Epicharmus,[24] it was Aristotle's doctrine of motion and stasis that gave rhetoricians the ultimate basis for their art. Reinforced by the dictum of the Stagirite (265a3-12, . . . those physicists are mistaken who say that all objects of sense are always in motion . . .), every rhetorician could henceforth, even in the presence of his old foes, boldly lift up his head and raise his voice.

---

[24] Kaibel, Georg, *Comicorum Graecorum Fragmenta,* I, 1, (Berlin, 1899). Norwood, Gilbert, *Greek Comedy* (London, 1931), pp. 83-113.

B. The philosophy which provided the *sine qua non* of a scientific rhetoric also provided a theoretical background for such a rhetoric. Briefly, it was this: Rhetoric is a composite and a hybrid art.

(1) The things with which rhetoric deals may in a sense be said to be 'physical,' or 'natural,' for they have a 'physical' generation in that they 'arise' or 'grow out of' natural circumstances and events; hence, they may also be said to have a 'nature.' In a sense, then, rhetoric is a natural, a physical, or a *meta*-physical science. The rhetorician is a *'physikos'* in that he "selects perceptible and changeable substance, and studies it in respect to the movement or to the other forms of change to which it is liable; he studies a part only of the real and investigates that part not *qua* real, but *qua* changeable." For "the part of the real which the *physikos* studies is 'composite substance' *(synthetos ousia),* i.e., a union of two elements, concrete of form and matter, and thus secondary and derivative in its being." (H. H. Joachim, *On Coming-To-Be,* pp. xviii, xix, xxxi).

(2) The things with which rhetoric deals are things done or things to be done, practical things; it is a practical science.

(3) Finally, rhetoric is a productive science, or an art, for it attains its specific purpose in making speeches concerning either things that have been done or things that ought to be done in life (192b8 and 1025b1ff), i.e., motions, movements, or actions.

Like all artificial production, rhetorical activity consists of two processes: *Noēsis* (Cogitation) and *Poiēsis* (Production proper).

The subject matter of both phases, or functional processes of rhetoric, is a stasis, that is to say, a temporary standing between contradictories or contrary statements, or a thing temporarily 'divided' between contrary willed and hence contrarily thinking, speaking, and acting agents.

In the process of rhetorical Noesis, Zetesis, or Analysis, the rhetor investigates the stasis professionally. Deliberately he inquires whether or not there is in the matter before him any valid rhetorical stasis. He 'thinks the matter through' and 'realizes the stasis intellectually,' as that in which the *amphisbētēsis,* or argument, ends and begins, or as we would say, begins and ends, i.e., wholly consists. Such a professional examination will reveal that every proposed matter is either asystatic, synestotic, or stasiastic. Only stasiastic matters are fit subjects for rhetorical treatment; astasiastic, or astatic, matters must be carefully avoided in the interests of a successful representation. The most common of the astatic and perhaps the easiest to detect are the asystatic, for these matters lack integration, completeness, unity, coherence; they are not 'whole,' but incomplete, irrational, alogical, unrelated and disassociated accumulations merely of useless materials, or *phlegmata,* i.e., 'unconstituted' excretions (539a18) of a body, in which there is no 'life,' and hence they are utterly worthless and unusable for rhetorical purposes. Of these, ancient rhetoric recognized two classes, the second having three types.

1. A matter which is lacking in essential *peristaseis* is asystatic because of its incompleteness; the known, or knowable, circumstances do not

constitute a perfect whole, do not provide a continuous medium for any movement; matters of this kind may be said to be inchoate, unfinished, imperfect, atelic.

2. Even though essential *peristaseis* are present in a matter, adequate in number and of the proper quality and kind, it may yet be asystatic if the movements in which the circumstances are involved do not meet specific requirements. a) A matter may be asystatic *kat' isotēta*, i.e., due to the 'likeness' of the movements involving the circumstances. Actually there are no two movements, but only one, in matters such as these: both parties direct one and the same motion at one another, due to the peculiarity of the circumstances anything said by the one party can with equal validity be said also by the other; these 'rasps' or 'saws' cut both ways equally well and it is impossible to detect a critical difference between the 'two' movements. b) A matter may be asystatic *kath' heteromerean*, i.e., due to its one-sidedness; for the purposes of a possible defensive movement all the circumstances are "on the other side," the *peristaseis* admit only one movement, not two. c) Lastly, a matter may be asystatic due to a difficulty involved in it. Critical analysis of a matter of this kind reveals an *aporon*, i.e., an aporia. The movements in a matter such as this are so indistinct, unstable, fluctuating, and confusing that it is impossible for any one to find a logical way through it. These are the *asystata* which the examining rhetor must be quick to recognize and to reject; their rhetorical inadequacy is associated either with the *peristaseis* or with the movements in the circumstances.

Matters which in Noesis are found not to be asystatic in either of these four ways are said to be synestotic, i.e., essentially complete, cohesive, coherent, and unified. But they need not for that reason be yet suitable for rhetorical treatment. The movements 'over,' 'around,' 'about,' or 'in' the circumstances may all be compatible with one another, i.e., progressively complementary one to the other either along one and the same straight line, or at angles less than 90 degrees. Like the tributaries of a river,[25] each individual movement makes its contribution to the whole and all merge and blend with one another so that there is no difference between them but all become one. In modern terminology we would say that these matters are fit subjects for discussion, but not for debate. Finally, the professional investigator will recognize certain synestotic matters which in truth and in fact are stasiastic: the *peristaseis* in these matters are essentially complete and adequate and the movements involving the circumstances are either diametrically opposite or at least 'anakamptically' contrary one to the other: these, *kat' exochēn*, are proper and fit subjects for the professional rhetor's praxis.

In eventual developments of this kind there will be "fighting language," or "a war of words" *(onomatōn stasiasantōn, Cratylus, 438d)* in that some

---

[25]Dewey, John, *Art as Experience* (New York, 1934), p. 41.

aver that *they* express the truth while others insist that *they* do and hence a
criterion other than words will be required in accordance with which decision
may be made between them.[26] In these encounters the parties are "not
unanimous concerning a matter of some magnitude" (1167a22); they are not
"like-minded" (1241a28), they do not "speak the same way, or say the same
thing" *(mē homologoumena,* 1135b28, 1280a19, 1358b31, 1363b6); they
'stasiazein,' i.e., 'make stasis' with one another and 'fight' *(machountai,*
1241a28), in that they make conflicting statements about one and the same
matter and say of a self-same thing that it is both so and not so; hence, they
amphisbētein (1010b20, 1280a19, 1299a29, 1300b27, 1281a9, 1363b6,
1358b31), putting 'pressure on one another' (1167a22), the one attacking and
the other defending (1358b12).

Having 'discovered' and probed the stasis in the matter before him, the
rhetorician proceeds to inquire of what 'nature' or kind the stasis is (89b34).
He classifies the stasis according to the classification which rhetorical theory
has developed after the pattern of Aristotle's classification of 'changes' and
'contrary motions in *Quantity, Quality,* and *Place'* and ultimately applies to it
proofs from the topics which rhetoric has devised for his purposes.

Corresponding to the diametrically opposite 'motions,' or 'changes'
(metabolai, 227a7, 229a9, 264b14), which Aristotle had distinguished in the
Category *Being,* rhetoricians recognized a stasis between contradictory
allegations of factuality which they designated *stasis stochasmos,* or *status
conjecturalis,* with reference to the claims of being and nonbeing between
which it intervenes. (According to Quintilian III, vi, 53, some styled it
genesis; Theodorus, according to Ps.-Augustine, 9, spoke of it as *peri tēs
ousias,* i.e., *de substantia,* or *concerning Being).* Graphically, this stasis in
'change' may be represented, thus:

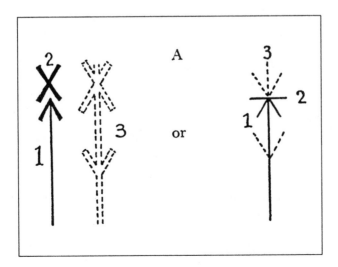

---

[26]Plato *VI,* by H. N. Fowler, L.C.L., (London, 1926), p. 184.

The three components depicted are: 1. A motion, or movement, toward one positive goal, i.e., *Existence,* an affirmative allegation, or a positive declaration as of fact, such as, "It is a fact that John hit Mary." 3. A motion or movement, away from the same positive goal, i.e., a negative statement of fact, a denial of factuality, such as, e.g., "It is not a fact that he hit her." 2. The 'standing-in-between' the diametrically opposite assertions, or the central station of opposite movements which cannot be indicated either in a graph or in words without presenting the conflicting vectors between which it is located, viz., "he hit her" ⋀ "he did not." Realizing the incompatibility of the two declarations, the mind, in doubt, converts these original motions into: 1. "Is it a fact that he hit her?" 3. "Or isn't it?" 2. The articulation: "Did he hit her, or not?"

On an abscissa representing time the stasis in 'change' may be graphed, thus:

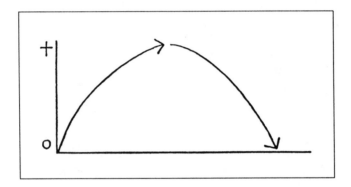

The opposite motions are (1) from zero (0) to plus (+) and (2) away from plus (+); no minus (-) is involved, i.e., no negative opposite to the positive goal.

In a modified graph of a function, the stasis appears as the cusp:

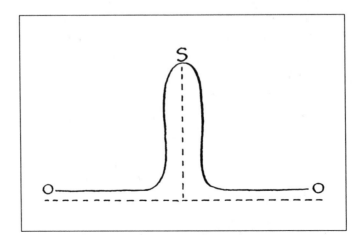

Let OS+ represent the affirmation and +SO the negation: the station, or stasis, is at S.

Analogous to the physical counter 'motions' which Aristotle had differentiated in the Categories *Quality, Quantity,* and *Place,* (225b5-226a25), the new rhetoric recognized stases between contrary statements, or in altercations concerning *Quantity, Quality,* or *Place.* The three stases may be represented in one diagram thus:

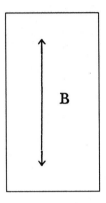

or individually, thus:

The three factors represented are: 1. A motion, i.e., an affirmation, or a declaration that a subject is positive in *Quantity, Quality,* or *Place.* 3. A motion, i.e., a negation, or a declaration that the subject is negative in *Quantity, Quality,* or *Place.* 2. The intervening stasis, or station central in the system of contrary motions, "It is so ⋀ It is not so."

In time, these three stases may be represented thus:

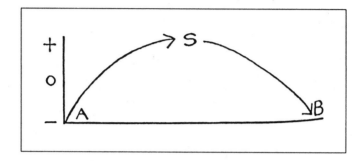

The motions are (1) toward the positive goal and (2) from the positive to the contrary negative. The stasis is at *S, between* the contrary motions AS and SB.

According to 229b1, these contrary movements may also be envisioned as passing either from the extremes to an intermediate or from the intermediate to the extremes. The rhetorical stases may accordingly also be represented as in either of the following diagrams:

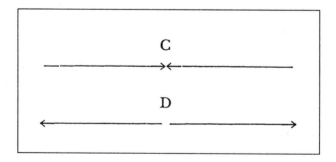

For didactic as well as for practical purposes, rhetoricians arranged and combined the four categories of rhetorical kinesis and stasis into a progressive series, sequence, or system, which may be represented, as follows:

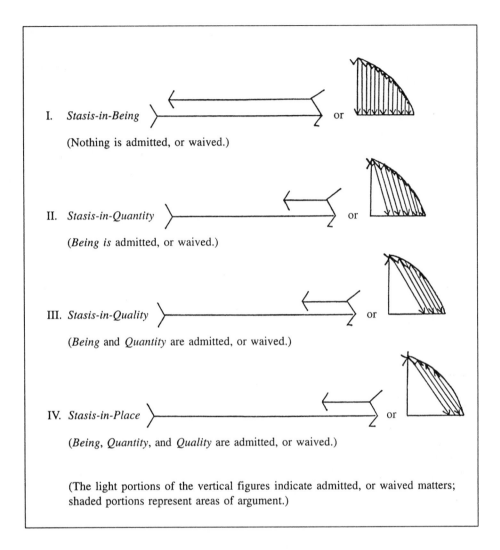

I. *Stasis-in-Being*

(Nothing is admitted, or waived.)

II. *Stasis-in-Quantity*

(*Being is* admitted, or waived.)

III. *Stasis-in-Quality*

(*Being* and *Quantity* are admitted, or waived.)

IV. *Stasis-in-Place*

(*Being, Quantity,* and *Quality* are admitted, or waived.)

(The light portions of the vertical figures indicate admitted, or waived matters; shaded portions represent areas of argument.)

Since Being is the principal category in Aristotelian logic, *Stasis* in *Being* is the first which the rhetor must consider in critically appraising a stasiastic matter; when he has satisfied himself that the stasis is not in *Being,* he inquires in turn whether it is in *Quantity, Quality,* or *Place.* To mistake, or misjudge the category of the stasis might seriously jeopardize a representation from the beginning, if not pre-determine its failure. A 'move' may be 'stasiated', i.e., 'stopped, converted, and repulsed' in from one to four ways; in every instance, however, it is the category of the counter-kinesis that determines the category of the stasis as well as the category of the resulting *amphisbētēsis;* in modern terms we might say that the category of the Answer "characterizes" (Cf. Walz, C., *Rhetores Graeci,* iv, 795, 18, and v, 592) the stasis as well as the argument-both-ways which results from it. The stasis (indicated by $\sum$ or $\wedge\!\wedge$ on the charts) is always the end, or peak of the first 'move' and the beginning of the second; hence, it is also a middle and the immediate, or proximate cause which generates, determines, and characterizes the consequent *amphisbētēsis,* or controversy, for every such *amphisbētēsis* starts as and from a stasis and 'grows out' of a stasis. In Stasis I, unqualified Being, or the subject's actual existence, is challenged, controverted, and rejected; there is no agreement whatever between the speakers on the subject and the area of dispute is considerable. In Stasis II, the subject's actuality or actual *Being* is admitted, or waived, but its quantification, or *Being-in-Quantity,* is checked, 'retorted' and denied and the area of disagreement is more limited. In Stasis III, the subject's *Being* and *Quantity* are admitted, or waived, but its qualitative *Being,* i.e., *Being-in-Quality* is 'arrested, re-directed, and repelled' and the extent of the dispute is correspondingly restricted. In Stasis IV, the subject's *Being, Quantity,* and *Quality,* are admitted, or waived; its *Being-in-Place* only is 'not allowed to pass,' but 're-turned' and 'hurled back.' To exemplify. The charge: "It is a fact that you stole my car," may be 'stasiated' and controverted entirely in *Being,* thus: "It is not a fact that I stole your car." Or, it may be denied and rejected in part only, i.e., quantitatively, thus: "That I stole your car is not a fact, I merely borrowed it." Again, the selfsame Charge may be 'stasiated qualitatively only,' thus: "That I stole your car is a fact, but under the circumstances it was a good thing that I did." Lastly, the Charge may be met, 'stasiated' and rebuffed by an Answer in the category of *Being-in-Place*, e.g., "It *is not in Place for you* to take this action, or to bring this charge *at this time,* or *in this court,* or *in this manner* etc." If the aggressive 'move' is not 'stasiated,' i.e., stopped, 're-volved,' and 're-jected,' either in *Being absolutely,* in *Being quantitatively,* in *Being qualitatively* or in *Being-in-Place,* there is no rhetorical stasis, no 'revolution,' and no *amphisbētēsis.* To *amphisbētein* is to make conflicting statements about a matter, to 'move,' or to argue it both ways; *ambigitur status* (Lucretius, III, 1074) means to activate a stasis from both sides, to agitate it, or to push it in contrary directions. To speak against a motion, to 'categorize' a statement, or to 'stasiate' a charge, is to negate, deny, or gainsay it, i.e., to say that it is not so either actually, quantitatively, or qualitatively, or to say that for some reason it is not in place.

We should note also that these four categories of rhetorical kinesis and stasis may be re-arranged, re-designated, widened or narrowed in scope, or further subdivided to suit the whims or wishes of any technical writer without in any way vitiating the essential character and validity of the stasis-theory in general.

V.

In the light of Aristotle's doctrine of physical kinesis and stasis certain statements by ancient rhetoricians concerning the stasis become more readily intelligible. For example, if we bear in mind the composite graph of the four basic stases, we have no difficulty in understanding how Cicero in *Tusculan Disputations,* III, 33, 79, could explain the term status with the parenthetic statement, *sic enim appellamus controversiarum genera,* i.e., for so we rhetoricians designate the (three or four) kinds, or classes, of controversies. By synecdoche, stasis, or status, the name of the part comes to stand for the whole, and the thing comes to stand for the class or the classes of the thing.

Wholly meaningful and proper, also, becomes the language used by Cicero in his *Topica* 25, 93: *stasis . . . in quo primum insistit quasi ad repugnandum congressa defensio,* i.e., stasis is where (the place at which) the defense, set to meet the attack, first steps into the affray, so to speak, for the purpose of fighting back (or making a 'retort,' or staging a 'come-back'). The lines of action, as here presented by Cicero, are orientated as they are in Aristotle's *Physics:* it is at ΛΛ that the prior motion comes to rest; the first speaker, i.e., the plaintiff, evidently intends his statement to be a final one, but his 'rest' is immediately disturbed, for the defendant, set, as it were, to meet the attack, steps in, puts his foot down, as it were, on the same ground, and insists on using the plaintiff's resting-place as the starting place of his contrary motion. Like the two brothers mentioned by Aristotle (1167a22, cf. Euripides, *Phoenissae,* 558), plaintiff and defendant both insist on having one and the same thing, each for his own purpose, both desire 'to have things their own way,' to rule, to dominate, to be supreme, and consequently, they *stasiazein,* or make stasis with one another, i.e., block one another, actualize a separation, or division, between them.

In the light of what has been set forth, we are able to appreciate the Latin term *constitutio* with which Roman rhetoricians interpreted the Greek *stasis.* The unknown *auctor ad Herennium* (I, 11, 8) described a rhetorical *constitutio* as the *prima deprecatio defensoris cum accusatoris insimulatione conjuncta,* i.e., the original deprecation of the accused joined with the accusation of the adversary. A *constitutio,* then, is a synthesis, a conjunction, co-stasis, or 'standing together' of specific statements, or declarations, between which there is an interval of conflict, or disagreement. The Latin term is analogous to the Greek *systasis* and a usable equivalent for both *systasis* and *systēma* as applied, for instance, in the theory of Greek music.[27] As authority for this use of the term, the *auctor* might also cite Aristotle, particularly in 646a8-647a5 where he discusses the processes of generation by which the various 'parts' of animal bodies are formed, or the 'aitia,' i.e.,

[27] *The Harmonics of Aristoxenus,* by Henry S. Macran, p. 98 & 168. "An Interval *(diastēma)* is the distance bounded by two notes which have not the same pitch," I, 15, p. 176. "Compound intervals as a matter of fact are in a sense scales *(systēmasin),*" I, 5, p. 168. "A scale *(systēma)* is to be regarded as the compound of two or more intervals," I, 16, p. 108. "The number and character of the scales *(systēmata)* are deduced from the intervals," p. 168. See also, *Musici Scriptores Graeci,* Carolus Janus (Leipzig, 1895), p. 179, 7; 180, 2; 243, 4; 261, 19; 292, 18, etc. See also, Boetii, *De Institutione Musica,* Godofredus Friedlein (Leipzig, 1867), p. 341: "Constitutio vero est plenum veluti modulationis corpus." Macran, p. 168, translates *tēn tou melous systasin* with "the constitution of melody" and systema with *system,* or scale. Note also, the German: "Die Konstitution der Musik." For an illuminating discussion of the importance of the *mesē* in the systems of Greek music, see Schlesinger, Kathleen, *The Greek Aulos* (London, 1939), p. 182ff.

causes, by which these parts have come to be as they are. The first generative process, or cause is a *synthesis,* while the second and third are *systaseis.* A *synthesis* is a mere juxtaposition, or mechanical mixture of elements; the first *systasis* is a chemical combination in which the qualities of the components are transformed and a new, wholly homogeneous body is created; the final *systasis* is the bringing, or coming together and the resulting 'standing together' of contrary informations of a homogeneous matter to constitute a functional member, or an instrumental organ of the body, as for example, a femur and a tibia are articulated to form a leg.[28] A *systasis, systema,* or *constitutio,* then, is a constitution, a 'physical' nature, or a natural body, i.e., in rhetoric, the physical incorporation, natural organization, organic make-up, or vital system of a controversy.

In terms of this science, rhetoricians spoke of the *peristaseis* (Who? What? When? Where? How? Why? By what means?) as the *stoicheia,* or elements of a rhetorical matter. Essential and indispensable as these are, they must be used in the rhetorical processes as they are found in the 'nature' of the matter. Of, or out of these elemental matters, or elements are constituted a Charge and an Answer as contrary informations of one and the same matter. Of, or out of these homogeneous, but contrary 'parts' is constituted and comes into being a 'non-uniform,' or 'anomoiomerous' instrumental 'part,' or organ of function (378b19). This constitution of contrary information is a vital organon of motion (336a18); it can move, or be moved in opposite, or contrary motions; rhetorically, it can be argued, i.e., set forth and advanced in argumentative speeches, for it has (26a26-261a26 and 336a20) innately inherent within it an originative source of kinesis as well as of stasis, or an impulse to change (Cf. Joachim, *On Coming-To-Be,* p. xxi and 256), that is to say, it could go, or be made to go this way or that way, but presently it is in dire need of assistance, for due to its equally potent conflicting impulses it is actually in stasis, or (as automotive engineers say of reciprocating pistons) "at top dead center," wholly equilibrized, immobilized, and paralyzed, unable to move either way. It cannot decide, determine, or dispose itself; cannot 'turn over,' get started, set off, come through, determine its course and pursue it effectively, *(diatithesthai,* cf. Sextus Empiricus, *Against the Rhetoricians.* II, 62); to do that is the work of the accomplished speaker, according to Hermagoras. The *constitutio* of the *auctor ad Herennium,* then, is the functionally dual *stasis* of Greek rhetoric interpreted mechanically, organically, physiologically, functionally, or bodily, as a part of a body, a member, a limb, or a joint in which there is both stasis and motion, as a *kampē* which Aristotle (702a22) described as the beginning of one thing and

---

[28]Duering, Ingemar, *Aristotle's De partibus animalium* (Goeteborg, 1943), p. 125, and *Aristotle's Chemical Treatise, Meteorologica, Book IV,* 1944, p. 11.

Peck, A. L., Aristotle *Parts of Animals,* Book II, L.C.L. Harvard, 1937, p. 106ff.

Joachim, H. H., *Aristotle on Coming-to-be and Passing-away* (Oxford, 1922); also "Aristotle's Conception of a Chemical Combination" in *Journal of Philology,* 1904, pp. 72-86.

the end of another constituting a *physikon sōma,* a bodily source and implement of motion (433b20 and 703a22), the psychical counterpart of which is the articulate question (1041b4), or, as Sextus Empiricus *(Against the Geometricians,* III, 4) styled it, the 'rhetorical' question. The implication clearly is that when rhetors deal with constitutions they are not dealing with elementary matters but with real existing things of considerable complexity and advanced development.

In terms of modern physics one might perhaps describe the *constitutio* of the auctor as the physical contrivance, or engine, by means of which, after it has been set into motion, rhetorical heat can be converted into oratorical energy and transmitted to the listener as the power of effective response.

In his first rhetorical treatise, the *De Inventione,* Cicero as a young man undertook to set forth in Latin his interpretation of the theory of Greek rhetoric which he had received from his teachers. As we read the text,[29] Cicero begins his exposition of rhetorical analysis by affirming his presumption concerning the genesis of a rhetorical matter: *Omnis res,* every real thing proposed for rhetorical action, in which there is observable a *controversia* of one of the four possible kinds, also has within it a *quaestio* of the same kind, out of which the controversy was generated, or developed. In other words, every *controversia* is a generation, a natural, organic development, an automotive, bilateral outgrowth from within, the outcome, product, and result of a generic process which starts from a vital center, a living nucleus, or an original stock; the antecedent of every *controversia* (⟵⟶) is a *contraversio.*[30] (→←) Translated into terms of Aristotelian *Physics* (255b31-256a2), Cicero is here declaring that in every occurrence of

'contrary movements' thus, $\updownarrow$ (or so, ⟵⟶), as depicted in graphs A and B,—which may also be interpreted as 'contrary movements,' thus, $\updownarrow$ (or so, ← →) as represented in graph D—there must necessarily also be 'counter movements,' thus, $\updownarrow$ (or so, ⟶←⟵), as pictured in graph C, from which

the evolution has proceeded. Further to elucidate Cicero's statement, we offer the following. In the generation of reciprocating motion which Cicero is discussing at least six moments, or stages, may be differentiated; represented in horizontal lines and described rhetorically, these moments might be visualized as follows, reading from the bottom, up:

6.　　　　⟵⟶ : *amphisbētēsis, controversia.*
5.　　　　←---- : a reiterated Answer, intensified to controvert the restated Charge.

---

[29]*De Inventione,* I, 8, 10ff., in Teubner edition by Ed. Stroebel, (Leipzig, 1915).
[30]Stroux, Johannes, *Contraversia, Philologus,* 84 (1929), pp. 368-376.

4.   ⟶ : a renewed Charge, modified and intensified to
                  controvert the Answer.
3. ⟶⟵– – – – : *stasis, zētēma, status, quaestio, prima conflictio.*
2.   ⟵– – – – : an Answer in which there is a denial of the Charge.
1. ⟶   : a positive assertion, an incrimination, a Charge.

Or, these six moments might be visualized in vertical lines and exemplified,
as follows:

6.   ↓ : "I borrowed it." "You did not borrow it."

5.   ↓ : "Most assuredly, I did borrow it."

4. | : "You most certainly did not borrow it."

3.   ↕ : "You stole it." "I borrowed it."

2.   ↕ : "I did not steal, I borrowed it."

1. | : "You stole my horse."

Both schematic representations indicate that 6 might be considered a
development of 3; the secondary, or consequent ⟵⟶ grows out of the
primary, or antecedent ⟶⟵; the immediate, or proximate cause of the ↕
is the ↕; if there had not been a ↕ or a ⟶⟵, no ↕ or ⟵⟶ could have
developed. Greek rhetoricians had designated the ultimate development as an
amphisbētēsis, i.e., a going both ways, or a going apart; the antecedent
configuration, they termed *stasis.* Every *amphisbētēsis,* the Greeks said,
begins as and from a *stasis;* unless a *stasis* has occurred, no *amphisbētēsis*
can begin to be. Roman rhetoricians, however, had accustomed themselves to
think and speak of the final development in this process as a *controversia,*

that is, a controversy. Hence, the question arose: Could the term *status,* the Latin equivalent of the Greek *stasis,* properly be used in Roman rhetoric? Was it correct to say that a *controversia* developed from a *status?* Did a stop, or a standstill actually occur before the contrary statements controverted one another? Some Roman rhetoricians decided that the term could so be used; others preferred to describe as *quaestio* that out of which a controversy arises. The term *quaestio* however, in this context was also open to criticism: it was already being used in a bewildering number of different senses; its predominant connotation for the student was grammatical and syntactical; pedagogically, it would therefore be more correct to apply the term to the individual, or particular question in controversy (as Cicero does in *De Inventione,* I, viii, 18); above all, neither was the term *quaestio* well suited for use in a context with genesis, or generation. But how otherwise might one describe and designate this *stasis, meson, aition?* Or, this *zētēma?* This *media quaestio* out of which a *controversia is generated?* "We," wrote Cicero, "call this *quaestio ex qua causa nascitur,"* a *"constitutio."* The term clearly is a Latin equivalent for the Greek *systasis* and admirably meets the requirements of the specific context in which he uses it. That a configuration of forces which might be represented graphically thus, or so, ——————→‹——————, should be called a *systasis,* or a *constitutio,* would seem intelligible to any educated Greek or Roman without argument. For the vectors obviously represent opposite, or contrary movements, or motions, on one and the same straight line, in head-on collision, meeting and stopping one another. Between such opposite, or contrary, *kinēsis,* or *motus,* there must needs be stasis, or status, single in number, but dual in function, a two-in-one, or a one-in-two. The two forces involved are clearly *"hama,"* or 'standing together' in the sense of 226b18; they are also *haptesthai,* or 'touching' in the sense of 226b25, i.e., 'standing in contact with one another' in that their extremes are 'together.' Clearly, then, this is not only a *stasis,* or a *status,* but also a *systasis* and a *constitutio,* i.e., a constitution in the sense of the formative, or generative action or process of constituting, as well as in the sense of the composite substance, or corporate being, concrete of matter and form, thereby constituted, made to consist, or brought into existence. That this terminology was well suited for use in context with generation and genesis may likewise easily be demonstrated.

In evidence, we present the following. (1) *Systasis* is a Greek noun, ending in *sis,* denoting a process; the verbs *synhistanai* and *synhistathai* are frequently used in Greek, also by Aristotle, closely associated with *genesis* and *gignesthai* (Cf. Aristotle *Generation of Animals,* A. L. Peck, L.C.L., Cambridge, 1943). From Peck's *Preface* we quote in part: (52) Genesis is a process of change; in fact, it is the most fundamental sort of change, viz., 'coming into being'; hence, the product resulting from a process of *genesis* is some *ousia* . . . (53) *Genesis* and its verb *gignesthai* are terms of frequent occurrence in Aristotle, and especially in *Generation of Animals.* In the title of the treatise, *genesis* is commonly translated "generation," and this is a convenient rendering of it there; but we must not forget that *genesis* also refers to the whole process of an animal's development until it has reached its completion; that is to say, *genesis* includes the whole subject of reproduction and embryology. . . . I have therefore commonly used "formation," "process of formation," and the like to render *genesis* and for *gignesthai* "to be formed," "to come to be formed," etc. (54) Another verb closely connected with *gignesthai* is the verb *synhistanai,* which might almost be regarded as the active voice of *gignesthai,* though *synhistanai* tends rather to refer *to the beginning of the process.* (Italics mine.) It is especially frequent in passages describing the initial action of the semen in constituting a "fetation" out of the menstrual fluid of the female. . . . *Synhistanai* therefore denotes the first impact of Form upon Matter, *the first step in the process of actualizing the potentiality of Matter.* (Italics mine.) Sometimes I have used "constitute," sometimes "set," sometimes "cause to take shape"; and for *synhistasthai,* which is also very frequent, "set" (intransitive), "take shape," "arise," etc. (55) Another possible rendering would have been "organize"; and indeed "organizers" is a term which has recently been introduced into embryology to denote substances which are responsible for bringing about the differentiation of the parts of the embryo.

(2) Aristotle himself uses the noun *systasis* in a comparable sense with reference to living animals, cf. 766a25: And when one vital part changes, the whole make-up of the animal *(systasis tou zōou)* differs greatly, in appearance and form (Peck, p. 391).

(3) In 767b18ff., Aristotle gives an enlightening account of his use of the term "movement" in connection with genesis and generation: "It comes to the same thing whether we say the 'semen' or 'the movement which makes each of the parts grow'; or whether we say 'makes them grow' or 'constitutes' and 'sets' them from the beginning—because the *logos* of the movement is the same either way." (Peck, p. 403.)

(4) Most significant, perhaps, and influential in determining Cicero's choice and use of the term *constitutio* in his rhetoric, was the fact that Aristotle himself used the term *systasis,* or *systaseis,* in speaking of the primates, or the primeval forms of animal life mentioned by Empedocles as the aboriginal "crossbreeds" from which all present forms of animal life have been propagated. (199b5: Thus in the original combinations—*en tais ex archēs ara systasesi*—the 'ox-progeny' if they failed to reach a determinate end must have arisen through the corruption of some principle corresponding to what is now the seed—*sperma.* Further, seed must have come into being first, and not straightway the animals: the words 'whole-natured first'— Empedocles, *Fragment* 62,4—must have meant seed. Ross, *Physics,* 199b.) As we know, e.g., from Fragments[31] #61 and #62, Empedocles had suggested a theory of prehistoric monsters, or primitive brutes, unmodified, mixed and contrary in form and nature, from which all present-day animals have

---

[31]Diels, Hermann, *Die Fragmente der Vorsokratiker* (Berlin, 1934), p. 334.

developed. William E. Leonard[32] translates Fragment #62, as follows:

> Many were born with twofold brow and breast,
> Some with the face of man on bovine stock,
> Some with man's form beneath a bovine head,
> Mixed shapes of being with shadowed secret parts,
> Sometimes like men, and sometimes women-growths.

Aristotle (199b9-12) raised the question whether there had been such *systaseis* in plants also, e.g., 'olive-headed vine-progeny' comparable to the 'man-headed ox-progeny' in animals. He concluded that there must have been, if there were such things among animals. Young Cicero apparently had likewise concluded that there must have been and must be such things among controversies. Hence, he wrote in his *Rhetorica* about the *constitutiones causarum* or the *constitutiones controversiarum*, and never mentioned the term stasis, or status.

(6) The reader's special attention is invited to the terms *amphiprosōpa* and *amphisterna* ('double faces' and 'double fronts') in the Greek original. They may remind one of the *amphisbaina*, a fabulous monster which 'goes' either or both ways, perhaps with a head at each end, mentioned, e.g., by Aeschylus in *Agamemnon*, 1233. We may recall that the Greek verb *amphisbētein* and the noun *amphisbētēsis*, in use since the Fifth Century, became Aristotle's standard expressions for 'arguing' and 'argumentation.' Perhaps these terms, too, imply that 'controversies' are 'mixed shapes of being,' *'Mischwesen,'*[33] or mongrels. In his *De Inventione* Cicero recognized four such mongrel forms of conflict-life: Every; *pragma, res,* real thing, or being in which there is controversy is an individual modification of an original mongrel strain of controversy; every "live" controversy at any time is a current specimen, or an individual development, of one of these primordial forms: 1. You did $\wedge$ I didn't. 2. You did this $\wedge$ I did that. 3. You did this $\wedge$ And a good thing it was. 4. You did this $\wedge$ You are 'out of order.' Accordingly, Cicero did not perpetuate the Greek doctrine of the *asystata* and the *synestōta*, but dismissed them both with the statement (I, 10, 18-21): "And one or the other of these original forms must necessarily be represented in every present cause; a matter in which none of them is found, cannot possibly be considered a controversy, and for that reason neither a cause." It is in agreement herewith also that he explained the names of the categories of controversy in their relation to *Poiēsis,* or speechmaking, rather than to *Noēsis* (*Cf. De Inventione,* I, viii-xv).

Here in his introduction to rhetorical analysis Cicero has incidentally also proposed a new term for general use in Latin rhetoric, i.e., *constitutio* should be used for *quaestio* in certain contexts. That this change in terminology,

---

[32]Leonard, William E., *The Fragments of Empedocles* (Chicago, 1908), p. 37.
[33]Diels, H., *Die Fragmente,* 1934, I, p. 334; in the 1903 edition, p. 200, he translates *"Mischgeschoepfe."*

however, did not imply any deviation in his theory, or basic thinking, becomes very clear from his subsequent remarks. "A constitution," he explains immediately, "is the original clash, or primary conflict of causes." Causes, according to 1013b25, are the origin, source, or beginning of every change and every stasis. Two causes of the same species, contrary in dynamis, are the origin, or beginning, of every natural stasis, or constitution: a cause of action and a cause of reaction, or reciprocation. The initial conflict of the causes is the constitution of the controversy. The superficial and observable moving apart or going asunder (←——— ———→) is the secondary phenomenon; the primary conflict with which the rhetor must concern himself first of all is the originative antagonistic standing ———→←———, or the genetic contrariness, in the immediate, or proximate causes of the whole development: no other understanding or analysis of a controversy is adequate for rhetorical purposes; no one can argue a controversery intelligently who does not thoroughly comprehend the conflict out of which it developed. This interpretation of a *Constitutio* is reiterated in I, xiii, 18: "The Question is the individual controversy which develops from the conflict in the causes, that is to say, e.g., the controversy: "You were not justified in doing it" "I was justified in doing it." The conflict of the causes is that in which the *constitutio* (or the 'standing together') consists, (i.e., not the *amphisbētēsis,* or the 'going apart'). Out of this conflict is born the controversy which we call the Question, e.g., in this case: "Was he justified in doing it, or not?"

Not even this 'primary' conflict, however, is without its genesis; it, too, had a generation by which it came into being and the nature of its generation is another strong reason why it should be called a *constitutio.* For the process by which it came to be as it is, was not a *synthesis,* or composition, out of elements, nor a *systasis,* or *constitution,* of contrary informations out of elemental matter, but a *systasis,* or the constitution of a heteromerous part out of contrary informations of the selfsame matter, as Aristotle himself had differentiated the processes in *Parts of Animals,* Book II. This *prima conflictio* which is the *constitutio* "profecta ex depulsione intentionis," i.e., has come out of, emerged, or resulted from a *depulsio,* i.e., a de-motion, or a motion downward, a denunciation, or a denial, of an *intentio,* i.e., an uprising, an anabatic, aggressive, presumptuous, attacking, and incriminating impulse, move, or act, commonly called a Charge. In other words, the primary conflict itself is a vertical reciprocation in formal speech. The causes of the conflict are the Answer and the Charge, contrary motions made orally, contrary functions performed rhetorically, either in unqualified contradictions (Cf. *De Interpretatione,* iv-vi) as when a 'change' is 'argued,' e.g., "It is a fact that you did this" ∧ "It is not a fact that I did it," or in contrary statements as, e.g., in "It is a fact that you did this" ∧ "I was justified in doing it."

In significant respects, then, according to Cicero, the genesis, or generation of a rhetorical subject—of which the reverse, or counterpart is a rhetorical analysis—is comparable, analogous, and like the generation of every other 'natural' physical being. The normal excitement, or turbulence, of some one individual living being, A, is intensified by a matter, or a circumstance in a matter. This intensification causes A to make a concentrated Charge against another individual, B, e.g., "You did this." B's reaction to A's excitement is an attempt to allay, neutralize, or offset it. The Answer to A's Charge might, for example, be either: "I did not do it," or "I was justified in doing it." The immediate effect of such reciprocation is a stasis, the momentary cessation of all excitement, or movement, an interval, or a latent stage in the process of becoming. The two opposite, or contrary *dynameis,* however, have come into contact with one another and are now 'together.' Out of this vital contact, association, or relation, a fresh *archē* (192b9-11), a new beginning, or a new being originates (Ross, *Physics,* p. 500). Out of the *apophasis* as the material, the *kataphasis* as the formal principle constitutes the 'fetation' out of which the controversy grows. The new Being which develops from this constitution, or embryo, is a "cross between" the originals. Accordingly, the course, or process of generation, by which a rhetorical subject, or an arguable *res* comes to be, is a re-production which involves the collaboration and interaction of opposites, or contraries, of one and the same species; due to their innately inherent incompatibility, however, the *dynameis* of contradictory, or conflicting, statements are unable to blend and unite with one another to constitute a unified, harmonious, integrated, or whole body: that which is born of conflict must needs be merely a contraversion, or a controversy. Let us restate the matter, thus: To begin with there must be a *Kataphasis,* e.g., "You did this!," and an *Apophasis,* e.g., "I did not!" These two opposite movements, or contradictory declarations, constitute the *prima conflictio* out of which a *secunda controversia* develops; that is to say, out of the initial constitution arises a more potent and more emphatic new *Kataphasis, e.g.,* "But you most certainly did," and likewise an intensified and more energetic new *Apophasis,* e.g., "I most assuredly did not!," and these two vitalized declarations exactly parallel and controvert one another. Or, in another instance, out of another original constitution, e.g., "You did this—I was justified in so doing," there may arise the new negative *Kataphasis:* "You were not justified in so doing" and the new positive *Apophasis:* "Most assuredly, I was justified in so doing." Thus, the 'start,' or the beginning of every rhetorical *pragma, res,* or real existing controversy is a Charge *(Kataphasis, Intentio)* and an Answer *(Apophasis, Depulsio, or Abnuentia),* or an Accusation and a Denial of the Charge. As opposites, or contraries, these declarations *stasiazein* with one another, make *stasis* with, or block one another, or effect the constitution of a conflict. This constitution, however, is not a final, but an initial, or an intermediary, 'sperm' stage in the process of becoming, or generation; it is alive and has the potentiality of ultimately developing, or being developed into a finished product. In its genetic development a new Charge arises out of the first Answer and a fresh Answer out of the old Charge; substantially neither is anything new, but merely a reiteration, restatement, or another version of the old. Accordingly, this 'generation' is actually a 're-generation,' or a transformed reproduction of the originals, merely a contra version of the initial conflict, not an accomplished, or successfully terminated and completed generation, but an original product in the process of becoming, unfinished and undetermined as yet, but alive and capable of being cultivated and ultimately developed by extraneous, artificial, or artistic means. Due to the blemish inherent in the movements, or seeds (199b4) the 'parent statements' fail to reach, or arrive at any conclusion, or determined end. The real thing by them produced, or brought into being, though alive and potential, is actually and by nature ambiguous, doubtful, questionable, variable, contrary, controversial, unsettled, undetermined, nothing specific and decided, but merely a controversy to which there is as yet no end, or termination. Graphically, this 'crossbreeding' of a controversy might be depicted, thus: (Let 1. indicate the prior, and 2. the consequent, as the controversy is generated by and from the conflict.)

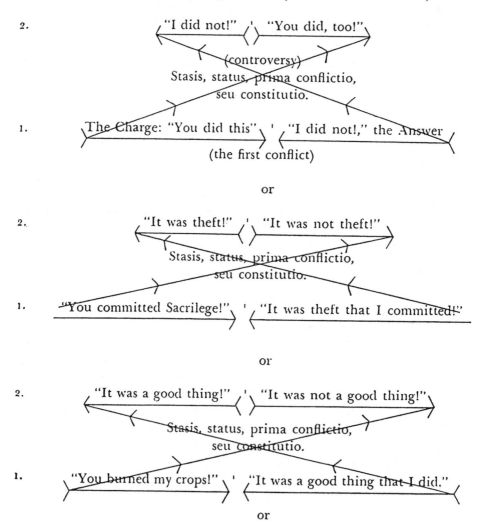

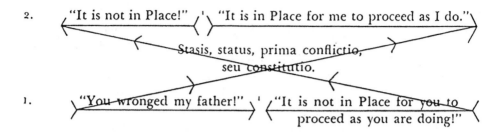

2.   "It is not in Place!"   "It is in Place for me to proceed as I do."

Stasis, status, prima conflictio,
seu constitutio.

1.   "You wronged my father!"   "It is not in Place for you to proceed as you are doing!"

Even though his term *constitutio* was never generally accepted in Latin rhetorical theory and though he himself later reverted to the use of the term *status*, *Tusculan Disputations* III, 33, 79, and *Orator* 14 and 35 would seem to indicate that Cicero never changed his basic point of view in this regard. The main difference in their interpretations of the rhetorical *constitutio* consists in this: what the *auctor* described as a mechanical-physiological organ of rhetorical action, Cicero described as an 'original' form of conflict, a sort of primordial "cross-breed" of contrariness out of which the individual and particular controversy generates or is propagated. Finally, in the light of this research, the description of stasis ascribed to Hermagoras (Quintilian III, vi, 21) becomes wholly meaningful to us. Hermagoras represented stasis as that which in rhetoric performs a most important twofold function,[34] i.e., as that which serves as the guiding principle of both rhetorical Noesis and Poiesis. In rhetorical analysis the subject matter is intellectually laid hold upon, or 'grasped' and investigated logically with reference to its stasis, i.e., to determine whether it be asystatic, synestotic, or stasiastic, and if stastic, what type of stasis it exhibits. In speechmaking, the stasis is rhetorically 'handled,' 'managed,' or treated in two speeches: opposing rhetors present to a third party as the judge both a *synechon* and an *aition*, i.e., an argument why the stasis should be maintained and established permanently as well as a reason why it ought to be resolved in a contrary motion. Both speakers strengthen their causes with proofs drawn from the special *topoi* which rhetoric has devised for their use. The judge considers the stasis in the light of both the *synechon* and the *aition*, i.e., he weighs the *krinomenon*, or the thing to be judged, and in accordance with his verdict, reached with the cooperation of the rhetors, will be the final disposition, conclusion, end, or settlement of the stasis (Cf. *diatithesthai*, Sextus Empiricus, *Against the Rhetoricians* II, 62). Hence, it was from actual rhetorical practice that Hermagoras derived his functional description of stasis (Quintilian, III, vi, 21, and *Rhetores Graeci*, vii, 173 and v, 78, 10) as that (1) with reference to which a subject matter is investigated and analyzed in Noesis, and (2) that with reference to which (in Poiesis) both speakers must present arguments in their speeches.

---

[34]Stroux, Johannes, *Summum Ius*, p. 129.

Quintilian's statements concerning the stasis are likewise found to be meaningful and correct. We may regret that he did not explain for us the fundamental relation between the physical and the rhetorical stasis, but we find no fault whatever with his explanation (III, vi, 1-5): "That which I call Stasis, some style the Constitution, others the Question, and still others, that which may be inferred from the Question, while Theodorus called it the fountain-head, or primary source (as of a river) to which everything in the debate is to be referred." (With Theodorus' explanation, compare *Physics*, 261a25: "it is the self-movement that we declare to be the first principle of things that are moved and impart motion and the primary source to which things that are in motion are to be referred," Ross, p. 261a). We understand also how Quintilian as a scholar might prefer to retain the historic Greek term *stasis* and how, as a practical rhetor, he would describe it as the main point in the argument on which the whole matter turns (III, vi, 21).

The explanation which Pseudo-Augustine gives to the statement which he 'borrowed' from his *Vorlage* also becomes more intelligible in the light of this study. His interpretation (Section 12, lines 13-18) may be represented diagrammatically, thus:

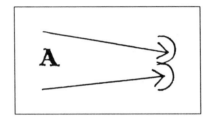

At first *(primo)*, i.e., at A, there is as yet no contact, and hence, no *pugna*, or fight, between the parties. However, as they advance and come closer to one another, there is imminent danger that they might come to blows. At the critical moment, the question intervenes, comes between them; it embraces each of the parties, as it were, in one of its arms, holds them apart and stops them (for if and when and as long as they struggle, there is motion, cf. 938a25, *machomenos de kineitai*). According to Pseudo-Augustine, the question is called the status because both parties stand still in it, i.e., stop advancing, desist from fighting, each insisting on what he has previously maintained, each equally in control of, and controlled by the other.

We conclude our study by asking again the age-old question: "What, then, is stasis?"[35] We answer: In Pre-Aristotelian Greek thought, in Aristotle's physical philosophy and in the *meta*physical rhetoric of Post-Aristotelian Peripatetics of the Third Century before Christ, it was the rest, pause, halt, or

---

[35]*Ti esti stasis;* See, *Commentarium Codicis Vaticani Gr. 107* in Hermogenis *peri staseon et peri heureseos* edidit Georgius Kowalski, (Lwów, 1939).

standing still, which inevitably occurs between opposite as well as between contrary 'moves', or motions. In rhetorical Noesis, it was frequently identified with the thing sought in the zetesis, i.e., the *zētēma, quaestio,* or the Question. To the *Auctor ad Herennium* it was the *constitutio,* i.e., the organ of rhetorical action, the instrument and implement of controversy, the body, or functional system of argument. To Cicero it was likewise a constitution, i.e., a natural start, or physical beginning, an original form, the originative and archemorphic conflict out of which individually modified controversies arise, an archetype of dispute, or argument. To Theodorus stasis was the originative head, or primary source, to which everything moved in the debate must be related. To Quintilian and to Pseudo-Augustine it was the main question in debate. At no time, however, did the term wholly lose its original physical denotation as that which is neither a kinesis, nor an eremēsis, but both, or the opposite, or contrary, of both, namely, the ambivalent, bi-functional stasis, station, or standing still, which necessarily must occur momentarily in-between opposite 'changes' and in-between contrary motions, movements, processes, functions, or forces in action.[36]

Further to trace the concept stasis through the ages is the task of the history of rhetoric. Our goal has been accomplished if we have succeeded in shedding any light of truth upon its origin and thereby restoring to the ancient term some of the dignity which it had before it fell into the hands of rhetoricians[37] who knew not Aristotle's natural science.

---

[36]That the political concept, stasis, is likewise an adaptation of the physical concept is indicated by Menecles (146-118 B.C.) Scholium on *Pindar Pythian Ode,* IV, 10a, in Jacoby, Felix, *Fragmente der Griechischen Historiker* (Berlin, 1929), III, 1, p. 83. Note also the unconvincing explanation offered by Barker, Ernest, *The Politics of Aristotle* (Oxford, 1948), p. 448: "Stasis . . . the word means the act of forming (and thence the body of persons forming) a combination for the attainment of some political end by legal or illegal means."

[37]Hermogenis *Opera,* Edidit H. Rabe, (Leipzig, 1913), p. 35; See also, Walz, *Rh. Gr.* V, 77, 592.

Bibliography

Standard Overviews

Baldwin, Charles Sears. *Ancient Rhetoric and Poetic.* NY: Macmillan, 1924.

Beck, Frederick A. G. *Greek Education.* NY: Barnes and Noble, 1964.

Bryant, Donald C. *Ancient Greek and Roman Rhetoricians.* Columbia, MO: Artcraft Press, 1968.

Clark, Donald Lemen. *Rhetoric in Greco-Roman Education.* NY: Columbia U.P., 1957.

Conley, Thomas M. *Rhetoric in the European Tradition.* NY: Longman, 1990.

Kennedy, George A. *The Art of Persuasion in Greece.* Princeton: Princeton U.P., 1963.

_____. *Classical Rhetoric and its Christian and Secular Tradition from Ancient to Modern Times.* Chapel Hill: U. of North Carolina Press, 1980.

Kroll, Wilhelm. "Rhetorik." *Paulys Real-Encyclopädie der classischen Alter-tumswissenschaft* Supp. 7 (1940): 1039-1138.

Murphy, James J., ed. *A Synoptic History of Classical Rhetoric.* Davis, CA: Hermagoras Press, 1983.

Origins of Greek Rhetorical Theory

Cole, Thomas. *The Origins of Rhetoric in Ancient Greece.* Baltimore: Johns Hopkins U.P., 1991.

_____. "Who Was Corax?" *Illinois Classical Studies* 16 (1991): 65-84.

Enos, Richard Leo, and Margaret Kantz. "A Selected Bibliography on Corax and Tisias." *Rhetoric Society Quarterly* 13 (1983): 71-74.

Farenga, Vincent. "Periphrasis on the Origin of Rhetoric." *Modern Language Notes* 94 (1979): 1033-55.

Hinks, D. A. G. "Tisias and Corax and the Invention of Rhetoric." *Classical Quarterly* 42 (1940): 61-69.

Kennedy, George A. "The Earliest Rhetorical Handbooks." *American Journal of Philology* 80 (1959): 169-78.

Schiappa, Edward. "The Beginnings of Greek Rhetorical Theory," *Rhetorical Movement: Essays in Honor of Leland M. Griffin,* ed. David Zarefsky. Evanston, IL: North-western U.P., 1993.

Smith, Bromley. "Corax and Probability." *Quarterly Journal of Speech Education* 7 (1921): 13-42.

Verrall, A.W. "Korax and Tisias." *Journal of Philology* 9 (1880): 197-210.

Wilcox, Stanley. "Corax and the Prolegomena." *American Journal of Philology* 64 (1943): 1-23.

_____. "The Scope of Early Rhetorical Instruction." *Harvard Studies in Classical Philology* 53 (1942): 121-55.

Homeric Rhetoric

Connors, Robert J. "Greek Rhetoric and the Transition from Orality." *Philosophy and Rhetoric* 19 (1986): 38-61.

Enos, Richard Leo. *Greek Rhetoric Before Aristotle.* Prospect Heights: Waveland, 1993.

Kennedy, George A. "The Ancient Dispute over Rhetoric in Homer." *American Journal of Philology* 78 (1957): 23-35.

Kirby, John T. "Rhetoric and Poetics in Hesiod." *Ramus* 21 (1992): 34-60.

Kirk, G. S. *Homer and the Oral Tradition.* Cambridge: Cambridge U.P., 1976.

Lentz, Tony M. *Orality and Literacy in Hellenic Greece.* Carbondale: Southern Illinois U.P., 1989.

Nadeau, Ray. "Delivery in Ancient Times: Homer to Quintilian." *Quarterly Journal of Speech* 50 (1964): 53-60.

Solmsen, Friedrich. "The Gift of Speech in Homer and Hesiod." *Transactions and Proceedings of the American Philological Association* 85 (1954): 1-15.

Swearingen, C. Jan. "Literate Rhetors and Their Illiterate Audiences: The Orality of Early Literacy." *Pre/Text* 7 (1986): 145-62.

Sophistic Rhetoric

Barrett, Harold. *The Sophists: Rhetoric, Democracy, and Plato's Idea of Sophistry.* Novato, CA: Chandler & Sharp, 1987.

Bett, Richard. "The Sophists and Relativism." *Phronesis* 34 (1989): 19-169.

Classen, C. J. *Sophistik* (Wege der Forschung 187). Darmstadt: Wissenschaftliche Buchgesellschaft, 1976.

Cope, E. M. "On The Sophistical Rhetoric." *Journal of Classical and Sacred Philology* 2 (1855): 129-169; 3 (1856): 34-80, 252-88.

Crowley, Sharon. "A Plea for the Revival of Sophistry." *Rhetoric Review* 7 (1989): 318-34.

Dupréel, Eugène. *Les Sophistes.* Neuchâtel: Éditions du Griffon, 1948.

Gomperz, Heinrich. *Sophistik und Rhetorik.* Aalen: Scientia, 1985. First published Leipzig: Teubner, 1912.

Jarratt, Susan C. *Rereading the Sophists: Classical Rhetoric Refigured.* Carbondale: Southern Illinois U.P., 1991.

Jarrett, James L. *The Educational Theory of the Sophists.* NY: Teachers College Press, 1969.

Kerferd, G. B. *The Sophistic Movement.* Cambridge: Cambridge U.P., 1981.

_____. *The Sophists and Their Legacy.* Wiesbaden: Franz Steiner Verlag, 1981.

Poulakos, John. "Rhetoric, the Sophists, and the Possible." *Communication Monographs* 51 (1984): 215-225.

Robinson, Thomas M. *Contrasting Arguments: An Edition of the Dissoi Logoi.* Salem, NH: Ayer, 1979.

Romilly, Jacqueline de. *The Great Sophists in Periclean Athens.* Trans. Janet Lloyd. Oxford: Clarendon Press, 1992.

Schiappa, Edward. *Protagoras and Logos: A Study in Greek Philosophy and Rhetoric.* Columbia: U. of South Carolina Press, 1991.

_____. "*Rhêtorikê*: What's in a Name? Toward a Revised History of Early Greek Rhetorical Theory." *Quarterly Journal of Speech* 78 (1992): 1-15.

Segal, Charles P. "Gorgias and the Psychology of the Logos." *Harvard Studies in Classical Philology* 66 (1962): 99-155.

Sprague, Rosamond Kent, ed. *The Older Sophists.* Columbia: U. of South Carolina Press, 1972.

Sutton, Jane. "Rereading Sophistical Arguments: A Political Intervention." *Argumentation* 5 (1991): 141-157.

Untersteiner, Mario. *The Sophists.* Trans. Kathleen Freeman. Oxford: Basil Blackwell, 1954.

Versényi, Lazlo. *Socratic Humanism.* New Haven: Yale U. Press, 1963.

Platonic Rhetoric

Burger, Ronna. *Plato's Phaedrus: A Defense of a Philosophical Art of Writing.* University, AL: U. of Alabama Press, 1980.

Erickson, Keith V. *Plato: True and Sophistic Rhetoric.* Amsterdam: Rodopi, 1979.

Guthrie, W. K. C. *A History of Greek Philosophy*, vols. 4 & 5. Cambridge: Cambridge U.P., 1962-1981.

Hunt, Everett Lee. "Plato and Aristotle on Rhetoric and Rhetoricians." In *Historical Studies of Rhetoric and Rhetoricians*, ed. Raymond F. Howes. Ithaca: Cornell U.P., 1961.

McComiskey, Bruce. "Disassembling Plato's Critique of Rhetoric in the *Gorgias* (447a-466a)." *Rhetoric Review* 10 (1992): 205-15.

Morrow, G. E. "Plato's Conception of Persuasion." *The Philosophical Review* 62 (1953): 234-50.

Murray, James S. "Disputation, Deception and Dialectic: Plato on the True Rhetoric (Phaedrus 261-266)." *Philosophy and Rhetoric* 21 (1988): 279-87.

Neel, Jasper. *Plato, Derrida, and Writing.* Carbondale: Southern Illinois U.P., 1988.

Nehamas, Alexander. "Eristic, Antilogic, Sophistic, Dialectic: Plato's Demarcation of Philosophy from Sophistic." *History of Philosophy Quarterly* 7 (1990): 3-16.

Plochmann, George Kimball and Franklin E. Robinson. *A Friendly Companion to Plato's Gorgias.* Carbondale: Southern Illinois U.P., 1988.

Quimby, Rollin W. "The Growth of Plato's Perception of Rhetoric." *Philosophy and Rhetoric* 7 (1974): 71-79.

Robinson, Richard. *Plato's Earlier Dialectic.* 2nd ed. Oxford: Clarendon Press, 1953.

Schiappa, Edward. "Did Plato Coin *Rhêtorikê?*" *American Journal of Philology* 111 (1990): 457-70.

Vickers, Brain. *In Defense of Rhetoric.* Oxford: Clarendon Press, 1988.

Welch, Kathleen E. *The Contemporary Reception of Classical Rhetoric: Appropriations of Ancient Discourse.* Hillsdale, NJ: Lawrence Erlbaum, 1990.

Isocratean Rhetoric

Benoit, William Lyon. "Isocrates on Rhetorical Education." *Communication Education* 33 (1984): 109-120.

_____. "Isocrates and Aristotle on Rhetoric." *Rhetoric Society Quarterly* 20 (1990): 251-59.

_____. "Isocrates and Plato on Rhetoric and Rhetorical Education." *Rhetoric Society Quarterly* 21 (1991): 60-72.

Berquist, Goodwin F., Jr. "Isocrates of Athens: Foremost Speech Teacher of the Ancient World." *Speech Teacher* 8 (1959): 251-55.

Cahn, Michael. "Reading Rhetoric Rhetorically: Isocrates and the Marketing of Insight." *Rhetorica* 7 (1989): 121-44.

Gillis, D. "The Ethical Basis of Isocratean Rhetoric." *Parola del Passato* 128 (1969): 321-48.

Hudson-Williams, H.LI. "Thucydides, Isocrates, and Rhetorical Composition." *Classical Quarterly* 42 (1948) 76-81.

Johnson, R. "Isocrates' Methods of Teaching." *American Journal of Philology* 80 (1959): 25-36.

Mathieu, Georges. *Les Idées Politiques d'Isocrate*. Paris: Belles Lettres, 1925.

Norlin, George [and LaRue Van Hook]. *Isocrates*. 3 vols. Cambridge, MA: Harvard U.P., 1928-1945.

Perkins, T. M. "Isocrates and Plato: Relativism vs. Idealism." *Southern Speech Communication Journal* 50 (1984): 49-66.

Usher, S. "The Style of Isocrates." *Bulletin of the Institute of Classical Studies* 20 (1973): 39-67.

Van Hook, LaRue. "Alcidamas Versus Isocrates; The Spoken Versus the Written World. *Classical Weekly* 12 (1919): 89-94.

Vries, G. J. de "Isocrates' Reaction to the Phaedrus." *Mnemosyne* 6 (1953): 39-45.

Wagner, Russell H. "The Rhetorical Theory of Isocrates." *Quarterly Journal of Speech Education* 8 (1922): 323-37.

Wilcox, Stanley. "Criticisms of Isocrates and His *Philosophia.*" *Transactions and Proceedings of the American Philological Association* 74 (1943): 113-33.

Aristotelian Rhetorical Theory

Aly, Bower. "Enthymemes: The Story of a Lighthearted Search." *Speech Teacher* 14 (1965): 265-275.

Anderson, Alan Ross and N. D. Belnap, Jr. "Enthymemes." *Journal of Philosophy* 58 (1961): 713-723.

Anderson, Floyd Douglas. "Aristotle's Doctrine of the Mean and its Relationship to Rhetoric." *Southern Speech Communication Journal* 34 (1968): 100-107.

Angelo, Frank J. "The Evolution of the Analytic Topoi: A Speculative Inquiry." In *Essays on Classical Rhetoric and Modern Discourse*. Ed. Robert J. Connors, Lisa S. Ede, and Andrea A. Lunsford. Carbondale: Southern Illinois U.P., 1984.

Arnhart, Larry. *Aristotle on Political Reasoning: A Commentary on the Rhetoric.* DeKalb: Northern Illinois U.P., 1981.

Berlin, James A. "Aristotle's Rhetoric in Context: Reading Historically." In *A Rhetoric of Doing: Essays Honoring James L. Kinneavy*, eds., Stephen P. Witte, Neal Nakadate, Roger D. Cherry. Carbondale: Southern Illinois U.P., 1992.

Bitzer, Lloyd F. "Aristotle's Enthymeme Revisited." *Quarterly Journal of Speech* 45 (1959): 399-408.

Brake, Robert J. "A Reconsideration of Aristotle's Concept of Topics." *Central States Speech Journal* 16 (1965): 106-112.

Brandes, Paul. *A History of Aristotle's Rhetoric.* Metuchen, NJ: Scarecrow Press,1989.

Brinton, Alan. "The Outmoded Psychology of Aristotle's Rhetoric." *Western Journal of Speech Communication* 54 (1990): 204-218.

Brockriede, Wayne E. "Toward a Contemporary Aristotelian Theory of Rhetoric." *Quarterly Journal of Speech* 52 (1966): 33-40.

Dearin, Ray D. "Aristotle on Psychology and Rhetoric." *Central States Speech Journal* 17 (1966): 277-282.

Erickson, Keith V. *Aristotle's Rhetoric: Five Centuries of Philological Research.* Metuchen, NJ: Scarecrow Press, Inc., 1975.

_____, ed. *Aristotle: The Classical Heritage of Rhetoric.* Metuchen, NJ: Scarecrow Press, 1974.

Fortenbaugh, William W. "Aristotle's Platonic Attitude Towards Delivery." *Philosophy and Rhetoric* 19 (1986): 242-254.

_____. *Aristotle on Emotion.* London: Duckworth, 1975.

Garver, Eugene. "Aristotle's Rhetoric as a Work of Philosophy." *Philosophy and Rhetoric* 19 (1986): 1-22.

Green, Lawrence D. "Aristotelian Rhetoric, Dialectic, and the Traditions of *Antistrophos*" *Rhetorica* 8 (1990): 5-27.

Grimaldi, William M. A. *Aristotle's Rhetoric: A Commentary.* 2 vols. NY: Fordham U.P., 1980, 1988.

_____. *Studies in the Philosophy of Aristotle's Rhetoric.* Wiesbaden: Franz Steiner, 1972.

Hill, Forbes. "The Amorality of Aristotle's Rhetoric." *Greek, Roman, & Byzantine Studies* 22 (1981): 133-47.

Huseman, Richard C. "Aristotle's System of Topics." *Southern Speech Journal* 30 (1965): 243-52.

Johnstone, Christopher Lyle. "An Aristotelian Trilogy: Ethics, Rhetoric, Politics, and the Search for Moral Truth." *Philosophy and Rhetoric* 13 (1980): 1-24.

Kennedy, George A. *Aristotle on Rhetoric: A Theory of Civic Discourse.* NY: Oxford U.P., 1991.

Miller, Carolyn R. "Aristotle's "Special Topics' in Rhetorical Practice and Pedagogy." *Rhetoric Society Quarterly* (1987): 61-70.

Ochs, Donovan. "Aristotle's Concept of Formal Topics." *Speech Monographs* 36 (1969): 419-25.

Olian, Robert J. "The Intended uses of Aristotle's Rhetoric." *Speech Monographs* 35 (1968): 137-48.

Roberts, W. Rhys. "References to Plato in Aristotle's Rhetoric." *Classical Philology* 29 (1924): 342-46.

Seaton, R.C. "The Aristotelian Enthymeme." *Classical Review* 28 (1914): 113-19.

Self, Lois. "Rhetoric and 'Phronesis': Aristotle's Ideal." *Philosophy and Rhetoric* 12 (1979): 130-45.

Solmsen, Friedrich. "The Aristotelian Tradition in Ancient Rhetoric." *American Journal of Philology* 62 (1941): 35-50, 169-90.

Thompson, Wayne. *Aristotle's Deduction and Induction.* Amsterdam: Rodopi, 1975.

_____. "Stasis in Aristotle's Rhetoric." *Quarterly Journal of Speech* 58 (1972): 134-41.

Warnick, Barbara. "Judgment, Probability, and Aristotle's Rhetoric." *Quarterly of Speech* 75 (1989): 299-311.

Post-Aristotelian Rhetorical Theory

Braet, Antoine. "The Classical Doctrine of *Status* and the Rhetorical Theory of Argumentation." *Philosophy and Rhetoric* 20 (1987): 79-93.

Fortenbaugh, William W., ed. *Peripatetic Rhetoric After Aristotle.* New Brunswick, NJ: Transaction Books, 1993.

Innes, Doreen C. "Theophrastus and the Theory of Style." *Theophrastus of Eresus: On His Life and Work.* New Brunswick: Transaction Books, 1985.

Kennedy, George A. "Theophrastus and Stylistic Distinctions." *Harvard Studies in Classical Philology* 62 (1957): 93-104.

Nadeau, Ray. "Classical Systems of Stases: Hermagoras to Hermogenes." *Greek, Roman, and Byzantine Studies* 2 (1959): 51-71.

_____. "Hermogenes' *On Stases*: A Translation with an Introduction." *Speech Monographs* 31 (1964): 361-424.

_____. Hermogenes on "Stock Issues' in Deliberative Speaking." *Speech Monographs* 25 (1958): 59-66.

_____. "Some Aristotelian and Stoic Influences on the Theory of Stases." *Speech Monographs* 26 (1959): 248-254.

Solmsen, Friedrich. "Tracing of Aristotelian and Peripatetic Influence on Later Rhetoricians." *American Journal of Philology* 92 (1941): 169-190.

Wisse, Jakob. *Ethos and Pathos from Aristotle to Cicero.* Amsterdam: Hakkert, 1989.

Index